HEARTS IN ART

HEARTS
IN ART

Andrew Hoggan

MAINSTREAM
PUBLISHING

EDINBURGH AND LONDON

First published in Great Britain in 1995 by
MAINSTREAM PUBLISHING COMPANY (EDINBURGH) LTD
7 Albany Street
Edinburgh EH1 3UG

ISBN 1 85158 736 5

A catalogue record for this book is available from the British Library

Illustrations by Craig Mitchell

Typeset in Palatino by Pioneer Associates Ltd, Perthshire
Printed and bound in Great Britain by Butler & Tanner Ltd, Frome

Foreword

As Chairman I was asked to provide a brief foreword for this excellent publication profiling Hearts players since the war.

My response, however, is as a supporter. Having previewed some of the excellent artwork and profiles I was taken down memory lane. Memories are evoked of standing on the terraces at Cappielow marvelling at Donald Ford's hat-trick of penalties, and many more similar occasions. The illustrations and statistics add up to what is a unique history of the club, told through the achievements of the players.

This publication is a must for all Hearts supporters. I am sure that it will settle many arguments in the pub – and probably provoke a few more as Hearts folk debate their favourite personalities on the park.

Chris Robinson
Chairman

Introduction

The foundations of this book were born from the *Hearts Review* magazine which I co-edited during the 1980s. My favourite article was the 'Past Master'. It described the careers of well-known Hearts players. When I ended my involvement with the *Review* I continued to research player careers, concentrating on post-war stars from 1946–47 to the present. As the collection of information grew, so did the desire to publish my research to make it accessible to all Hearts fans.

The illustrations which accompany the text are by my good friend, Craig Mitchell. I was delighted when he agreed to draw portrait pictures of each player. I am sure you will agree they are of a fine standard with some uncanny likenesses. Some of the pictures originally appeared in *Hearts Review* but the majority were specially drawn for this book. My thanks to Craig for his efforts and the time he devoted to this work.

This book is the culmination of five years of research. There were times when it felt like an impossible task. The majority of the statistical data was researched from newspaper archives and Hearts' Official Programme from 1946 to the present. Both the papers and the programme carried numerous errors or omissions, particularly in the 1950s. I am grateful to Willie Smith and David Speed who took time to help verify or amend the figures I collated. Graham Blackwood, John Ure and Alex Jones also provided invaluable help and assistance from their collections of Hearts memorabilia. My thanks also to everyone who appears in the full acknowledgment list.

The following A to Z guide covers the career of every Hearts player who made a competitive League or Cup appearance for the club since 1946–47. It does not include players who only appeared in East of Scotland Shield or Penman Cup ties. The former became a bit of a joke in the 1980s with mostly reserve teams fielded in what was still classed a first-team match. The latter had a similar reputation in the 1950s. However, players who made competitive League and Cup appearances have East of Scotland and Penman Cup matches included in their records.

Readers will notice that some birthplaces, birthdates, honours won and career moves are missing. If anyone can help fill the blanks or bring details fully up to date, I'd be delighted to hear from them so that they can be included in any future revised editions of this book.

I hope you will find this publication a help in reliving memories of some great and not-so-great players and useful as a statistical record of their careers. Who knows, some details may solve that pub argument or even, dare I say it, start new ones! Enjoy it!

Acknowledgments

Graham Blackwood, Alex Jones, Willie Smith, David Speed, John Ure (Hearts), David Allan (Cowdenbeath), Peter Rundo (Dundee United), Andrew Wilkie (East Fife), Peter McLeish (Hamilton), Gordon Allison (Kilmarnock), Jim Jeffrey (Motherwell), John Norman (Partick Thistle), Harry Smith (Raith), Robert McElroy (Rangers), Allan Grieve (Stirling), John Byrne (St Mirren), C. Lindsay (Third Lanark), and to all the other members of the Association of Football Statisticians who took the time to reply despite being unable to help.

The staff at the National Library, George IV Bridge, Edinburgh, and at the Mitchell Library in Glasgow; Douglas Spence (*Sunday Post*); David McCarthy (*Edinburgh Evening News*); all former players, friends and relatives of former players who helped with information and supplied pictures. Many others made small contributions here and there and my thanks to them also. Finally to Bill Campbell and all at Mainstream for their help and assistance in putting this publication into print.

If anyone can supply any additional information on any of the players, please write to Andrew Hoggan, c/o Mainstream Publishing, 7 Albany Street, Edinburgh EH1 3UG.

List of Abbreviations and Notes

ASC	Anglo-Scottish Cup match
EC	European Cup match
ECWC	European Cup-Winners' Cup match
LC	League Cup match
Lge	League match
PL	Premier League
SC	Scottish Cup match
S. Lge	South League match
Tex. C	Texaco Cup match
H	Home fixture
A	Away fixture
N	Neutral venue
BC	Boys Club
YC	Youth Club
YMCA	Young Men's Club Association
r-up	runners-up
'S'	Schoolboy signing
U-18, U-23	Under-18, Under-23, etc
Apps	appearances
Gls	goals scored

Appearance records: The + symbol indicates substitute appearances (e.g. 24+5 means 24 starts and 5 substitute appearances).

Transfer fees: All figures are either those quoted in official Hearts publications such as books and match programmes, or are from newspaper reports. Where these sources contradict each other, we have used our judgment to ascertain the fee more likely to be correct.

New Debutants 1994–95: Stuart Callaghan, Alan Lawrence and David Winnie made competitive debuts in August 1995. They just missed our printing deadline, but will be included in future editions of this book.

Terrible Trio figures: Further intensive research resulted in changes to the goalscoring records of Conn, Bauld and Wardhaugh from previously published information on these players. Hearts historians now believe the revised figures to be 100 per cent accurate.

Midfield

BORN: Dundee, 8 July 1955

HEIGHT: 5' 10"   WEIGHT: 11st (1981)

COMPETITIVE DEBUT: v Clydebank, 19th Sept 1981 (Div. I) (H), 1–0

CAREER: Harris Acad; Butterburn YC, 1969; Lochee United; Dundee United, 1974; **Hearts, Sept 1981** (£55,000); St Johnstone, June 1982 (£65,000); Saints player/coach, Aug 1985; retired in May 1986

HONOURS: Scottish Div. I. winner 1982–83 (St Johnstone)

A fringe player with Dundee United for seven years, Derek joined Hearts at the same time as Willie Pettigrew. A real grafter in the midfield engine, he supplied the forwards with many goalscoring opportunities from defence-splitting passes. Light and nippy on his feet, Addison made the most of his deceptive running style to glide past opponents. His single season could be considered successful in a playing sense, despite the team's failure to win promotion. Financial pressure on Hearts necessitated his sale. He went on to make 113 competitive appearances for St Johnstone before retiring.

Defender

BORN: Windygates, Fife, 2 March 1930

DIED: January 1995

HEIGHT: 5' 9"   WEIGHT: 11st 6lb (1953)

COMPETITIVE DEBUT: v Motherwell, 29 Jan 1949 (Lge) (H), 5–1

CAREER: Guested with Forfar during the war; Windygates Juveniles; **Hearts, July 1947;** East Fife, May 1955 (free transfer)

Often used as a utility player covering at centre-half and both full-back positions. His biggest match for Hearts was the 1953 Scottish Cup semi-final when he appeared in place of Tam McKenzie at left-back before a crowd of 116,262. Adie played most of season 1953–54 at left-back and was unlucky not to win a Championship medal, with Celtic just pipping Hearts to the title. John was a keen, quick tackler and his upfield clearances initiated many attacking moves. Freed at the end of season 1954–55, he became a stalwart of East Fife's defence.

In later years John moved into business as a general merchant in

Buckhaven, then took over the Bayview Bar with his brother-in-law, Walter Robertson, an ex-East Fife player. He died in 1995.

KENNY AIRD

Outside-right

BORN: Glasgow, 13 April 1947

HEIGHT: 5′ 5″   WEIGHT: 10st (1973)

COMPETITIVE DEBUT: v Abroath, 3 March 1973 (Lge) (A), 0–3

CAREER: Boys Brigade football; Cranhill Secondary School; Drumchapel Amateurs; Celtic, *c.* 1963; St Mirren, *c.* 1965; St Johnstone, 1967; **Hearts, Feb 1973** (£17,500); retired in May 1977 following a free transfer

HONOURS: Scottish Cup r-up 1975–76 (Hearts); Scottish League Cup r-up 1969–70 (St Johnstone)

Popular and energetic winger. The Hearts fans sang his praises with a particular chant dedicated to him. Before he came to Tynecastle, Kenny wandered around before settling with St Johnstone where he made 160 League appearances.

Hearts signed the entertaining winger to boost the supply of cross balls for the main strikers to feed on. Kenny was in fine form early in season 1973–74 until an injury against Celtic sidelined him and upset the team's rhythm. Injuries then continued to hamper the wee man. His best season for appearances and goals was 1975–76 when Aird picked up a Scottish Cup runners-up medal. Kenny starred in the team which demolished Locomotiv Leipzig 5–1 the following season, setting up Willie Gibson for the second goal that night.

Aird's Hearts career ended on a sad note when his retiral coincided with the club suffering relegation.

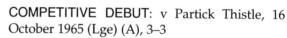

RAB AITCHISON

Half-back

BORN: Edinburgh, 11 November 1943

HEIGHT: 5′ 11″   WEIGHT: 11st (1965)

COMPETITIVE DEBUT: v Partick Thistle, 16 October 1965 (Lge) (A), 3–3

CAREER: Leith Schools; Edinburgh Emmet; St Bernard's A; Newtongrange Star; **Hearts, Nov 1963**; Arniston Rangers, Apr 1967 (free transfer); Bonnyrigg Rose, *c.* 1975; retired *c.* 1980

HONOURS: Scotland Junior international; Scottish Junior Cup winner 1977–78 (Bonnyrigg)

A native of Leith, Rab played his early games in Edinburgh football circles and won a Lord Weir

Cup medal with St Bernard's. He signed for Hearts as a wing-half but found it difficult to gain a first-team place due to intense competition, managing only a handful of appearances over two seasons. He became a bigger success in the ranks of junior football after his release in 1967. In addition to international honours, he won a Junior Cup medal in the twilight of his playing career. He later moved into management with a number of East of Scotland junior clubs.

THOMSON ALLAN

Goalkeeper

BORN: Longridge, 5 October 1946

HEIGHT: 5′ 10″   WEIGHT: 11st 10lb (1979)

COMPETITIVE DEBUT: v Rangers, 24 February 1979 (PL) (H), 3–2

CAREER: Holycross Academy; Edina Hearts; Hibernian, Oct 1963; Dundee, July 1971; Meadowbank, Jan 1979 (on loan); **Hearts, Feb 1979** (free transfer); Falkirk, 1980; Meadowbank, 1981; retired in 1982

HONOURS: 2 full Scotland caps; Scotland Youth international; 1 Scottish League cap; Scottish League Cup winner 1973–74 (Dundee); r-up 1968–69 (Hibs)

Agile goalkeeper with a good eye and sharp reflexes. Thomson joined Hearts as a part-timer when working with British Leyland at Bathgate. He built up a reputation as a solid, reliable, consistent goalkeeper with Hibs and Dundee. His form peaked in 1974 and coincided with domestic and full international honours. Willie Ormond was the Scotland boss who picked Allan. He remembered his talents when looking to stem the tidal wave of goals against and defeats which Hearts were suffering in season 1978–79. His transfer was negotiated for a small signing-on fee. Thomson performed well for Hearts in a brief spell but didn't display the form he was renowned for. He moved to Falkirk in 1980.

ALAN ANDERSON

Centre-half

BORN: Edinburgh, 21 December 1939

HEIGHT: 6' 1"   WEIGHT: 12st 7lb (1969)

COMPETITIVE DEBUT: v Dunfermline, 2 January 1964 (Lge) (H), 2–1

CAREER: David Kilpatrick School (Leith); United Crossroads; Dalkeith Thistle; Falkirk, 1959; Millwall, Sept 1959; Scunthorpe United, July 1962 (£10,000); **Hearts, Nov 1963** (£1,500); retired in May 1976

HONOURS: Full Scotland international; Scottish League r-up 1964–65 (Hearts); Scottish Cup r-up 1967–68 (Hearts); Texaco Cup r-up 1970–71 (Hearts); English Division IV winner 1961–62 (Millwall)

Nicknamed 'Double A' by the fans, Alan was a typical stopper centre-half with a powerful physique, a dominating and assured figure in defence. In attack he used his height at corners and set-pieces to score a creditable number of goals with his head.

A native of Leith, Alan served his time as an apprentice compositor. He found his way to Tynecastle for a bargain fee and gave tremendous service over 13 seasons, displaying leadership qualities which saw him captain the side as he matured into a seasoned campaigner.

During his playing days he took over the Royal Oak public house in Infirmary Street. The bar was renamed The Pivot and a supporters club ran regularly from the pub during his later years with Hearts. He retired to concentrate on his pub full time and later managed the Wheatsheaf Inn in Dalkeith.

DAVID ANDERSON

Goalkeeper

BORN: 1948

HEIGHT: 6' 2"   WEIGHT: 12st (1964)

COMPETITIVE DEBUT: v Hibernian, 13 May 1964 (Summer Cup), (A) 0–1

CAREER: Bonnyrigg Rose; **Hearts, Oct 1963**; Dunfermline, 1966; Dumbarton, 1969; retired in 1974

HONOURS: Scotland Schoolboy and Junior international

A native of Loanhead on the boundary of Edinburgh, David came to Hearts as a 15-year-old and even at that early age he was tipped for the top thanks to a strapping physique and sound goalkeeping ability. His initial season in reserve football confirmed his potential but the consistency of Jim Cruickshank, who himself had just broken through, meant no League or Cup appearances for young Anderson. His chance came in a Summer Cup tie but a full year passed before he played two more games in the same competition. These proved to be his only games, with a record of one win, one draw and one defeat, with four goals conceded.

After spells with Dunfermline and Dumbarton, David was forced to retire at the age of 26, after suffering a series of blackouts. He was later diagnosed as suffering from a brain aneurysm, the same condition which killed the late Davie Cooper. Sadly, Anderson's condition has worsened over the years and he is now partially blind and semi-paralysed.

DOUGLAS ARMSTRONG

Half-back

BORN: Edinburgh, 13 June 1925

HEIGHT: 6'   WEIGHT: 11st 5lb (1953)

COMPETITIVE DEBUT: v Rangers, 20 October 1951 (Lge) (A), 0–2

CAREER: North Merchiston Boys Club; Edinburgh Ashton; Haddington Athletic, 1947; **Hearts, Jan 1948**; Third Lanark, May 1956 (free transfer)

HONOURS: Scotland Junior international

Slim half-back who worked tirelessly in front of the defence in the early '50s. Dougie was used mostly as a covering player, hence his meagre 53 competitive appearances over eight years. He was a reliable squad player who almost established himself in 1953 until John Cumming moved into the half-back line. A cartilage operation in January 1956 slowed Dougie up and he was released in May 1956.

IAN BAIRD

Centre-forward

BORN: Rotherham, 1 April 1964

HEIGHT: 5′ 10″   **WEIGHT:** 12st 9lb (1991)

COMPETITIVE DEBUT: v Dunfermline, 10 August 1991 (PL) (A), 2–1

CAREER: Southampton, Apr 1982; Cardiff (on loan); Newcastle United (on loan); Leeds United, Mar 1985 (£75,000); Portsmouth, June 1987 (£285,000); Leeds United, Mar 1988 (£185,000); Middlesbrough, Jan 1990 (£350,000); **Hearts, July 1991** (£350,000); Bristol City, July 1993 (£295,000)

HONOURS: Premier League r-up 1991–92 (Hearts)

The far-travelled Baird arrived at Hearts two years after a previous bid for his signature had been unsuccessful. He soon impressed all with his robust style and was quickly nicknamed 'Yogi' by the supporters. However, indifferent form and a failure to score often enough saw many fans turn against him. Worse was to follow with a ridiculous sending-off against St Mirren in a Scottish Cup tie. Persistent injury problems made matters worse and Ian did himself no favours by attempting to play through the pain barrier. In season 1992–93 criticism of the player intensified and it was clear his future lay elsewhere. To his credit, Baird put the supporters' opinions to the back of his mind and hit five goals in seven matches during November and December 1992. Long before the season's end, however, he had sold his house in Edinburgh and his family had returned south. His last match for Hearts ended with another ordering-off. He allegedly gestured to the Aberdeen fans after an equaliser. The club video exonerated him and no fine was levied.

Ian later signed for Bristol City, with the fee set at £295,000 by a transfer tribunal.

EAMONN BANNON

Midfield

BORN: Edinburgh, 18 April 1958

HEIGHT: 5′ 9″   **WEIGHT:** 11st 11lb (1991)

COMPETITIVE DEBUT: v SV Hamburg, 3 November 1976 (ECWC) (H), 1–4

CAREER: Links Boys Club; **Hearts, July 1976;** Chelsea, Jan 1979 (£215,000); Dundee United, Oct 1979 (£165,000); **Hearts, May 1988** (£225,000); Hibernian player/coach, July 1993 (free transfer); **Hearts assistant manager, July 1994;** Stenhousemuir (player) Aug 1995

HONOURS: 11 full Scotland caps; 7 U-21 Scotland caps; 1 Scottish League cap; UEFA Cup r-up 1986–87 (Dundee United); Premier League winner 1982–83 (Dundee United); r-up 1989–90, 1991–92 (Hearts); Division I r-up 1977–78 (Hearts); Scottish Cup r-up 1980–81, 1984–85, 1986–87, 1987–88 (Dundee United); Scottish League Cup winner 1979–80, 1980–81 (Dundee United); r-up 1981–82, 1984–85 (Dundee United)

Matured at an early age into a cool, collected and thoughtful top-class player. Eamonn's main attributes were pinpoint passing, deceptive body movement which helped him glide past opponents with the assistance of a neat turn of pace, and a cannonball shot. He scored many goals from the midfield in Hearts' promotion campaign in season 1977–78, most notably the all-important goal which clinched promotion at Arbroath in April 1978.

Hearts' horrendous financial plight forced his sale to Chelsea, where he failed to settle. He was transferred to Dundee United, who benefited from Eamonn in his prime. His return to Tynecastle in May 1988 allowed Hearts fans to enjoy his skills during the twilight of a successful career. Eamonn's experience was invaluable on the European stage as Hearts reached the UEFA Cup quarter-finals in 1988–89. Bannon was used more sparingly as he advanced to his mid-30s. Injury kept him out more often and, when fit, he was often a substitute.

A managerial change in May 1993 saw Eamonn granted a free transfer and, after considering offers from Ayr United, St Mirren and Gateshead, he was surprisingly named as the new Hibernian reserve team player/coach in July 1993. He returned to Hearts for a third time in July 1994.

ROY BARRY

BORN: Edinburgh, 19 September 1942

HEIGHT: 5' 10"   WEIGHT: 11st 9lb (1964)

Centre-half

COMPETITIVE DEBUT: v Raith Rovers, 12 August 1961 (LC) (H), 1–0

CAREER: Musselburgh Athletic Juniors; **Hearts, July 1961**; Dunfermline, Sept 1966 (£13,000); Coventry City, Oct 1969 (£40,000); Crystal Palace, Sept 1973 (£45,000); Hibernian, Feb 1975; East Fife player/manager, 1976; retired in 1978; Oxford United assistant manager.

HONOURS: Scottish League r-up 1964–65 (Hearts); Scottish Cup Winner 1967–68 (Dunfermline); Scottish League Cup winner 1962–63 (Hearts)

Roy made an early breakthrough at Hearts but was basically a fringe player in his first season. He established himself at centre-half in 1962–63, but encountered problems with his on-field discipline, his hot temper often landing him in trouble with referees. Roy's red hair made him stand out from the other players and, when Hearts were toiling in some games, fans had a nasty habit of cat-calling him. His commitment and effort were never in doubt, however. He tackled with conviction and cleared his lines with minimum fuss. He lost his place to Alan Anderson and began to figure more as a link man in Hearts' infamous 4–2–4 formation. From his new position Roy was a driving force in season 1964–65, scoring seven goals in the League. He became a victim of his own versatility and this had an unsettling effect. He moved to Dunfermline and captained them to a Scottish Cup win against Hearts. He later tried his luck in England before joining Hibs in 1975, and moving into management in 1976 with East Fife.

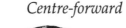

WILLIE BAULD

Centre-forward

BORN: Newcraighall, 24 January 1928

DIED: Edinburgh, 11 March 1977

HEIGHT: 5' 8"   WEIGHT: 11st 4lb (1952)

COMPETITIVE DEBUT: v East Fife, 9 October 1948 (LC) (H), 6–1 (scored a hat-trick)

CAREER: Niddrie Marehill; Edinburgh Waverley; Musselburgh Union; **Hearts, May 1946**; Newtongrange Star (on loan); Edinburgh City (on loan); **Hearts, 1947**; retired in May 1962; opened a newsagent's close to Tynecastle.

HONOURS: 3 full Scotland caps; 13 Scottish League caps; Scottish League Championship winner 1957–58, 1959–60 (Hearts); Scottish Cup winner 1955–56 (Hearts); Scottish League Cup winner 1954–55, 1958–59 (Hearts); r-up 1961–62 (Hearts); awarded a testimonial match in November 1962

The undisputed 'King of Hearts', as he was affectionately known, Willie was hero-worshipped throughout his Tynecastle career and his legend lives on as older generations still talk of his feats. Hearts almost lost his signature to Sunderland after a mix-up which was fortunately resolved in our favour. After loan spells to prime him for first-team football, Bauld exploded onto the Scottish football scene in spectacular fashion with a superb debut hat-trick against East Fife. This was no flash in the pan – he repeated the feat a week later in a 4–1 win against Queen of the South. Bauld had arrived in a big way and, with Alfie Conn and Jimmy Wardhaugh, the 'Terrible Trio' was born. He soon displayed an array of skills: a quick-thinking footballing brain, neat touch play, powerful shooting and, above all else, an exceptional heading ability. Willie could hang in mid-air seemingly motionless before bulleting headers into the opposition net or providing knock-downs for Conn or Wardhaugh to score.

International recognition arrived in 1950 when Willie won the first of only three caps – scant reward for such an exceptional talent. On the domestic front the Trio scored goals by the barrowload as Hearts swept the board from the mid to late-1950s. Bauld's 183 League goals is bettered only by Jimmy Wardhaugh's 206. His goals record would surely have been greater if continual knee injuries had not forced his absence from so many games.

Willie was used sparingly in his last two seasons as youngsters were tried out in a transitional spell. He announced his retirement in May 1962 and was awarded a testimonial match against Sheffield United. A bitter disagreement developed when Hearts made charges to Willie over such items as the match ball from this game. This was no way to treat royalty and the King shunned Tynecastle for 12 years. He returned to a hero's welcome and an emotional standing ovation in January 1975 at the invitation of club chairman Bobby Parker, a former colleague. Willie, however, insisted he attended the match to lend support to his young nephew, who had been selected as mascot for the Cup tie with Kilmarnock.

His death from heart failure at the age of 49 stunned all Hearts supporters and thousands attended his funeral to pay their respects to an all-time great and a true, loyal club servant.

BOBBY BAXTER
Centre-half

BORN: Edinburgh, 23 January 1911

DIED: Edinburgh, April 1991

HEIGHT: 5' 10"   WEIGHT: 11st 10lb (1946)

COMPETITIVE DEBUT: v Partick Thistle, 18 August 1945 (Lge) (A), 3–1

CAREER: Musselburgh Bruntonians; Middlesbrough, 1931; **Hearts, 1939–40** (guest); Hibernian, 1940; **Hearts, June 1945** (£2,000); Leith Athletic manager, May 1948; Cowdenbeath manager, July 1951

HONOURS: 3 full Scotland caps; 2 wartime caps for Scotland

A highly rated centre-half down south with Middlesbrough, with whom he made 266 appearances. He hit peak form in season 1938–39 and was rewarded with three caps for Scotland. He returned to Edinburgh at the start of the war to work in the pits. He guested with Hearts and the 'Uncrowned King of Gilmerton' almost led them to the wartime East and North League title.

Unfortunately, managerless Hearts slipped up when Hibs pinched his services for season 1940–41, and he remained at Easter Road until June 1945. Hearts renegotiated his transfer and the veteran 34-year-old helped bolster Hearts' young defence. He was appointed skipper and his influence and coaching knowledge were of great benefit. Bobby was a skilful, constructive player who always attempted to play out of trouble rather than resort to hoofing the ball upfield. He faded from the playing side in 1947 and coached at Tynecastle for one year before moving into management. In later years he was the manager of the Edinburgh Monarchs speedway team.

BILLY BENNETT
Midfield

BORN: Newburgh, 5 July 1955

HEIGHT: 5′ 8″   WEIGHT: 11st (1975)

COMPETITIVE DEBUT: v Arbroath, 16 November 1974 (Lge) (A), 1–3

CAREER: Bell Baxter School; Letham Boys Club (Perth); **Hearts, c.1973**; Berwick Rangers, c.1976; Forfar Athletic, May 1978; Arbroath, 1989; Cowdenbeath, 1991; retired in 1993

HONOURS: Division II winner 1983–84 (Forfar); r-up 1991–92 (Cowdenbeath)

Battling midfielder or defender who loved to charge into attack. After being introduced for the first time in an East of Scotland Shield tie against Berwick, Billy was given his League debut a week later. Hearts crashed to an embarrassing defeat and three defensive changes were made, with Bennett a casualty. He never played for the first team again, despite a reasonable showing in his first game. After a short spell at Berwick he moved to Forfar and took a full-time job as a financial representative. He skippered the Loons for several seasons, leading them to a creditable 0–0 draw against Rangers in the 1984 League Cup semi-final, before losing the replay 3–0. He completed his career with the 'Blue Brazil' and played his part in assisting them to promotion in 1991–92.

NEIL BERRY
Midfield/defender

BORN: Edinburgh, 6 April 1963

HEIGHT: 5′ 11″   WEIGHT: 12st 7lb (1985)

COMPETITIVE DEBUT: v Dundee United, 15 December 1984 (PL) (A), 2–5

CAREER: Firhill School (Edinburgh); Bolton Wanderers, 1981; **Hearts, Dec 1984** (free transfer)

HONOURS: Scotland Youth international; Premier League r-up 1985–86, 1987–88 (Hearts); Scottish Cup r-up 1985–86 (Hearts)

After joining Bolton straight from school Neil failed to establish himself down south. He returned to Hearts in December 1984 and made a quick debut at Tannadice, having the misfortune to score an own-goal that day as Hearts lost heavily. However, Berry soon settled at Tynecastle. His powerful ball-winning qualities and distribution skills were among the many reasons why Hearts put together such a great run in season 1985–86. Neil featured regularly over the next three seasons either in midfield or at full-back or central defence when required.

From seasons 1989–90 to 1991–92 'Chuck' endured a succession of horrendous injuries. The latter season was a total wash-out due to a severe ankle complaint. He continued to feature in the next two seasons, although more often in defence.

JIM BETT
Midfield

BORN: Hamilton, 25 November 1959

HEIGHT: 5' 11"   WEIGHT: 12st 4lb (1994)

COMPETITIVE DEBUT: v Partick Thistle, 8 October 1994 (PL) (A), 1–0

CAREER: Hamilton Schools; Dundee (S-form); Airdrie, *c*.1976; Valur, Iceland, May 1978 (£1,500); SK Lokeren, Belgium, 1979; Rangers, 1980 (£150,000); SK Lokeren, 1983 (£200,000); Aberdeen, June 1985 (£300,000); Reykjavik, Iceland, May 1994 (free transfer); **Hearts, Sept 1994** (free transfer); Dundee United Aug 1995

HONOURS: 25 full Scotland caps; 7 U-21 Scotland caps; Scotland Schoolboy international; Scottish Cup winner 1980–81 (Rangers), 1985–86, 1989–90 (Aberdeen); r-up 1981–82, 1982–83 (Rangers); Scottish League Cup winner 1981–82 (Rangers), 1989–90 (Aberdeen); r-up 1982–83 (Rangers), 1987–88, 1988–89 (Aberdeen); Icelandic Cup winner 1994 (Reykjavik)

Stylish and highly skilful midfielder who won almost all the game's top honours in Scotland. A superb passer of the ball, Bett was once described as 'a right-footed Jim Baxter'. He joined Hearts initially on a short-term contract to provide more competition in the midfield area. After making a notable contribution in 1994–95, he declined another short-term contract in August 1995.

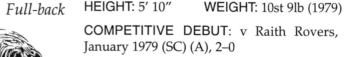

IAN BLACK

Full-back

BORN: Edinburgh, 4 February 1960

HEIGHT: 5′ 10″   **WEIGHT:** 10st 9lb (1979)

COMPETITIVE DEBUT: v Raith Rovers, 27 January 1979 (SC) (A), 2–0

CAREER: Musselburgh Windsor; **Hearts, 1977**; Hibernian, 1980 (free transfer); East Fife; Berwick Rangers; Ormiston Primrose, 1982

Forceful, hard-tackling full-back who also packed a powerful shot. Ian broke through in 1978–79 season just after Eamonn Bannon's transfer. His debut at Starks Park was memorable, with Hearts winning 2–0, Ian playing in the midfield that afternoon. After a couple of substitute appearances he had a short run in the left-back position until the end of the season. He made a few more appearances the next term but the arrival of several new defenders restricted his chances. He was released in 1980 and joined Hibs for a short spell.

KENNY BLACK

Defender/midfield

BORN: Stenhousemuir, 29 November 1963

HEIGHT: 5′ 8″   **WEIGHT:** 10st 11lb (1988)

COMPETITIVE DEBUT: v Dundee United, 11 August 1984 (PL) (A), 0–2

CAREER: Gairdoch United; Rangers, 1980 (farmed out to Linlithgow Rose then called up in 1981); Motherwell, Dec 1983 (exchange deal); **Hearts, June 1984** (£30,000); Portsmouth, May 1989 (£350,000); Airdrie, Oct 1991 (£100,000)

HONOURS: Premier League r-up 1985–86 (Hearts); Scottish Cup r-up 1985–86 (Hearts), 1994–95 (Airdrie); B&Q Cup winner 1994–95 (Airdrie); Tennents Sixes winner 1984–85 (Hearts)

A tough, no-nonsense versatile defender or midfielder who gave five years of valuable service to Hearts. A virtual ever-present in the side, the fans either loved or hated his style of play. Never one to hide in games even when luck was against him, Kenny possessed a fine left foot which he used to good effect in free-kick or penalty situations. Kenny was an accurate passer of the ball and battled admirably in every role he filled. He is one of the few Hearts players to record a Premier League hat-trick, against Dumbarton in January 1985.

After failing to settle with Portsmouth he rejoined his former manager at Hearts when he signed for Alex Macdonald's Airdrie.

Forward

BORN: Edinburgh, 20 August 1934

HEIGHT: 5' 6"   WEIGHT: 10st 2lb (1955)

COMPETITIVE DEBUT: v Hibernian, 20 September 1952 (Lge) (A), 1–3

CAREER: Milton House Amateurs; Merchiston Thistle; Kelty Rangers; **Hearts, Oct 1950**; Ipswich Town, June 1962 (£10,000); Colchester United, May 1965

HONOURS: Scottish League winner 1957–58, 1959–60 (Hearts); Scottish League Cup winner 1959–60 (Hearts); r-up 1961–62 (Hearts)

A fringe member of Hearts' first-team squad for five seasons. Bobby returned from National Service in Malaysia in August 1957 and soon won a place in the first team at inside-forward or on either wing. His pace and determination made him a much feared striker. Blackwood had fine ball-control skills and could find the net with deadly accuracy. His form peaked in season 1959–60, scoring 12 League and 5 League Cup goals and his contribution was one of the main reasons why Hearts won both competitions. Bobby kept on scoring during the transitional 1960–61 season but his goal touch deserted him in 1961–62.

Newly crowned English Champions, Ipswich Town, took Blackwood south in June 1962 and he starred at Portman Road for three seasons. He moved to Colchester in 1965 and made 104 League appearances. He twice suffered a broken jaw in successive seasons after clashing with the same player, Dennis Allen of Reading! Bobby now resides in the Edinburgh area.

Forward

BORN: Bridge of Allan, 22 September 1949

HEIGHT: 5' 9"   WEIGHT: 12st 2lb (1983)

COMPETITIVE DEBUT: v St Johnstone, 20 August 1983 (PL) (A), 1–0 (scored)

CAREER: Fallin Boys Brigade; Bannockburn; Airth Castle Rovers; Partick Thistle, 1968; Norwich City, Feb 1972 (£30,000); Sheffield United, Feb 1973 (£30,000 plus another player); Celtic, Feb 1974 (£25,000); Arbroath, Jan 1975 (£12,000); St Mirren, Jan 1978 (£25,000); Hong Kong Rangers, 1981; **Hearts, Aug 1983** (free transfer); Arbroath player/manager, Feb 1985; St Mirren assistant manager, Dec 1986; Dundee United coach; Airdrie manager; FC Dynamo (Zambia) manager, 1991; St Mirren manager, June 1992

HONOURS: 2 full Scotland caps; 3 Scotland U-23 caps; Scottish League Cup winner 1971–72 (Partick); English League Division II winner 1971–72 (Norwich City); Tennents Sixes winners 1984–85 (Hearts)

A bustling, 'up-and-at-'em' striker, Jimmy was courageous enough to put his foot or head where others wouldn't dare. He terrorised defenders by running at and taking them on with considerable success. An electrician to trade, Jimmy wandered around during his career before joining Hearts at the veteran stage. He is well remembered by Hearts fans for a late goal from a diving header which sunk Hibs in September 1983. He also scored our 6,000th League goal, against Dundee United in December 1984. Jimmy had a grand rapport with the Tynecastle faithful who humorously chanted: 'He's fat, he's round, he bounces on the ground – Jimmy Bone!!!'

He made a telling contribution to ensure Hearts' Premier League place in 1983–84 to the point where they qualified for European football. He thus achieved one of his ambitions when he appeared against Paris St-Germain in 1984.

Bone's experience, hints and tips helped mould John Robertson and several other youngsters into future stars, and he has since gained comprehensive managerial experience at home and abroad with several clubs.

ADRIAN BOOTHROYD

Defender

BORN: Bradford, 8 February 1971

HEIGHT: 5′ 9″   **WEIGHT:** 11st 5lb (1993)

COMPETITIVE DEBUT: v St Johnstone, 12 December 1992 (PL) (A), 1–1 (came on as substitute)

CAREER: Bradford Boys; Huddersfield, July 1989; Bristol Rovers, June 1990 (£30,000); **Hearts, Dec 1992** (free transfer); Mansfield Town, Dec 1993 (free transfer)

Adrian was signed by Joe Jordan on the eve of his debut match at Perth. When the tannoy announced the teams, the chorus said, 'Who?' at the mention of his name. Ade took to the field late in the game and almost fluked a debut goal. One month later, with a few more substitute appearances behind him, Boothroyd came on in a Scottish Cup tie against Huntly. He scored two excellent goals which earned widespread media attention. The first was a run from the halfway line where he beat three defenders before cracking the ball home and the second a looping header. The quality of the opposition had to be questioned, however.

The managerial change in May 1993 was the beginning of the end for Ade. He appeared on the German tour and scored in one game but never played another competitive game. His release came as no surprise.

BORN: Pittenweem, Fife, 7 March 1934

HEIGHT: 5′ 7″   WEIGHT: 11st 1lb (1960)

COMPETITIVE DEBUT: v Partick Thistle, 13 August 1955 (LC) (A), 2–0

CAREER: Chelsea, June 1951; **Hearts, July 1955** (£1,000); Newport County, Aug 1961 (free transfer); Hamilton Accies, July 1965

HONOURS: Scottish League winner 1957–58, 1959–60 (Hearts); Scottish League Cup winner 1959–60 (Hearts)

ANDY BOWMAN

Half-back

A tough, uncompromising half-back, Andy was a committed tackler and linked well with the attack. He joined Chelsea aged 15 but struggled to settle or make any impact. When Hearts made an offer Andy was delighted to return home. He made a quick debut and figured in six League Cup ties in 1955–56. He then made way for Dave Mackay and John Cumming to renew their half-back partnership. He enjoyed a good number of games in 1957–58, appearing in just over half of the League campaign. His forceful style complemented a workmanlike defence.

Bowman's appearances were restricted in 1958–59 but he did play in one game against Liege in the European Cup. He played regularly in 1959–60 and the following season saw him in action twice against Benfica. However, he lost his place in 1960–61 and later moved to Newport on a free transfer. His son David followed in his footsteps when he starred for Hearts in the early 1980s.

BORN: Tunbridge Wells, 10 March 1964

HEIGHT: 5′ 8″   WEIGHT: 10st 8lb (1982)

COMPETITIVE DEBUT: v Airdrie, 30 July 1980 (ASC) (A), 0–3 (came on as substitute)

CAREER: Parsons Green School, Edinburgh; Salvesen Boys Club; **Hearts, June 1980**; Coventry City, Dec 1984 (£170,000); Dundee United, June 1986 (£125,000)

HONOURS: 1 full Scotland cap; 1 Scotland U-21 cap; Scotland Schoolboy international; European Youth Championship winner 1982; UEFA Cup r-up 1986–87 (Dundee United); Scottish Cup winner 1993–94 (Dundee United); r-up 1986–87, 1987–88, 1990–91 (Dundee United)

DAVID BOWMAN

Midfield

Dave broke into Hearts' first team almost immediately as a 16-year-old. This was mainly due to a lack of quality and strength in depth at the time, but does not detract from his ability. He combined a mix of robust powerplay with subtle passes and neat touches and could pack a hard shot. He turned in many consistent, mature performances for such a young player. This is borne out by his achievement of being the youngest Hearts player to chalk up a hundred competitive appearances. His prompting and influence in 1982–83 helped Hearts return to the Premier League. Dave also contributed his best goal tally that term.

After helping the club to consolidate Premier League status and appearing in the 1984–85 UEFA Cup matches, Dave was surprisingly sold. Coventry City took him south at the age of 20 and many Hearts fans questioned the wisdom in selling such a talented youngster. He returned to Dundee United in 1986 and has shown his versatility in serving them well over the years. Domestic and full international honours came his way on Tayside. Dave is the son of Andy Bowman, the 1950s star.

CRAWFORD BOYD

Defender

BORN: Kilwinning, 19 March 1952

COMPETITIVE DEBUT: v Motherwell, 19 September 1979 (Div. I) (A), 2–4

CAREER: Largs Thistle; Queen of the South, 1972; **Hearts, Sept 1979** (£25,000); Queen of the South, Feb 1981 (free transfer); Irvine Meadow player/manager, 1985; Largs Thistle, 1985

HONOURS: Division I winner 1979–80 (Hearts)

Crawford had dutifully served Queen of the South for many seasons and feared he would never obtain the chance to play at a bigger club. He felt Queens always put too high a transfer fee on his head. Willie Ormond granted Crawford his wish in 1979. A long-running dispute between Boyd and the Queens management ended when a £25,000 fee took him to Hearts.

Boyd had limitations but performed competently in the centre of defence. Some of his pass-backs are well remembered for all the wrong reasons – one 40-yard lob which hit John Brough's crossbar at Shawfield in a match against Clyde particularly stands out. Crawford found difficulty in adjusting to the standards required for the Premier League and Bobby Moncur saw fit to drop him. He returned to Queen of the South as a part-timer and to his old job at Hunterston Power Station.

BORN: St Helens, Lancashire, 23 April 1917

DIED: 1981

Right-winger

COMPETITIVE DEBUT: v Ayr United, 9 October 1937 (Lge) (H), 7–0

CAREER: St Helens Town; Preston North End, May 1934; **Hearts, Oct 1937** (£1,500); Northampton Town, Sept 1946 (£2,250, along with Archie Garrett); Northampton coach, 1949

HONOURS: Scottish League r-up 1937–38 (Hearts)

An exciting right-winger who terrorised defences with his direct attacking style. Jimmy could create and take goal chances and linked beautifully in a famous forward line of Briscoe, Walker, Garrett, Black and Warren just before the Second World War. His best years were without doubt prior to the war. When hostilities ceased Jimmy was at the veteran stage and aged 31. He made only two appearances in 1946–47 before moving to Northampton.

BORN: Edinburgh, 31 March 1960

HEIGHT: 5' 11"   WEIGHT: 12st 10lb (1979)

Goalkeeper

COMPETITIVE DEBUT: v Arbroath, 8 April 1978 (Div. I) (H), 3–2

CAREER: Calvary Park; **Hearts, Aug 1977**; Partick Thistle, Dec 1983 (free transfer); Dunbar Juniors, 1989

HONOURS: 1 U-21 Scotland cap; Division I winner 1979–80 (Hearts)

Brave goalkeeper who was able to produce marvellous reflex saves. His main shortcoming was an inability to come for cross balls successfully. John was a firm favourite with the fans in the late 1970s and early 1980s when many amazing displays by him saved Hearts from some total hammerings. An especially good spell of form won him his only international honour, against Denmark's U-21 side at Pittodrie in 1980. Brough lost his place to Henry Smith in July 1981, managing a mere six competitive games thereafter before moving to Partick.

GORDON BROWN

Midfield

BORN: Edinburgh

HEIGHT: 5' 11"   **WEIGHT:** 10st 8lb (1977)

COMPETITIVE DEBUT: v Dundee United, 16 November 1977 (LCqf) (H), 2–0 (came on as a substitute)

CAREER: Currie Hearts; **Hearts, 1976** (freed in 1979); Newtongrange Star; Bonnyrigg Rose; Easthouses Lily; Easthouses Lily manager, May 1994

Teenage midfielder who made four substitute appearances in competitive matches in 1977–78. Gordon's highlight would probably be his debut match when Hearts knocked Dundee United out of the League Cup. The match was sealed in a penalty shoot-out. After his release Gordon played in the ranks of junior football for several years.

JIMMY BROWN

Goalkeeper

BORN: Buckhaven, 19 July 1925

HEIGHT: 5' 9"   **WEIGHT:** 12st 7lb (1953)

COMPETITIVE DEBUT: v Dumbarton, 10 October 1942 (S.Lge) (A), 2–2

CAREER: Wemyss Schoolboys; Bayview Youth Club; **Hearts, June 1942**; Southend United, 1952 (on loan); Kilmarnock, Aug 1953 (free transfer); St Mirren, Nov 1960; East Fife, Nov 1962; Stranraer, Dec 1962; Falkirk, Jan 1963; Polish White Eagles (Canada), 1963

HONOURS: Represented Scotland on a tour of the USA and Canada in 1949; Scottish Cup r-up 1956–57 (Kilmarnock); Scottish League Cup r-up 1960–61 (Kilmarnock)

Jimmy was instantly recognisable with his chunky thighs and was famed for wearing flashy coloured tops and baseball caps which were unusual in the immediate post-war years. He was a dependable and agile custodian who clutched the ball with his elbows pointing outwards, no doubt as a guard against the shoulder-charging which was permitted in those days. Jimmy had a strange pre-match ritual: after running to his goal he would habitually pull on the crossbar before touching each goalpost. He was unchallenged for the goalie's jersey for almost ten years until dispossessed by Jimmy Watters. His shut-out record is fourth best in Hearts' history.

Jimmy once scored a penalty against Queens Park in a reserve match in

1947. He also saved the odd one or two at the other end during his career. He suffered a badly dislocated shoulder in a match against Queen of the South in February 1950. He recovered, but suffered recurrent problems over the next two years. A broken collar-bone in season 1952–53 didn't help and, with Jimmy Watters established in the team, Hearts granted him a free transfer and a fresh start in April 1953. He went on to make 315 appearances at Rugby Park and then had several moves at the veteran stage. Jimmy later became a publican in Kilmarnock and Stewarton, coaching Stewarton United for a short period. He returned to live in his native Fife in the early 1980s.

JIMMY BROWN

Midfield/defender

BORN: Edinburgh, 11 August 1950

HEIGHT: 5' 9"   WEIGHT: 10st 1lb (1977)

COMPETITIVE DEBUT: v Airdrie, 4 January 1969 (Lge) (A), 1–1

CAREER: Boroughmuir High School; Murieston Boys Club; Salvesen Boys Club; **Hearts, Aug 1967**; Hibernian, May 1979 (free transfer); Dunfermline Athletic, 1981 (free transfer); forced out of the game through injury, *c.* 1982

HONOURS: Scotland Juvenile, Youth and Amateur International; 1 Scottish League cap; Division I winner 1980–81 (Hibernian); Scottish Cup r-up 1975–76 (Hearts); Texaco Cup r-up 1970–71 (Hearts)

Jimmy's never-say-die attitude, tough tackling and effective ball distribution won him many plaudits in a long Hearts career. At times he appeared untiring – a true workhorse who always gave 100 per cent. He was nicknamed 'Bomber' by the Hearts fans, which immediately creates an image of the type of player he was. Brown captained the team for several seasons through a difficult time as the club slid into decline. One bright spot came in 1976 when he won full international recognition as a squad member for a World Cup qualifying tie against Wales but sadly he missed being selected.

Following relegation, Jimmy turned part-time for season 1977–78, combining football with finance company work. In November 1977 he suffered a terrible double fracture to his leg which put him out for five months and almost ended his career. He demonstrated true grit by making a full recovery in time to return to Premier League action after promotion was secured.

A second relegation in 1979 spelled the end of Jim Brown's Hearts career and he moved to neighbours Hibs, who were also toiling. He captained the Easter Road side before another move to Dunfermline, where a crude challenge (which led to legal action) ended his career.

Goalkeeper

BORN: Lanark

HEIGHT: 5′ 10″   **WEIGHT:** 11st (1960)

COMPETITIVE DEBUT: v Raith Rovers, 31 August 1955 (LC) (A), 2–0

CAREER: Lanark United; **Hearts, Oct 1952;** Queen of the South, Apr 1961 (free transfer); quit football, *c.*1963; Hamilton Accies, 1965

Wilson Brown signed for Hearts as a teenager but spent most of his time on National Service with the Royal Scots. He was fortunate to be stationed at Glencorse Barracks near Edinburgh and managed to turn out for the reserve side.

After being demobbed he turned full time and made a breakthrough in the League Cup ties of 1955–56. Wilson played second fiddle more often to the established Willie Duff. Even when Duff moved on, Gordon Marshall emerged from the ranks to challenge for the goalkeeper's position. Wilson continued to strive for first-team action but only managed a few matches each season. He eventually became disillusioned with his situation and quit in the early 1960s.

Goalkeeper

BORN: Edinburgh, 9 August 1964

HEIGHT: 6′ 3″   **WEIGHT:** 14st (1987)

COMPETITIVE DEBUT: v Motherwell, 15 April 1987 (PL) (A), 1–0

CAREER: Linlithgow Rose; Rangers, 1980; **Hearts, May 1986** (free transfer); quit football to join the police, Aug 1988

HONOURS: Scotland Schoolboy international

Andy joined Hearts after spending almost his entire Rangers career as an understudy. His short spell at Tynecastle was similar, as Henry Smith's deputy. An injury to Smith in April 1987 gave Andy a debut chance. In his one and only competitive appearance he competently dealt with all Motherwell's goal attempts and recorded a clean sheet. Henry Smith's continual domination of the goalkeeper's position eventually prompted Andy to pursue a career outside football.

Forward

BORN: Kelty, 1 June 1929

HEIGHT: 5′ 10″   WEIGHT: 10st 7lb (1949)

COMPETITIVE DEBUT: v Partick Thistle, 6 November 1948 (Lge) (H), 1–3

CAREER: Kelty Public School; Bayview Youth Club; Lochgelly Violet; **Hearts, 1948**; freed, April 1952

Bobby joined Hearts on a part-time basis. He was studying for a mining engineering qualification at Edinburgh University when he signed in 1948, graduating with a BSc in June 1951. He made his debut when Archie Williams came down with flu. Bobby's best attributes were speed, positional sense and an ability to hit the ball on the run. He turned out consistently in reserve football throughout his four years at Tynecastle. By all accounts he was a fair player but found difficulty in gaining selection ahead of established stars.

Full-back

BORN: Lanark, 13 December 1965

HEIGHT: 5′ 11″   WEIGHT: 12st 2lb (1987)

COMPETITIVE DEBUT: v Rangers, 3 October 1987 (PL) (H), 0–0

CAREER: Rangers, 1981; Leeds United; Hamilton and Bradford, 1986–87 (on loan); **Hearts, July 1987** (£175,000); Dunfermline, Dec 1988 (£25,000); Hamilton, July 1990; Kilmarnock, 1991; Ayr United, June 1993; Dumbarton, Aug 1995

HONOURS: Scotland Schoolboy and U-21 international; Scottish League Cup winner 1983–84 (Rangers)

Popularly known as 'Shuggie', the West Coast nickname for Hugh. He joined Hearts at the same time as Dave McPherson, and it was rumoured that Hearts were forced to sign him or risk losing McPherson's signature. It seemed an unlikely scenario but Burns took a while to make his competitive debut. He was easily recognised with his bleached hair and strong, thick thigh muscles. He tackled with great vigour and liked to overlap on the wing to support the forwards. Hugh's main failing was poor heading ability – his heavy legs restricted his jumping and midfielders often dropped balls over his head to attackers. The management realised this shortcoming and after a loan spell to Dunfermline, the Fifers arranged his permanent transfer.

SANDY BURRELL

Full-back

BORN: Edinburgh, 25 May 1955

HEIGHT: 5' 7"   **WEIGHT:** 11st 1lb (1976)

COMPETITIVE DEBUT: v Oldham Athletic, 30 September 1974 (Tex. C) (H), 1–1

CAREER: Lasswade High School; Royston Boys Club; **Hearts, 1971**; Falkirk, May 1977 (free transfer); Meadowbank Thistle, 1982 (free transfer); Newtongrange Star, 1984; Sherwood Boys Club coach in 1990s

HONOURS: Scottish Cup r-up 1975–76 (Hearts)

Promising full-back who never quite realised his early potential. His first-team opportunities were restricted due to an abundance of talented full-backs in the mid-1970s. Sandy was a competent defender who could distribute well to the midfield and break up opposition attacks with assured tackling and intelligent anticipation.

Sandy's most important match for Hearts was the 1976 Cup final where he appeared at left-back. He was substituted at half-time, however, making way for winger Kenny Aird as Hearts attempted to fight back from a two-goal deficit.

Burrell was freed after Hearts' relegation in May 1977. He played on in senior and junior circles well into his 30s and later assisted with local youth teams in his home town of Bonnyrigg.

DREW BUSBY

Forward/midfield

BORN: Glasgow, 8 December 1947

HEIGHT: 5' 8"   **WEIGHT:** 12st 12lb (1978)

COMPETITIVE DEBUT: v Partick Thistle, 11 August 1973 (LC) (H), 2–0

CAREER: Vale of Leven Academy; Coventry City, 1964; Dumbarton Castle Rovers; Third Lanark, 1966; Vale of Leven, 1967; Airdrie, July 1970; **Hearts, May 1973** (£35,000); Toronto Blizzard, May 1979; Morton, Aug 1980; Queen of the South player/manager, Jun 1982 until 1984; later scouted for St Mirren and worked in the licensed trade

HONOURS: Scottish Cup r-up 1975–76 (Hearts)

After several false starts to his career and claiming credit as the man who scored Third Lanark's last goal, Drew came to prominence with Airdrie in the early 1970s where he struck up a deadly and profitable scoring partnership with Drew Jarvie. The Diamonds' relegation in 1973 sparked intense interest in Busby's future and it looked like Sunderland would win the race to sign him. As it transpired, Hearts paid a then record fee to sign him as a strike partner for Donald Ford.

The gutsy, robust attacker quickly won acclaim from all quarters and the supporters came to idolise him for his total commitment to Hearts. Drew was famed for his thunderbolt shot and awesome heading abilities – and look out any keeper who had to face a Busby penalty. He was equally effective when moved into midfield, where his beaverish style broke down opposition attacks and put Hearts on the offensive.

Drew is remembered for many fine goals, such as a cracker in the 4–1 win against Hibs and a Texaco Cup winner against Everton at Goodison, not forgetting a memorable double against Rangers in a 3–0 Ibrox win – all in September 1973. He hit several hat-tricks and numerous doubles, most notably two 25-yard bullets against Celtic in October 1978. His former manager, the late Willie Ormond, summed up Drew by calling him 'the most underrated player with the club, whose workrate is quite incredible'.

PADDY BYRNE

Midfield

BORN: Dublin, 15 May 1956

HEIGHT: 5' 7"   WEIGHT: 11st 3lb (1982)

COMPETITIVE DEBUT: v Airdrie, 8 August 1981 (LC) (A), 1–0

CAREER: Bohemians, 1972; Philadelphia Furies (USA), 1978; Leicester City, July 1979; **Hearts, July 1981**; Shamrock Rovers, Sept 1983; Shelbourne; Shelbourne manager, 1990s

HONOURS: Republic of Ireland Youth international; 1 Irish League cap; League of Ireland winner 1974–75 (Bohemians); English Division II winner 1979–80 (Leicester)

Stocky midfielder with a slow but deceptive manner of play, Paddy was a creative player who opened up defences with accurate passes. He was a virtual ever-present in 1981–82 and scored eight League goals, a good return for a midfield man. Unfortunately Paddy's family could not settle in Edinburgh and they returned to Dublin, where he had a successful business interest. Season 1982–83 saw Paddy commute from Dublin to play each week and he made a worthy contribution to help Hearts win promotion. He then expressed a desire to remain in Ireland and Hearts reluctantly agreed to release him.

RALPH CALLACHAN

Midfield

BORN: Edinburgh, 29 April 1955

HEIGHT: 5' 11"   **WEIGHT:** 10st 2lb (1975)

COMPETITIVE DEBUT: v Dunfermline, 17 April 1974 (Lge) (A), 3–2

CAREER: Brunstane Primary School; Tynecastle Boys Club; **Hearts, Sept 1971**; Newcastle United, Feb 1977 (£90,000); Hibernian, Aug 1978 (cash/exchange deal); Meadowbank Thistle, Nov 1986 (free transfer); Berwick Rangers, Oct 1988, as player/assistant manager

HONOURS: Scotland Youth and Amateur international; Division I winner 1980–81 (Hibernian); Scottish Cup r-up 1975–76 (Hearts), 1978–79 (Hibernian); Scottish Cup (Second XI) winner 1972–73 (Hearts)

Slim-built midfield grafter with fine ball-playing skills. Ralph's deceptive style and creativity produced many goalscoring opportunities for his front-line colleagues in addition to the chances he scored too. Hearts lost Ralph through a bad knee injury early in season 1976–77 and his lengthy absence, coupled with his controversial and seemingly unnecessary transfer in February 1977, was a major factor in Hearts' eventual relegation that year.

Ralph was actually signed by the Newcastle directors who had just sacked manager Gordon Lee. Consequently, his spell on Tyneside was short-lived and he returned to city rivals Hibs where he became the star player in a struggling side.

Callachan completed a capital hat-trick of clubs on joining Meadowbank in 1986 and later took up a managerial position at Berwick, combining this with his licensed trade interests.

BOBBY CAMPBELL

Full-back

BORN: Forres, 7 October 1936

HEIGHT: 5' 9"   **WEIGHT:** 11st 2lb (1956)

COMPETITIVE DEBUT: v East Fife, 5 September 1953 (Lge) (H), 2–2

CAREER: St James Youth Club; Lossiemouth United; Lossiemouth (seniors); **Hearts, Aug 1953**; Cowdenbeath, 1957 (free transfer)

A painter and decorator to trade, the young Highlander had the satisfaction of making a first-team debut after only two reserve appearances – but then returned to reserve-team obscurity. In 1954 he left to carry out his

National Service with the navy. He made one more appearance after his return in April 1956 but thereafter was unable to obtain a regular place due to the superb form of the club's full-backs. Bobby was freed in 1957 and later appeared against Hearts in the 1958 League Cup semi-final as a centre-half. The Maroons won 9–3 that evening.

GEORGE CAMPBELL
Inside-forward

HEIGHT: 5' 10"   WEIGHT: 10st 4lb (1956)

COMPETITIVE DEBUT: v Aberdeen, 17 September 1955 (LCqf) (H), 2–4

CAREER: Dunbar United; **Hearts, Aug 1954**; freed in April 1958

An intellectual young man, George studied for a BSc at Edinburgh University. He made his debut in season 1955–56 after impressing in reserve-team football. At the start of 1956–57 he deputised for Alfie Conn in three League Cup matches and performed well, scoring two goals. Intense competition for positions in the forward line and an abundance of more talented players resulted in Campbell's release in April 1958.

JIMMY CANT
Sweeper/defender

BORN: Edinburgh, 24 September 1953

HEIGHT: 5' 9"   WEIGHT: 11st 4lb (1973)

COMPETITIVE DEBUT: v Dundee, 28 April 1973 (Lge) (A), 2–2

CAREER: Peebles Rovers; **Hearts, 1970**; Montrose, Dec 1976 (free transfer); Raith Rovers, 1977

A product of Hearts' youth policy in the early 1970s, Jimmy progressed through the Hearts Colts XI and became a regular in reserve football in 1972–73. He established himself during 1973–74 with some mature performances. Injury put him out of action for a short time but he was back to his best in the 1974–75 League Cup competition. He scored three goals in the sectional ties, including a double against Morton in what was probably his best game for the club. He looked a fine prospect with his cool, confident approach. Tragically, his form totally deserted him in 1975 and further injuries restricted him to a mere four games in 1975–76. He could not recover his form or confidence and was granted a free transfer in December 1976. He later played representative football for Australia.

Forward

BORN: Edinburgh, 22 February 1953

HEIGHT: 5′ 8″   **WEIGHT:** 10st (1973)

COMPETITIVE DEBUT: v St Mirren, 21 February 1970 (Lge) (H), 1–0

CAREER: Firhill School; Salvesen Boys Club; **Hearts, 1969**; Derby County, Mar 1975 (£25,000); free transfer, Oct 1977

HONOURS: 1 Scotland Amateur Youth cap

Having quit his job as an apprentice electrician to join Hearts at the age of 16, the blond-haired striker was tipped for the top but never quite fulfilled his potential. He was a prolific scorer for the reserves and made occasional appearances in the first team, managing to hold a place during an unmemorable season 1972–73 when he scored five times in 27 games. A serious knee injury in the autumn of 1973 resulted in a cartilage operation which kept him out for a full year. When he was ready for action he found Ford, Busby and Gibson among others ahead of him in the strikers' queue. He appeared briefly in 1974-75 but his days were numbered after he submitted several transfer requests. Dave Mackay took him to Derby but cartilage problems continued to trouble him down south.

Versatile

BORN: Derby, 14 October 1964

HEIGHT: 6′   **WEIGHT:** 11st 5lb (1986)

COMPETITIVE DEBUT: v Dundee, 22 September 1984 (PL) (H), 0–2 (came on as substitute)

CAREER: Hearts, Mar 1983; Cowdenbeath, Aug 1986; St Johnstone, July 1988 (£4,000)

HONOURS: Division I winner 1989–90 (St Johnstone)

Paul was introduced for an East of Scotland Shield tie in 1982–83 but did not push for a first-team place until 1984–85. His limited number of games came mainly as a substitute or as cover for his teammates' injuries or suspensions. His single goal was a well-taken header in a League Cup tie against Stirling Albion.

Paul decided to try his luck with Cowdenbeath, who clinched his signature in a deal which involved them relinquishing their rights to possible future returns should Craig Levein ever transfer to another club. After two years at Central Park Paul moved to Perth where he carved out a successful career in defence and midfield.

Forward

BORN: Airdrie, 28 October 1956

HEIGHT: 6'   WEIGHT: 12st 7lb (1989)

COMPETITIVE DEBUT: v Morton, 20 October 1984 (PL) (A), 2–3 (scored)

CAREER: Caldervale High School; Airdrie, 1974; West Ham United, June 1982 (£180,000); Rangers, Mar 1983 (£165,000); **Hearts, Oct 1984** (£30,000); Partick Thistle manager, Nov 1989; Dunfermline, Jan 1990; **Hearts coach, Apr 1990**; **Hearts manager May 1993–June 1994**; Motherwell Youth coach, Sept 1994; Hamilton assistant manager, Jan 1995

HONOURS: 3 Semi-Pro XI Scotland caps; Premier League r-up 1985–86 (Hearts); Scottish Cup r-up 1982–83 (Rangers), 1985–86 (Hearts); Scottish League Cup winner 1983–84 (Rangers); Tennents Sixes winner 1984–85 (Hearts); SPFA Player of the Year 1981–82 (Airdrie); Division I leading scorer 1979–80 (Airdrie)

Sandy Clark was a prolific scorer with his home-town team. Hearts made a £70,000 bid for his services in 1979 and were turned down – as was a £150,000 offer from Hibs shortly afterwards. After 89 goals in 234 games for Airdrie, he moved to West Ham. He hit only seven goals in 26 matches at Upton Park before moving to Ibrox, where he won his only senior winners' medal.

Hearts got a bargain when they signed 28-year-old Sandy from Rangers in 1984 and he scored the winner on his debut at Cappielow. A totally honest, hard-working professional, Clark proved an excellent target-man to feed John Robertson and John Colquhoun. A strong runner with excellent ground skills, he also utilised his power in the air to great effect. His wholehearted approach endeared him to the supporters, who dubbed him 'The Forehead'. He enjoyed an outstanding season in 1985–86 and performed consistently until a painful achilles injury in August 1988 effectively ended his first-team career.

After a brief spell as Partick manager and a three-month playing sojourn with Dunfermline, Sandy returned to Hearts and successfully ran the youth and reserve sides. This culminated in the Premier Reserve League title and the BP Youth Cup arriving at Tynecastle in 1992–93. He took over from Joe Jordan in May 1993 as first-team boss but at the end of a difficult first season he was dismissed when the new Robinson/Deans regime took control of Hearts.

DAVID CLUNIE

Full-back

BORN: Edinburgh, 16 March 1948

HEIGHT: 5′ 11″   **WEIGHT:** 11st (1970)

COMPETITIVE DEBUT: v Dundee, 1 October 1966 (Lge) (H), 3–1 (came on as substitute)

CAREER: Forrester School; Salvesen Boys Club, 1961; **Hearts, Dec 1964**; St Johnstone, May 1977 (free transfer); retired in May 1978

HONOURS: Scotland Schoolboy international; 2 Scotland U-23 caps; 1 Scottish League cap; Texaco Cup r-up 1970–71 (Hearts)

Dave made the majority of his appearances as a full-back but also proved a sound deputy when asked to cover at sweeper or in midfield. He was solid in the tackle and noted for his passing ability. He also utilised his long throw-in technique to good effect.

In 1967 a mystery illness almost ended his career before it started, but he overcame his ailment. In season 1968–69 he finally broke into the team. His form peaked in the early 1970s and he won international honours. Clunie was a steady player throughout his Tynecastle career and a loyal servant.

He became a victim of Hearts' relegation clear-out in 1977. He moved to St Johnstone and played in 37 competitive games there before retiring at the early age of 30 in May 1978. He later assisted clubs in the Edinburgh amateur leagues as a manager and coach.

JOHN COCHRANE

Inside-left

BORN: Yoker, Glasgow

HEIGHT: 5′ 8″   **WEIGHT:** 10st 6lb (1953)

COMPETITIVE DEBUT: v Hamilton Accies, 17 March 1954 (Lge) (H), 3–0 (scored)

CAREER: Blythswood Secondary School; Renfrew Rovers U-17; Renfrew Waverley; Ardrossan Winton Rovers; **Hearts, July 1950**; freed in Apr 1954

HONOURS: Scotland Juvenile international

John was an apprentice tinsmith to trade when he signed for Hearts in 1950. He had neat, precise ball skills and a knack of easily wrong-footing opponents. It was said his main failing was an inability to finish, though he made a scoring debut in a 3–0 midweek match and held his place for a weekend trip to Pittodrie. Although he played well, Alfie Conn's return from injury meant

Cochrane going back to reserve football. He reappeared in the end-of-season Penman Cup matches and scored in the final – a 4–2 defeat against Stenhousemuir. John had earlier been informed he would receive a free transfer and he left the club immediately after that match.

JOHN COLQUHOUN
Forward

BORN: Stirling, 14 July 1963

HEIGHT: 5' 7"   WEIGHT: 10st (1987)

COMPETITIVE DEBUT: v Celtic, 10 August 1985 (PL) (H), 1–1 (scored)

CAREER: Grangemouth International; Stirling Albion, 1980; Celtic, Nov 1983 (£60,000); **Hearts, May 1985** (£50,000); Millwall, Jun 1991 (£400,000); Sunderland, July 1992 (£220,000); **Hearts, July 1993** (part-exchange deal for Derek Ferguson)

HONOURS: Premier League r-up 1985–86, 1987–88, 1989–90 (Hearts); Scottish Cup r-up 1985–86 (Hearts); Tennents Sixes winner 1990–91 (Hearts)

Tricky winger with an electric burst of pace, accurate crossing ability and deadly finishing, John is also capable of maintaining his composure in one-to-one situations. Many of his goals rank in the spectacular category with jealous opposing managers describing some long-range efforts as flukes – but John has scored too many goals of this type for them all to be flukes!

He was acquired from Celtic for a bargain fee and gave first-class service to Hearts. He linked well with John Robertson and Sandy Clark, particularly in 1985–86. John was a virtual ever-present for six seasons despite harsh treatment from opposing defenders. His form dipped in 1990–91 and he looked stale and in need of a fresh challenge. A big fee took him south but after two years, two clubs and a struggle to play regularly, 'JC' was delighted to come back to Gorgie. His form was mixed in 1993–94 but improved in 1994–95 as he took time to readjust to Scottish football.

ALFIE CONN Snr

Inside-right

BORN: Prestonpans, 2 October 1926

HEIGHT: 5′ 7″   **WEIGHT:** 10st 10lb (1951)

COMPETITIVE DEBUT: v Dumbarton, 14 October 1944 (S.Lge) (H), 4–0

CAREER: Bathgate Academy; Prestonpans YMCA; Inveresk Athletic; **Hearts, June 1944**; Raith Rovers, Sept 1958 (£2,250); Johannesburg Ramblers (South Africa) player/manager, 1960; Gala Fairydean, 1960; Raith Rovers manager, 1962

HONOURS: 1 full Scotland cap; 2 Scottish League caps; Scottish Cup winner 1955–56 (Hearts); Scottish League Cup winner 1954–55 (Hearts)

Small, stocky inside-forward who utilised a cannonball shot to great effect, Alfie was a member of the feared 'Terrible Trio'. He made an early breakthrough but did not really establish himself until the Trio was born in October 1948. Alfie is Hearts' fourth highest post-war League goalscorer, with 121 goals. Although small in physique, he was a tricky, elusive player who worked aggressively in the forward line. He often upset opposition defences with his spirited style.

Conn was reputed to be a notorious practical joker but his antics were appreciated. His gags were said to be priceless for the way in which they helped ease the tension before big games. Injury problems meant lengthy layoffs in his last few seasons at Hearts. He did, however, manage to score four of the record 132 goals in 1957–58 in only five appearances! In later life Alfie had the enjoyment of watching his son, Alfie Jnr, make a big impact in professional football north and south of the border. He worked in the building trade then as a sales director with an international paint company.

ALFIE CONN Jnr

Forward

BORN: Kirkcaldy. 5 April 1952

HEIGHT: 5′ 10″   **WEIGHT:** 11st 6lb (1980)

COMPETITIVE DEBUT: v Partick Thistle, 9 August 1980 (PL) (A), 2–3

CAREER: Musselburgh Windsor BC; Rangers, Oct 1968; Tottenham Hotspur, July 1974 (£140,000); Celtic, Mar 1977 (£65,000); Pittsburgh (USA), 1979; **Hearts, July 1980** (free transfer); Blackpool, Mar 1981 (free transfer); Motherwell, 1981; retired in 1983

HONOURS: 2 full Scotland caps; 3 Scotland U-23 caps; Scotland Schoolboy international;

ECWC winner 1971–72 (Rangers); Scottish League winner 1976–77, 1978–79 (Celtic); Scottish Cup winner 1972–73 (Rangers), 1976–77 (Celtic); Scottish League Cup winner 1970–71 (Rangers)

Alfie Conn followed in his famous father's footsteps by playing at the top level in senior football. He won all the major domestic honours with both halves of the Old Firm, including European success with Rangers. He found his way to his father's old club via a spell in the USA. He was only 28 when Hearts signed him but his best years were long gone and he made only a modest contribution in a brief nine-month stay. Conn was instantly recognisable with his socks rolled down (no shinguards) and his jersey hanging over his shorts. He possessed good dribbling and close-control skills with the ball seemingly glued to his foot. It was unfortunate that Hearts fans only saw fleeting glimpses of these fine talents.

JIM COWELL

Winger

BORN: Bellshill, 28 July 1961

HEIGHT: 6′   WEIGHT: 11st 9lb (1985)

COMPETITIVE DEBUT: v St Mirren, 11 May 1985 (PL) (A), 2–5 (came on as substitute)

CAREER: Shettleston Juniors; **Hearts, 1985**; Ayr United, Nov 1985; Clyde; Falkirk, Jan 1990; East Fife, Nov 1990; Dumbarton, Dec 1991; Elgin City; Bo'ness United, Aug 1994

Unusually tall for a winger, Jim failed to make the grade with Hearts. One League appearance as a substitute on the last day of season 1984–85 and another in a friendly against Eintracht two weeks earlier sums up his Hearts career. He did little to impress in either game and soon moved on to enjoy senior first-team action elsewhere.

GEORGE COWIE

Full-back

BORN: Findochty, 9 May 1961

HEIGHT: 5′ 9″   **WEIGHT:** 10st 7lb (1983)

COMPETITIVE DEBUT: v St Johnstone, 20 August 1983 (PL) (A), 1–0

CAREER: Buckie Thistle; West Ham United, Aug 1978; **Hearts, June 1983** (free transfer); Dunfermline, June 1987 (£15,000); forced to retire through injury in 1988, though attempted a brief comeback with Morton; manager of Forres Mechanics, Jan 1993

HONOURS: Scotland Youth international (captain); Premier League r-up 1985–86 (Hearts)

A quicksilver full-back, wholehearted in his approach, George tackled with complete determination and possessed his fair share of skill. He performed consistently at left-back throughout season 1983–84 and recorded three goals due to his willingness to push forward into the attack. Competition from Brian Whittaker and some injury problems saw George in and out of the first-team picture thereafter. To his credit he could always be depended upon when recalled to deputise at either full-back or in midfield. Serious injury eventually forced him out of the game and Hearts provided the opposition for his testimonial match with Dunfermline.

CHARLIE COX

Right-half

BORN: Clydebank, 19 February 1926

HEIGHT: 5′ 8″   **WEIGHT:** 10st (1950)

COMPETITIVE DEBUT: v Celtic, 22 September 1945 (Lge) (H), 2–2

CAREER: Dumbarton Academy; Yoker Juniors; **Hearts, May 1944**; Motherwell, Dec 1951 (£6,500 plus Tommy Sloan); retired through injury in 1959; Motherwell coach for a short spell

HONOURS: 1 full Scotland cap; Scottish Cup winner 1951–52 (Motherwell); Scottish League Cup r-up 1954–55 (Motherwell)

A cultured and constructive half-back who played hard but fair, Charlie picked up many knocks due to his robust style and fearless tackling. It was said by sports writers that he couldn't last the pace but, to be fair, he often battled on when carrying knocks.

Charlie played in many memorable matches and one of the best remembered was against Rangers on 17 February 1946. He suffered an early injury and, after playing on the left wing, popped up to score the decisive goal in a 2–0 win. It prompted the *Evening News* headline 'A lame duck sinks Rangers!'

Charlie was a part-timer also working as a commercial traveller in the licensed trade. When Tommy Walker took over as manager he introduced a policy whereby all players should turn full-time. The wage increase was £2 a week which took Charlie to £14, less than he could earn combining his part-time job with football. He subsequently joined Motherwell, where he enjoyed Scottish Cup success only four months after his transfer and gave good service until 1959.

SCOTT CRABBE

Forward

BORN: Edinburgh, 12 August 1968

HEIGHT: 5' 7"   WEIGHT: 10st (1991)

COMPETITIVE DEBUT: v Clydebank, 3 January 1987 (PL) (A), 3–0

CAREER: Forrester School; Tynecastle BC; **Hearts, Aug 1985**; Dundee United, Oct 1992 (swap deal for Allan Preston and £215,000 to Hearts)

HONOURS: Scotland U-17, U-19 and U-21 international; Premier League r-up 1989–90, 1991–92 (Hearts); SPFA Young Player of the Year 1989–90

Scott was a die-hard Hearts fan who realised his dream in graduating from the Tynecastle terracing to the first team. He was a firm favourite with the fans, who delighted in Crabbe kissing the club crest on his jersey each time he scored a goal. A highly skilful striker with an array of fine attributes, he was particularly lethal in free-kick situations near to goal. His drawback was a lack of pace. When his form suffered, Scott found difficulty in maintaining his confidence and prior to his transfer this became increasingly noticeable.

After striving for four years to obtain a first-team place, Crabbe looked to be heading out of Tynecastle in the summer of 1989. However, he worked hard at his strength and fitness and 1989–90 saw him explode onto the scene with 17 goals and U-21 international honours. The next season saw Crabbe sidelined initially with food poisoning; then injuries and a loss of confidence made it a disastrous term. St Johnstone enquired about his services in August 1991 and Hearts had accepted a £285,000 fee. Crabbe, with his strong feeling for the club, killed the deal stone dead by refusing to talk with Saints. He then proceeded to score 17 competitive goals for Hearts in 1991–92 and establish himself once more.

He fell out of favour early in 1992–93 and Dundee United expressed an interest. A deal was agreed but almost fell through when Jim McLean tried to force Crabbe into an instant decision. He turned United down and took his place on the subs bench for Hearts' Euro tie with Slavia Prague. He didn't play, but at the end of the famous 4–2 win, he ran to the fans to say his farewell and, in an emotional scene, kissed his Hearts jersey and threw it to the crowd. He left the ground immediately to sign for United, gutted to leave his boyhood favourites. A true Jambo!

JOHN CRAIG

Midfield

BORN: Glasgow

HEIGHT: 5' 7"   **WEIGHT:** 10st 3lb (1978)

COMPETITIVE DEBUT: v Partick Thistle, 9 September 1978 (PL) (A), 2–3

CAREER: Aberdeen; Partick Thistle; **Hearts, Sept 1978** (exchange deal for Donald Park); Morton, May 1979 (free transfer)

Arrived at Tynecastle along with Denis McQuade in a deal which took Donald Park to Partick Thistle. Unfortunately, the large majority of Hearts supporters did not take to John Craig. He struggled to find any consistent good form and was soon out of favour. He clearly didn't fit into the team plan at Tynecastle and nobody was surprised at his release.

COLIN CRAMB

Forward

BORN: Lanark, 23 June 1974

HEIGHT: 5' 11"   **WEIGHT:** 11st 5lb (1995)

COMPETITIVE DEBUT: v Dundee United, 21 March 1995 (PL) (A), 1–1 (came on as substitute)

CAREER: Shotts YM; Craigneuk Colts; Jerviston Boys Club; Hamilton Accies Boys Club; Hamilton Accies, May 1991; Southampton, 1993 (£100,000); Falkirk, Aug 1994 (£70,000); **Hearts, March 1995** (£50,000)

HONOURS: B&Q Cup Winner 1992–93 (Hamilton)

Colin came to prominence with Hamilton as a 17-year-old. His physical presence, aerial ability and deadly accuracy in front of goal soon attracted interest from English eyes. Southampton paid big money for his services but he failed to settle at The Dell.

He returned to Scotland and signed for Falkirk, where he started well. However, he fell out of favour after allegations of 'high jinks' on a club tour abroad. Thereafter, the media saddled him with a 'bad boy' tag. When Mo Johnston moved to Falkirk on a free transfer, Colin moved in the opposite direction to Tynecastle. His arrival will ensure keen competition for the striker positions. Let's hope Hearts can help unlock his undoubted potential.

IAN CRAWFORD

Outside-left

BORN: Edinburgh, 14 July 1934

HEIGHT: 5' 7"   WEIGHT: 10st 10lb (1959)

COMPETITIVE DEBUT: v Motherwell, 18 April 1955 (Lge) (H), 3–2

CAREER: St Anthony's School; Merchiston Thistle; Hibernian, 1951; Hamilton Accies, Oct 1953; **Hearts, Aug 1954**; West Ham, June 1961 (£10,000); Scunthorpe United, Feb 1963; Peterborough, July 1964; retired in 1968

HONOURS: 1 Scotland U-23 cap; Scottish League winner 1957–58, 1959–60 (Hearts); Scottish Cup winner 1955–56 (Hearts); Scottish League Cup winner 1958–59, 1959–60 (Hearts)

Ian was surprisingly rejected by both Hibs and Hamilton as a teenager but developed into a highly rated outside-left with Hearts. His pace and powerful running created chances for others, but he could find the target too. Such was his value to Hearts in the second half of 1955–56 that he received special leave from the Cameronian Highlanders as he was then doing his National Service. It definitely proved worthwhile: he starred in the Scottish Cup campaign and won immortality in club history with two goals in the 1956 final against Celtic. His form won constant plaudits from all quarters and he scored a remarkable number of goals for a winger, once hitting four against Cowdenbeath in the 1959 League Cup semi-final.

Crawford won every domestic honour with Hearts and maintained his form in the transitional 1960–61 season. It came as a surprise when West Ham's bid for his transfer was accepted by Hearts. He played on well into his 30s and appeared in 172 League matches for his last club, Peterborough.

Ian was known to be living in Norway in 1994.

Goalkeeper

BORN: Glasgow, 13 April 1941

HEIGHT: 5′ 11″   **WEIGHT:** 11st 6lb (1967)

COMPETITIVE DEBUT: v Ayr United, 15 October 1960 (Lge) (A), 0–1

CAREER: Queens Park School; Drumchapel Amateurs, 1958; Queens Park, 1959; **Hearts, May 1960**; Dumbarton, Aug 1977 (free transfer); retired in 1978

HONOURS: 6 full Scotland caps; 3 U-23 caps; Scotland Schoolboy and Amateur international; 3 Scottish League caps; Scottish League r-up 1964–65 (Hearts); Scottish Cup r-up 1967–68, 1975–76 (Hearts); Scottish League Cup r-up 1961–62 (Hearts); Texaco Cup r-up 1970–71 (Hearts)

A fine servant to Hearts in a memorable 17-year career, 'Cruickie' was an agile keeper with safe hands, good positional sense and great courage. He won deserved respect for his consistent displays and was hero-worshipped by the Hearts fans. After three years as understudy to Gordon Marshall, Jim won automatic selection in season 1963–64 and was a mainstay for many years thereafter. His main competitor in later years was Kenny Garland but Jim outlasted the talented Fifer despite spells of playing second-fiddle.

Perhaps one of the most outstanding moments in Jim's career was his treble save from Hibs' Joe Davis in 1967 when he stopped a penalty and the two rebounds thereafter. Those who witnessed the feat will never forget it. Jim had a reasonable success rate at stopping penalties and his League records of 394 appearances and 102 shut-outs were unbroken until Henry Smith took over.

Despite his loyal years of service Jim did not receive a testimonial from the club. The fans, however, recognised his contribution by honouring him at a gala night in December 1975.

BORN: Carluke, 17 March 1930

HEIGHT: 5' 9"   WEIGHT: 11st 1lb (1953)

COMPETITIVE DEBUT: v Celtic, 30 December 1950 (Lge) (A), 2–2

CAREER: YMCA football; Castlehill Colliery; Carluke Rovers; **Hearts provisional, 1948** (called up Jan 1950); retired in 1967; **Hearts trainer/physio for 10 years until 1977**; employed in the steel industry

HONOURS: 9 full Scotland caps; 2 Scotland B caps; 7 Scottish League caps; Scottish League winner 1957–58, 1959–60 (Hearts); r-up 1964–65 (Hearts); Scottish Cup winner 1955–56 (Hearts); Scottish League Cup winner 1954–55, 1958–59, 1959–60, 1962–63 (Hearts); r-up 1961–62 (Hearts); Rex Kingsley's Footballer of the Year 1961

JOHN CUMMING

Left-half

John Cumming is unquestionably an all-time great in the history of Hearts. The 'Lionheart' was an inspirational force in the halcyon era between 1954 and 1962 and was the only player who gained a medal from each of the seven domestic honours secured during these years.

His indomitable spirit was never more evident than during the 1956 Scottish Cup final victory. A sickening clash of heads with Celtic's Willie Fernie saw John sustain a vicious gash on his forehead. Bleeding profusely, but using a sponge to mop up the damage, he carried on in typical fashion to make sure of a winner's medal. He later had four stitches inserted in the wound.

John made his debut on the left wing but later settled into the left-half berth where he performed with distinction, before proving his versatility again in the twilight of his career – even appearing in goal during one reserve match!

In his 612 first-team appearances, Cumming was never once booked by the ref, which pays glowing tribute to his hard but fair image. He was granted a testimonial in May 1980 when a Hearts XI beat a North East XI 4–3 and in the match programme his former colleague, Dave Mackay, paid him a glowing tribute by stating that John was the best half-back partner he ever had. Fine praise indeed!

KEN CURRIE

Inside-forward

HEIGHT: 5′ 9″   **WEIGHT:** 10st 10lb (1948)

COMPETITIVE DEBUT: v Celtic, 8 January 1944 (S.Lge) (A), 0–4

CAREER: Bayview Youth Club; **Hearts, 1942;** Third Lanark, July 1951 (£1,500)

Hard-working inside-forward who broke into the first team in season 1946–47, Currie reserved some of his best performances for League Cup ties, scoring most of his goals in this competition. Ken was a part-timer who also worked for a firm of chartered accountants. His best season for appearances was 1947–48, but with Hearts toiling to get results, Dave McLean brought in new men to boost the firepower up front.

A serious back injury kept Ken out of action throughout most of 1948–49. He returned to fill the left-half position in April 1949 and excelled there for several games. He came down with appendicitis in October 1950 and an operation was required. He never played for the first team again and was made available for transfer in April 1951. Hearts initially wanted a £4,000 fee but Ken appealed to the Scottish League Management Committee and eventually the asking price was reduced to £1,500.

TOMMY DARLING

Full-back

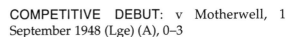

BORN: Clackmannan, 14 July 1929

HEIGHT: 5′ 7″   **WEIGHT:** 10st (1949)

COMPETITIVE DEBUT: v Motherwell, 1 September 1948 (Lge) (A), 0–3

CAREER: Dalkeith Thistle; **Hearts, 1948;** Cowdenbeath, May 1952 (free transfer)

A stocky full-back who hailed from Dalkeith and was employed as a miner, Tommy made four consecutive appearances at left-back at the start of season 1948–49. An injury to Dougal Matheson gave Tommy his chance and he performed competently. But these were his only appearances and he was given a free transfer in May 1952.

BORN: Kintore, Aberdeen, 25 October 1934

HEIGHT: 5′ 8″   WEIGHT: 11st 4lb (1963)

COMPETITIVE DEBUT: v Partick Thistle, 4 February 1961 (Lge) (A), 1–4

CAREER: Inverurie Juniors; Chelsea, 1950; Fraserburgh; Inverurie Juniors; Aberdeen, 1955; **Hearts, Feb 1961** (£8,000); Dundee United, Oct 1963 (£6,000); Partick Thistle, Feb 1964 (swap deal)

HONOURS: Scotland U-23 international; Scottish Cup r-up 1958–59 (Aberdeen); Scottish League Cup winner 1962–63 (Hearts); r-up 1961–62 (Hearts)

NORMAN DAVIDSON
Centre-forward

Norrie joined Hearts at a difficult time when Tommy Walker was attempting to find replacements for the departed stars of the 1950s. The centre-forward's appearances were significantly restricted for a variety of reasons but once in the side he had a knack of scoring regularly – 26 goals in domestic competitions. He netted a glorious header in the replayed 1961 League Cup final when Hearts went down 3–1 to Rangers. Norrie is better remembered for scoring the solitary goal which secured the League Cup against Kilmarnock in 1962, sliding in to touch Willie Hamilton's cut-back into the net. One year later, in October 1963, Norrie was allowed to join Dundee United in view of 'emerging young strikers on the books'!

BORN: Edinburgh

HEIGHT: 5′ 9″   WEIGHT: 11st (1966)

COMPETITIVE DEBUT: v Airdrie, 17 September 1966 (Lge) (H), 1–1

CAREER: Falkirk; Bonnyrigg Rose; **Hearts, 1966**; Raith Rovers, 1967 (free transfer); freed in Apr 1970

TOMMY DAVIDSON
Forward

Red-haired striker who put in plenty of endeavour on his debut despite missing a couple of good scoring chances. Tommy's next games were as a substitute against Clyde in late October 1966, then at inside-right in a 1–2 defeat at Pittodrie. These were his only games for the first team and he later rejoined Tommy Walker at Raith.

JIM DENNY
Defender

BORN: Paisley, 13 March 1950

HEIGHT: 5′ 9″   **WEIGHT:** 10st 8lb (1980)

COMPETITIVE DEBUT: v St Johnstone, 5 September 1979 (Div. I) (H), 2–1

CAREER: Yoker Athletic; Rangers, 1970; **Hearts, Sept 1979** (£15,000); Stirling Albion, May 1981 (free transfer); Irvine Vics, 1982; Troon Juniors, 1985

HONOURS: Division I winner 1979–80 (Hearts); Scottish Cup winner 1970–71 (Rangers)

Jim Denny arrived at Tynecastle during one of the worst periods in Hearts' history. He had been used as a squad player for most of his time with Rangers and was signed by Willie Ormond to boost the defence in our promotion campaign. Jim made most of his appearances at full-back but demonstrated his versatility in midfield and at sweeper. He lost his place as Hearts plummeted towards relegation for the third time, and was part of the subsequent clear-out in May 1981.

JACKIE DEWAR
Outside-left

BORN: Crieff, 1 November 1929

HEIGHT: 5′ 8″   **WEIGHT:** 10st 2lb (1947)

COMPETITIVE DEBUT: v East Fife, 5 March 1947 (LCqf) (A), 5–2

CAREER: Bayview Youth Club; **Hearts, July 1945**; Dundee United, Sept 1947 (free transfer)

A hard-working, elusive winger, Jackie made his debut as a teenager and showed good form in his first two games. His next two games saw Hearts knocked out of the Scottish Cup and League Cup, the latter a 6–2 semi-final defeat against Aberdeen at Easter Road. Jackie then scored in three consecutive League matches against Queens Park, Morton and Rangers. His goal at Ibrox helped ensure a 0–2 win. His last two appearances were Penman Cup ties against Leith Athletic.

BORN: Middleton, 17 November 1921

HEIGHT: 5' 8"   WEIGHT: 10st 5lb (1948)   *Forward*

COMPETITIVE DEBUT: v Third Lanark, 4 October 1947 (Lge) (H), 1–3

CAREER: Queens Park School; Clyde, 1945; **Hearts, Sept 1947** (£15,000); Northampton, Nov 1949 (c.£8,500); Leicester City, Oct 1951 (£10,000)

Signed by Dave McLean to help Hearts fight clear of the relegation zone in 1947–48, Arthur made a quiet debut. He was a willing worker but not one to catch the eye or win the limelight. He settled at inside-left and turned in some steady performances to assist in the struggle against demotion. He was good in the air and was noted for his versatility, being able to play anywhere up front or in the half-back line. He had a fine goalscoring record with his previous club, Clyde, but somehow could not find his scoring boots at Tynecastle. The birth of the Terrible Trio meant the end of Arthur's Hearts career. After making only one competitive appearance in 1949–50, he tabled a transfer request in October 1949 and moved to Northampton a month later.

BORN: Broxburn, 8 November 1956

HEIGHT: 5' 10"   WEIGHT: 10st 10lb (1980)   *Forward*

COMPETITIVE DEBUT: v Dumbarton, 9 February 1980 (Div. I) (A), 1–1 (came on as substitute)

CAREER: Fauldhouse Juniors; East Stirling, 1977; Chelsea, Feb 1979 (£60,000); Dundee United, Sept 1979; **Hearts, Feb 1980** (free transfer); St Johnstone, Sept 1980; Partick Thistle, 1982; Meadowbank, 1983; Dunfermline, 1984; Whitburn Juniors, 1985

Jim attracted widespread attention as a goal-scorer with East Stirling, but a move to Chelsea didn't work out and he made no impact on his return to Scotland with Dundee United. Caretaker boss Alex Rennie brought Docherty to Hearts in order to boost competition for the forward line. Jim scored plenty of goals in the reserve side yet found promotion to the first team difficult. At the start of season 1980–81 Docherty scored three hat-tricks for the reserves and his form and confidence improved, but he still couldn't find a place in new manager Moncur's plans. He moved on to St Johnstone and was destined to keep moving thereafter.

JOHN DOCHERTY
Inside-forward

BORN: Glasgow, 28 February 1935

HEIGHT: 5' 9"   WEIGHT: 11st 11lb (1961)

COMPETITIVE DEBUT: v Aberdeen, 15 March 1961 (Lge) (A), 2–0

CAREER: Stirling Albion; St Johnstone, 1958; **Hearts, March 1961**; Colchester United, Jun 1963 (free transfer); Chelmsford, 1965

Bustling inside-forward who joined Hearts for a moderate fee. John played 94 League matches at Muirton Park but a failure to perform consistently to the standard expected at Hearts saw him appear infrequently. Injury problems did not help. The highlight of Docherty's short spell at Tynecastle would probably be the three European ties he played in during 1961–62. He later transferred to Colchester where he made 77 appearances before moving to non-league football in 1965. He now lives in West Lothian.

GEORGE DONALDSON
Midfield

BORN: Edinburgh, 24 November 1954

HEIGHT: 5' 9"   WEIGHT: 10st 4lb (1975)

COMPETITIVE DEBUT: v Morton, 24 August 1974 (LC) (H), 2–0 (came on as substitute)

CAREER: Gilmerton Primary School; Tynecastle Boys Club; Rangers, 1970; **Hearts, Apr 1974** (free transfer); Clydebank, 1977; Meadowbank, 1979

A dazzling young starlet who looked to have the football world at his feet, Donaldson was a Rangers reserve tipped for the top. The dream turned sour for the strong, stockily-built midfielder when he was surprisingly freed in April 1974. Several clubs were credited with an interest in his signature but George decided to accept an offer from his home-town team. He operated in a midfield role for Hearts but found his fortunes there all too similar to his Ibrox experience. He never really enjoyed an extended run and was used as a deputy for other players. After appearing a few times in 1975–76, he faded from the scene the following season and was released in 1977.

BORN: Glasgow, 3 December 1926

HEIGHT: 5' 11"   WEIGHT: 11st 9lb (1952)

COMPETITIVE DEBUT: v Motherwell, 27 August 1947 (Lge) (A), 1–3

CAREER: John Street School (Glasgow); Shawfield Juniors; **Hearts, Sept 1946**; Kilmarnock, Dec 1954 (£4,300); retired in 1960

HONOURS: 1 full Scotland cap; Scotland Junior international; 3 Scottish League caps; Junior Cup winner 1946–47 (Shawfield)

Bobby started his career as a wing-half before adapting to the centre-half position with Hearts. He signed provisional forms in September 1946 and shortly afterwards represented the Scottish

BOBBY DOUGAN

Centre-half

Central League against the Irish Intermediate League. Bobby was called up in August 1947 and made a quick debut. He earned rave notices as a cultured, ball-playing star (which was unusual for a half-back in those days). Dougan never panicked, even in tricky situations. Instead of resorting to the hefty boot upfield, he alarmed the Tynecastle punters by always playing his way out of trouble, and achieved this with considerable success. He was an immaculate performer, displaying controlled, intelligent football and exceptional passing abilities.

Dougan was a mainstay in Hearts' first team from October 1948 to September 1951 until a serious ankle injury in a representative game for Scotland put him out of action for virtually a whole year. He made a successful comeback which culminated in a third League cap in March 1953. Injury returned to haunt him when a terrible knee injury necessitated a cartilage operation in 1954. His knee took some time to recover, with several breakdowns hindering the problem. The injury took its toll on Bobby's effectiveness, and his value to the team was greatly reduced. Subsequently, he was allowed to join Kilmarnock, where he overcame his injury problems and gave fine service until his retirement in 1960.

WILLIE DUFF

Goalkeeper

BORN: Winchburgh, 6 February 1935

HEIGHT: 5′ 11″   **WEIGHT:** 13st (1955)

COMPETITIVE DEBUT: v Dundee, 14 August 1954 (LC) (H), 3–1

CAREER: Juniper Green YMCA; Slateford Athletic; Easthouses Lily; **Hearts, Aug 1952** (£200); Charlton Athletic, Jan 1958 (£6,500); Peterborough, 1963; Dunfermline Athletic, 1970s

HONOURS: 1 U-23 Scotland cap; 1 Scottish League cap; Scottish Cup winner 1955–56 (Hearts); Scottish League Cup winner 1954–55 (Hearts)

A joiner to trade, Willie was a brave, reliable custodian who displayed solid consistency in 1954–55 and 1955–56. Early in season 1956–57, Duff departed Tynecastle to start his National Service with the Royal Horse Artillery in Surrey. He turned out for Charlton Athletic during his stay in the London area, and his steady displays prompted them to secure his permanent transfer. He later set up a joinery business in Edinburgh, and was known to be living in America in December 1992.

RAY DUNLOP

Goalkeeper

BORN: Paisley, 23 November 1950

HEIGHT: 5′ 11″   **WEIGHT:** 12st 3lb (1977)

COMPETITIVE DEBUT: v Dumbarton, 13 August 1977 (Div. I) (A), 2–2

CAREER: Yoker Athletic; Stenhousemuir, 1973; **Hearts, June 1977** (£10,000); Queen of the South, Apr 1979 (free transfer)

HONOURS: Division I r-up 1977–78 (Hearts)

Ray was an electrician to trade while playing part-time with Stenhousemuir, and then had the unenviable task of replacing a Tynecastle legend – Jim Cruickshank. With Hearts facing their first season out of the top flight, Ray would be under pressure to keep eager Division I strikers at bay. He performed well, with 14 shut-outs in his 34 League appearances. One memorable League Cup quarter-final saw him make two inspired saves in a penalty shoot-out against Dundee United. Later in the season 1977–78 he was sent off in a Scottish Cup match against Morton and also missed the promotion run-in with John Brough deputising. Thomson Allan's arrival increased competition later in 1978–79 and Dunlop was released in April 1979.

BORN: Cowdenbeath, 18 April 1930

HEIGHT: 5′ 7″   WEIGHT: 10st 9lb (1952)

COMPETITIVE DEBUT: v Celtic, 29 September 1951 (Lge) (A), 3–1

CAREER: Hill of Beath Ramblers; **Hearts, Jun 1947**; Dunfermline, Dec 1952; Gillingham, May 1953

HONOURS: Scotland Boys Club international

JOHN DURKIN

Outside-right

John made a superb debut, tearing Celtic's defence apart with some fine wing play, and setting up Willie Bauld's opening goal with a pinpoint cross. However, Durkin's next few games were criticised by the press, who commented that he lacked pace and the necessary experience. He was dropped after three games and did not play first-team football again until the last sectional League Cup tie of season 1952–53, when he scored his only goal.

John was highly rated in his earlier seasons but never quite fulfilled his potential. He was released in December 1952 in light of adequate cover for the right-wing berth. He was at Dunfermline for only six months before moving to Gillingham, where he scored five goals in 30 games.

BOBBY ELGIN

Outside-left

BORN: Edinburgh, 23 June 1949

HEIGHT: 5' 9"   WEIGHT: 10st 12lb (1968)

COMPETITIVE DEBUT: v Morton, 29 April 1968 (Lge) (A), 0–1

CAREER: Musselburgh Grammar School; Edinburgh Athletic; **Hearts, 1964**; Stockport County, July 1969

Fair-haired winger who waited almost four years to make his competitive debut, which was marred by a dreadful team performance: Morton won 1–0 against a team still suffering a Cup final hangover after losing to Dunfermline. Bobby made little impression in the two games he played on Hearts' 1968 tour of Ireland and it was a similar story in the single League Cup match he played in 1968–69. He moved to Stockport, where he managed more first-team games. Today he is employed by Lothian and Borders Police and is based in Dalkeith.

MAURICE ELLIOTT

Forward

BORN: Torthorwald, 23 November 1942

HEIGHT: 5' 8"   WEIGHT: 11st 4lb (1963)

COMPETITIVE DEBUT: v Kilmarnock, 18 March 1961 (Lge) (H), 0–1

CAREER: Dumfries Academy; Queen of the South, 1960; **Hearts, March 1961**; Queen of the South, Jan 1964

HONOURS: Scottish League Cup r-up 1961–62 (Hearts)

Maurice joined Hearts from his home-town team as a part-timer, thus enabling him to continue with his quantity surveying apprenticeship. But his part-time status and a series of knee and ankle injuries are perhaps the reasons why he failed to fulfil his early promise. His limited appearances did, however, include a League Cup final against Rangers at Hampden on 28 October 1961 (1–1) and two European ties against Inter Milan. Elliott's only competitive goals for Hearts were in League matches against Celtic and Partick Thistle. He returned to Palmerston Park in January 1964, where his first appearance was against (of all clubs) Hearts! Maurice played inside-left that day and another ex-Heart, Jim Rodger, was his wing partner.

BORN: London, 19 February 1962

HEIGHT: 6' 1"   WEIGHT: 14st 1lb (1993)

Forward

COMPETITIVE DEBUT: v Rangers, 7 August 1993 (PL) (A), 1–2

CAREER: Norwich City; Notts Forest, Aug 1981 (£1,000,000); Southampton; Notts County; Brighton; Manchester City; West Ham; Orient; Leatherhead; Torquay United; Airdrie, Jan 1993; Trelleborg; **Hearts, July 1993** (free transfer); Canadian football, Apr 1994

HONOURS: England U-21 and B international

The first black footballer to play for Hearts in modern times, Justin's personal life and wanderlust have often attracted more attention than his footballing ability. He made an impressive debut at Ibrox and was unlucky not to score. His principal role was that of target man to feed John Robertson and John Colquhoun, a tactic which unfortunately was too predictable to succeed. He was, however, very good at displaying immense strength in holding off defenders and then looking to create openings. But his inability to score prompted Sandy Clark to sign Mo Johnston. Justin's Hearts career looked to be over and Dundee United, Dundee and Airdrie all made attempts to sign him. Fashanu was then fined for missing training, with worse to follow when he was allegedly involved in a sex scandal. The media had a field day and Fashanu was sacked for 'unbecoming conduct'. He fled to America as allegations broke about a trail of debt he had built up in Edinburgh.

BORN: Glasgow, 22 April 1930

HEIGHT: 5' 10"   WEIGHT: 11st 7lb (1952)

Right-back

COMPETITIVE DEBUT: v Dundee, 18 October 1952 (Lge) (A), 1–3

CAREER: Tollcross YMCA; Benburb Juniors; **Hearts, Aug 1951**; Hamilton, May 1953; Accrington, May 1954; Rochdale, Sept 1955; Oldham Athletic, July 1959

Hearts beat off competition from Rangers, Queen of the South and Grimsby to win Charlie's signature on a provisional basis. The miner at Barony Pit in Ayrshire was called for his debut when Bobby Parker was selected as a travelling reserve for a Wales v Scotland match.

Ferguson found the going tough against Dundee's lively left-winger, Christie, and it proved to be Charlie's only game.

DANNY FERGUSON

Defender

BORN: Prestonpans, 5 February 1939

DIED: Prestonpans, 15 April 1977

HEIGHT: 5' 11"   WEIGHT: 11st 6lb (1965)

COMPETITIVE DEBUT: v Third Lanark, 3 December 1960 (Lge) (A), 3–0

CAREER: Ormiston Primrose; Hamilton Accies, Aug 1958; **Hearts, March 1959** (£10,000 – joint fee which included R. Walker); Durban United, May 1967; Morton, 1969; Cowdenbeath, Aug 1970

HONOURS: Scottish League r-up 1964–65 (Hearts); Scottish League Cup winner 1962–63 (Hearts); r-up 1961–62 (Hearts)

Danny became a victim of his own versatility as his career progressed. He was asked to cover in many defensive positions. On one occasion he even starred at centre-forward in a Scottish Cup tie against Tarff Rovers, hitting a hat-trick that day in a 9–0 rout. After completing his National Service, Danny began to establish himself in season 1961–62. He was club captain by season 1963–64 and in the following term played an influential role in the side which came close to a League Championship success. One consolation was the distinction of scoring Hearts' 5,000th League goal, against Morton on 10 March 1965.

A terrible leg injury in January 1966 against Real Zaragoza in the away leg of a Fairs Cup tie put Danny out of action for ten months. He fought his way back but couldn't recapture his form and was released in May 1967. After a short spell in South Africa with Durban United, he returned to play out his senior career with first Morton then Cowdenbeath. He worked in the licensed trade for a few years after retiring from football, but tragically died from illness at a very young age.

Midfield

BORN: Glasgow, 31 July 1967

HEIGHT: 5' 8"   WEIGHT: 10st 11lb (1991)

COMPETITIVE DEBUT: v Cowdenbeath, 21 August 1990 (LC) (A), 2–0

CAREER: Roystar Boys Club; Burnbank Boys Club; Gartcosh United; Rangers, 1982; Dundee, 1990 (on loan); **Hearts, July 1990** (£750,000); Sunderland, July 1993 (£500,000 plus John Colquhoun to Hearts); Falkirk, Sep 1995 (£300,000)

HONOURS: 2 full Scotland caps; Scotland Youth and U-21 international; Scottish League winner 1986–87, 1988–89 (Rangers); r-up 1991–92 (Hearts); Scottish League Cup winner 1986–87, 1987-88 (Rangers)

A fine footballer with precise passing ability, good close-control skills and neat footwork. On his day Ferguson could dictate the course of any match but with Hearts this was too infrequent. Derek displayed exceptional potential as a youth and made his Rangers debut as a 15-year-old. Controversy followed him off the field and, when Rangers finally decided to offload him, he became Hearts' record signing. The ball-playing midfielder often fell victim to crunching tackles in the physical Premier League arena.

Derek endured a goalscoring drought at Tynecastle. He either lacked the ability or confidence to shoot in a genuine goalscoring situation, often electing for a pass to a colleague. His best performance probably came against Rangers in the 1993 Scottish Cup semi-final. He ran the proceedings from start to finish but luck was not on Hearts side that day. After his contract expired he signed for his former Rangers colleague, Terry Butcher, at Sunderland.

Forward

BORN: Newarthill, 4 August 1962

HEIGHT: 5' 7"   WEIGHT: 10st 7lb (1990)

COMPETITIVE DEBUT: v Celtic, 13 August 1988 (PL) (A), 0–1

CAREER: Fir Park Boys Club; Dundee, 1978; Rangers, June 1984 (£200,000); Dundee United, July 1986 (£145,000); **Hearts, July 1988** (£325,000); Motherwell, Dec 1990 (£100,000); Airdrie, Sept 1993 (£50,000); Portadown, 1994 (£20,000)

HONOURS: 4 Scotland U-21 caps; Scottish Cup winner 1990–91 (Motherwell); r-up 1986–87, 1987–88 (Dundee United); Scottish League Cup winner 1984–85 (Rangers)

Ferguson made his mark as a youngster with Dundee before big-money transfers took him to Rangers, then Dundee United. Hearts paid a fee equivalent to their record for Ferguson in July 1988 to replace the departed golden boy, John Robertson. Fergie's career got off to a good start with a hat-trick against St Johnstone and a double against Dunfermline in League Cup ties. However, Hearts struggled in the League and Ferguson was branded lazy by some fans. Workrate had never been his hallmark: Iain liked the ball at his feet and from there he used skill to take on opponents and create scoring chances. Most of his goals were spectacular, none more so than a free-kick rocket against Bayern Munich in a UEFA Cup quarter-final at Tynecastle.

It was a popular belief that Ferguson's style clashed with that of John Robertson on the wee man's return to Gorgie. Iain found himself out of favour and had loan spells with Bristol City and Charlton with the hope of a permanent transfer. Nothing materialised and he returned to Hearts and scored another two fine goals at Pittodrie and Fir Park on League business. His goal against Motherwell probably influenced their decision to sign him in December 1990, where he later won a Scottish Cup winners' medal, heading their opening goal in the 4–3 final victory.

IAN FERGUSON

Forward

BORN: Dunfermline, 5 August 1968

HEIGHT: 6' 1"   WEIGHT: 12st (1992)

COMPETITIVE DEBUT: v Aberdeen, 9 October 1991 (PL) (H), 1–0 (came on as substitute)

CAREER: Lochgelly Albert; Raith Rovers, Aug 1987; **Hearts, Oct 1991** (£100,000); St Johnstone, Nov 1993 (£110,000)

HONOURS: Premier League r-up 1991–92 (Hearts)

Tall, slim, gangling striker who was nicknamed 'Rodney' by some supporters, Ian made most of his early appearances as a substitute. Ian played with total endeavour. He was a capable dribbler and his unusual running style took him past opponents and into scoring positions. He had an unorthodox tackling technique whereby he would slide in, win the ball and bounce to his feet in a single movement. Fergie could challenge effectively in the air and could ghost into good scoring positions. Two of his most memorable goals were scored against Hibs. The first was a raging volley in the 1992 New Year fixture at Tynecastle, and was followed by the winner at Easter Road in March 1992.

Other important strikes included a fine volley against Falkirk in a Scottish Cup quarter-final, and another goal against the Bairns in May 1992 helped secure European qualification.

The fact that Ferguson's substitute appearances outnumbered his starts perhaps tells its own story about his efforts to win a permanent place in the attack. He never really figured seriously in Sandy Clark's plans after Joe Jordan's departure. Ian was playing well for St Johnstone, until a knee ligament injury sidelined him in August 1994.

ALAN FINLAY
Inside-forward

BORN: Edinburgh, 9 January 1939

HEIGHT: 5′ 7″   **WEIGHT:** 9st 10lb (1960)

COMPETITIVE DEBUT: v Kilmarnock, 12 November 1960 (Lge) (A), 1–2 (scored)

CAREER: Dunbar United; **Hearts, Aug 1956**; Newport County, Apr 1961 (free transfer); Duns, 1962

Fair-haired inside-forward who took four years to break through for a League debut. Alan first appeared on the 1960 tour of Canada and by all accounts played well in his two games. Hearts' erratic form in 1960–61 resulted in young players being brought in to show what they could do. Alan made ten competitive appearances but found himself freed in the general clear-out in April 1961.

BOBBY FLAVELL
Forward

BORN: Annathill, 1 September 1921

HEIGHT: 5′ 6″   **WEIGHT:** 11st 8lb (1949)

COMPETITIVE DEBUT: v St Mirren, 20 December 1947 (Lge) (A), 0–1

CAREER: Eastfield Heatherbell; Kirkintilloch Rob Roy; Airdrie, 1940; (guest for Brentford, Arsenal and Spurs during the war); **Hearts, Dec 1947** (£10,000); FC Millionerios (Columbia), June 1950; returned to **Hearts, Dec 1950**, to a fine and suspension; Dundee, Sept 1951 (£6,000); Kilmarnock, Dec 1954; St Mirren, July 1956; St Mirren coach, 1958; Ayr United manager, Nov 1961; St Mirren manager, Dec 1961; Ayr United manager, 1963–64; Albion Rovers manager for a short spell in 1969, then later a director; Berwick Rangers chief scout, 1980

2 full Scotland caps; wartime international; 2 Scottish League caps; Scottish Cup r-up 1951–52 (Dundee); Scottish League Cup winner 1951–52, 1952–53 (Dundee)

Stocky centre-forward bought to revive Hearts' flagging fortunes in 1947–48 as they battled against relegation. Comparisons were drawn with a famous striker of the previous generation, Hughie Gallacher. Flavell was similar in physique and the speed with which he could snap up a chance. After Hearts' poor start to season 1948–49 Flavell tabled a transfer request in the September and, after repeated requests, was placed on the list one month later. He fought his way back into favour and performed well on the left wing as a feeder for the newly established Terrible Trio, as well as contributing a number of goals himself.

Bobby sensationally walked out on Hearts in June 1950, signing for the Millionerios club in Columbia for a supposed king's ransom, shamefully breaching his contract in the process. He returned in December 1950 and one month later was fined £150 and banned until the end of the season. He could not reconcile his differences with Hearts and was transferred to Dundee, where he enjoyed two League Cup successes. Wanderlust prevailed thereafter.

GEORGE FLEMING
Midfield

BORN: Edinburgh, 22 September 1948

HEIGHT: 5′ 6″   **WEIGHT:** 9st 3lb (1967)

COMPETITIVE DEBUT: v Dundee United, 10 December 1966 (Lge) (H), 2–1

CAREER: Forrester High School; Salvesen BC; **Hearts, Dec 1964**; Dundee United, Feb 1972 (£7,000); St Johnstone player/coach, 1980; Arbroath manager, Dec 1983–85

HONOURS: Division I winner 1982–83 (St Johnstone); Scottish Cup r-up 1973–74 (Dundee United); Scottish League Cup winner 1979–80 (Dundee United); Texaco Cup r-up 1970–71 (Hearts)

George won many accolades in an eight-year association with Hearts from 1964–72: 'Mr Perpetual Motion' due to his unstinting capacity for hard work; 'the play-anywhere forward' relating to his total versatility; and the more renowned 'Last-Gasp Fleming' down to his knack of scoring many a late goal at crucial times in important matches. It wasn't all sweetness and light, however: George had his critics too and there were spells where he was in and out of the side. When he lost his place to Tommy Murray in 1971, the writing was on the wall. He tabled a transfer request and five months later got his wish with a move to Dundee United. Many were sad to see him go as George was a self-confessed Hearts fan and always gave 100 per cent even when things weren't working for him. He was once described as 'an exasperating player, either dazzling or dismal'.

George became an important player in Jim McLean's early Dundee United sides and enjoyed his only domestic Cup-winning success at Tannadice. He later played at the veteran stage with St Johnstone, where he helped nurture the young stars at Muirton Park – notably one lad called McCoist.

JIM FLEMING

Forward

BORN: Alloa, 7 January 1942

HEIGHT: 5' 10"   WEIGHT: 12st 4lb (1969)

COMPETITIVE DEBUT: v St Mirren, 18 March 1967 (Lge) (A), 0–3

CAREER: Partick Thistle, 1958; Luton Town, Nov 1960; Dunfermline, 1965; **Hearts, March 1967** (swap deal for Don Kerrigan); freed in Apr 1969

A leader of the Hearts attack who displayed 'meritorious foresight', Jim was always on hand when a goal chance presented itself and his foraging upset even the most resolute defenders. He could have been a big success at Tynecastle had injuries not intervened. He played in all but one of Hearts' games towards the end of season 1966–67, but had to wait until a League Cup tie against Stirling Albion in August 1967 to record his first goal. He held his place until an injury ruled him out in January 1968. He suffered a recurrence in his second match back and thankfully the close season gave him a prolonged recovery period. Disaster was to strike again when Fleming retired in the first pre-season game with another injury. He was soon back though, scoring in a 1–3 derby win at Easter Road in September. He was on target again in a 1–2 win at Pittodrie in October but was taken off injured in that match and was out for a further two months. His last appearance was against Partick in March 1969, and he left the club on a free transfer shortly afterwards.

DONALD FORD

Forward

BORN: Linlithgow, 25 October 1944

HEIGHT: 5' 7"   **WEIGHT:** 9st 6lb (1968)

COMPETITIVE DEBUT: v Celtic, 26 September 1964 (Lge) (H), 4–2

CAREER: Vale of Avon, *c*.1962; Bo'ness United, Apr 1964; **Hearts, July 1964** (as an amateur, turning professional in Feb 1967); Falkirk, May 1976 (free transfer); retired 1977

HONOURS: 3 full Scotland caps; 9 Scotland Amateur caps; 3 Scottish League caps; Scottish League r-up 1964–65 (Hearts); Scottish Cup r-up 1967–68 (Hearts); Texaco Cup r-up 1970–71 (Hearts)

A chartered accountant by profession, Donald was a member of the Scottish Sports Council and served as a councillor in his home town of Linlithgow. As well as being a more than useful cricketer, Donald also played football for Hearts. He was a small, slimly-built striker, quick on his feet and able to demonstrate quality shooting abilities. He had a knack of being in the right place at the right time to poach goals from rebounds or knockdowns. He holds a unique distinction as the only Hearts player to score a hat-trick of penalties in a League match, achieving this feat against Morton at Cappielow in September 1973. Other goalscoring highlights included the late strike which knocked Rangers out of the Scottish Cup in 1968. Four fine goals against Airdrie in a 1970 Texaco Cup tie and a sensational treble inside a fifteen-minute spell against Aberdeen at Pittodrie in November 1971, are just a few of his many strikes. What made the latter hat-trick so remarkable was that Hearts were trailing by two goals and reduced to ten men – and there were only 17 minutes left on the clock. Donald had other ideas and his 88th-minute winner brought the house down.

His last season with Hearts could be described as an injury nightmare and it ended with a free transfer. In his only match against Hearts, Donald scored for Falkirk in a 4–3 win for the Bairns. After one season at Brockville he retired, aged 32. He later worked for Radio Forth.

BORN: Tyldesley, England, 11 September 1963

HEIGHT: 5' 10"   WEIGHT: 11st 11lb (1991)

Forward

COMPETITIVE DEBUT: v Dundee United, 23 August 1986 (PL) (A), 0–1

CAREER: Bolton Wanderers, Aug 1981; Preston North End, June 1985; **Hearts, Aug 1986** (free transfer); Hartlepool, Oct 1994 (on loan); Partick Thistle, Dec 1994 (swap for Willie Jamieson)

HONOURS: England Youth international; Premier League r-up 1987–88 (Hearts); Tennents Sixes winner 1990–91 (Hearts)

Hard-working and determined forward with blistering pace, Wayne was more of a chance-maker than goal-taker, his accurate low crosses bringing many goals for his colleagues. He could have been a major star if he had been able to show more composure when presented with a scoring opportunity. He enjoyed most success on the European stage, with four goals in his 11 appearances. He had several nick-names, some more complimentary than others. His colleagues referred to him as 'Fozzie', while the fans called him 'Super-Wayne' or 'Tyson'. The latter nickname was linked to an incident with Motherwell's Steve Kirk when Foster's temper reached boiling-point.

Wayne made a notable contribution in his first two seasons and again when Joe Jordan first took control. He then faded from the scene for long spells, making only isolated appearances, mostly as a substitute. A Scottish Cup tie against Hibs on 20 February 1994 catapulted him back into the spotlight in a big way. He came on for John Robertson and, with four minutes remaining, scored a glorious winner, showing commendable composure as he raced in on Leighton before smashing a low shot into the net. It was Foster's first goal in nearly three years and extended an unbeaten run against Hibs to 21 games. Coincidentally, it was Wayne's 21st competitive goal for Hearts and he celebrated in a frenzy by almost jumping into the crowd of delirious fans.

After a loan spell with Hartlepool he joined Partick in December 1994, but he'll always be remembered for the day he dumped the Hibees out of the Cup!

STEPHEN FRAIL

Defender

BORN: Glasgow, 10 August 1969

HEIGHT: 5' 9"   **WEIGHT:** 10st 9lb (1994)

COMPETITIVE DEBUT: v Kilmarnock, 2 April 1994 (PL) (A), 1–0

CAREER: Possilpark YM; Dundee, Aug 1985; **Hearts, Mar 1994** (£130,000)

HONOURS: B&Q Cup winner 1990–91 (Dundee)

Flame-haired midfielder who was signed just one hour before the 1993–94 transfer deadline. He scored two crucial goals to help Hearts retain Premier League status as they became embroiled in the relegation dogfight. The first goal was a raging 20-yard drive, which came near the end of a clash with Celtic at Parkhead, earning a point in a 2–2 draw. His other goal was the opener in a 2–0 home win against Dundee United. Stephen has helped to fill the problem area of the right side of Hearts' defence. His attacking style, general endeavour and sound defensive qualities lend themselves well to Hearts' pattern of play. He is a sound all-round player who should reach his peak at Tynecastle.

Stephen had been enjoying a rich vein of form during 1994–95 which saw him tipped as a possible Scotland international. A recurrence of a serious knee ligament injury in March 1995, however, was to put him out of action for an estimated ten months.

ANDY FRASER

Half-back

BORN: Newtongrange, 29 August 1940

HEIGHT: 5' 10"   **WEIGHT:** 11st 4lb (1960)

COMPETITIVE DEBUT: v Kilmarnock, 8 August 1959 (LC) (H), 4–0

CAREER: Craiglee Thistle; Newtongrange Star; **Hearts, April 1958**; Hartlepool, April 1961 (free transfer)

Andy Fraser made his debut when Andy Bowman was out of action at the start of season 1959–60. He played reasonably well but after only three games made way for the more experienced Jimmy Murray. After playing on in reserve football, Andy was recalled in November 1960 for a League match with Raith Rovers. It proved to be his last first-team game.

Andy can at least boast that he never played on a losing first-team side, notching up three wins and a draw in his four appearances.

BILLY FRASER
Outside-left

BORN: Edinburgh, 12 August 1945

HEIGHT: 5' 6"   WEIGHT: 10st 7lb (1965)

COMPETITIVE DEBUT: v Clyde, 21 August 1965 (LC) (H), 1–2

CAREER: Huddersfield Town, Apr 1963; **Hearts, Aug 1965** (free transfer); Washington Diplomats, 1970–71

A winger who made little impact at Tynecastle, Billy made only two competitive appearances for Hearts. Besides his debut, he played one League match against Partick Thistle and had the satisfaction of scoring. Billy later played against Hearts for the Washington Diplomats when the Maroons toured America in 1971.

CAMMY FRASER
Midfield

BORN: Dundee, 22 July 1957

HEIGHT: 5' 10"   WEIGHT: 11st 7lb (1979)

COMPETITIVE DEBUT: v Morton, 12 April 1975 (Lge) (A), 0–0

CAREER: Lintrathen High School; Dundee United S signing; Invergowrie Boys Club; **Hearts, Sept 1973**; Dundee, Sept 1980 (£60,000); Rangers, June 1984 (£165,000); Raith Rovers, Oct 1987; Dundee, Mar 1991; Montrose, Dec 1991; Lochore Juniors, 1993

HONOURS: Division I winner 1979–80 (Hearts); Scottish League Cup winner 1984–85, 1986–87 (Rangers); r-up 1980–81 (Dundee)

A fine ball-winning midfielder with good distribution and foresight on the field. Cammy displayed super confidence in his abilities even as a youthful teenager, before establishing himself as an automatic first-choice in season 1976–77. He shone brightly as an emerging star but was unfortunate to feature in a Hearts team sliding into decline and suffered the early part of the Yo-Yo years.

Fraser soon became renowned as a goalscoring midfield man to watch out for and became a driving force in Hearts' 1980 Division I Championship-winning side. Bobby Moncur arrived as the new manager in January 1980 and

Cammy fell out of favour to the point where he became unsettled. His move to Dundee came as no surprise but Hearts definitely lost a player who could have made a contribution to the revival in fortunes which took place in later years.

Cammy later skippered Dundee and earned rave notices which soon attracted Rangers and a big-money move to Glasgow. He matured further at Ibrox and displayed the type of playing arrogance associated to the man who later took over as Ibrox manager – Graeme Souness. This attribute brought its reward with two League Cup winners' medals.

Injury forced him out of the game on a couple of occasions but he was able to return with Raith Rovers at the age of 30, despite warnings that he could end up with arthritis. Cammy has continued to play on into his late 30s and was known to be representing Lochore Juniors in 1993.

JOHN GALLACHER
Centre-half

BORN: Falkirk, 12 December 1951

HEIGHT: 6'   WEIGHT: 11st 12lb (1977)

COMPETITIVE DEBUT: v Hibernian, 1 May 1970 (EoSS) (H), 3–2

CAREER: Falkirk High School; Gairdoch United; Queens Park, 1969; **Hearts, Apr 1970**; Dumbarton, May 1978 (free transfer); retired in 1982

HONOURS: Scotland Schoolboy and Amateur international; Scottish Cup r-up 1975–76 (Hearts)

John studied to become a teacher at Edinburgh University and combined football with a post at a Falkirk school. He had the misfortune to fracture his ankle on his debut, and thereafter he took several seasons to break into the team due to the consistency of veteran Alan Anderson. He began to establish himself in 1974–75 until a bad leg injury against Falkirk in a League Cup quarter-final sidelined him indefinitely.

John returned to re-establish himself towards the end of 1975–76 as Alan Anderson's career drew to a close. The slim, elegant defender had a near 100 per cent record in 1976–77 as Hearts dazzled in Cup competitions but struggled in the League. John scored eight goals in his best-ever season, yet Hearts were relegated. A mystery foot injury early in the new term effectively ended his season and was a contributory factor to his release in May 1978. John wished to retain his part-time teaching post and this clashed with Willie Ormond's plans to have a full-time staff in 1978–79.

BORN: Oswestry, 30 May 1965

HEIGHT: 5′ 11″   **WEIGHT:** 12st 7lb (1989)

COMPETITIVE DEBUT: v Dundee United, 18 November 1987 (PL) (A), 3–0 (came on as substitute)

CAREER: Tynecastle Boys Club; Elphinstone Primrose; Mansfield Town, Sept 1983; Halifax Town, Jan 1986; **Hearts, Nov 1987** (£60,000); Celtic, June 1989 (£500,000); Leicester City (on loan), Jan 1995

HONOURS: 1 full Scotland cap; Scotland Youth and U-21 international; Premier League r-up 1987–88 (Hearts); Scottish League Cup r-up 1994–95 (Celtic)

MIKE GALLOWAY
Midfield

Mike was plucked from the obscurity of English Division IV Halifax Town and was a smash hit at Tynecastle in what was an all-too-brief 18-month spell. He added a quality missing from the Hearts midfield through the years – hardness and the will to win coupled with goalscoring ability. Galloway took no prisoners: he was tenacious in the tackle, powerful in the air and packed a rocket shot in his right boot. He was versatile, too, deputising at full-back, central defence and centre-forward.

If his first season was good, the next was even better. Mike was a deadly weapon on the European stage as Hearts battled to the UEFA Cup quarter-finals. Mike scored in each leg of the first-round tie with St Patrick's Athletic. He then headed the only goal of the next round ties against Austria Vienna in the famous Prater Stadium. Incredibly, he scored in both legs of the third round against Velez Mostar. His goal in Mostar was a superb looping header. His form was noted by Celtic boss Billy McNeill and he dangled a half-million-pound carrot which Hearts decided to accept.

Sadly, Galloway was badly injured in a car crash in August 1995. Hopefully, with the right medical treatment, he'll make a full recovery.

KENNY GARLAND

Goalkeeper

BORN: Cupar, 19 March 1948

HEIGHT: 6′ 2″   WEIGHT: 12st 1lb (1970)

COMPETITIVE DEBUT: v Stirling Albion, 16 August 1967 (LC) (A), 1–0

CAREER: Bell Baxter School (Cupar); Strathmiglo United (as a left-half); Cupar TM Juveniles; Newburgh Juniors, 1964; **Hearts, 1966**

Kenny was originally an apprentice compositor with a Cupar printing firm. He distinguished himself early in his Hearts career by saving a hat-trick of penalties in a reserve game against St Johnstone in August 1967: Hearts had found the first serious contender for Jim Cruickshank's No. 1 jersey after four years. Kenny saved a penalty on his League debut against Rangers to earn a point in a 1–1 draw and held his place for four months. He then embarked on a struggle to oust Jim Cruickshank without much success. Garland only managed odd appearances until a lengthy run in the latter part of season 1971–72. Kenny was unfortunately involved in Hearts' catastrophic New Year 1973 match and many fans pointed a finger at his alleged ineptitude that fateful day. In fairness, the result was a total team disaster – Hibs hit the heights while Hearts had an all-time low.

By the mid-1970s young David Graham was also fighting for a first-team place and on occasions Kenny found himself third choice. Frustration got the better of him and he quit football in August 1975, aged 27. The big keeper endured long spells of playing second-fiddle to his rival Jim Cruickshank, but Kenny is remembered for his reflexes when faced with a spot kick. His success rate in saving penalties speaks for itself. He retired in August 1975 to join the police.

BORN: Lesmahagow, 17 June 1919

DIED: Bristol, 10 April 1994

HEIGHT: 5′ 11″   WEIGHT: 11st 7lb (1938)

COMPETITIVE DEBUT: v Hamilton Accies, 17 December 1938 (Lge) (H), 2–3

CAREER: Lesmahagow Juniors; Preston North End, 1934; **Hearts, Dec 1938** (£4,000); Northampton, Sept 1946 (joint fee £2,250 including Jimmy Briscoe); Birmingham City, Nov 1947 (£10,000); Northampton, Dec 1948; retired in 1950

Archie made his name as a young teenager prior to the Second World War. He had a long loping stride and a sweeping but powerful shooting ability. He was deadly accurate in front of goal and was just entering his best years when the war interrupted. At the age of 27 Archie was restored to the first team for the start of season 1946–47 and reminded pre-war fans of his abilities by scoring three goals in his four matches in August 1946. A month later he moved to England. After his retiral from football in 1950, Archie worked with the GPO in Bristol until the early 1980s.

BORN: Edinburgh, 26 March 1964

HEIGHT: 5′ 10″   WEIGHT: 9st 10lb (1981)

COMPETITIVE DEBUT: v Kilmarnock, 8 May 1982 (Div. I) (A), 0–0

CAREER: Salvesen Boys Club; **Hearts, 1980**; Derry City, Feb 1985 (free transfer)

Tall, very thinly-built full-back with the unusual nickname 'Bamber'. He was easily identified by his gangling, awkward presence on the field. Stuart made all his appearances as a teenager during a transitional rebuilding period. He could play competently on either side of the park, and although often criticised for making mistakes, Gauld could made good use of the ball. He didn't quite reach the standard needed for the Premier League. A stronger physique might have assisted him but it is to his credit that he was able to build a successful career in Northern Ireland. He also played in European competitions with Derry.

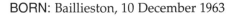

MARK GAVIN

Forward

BORN: Baillieston, 10 December 1963

HEIGHT: 5′ 9″   **WEIGHT:** 11st (1988)

COMPETITIVE DEBUT: v Morton, 26 March 1988 (PL) (H), 2–0 (came on as substitute)

CAREER: Leeds United, 1982; Bolton Wanderers, 1986; Rochdale, 1987; **Hearts, Jan 1988** (£30,000); Bristol City, Oct 1988 (£35,000); Watford, 1989 (£250,000); Exeter City, Mar 1993

HONOURS: Freight Rover Trophy winner 1985–86 (Bolton)

A man of many clubs, moving almost every year of his career in his mid-20s. Mark was a speedy winger with good close control who liked to patrol the left wing where he could supply accurate crosses to his front-line partners. He made only 17 appearances in a brief eight-month spell with Hearts. He showed enough signs of talent to suggest he would be a useful asset to the club but, with similar type players like John Colquhoun, Alan Moore and the emerging Scott Crabbe, opportunities were limited for Mark. As a result, permission was quickly granted when Bristol City made their approach and a quick deal was concluded.

WILLIE GIBSON

Forward

BORN: St Andrews, 3 April 1953

HEIGHT: 5′ 8″   **WEIGHT:** 10st 12lb (1975)

COMPETITIVE DEBUT: v Morton, 29 December 1973 (Lge) (H), 0–2 (came on as substitute)

CAREER: Buckhaven High School; Methil Star Colts; Lochore Welfare; **Hearts, July 1971**; Partick Thistle, July 1981 (£35,000); Raith Rovers, 1981; Cowdenbeath, 1982; retired in 1983

HONOURS: Division I winner 1979–80 (Hearts); Scottish Cup r-up 1975–76 (Hearts)

The slim Fifer was an immensely talented footballer with wonderful touch skills to match a deadly finishing ability in front of goal. He was capable of slipping defenders in order to find good goalscoring positions where he could find the net accurately with a shot or header. Willie first made an impact towards the end of season 1973–74, linking brilliantly with Drew Busby. Feeding on the crosses supplied by wingers Aird, Prentice and Park, he quickly established himself.

Gibson scored several hat-tricks as a Heart, the best remembered in a

November 1976 match against Celtic. His treble had Hearts 3–1 ahead – but the unbelievable happened with Celts fighting back to win 4–3. A few weeks prior to this match Willie netted two outstanding goals in one of his best ever performances: Hearts demolished Locomotiv Leipzig 5–1 and he simply sparkled that night. Despite being a member of three relegated squads, Willie's impressive goalscoring record pays testimony to his contribution during a difficult period.

Willie was transferred to Partick Thistle in 1981 but couldn't recapture his form. Further moves proved equally unsuccessful and he retired at the age of only 30 in 1983. His inability to succeed elsewhere could perhaps be linked to not receiving the high standard of ball supply to which he became accustomed with Hearts.

BOSTON GLEGG

Forward

BORN: Stenhousemuir, 29 November 1942

HEIGHT: 5' 4"   WEIGHT: 10st 1lb (1960)

COMPETITIVE DEBUT: v Clyde, 31 August 1960 (LC) (H), 6–2 (scored)

CAREER: Gairdoch Juveniles; Stenhousemuir; **Hearts, May 1960**; Stenhousemuir, 1961

HONOURS: Scotland Amateur international

Small striker who made his debut on the right wing. Newspaper reports suggest he performed reasonably well but lacked the build and experience to be considered first-team material. He kept his place for the next match against Motherwell but was clearly out of his depth and was dropped in place of the experienced Ian Crawford. These were the only appearances for the lad with the unusual name and he returned to the reserves before rejoining Stenhousemuir.

FREDDIE GLIDDEN

Centre-half

BORN: Newmains, 9 July 1928

HEIGHT: 5' 11"   **WEIGHT:** 12st 7lb (1956)

COMPETITIVE DEBUT: v Queen of the South, 10 November 1951 (Lge) (H), 4–3

CAREER: Stoneyburn Public School; Bathgate Academy; Murrayfield Rovers; West Calder Juveniles; Whitburn Juniors; **Hearts (provisional), 1946**; Newtongrange Star (farmed out); **Hearts (call up), 1948**; Dumbarton, Mar 1959 (free transfer); retired in 1962

HONOURS: Scotland Junior international; Scottish League winner 1957–58 (Hearts); Scottish Cup winner 1955–56 (Hearts); Scottish League Cup winner 1954–55, 1958–59 (Hearts)

Freddie's juvenile and junior career saw him star in several front-line positions. After signing provisional forms for Hearts he was farmed out to Newtongrange Star where he blossomed as a right-half. After two years at 'Nitten', Glidden was called in to Tynecastle and the commanding defender made steady progress in the third and second teams.

Freddie made his competitive debut at right-half and provided cover in several defensive positions before eventually making the centre-half berth his own following Bobby Dougan's departure. From a full haul of domestic honours his proudest moment was captaining Hearts to the Scottish Cup in 1956. Glidden was an inspiring leader, good in the air and strong in the tackle. He had an amazing appetite for the game even when the going was heavy. The saddest moment of his career was leaving Hearts but he could look back with pride at the sterling service he provided and the honours it brought. In later years he worked as a sub-postmaster in Edinburgh.

BORN: Edinburgh, 14 May 1944

HEIGHT: 6'   WEIGHT: 11st 1lb (1964)

COMPETITIVE DEBUT: v Celtic, 21 October 1961 (Lge) (H), 2–1

CAREER: Heriots School; Edina Hearts; Edinburgh Athletic; **Hearts, July 1961**; Durban United (South Africa), May 1967; **Hearts, Oct 1968**; Dundee United, Mar 1969 (£8,000); Hibernian, Jan 1972 (£12,000); Dundee, Dec 1974 (£13,000); retired in 1976

HONOURS: Scottish League r-up 1964–65 (Hearts); Scottish Cup r-up 1971–72 (Hibs); Scottish League Cup winner 1972–73 (Hibs); r-up 1961–62 (Hearts)

ALAN GORDON

Forward

An excellent all-round attacker with a proven goalscoring record in his 15-year career at senior level, Alan was a precocious young talent breaking through to make his debut aged only 17. The match following his debut was the 1961 League Cup final against Rangers – quite an introduction to face the Old Firm in consecutive weeks! Over the next few years Alan was gradually blooded into the first team. Supporters were often critical of the fair-haired teenager, stating that he couldn't last 90 minutes. However, he continued to develop and finally blossomed as a goalscoring star in Hearts' 1964–65 League campaign, striking 23 times to silence the critics. He maintained his form during the next two seasons despite competition for his place from Don Kerrigan.

In May 1967 Alan asked to be released from his contract as he had found employment linked to playing for Durban United in South Africa. Hearts agreed to his request on the understanding that he would remain a Hearts player on his return to Scotland. In later years it was revealed he had actually been 'tapped' by the South Africans. He returned to Edinburgh in 1968 and won back his first-team place at Tynecastle and was soon scoring goals once more. He moved to Dundee United and did well on Tayside, but the appointment of Jim McLean and the new man's policy of players living in the Dundee area hastened his departure due to Alan's business interests in Edinburgh. He moved to Hibs where he won honours and completed a unique career by finishing his footballing years at Dundee, thus being able to claim that he represented the principal senior sides in Edinburgh and Dundee.

IAN GORDON

Full-back

BORN: Possilpark, Glasgow, 13 May 1929

HEIGHT: 5′ 10″ **WEIGHT:** 11st (1952)

COMPETITIVE DEBUT: v Rangers, 20 October 1951 (Lge) (A), 0–2

CAREER: Albert Road School; Rob Roy Juveniles; Parkhead Juveniles; Kilsyth Rangers; **Hearts, Aug 1951**; Airdrie, Jan 1954

HONOURS: Scotland Junior international

Ian made his debut at Ibrox opposite Rangers' Scotland international right-winger Willie Waddell, and handled his illustrious opponent well during his fiery baptism. Ian was an assured left-back who could position himself shrewdly to meet an oncoming winger or intercept a pass. He was employed as an apprentice mining surveyor and joined Hearts as a part-timer. Ian played as a forward for Rob Roy and was a consistent scorer. He was capped twice at Junior level against Ireland and Wales, and Hearts moved to sign the promising youngster. Originally a centre-half, Gordon made all his Hearts appearances at full-back.

DAVID GRAHAM

Goalkeeper

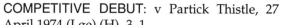

BORN: Edinburgh

HEIGHT: 5′ 11″ **WEIGHT:** 11st 4lb (1974)

COMPETITIVE DEBUT: v Partick Thistle, 27 April 1974 (Lge) (H), 3–1

CAREER: Carrickvale Secondary School; Haddington Athletic; Carrickvale Thistle; **Hearts, 1969**; freed in July 1976

HONOURS: 8 Scotland Professional Youth caps

A very talented young goalkeeper who was good enough to keep Alan Rough out of the Scottish Professional Youth squad, David was initially a part-timer, holding down a job with an Edinburgh typewriter firm. Despite his talent, Jim Cruickshank and Kenny Garland blocked the first-team door. He was unlucky with injuries, too, suffering dislocated fingers and twice breaking his arm. Early in his career he took the unusual step of appearing as a substitute on the left wing in reserve games – on one occasion he even scored against Dundee United reserves.

His long overdue League debut arrived at the end of season 1973–74 and he kept two clean sheets in his three games. The more established men were still destined to keep him out, however, and in May 1976 David was handed a free transfer. He was recalled when Jim Cruickshank refused to go on Hearts' world tour after a contract dispute. David agreed to travel and performed admirably. He was offered a new contract on his return but turned it down and quit senior football.

WILLIAM GRANT

Outside-left

HEIGHT: 5′ 10″   WEIGHT: 10st 5lb (1954)

COMPETITIVE DEBUT: v St Mirren, 22 April 1955 (Lge) (H), 1–1

CAREER: Armadale Thistle; **Hearts, 1953**; freed in 1955

Willie made one appearance for Hearts, in a midweek League match as deputy for Jim Souness. The well-built, speedy youngster performed well at outside-right despite being a natural left-winger. An abundance of talented wingers at the club led to Grant's release in 1955.

DAVID HAGEN

Forward

BORN: Edinburgh, 5 May 1973

HEIGHT: 5′ 11″   WEIGHT: 13st (1994)

COMPETITIVE DEBUT: v Falkirk, 3 December 1994 (PL) (H), 1–1 (came on as substitute)

CAREER: Grahamston Boys Club; Rangers, Aug 1989; **Hearts, Dec 1994** (£150,000)

HONOURS: Scotland Youth and U-21 international

A versatile forward, capable of filling any striking position, David's tricky, strong-running style can upset the most assured defenders. He struggled to win a first-team place at Ibrox with a host of big-name stars ahead of him in the strikers' queue, but he did manage to make 14 appearances in two seasons. Hearts won the race to sign the talented youngster ahead of Mark McGhee's Reading. Hagen's ex-Ibrox colleague Dave McPherson helped convince him it would be a good decision to opt for Hearts. Now we all look forward to him being a big hit at Tynecastle.

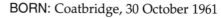

ALEX HAMILL

Midfield

BORN: Coatbridge, 30 October 1961

HEIGHT: 5' 8"   **WEIGHT:** 10st 7lb (1981)

COMPETITIVE DEBUT: v Kilmarnock, 6 December 1980 (PL) (H), 2–0

CAREER: Tottenham Hotspur; **Hearts, Nov 1980** (free transfer); Hamilton Accies, May 1982 (free transfer); Forfar Athletic, Oct 1986; Cowdenbeath assistant manager, May 1994; East Fife, Feb 1995

Versatile player who could fill in at full-back or in a wide attacking role, Alex made most of his appearances in midfield. A composed individual, he always looked to find teammates with a pass. He was prone to being caught and tackled in possession of the ball, though Hamill liked to push forward and managed a couple of goals in his two seasons. When Alex MacDonald took control he quite clearly had no plans for the curly-haired midfielder and Hamill faded from the first-team scene. He later provided Hamilton and Forfar with many years of service.

BRIAN HAMILTON

Midfield

BORN: Paisley, 5 August 1967

HEIGHT: 6'   **WEIGHT:** 11st 4lb (1995)

COMPETITIVE DEBUT: v Motherwell, 8 January 1995 (PL) (A), 2–1 (scored)

CAREER: Pollok United Boys Club; St Mirren, 1985; Hibernian, July 1989 (£275,000); **Hearts, Jan 1995** (£260,000)

HONOURS: Scotland Youth international; 2 Scotland U-21 caps; Scottish Cup winner 1986–87 (St Mirren); Scottish League Cup winner 1991–92 (Hibs); Tennents Sixes winner 1989–90 (Hibs)

Brian made his name with St Mirren, where he won a Scottish Cup medal as a 19-year-old. His manager at Love Street, Alex Miller, moved to become Hibs boss and Brian soon followed for a large fee. He won further honours at Easter Road before becoming involved in a contract dispute late in 1994. Brian was at the point where he said he would rather lick stamps in his wife's post office than play for Hibs when, out of the blue, he crossed the city to sign for

Hearts. Tommy McLean offered £175,000, while Hibs demanded £425,000. A tribunal set his fee at £260,000.

Brian scored a fine goal on his debut at Fir Park. He ran onto a defence-splitting Kevin Thomas pass and displayed great composure to beat the keeper from 12 yards. Not a noted goalscorer by any means, his real strength lies in the immense power of work he puts in on his midfield beat. A good passer of the ball, he also breaks up opponents' attacks with his committed tackling.

GEORGE HAMILTON

Inside-right

BORN: Irvine, 7 December 1917

HEIGHT: 5' 10"   **WEIGHT:** 11st 6lb (1948)

COMPETITIVE DEBUT: v Hibernian, 1 January 1948 (Lge) (A), 1–3

CAREER: Irvine Meadow, 1934; Queen of the South, 1937; Aberdeen, Apr 1938 (£3,000); guest for Ayr United and Rangers during the war; **Hearts, Dec 1947** (£8,000 plus Archie Kelly to Aberdeen); Aberdeen, Jun 1948 (£12,000); Hamilton Accies, Sept 1955 (£2,000); retired in Dec 1955

HONOURS: 5 full Scotland caps; 3 Scottish League caps; Scottish Cup winner 1946–47 (Aberdeen); r-up 1952–53, 1953–54 (Aberdeen); Scottish League Cup winner 1945–46 (Aberdeen); r-up 1946–47 (Aberdeen)

A skilled passer of the ball with intricate footwork, George's greatest strength was his heading ability. He was once described as a true sporting gentleman. This accolade surprised George, who said in later years: 'I often used to think I was one of the dirtiest players on the field. There were times when I used my backside more than my boots to keep defenders away. Maybe it was because I never argued with referees.'

Hearts had struggled in the first half of 1947–48 and as they looked for solutions to fight clear of relegation they remembered George Hamilton. He had scored a tremendous hat-trick against Hearts in the 1947 League Cup semi-final and Dave McLean saw him as an ideal short-term buy. His spell at Tynecastle did not last long. The move did not live up to expectations and George asked for a transfer, whereupon he returned to Aberdeen.

JOHNNY HAMILTON

Winger

BORN: Larkhall, 22 January 1935

HEIGHT: 5′ 6″   **WEIGHT:** 10st 7lb (1960)

COMPETITIVE DEBUT: v Airdrie, 1 October 1955 (Lge) (A), 4–1

CAREER: Larkhall Academy; Larkhall Rangers; Kirkmuirhill Juveniles; Burtonshaw Welfare; Lesmahagow Juniors; **Hearts, Apr 1955**; Watford, Apr 1967 (free transfer); Berwick Rangers, 1970; retired in 1973; **Hearts youth coach, Nov 1974–79**

HONOURS: Scotland U-23 international; Scottish League winner 1957–58, 1959–60 (Hearts); r-up 1958–59, 1964–65 (Hearts); Scottish League Cup winner 1958–59, 1959–60, 1962–63 (Hearts); r-up 1961–62 (Hearts); English Division III winner 1968–69 (Watford)

Affectionately known as 'Wee Hammy', Johnny was one of Hearts' most popular post-war personalities. A lively winger, his speedy bursts down the touchline were a joy to behold in Hearts' halcyon 1950s era. Hammy's deceptive galloping runs always bamboozled defenders and a famous cry was 'Open the gates, here comes Pigalle Wonder!' – a reference to a top greyhound of the time.

Hamilton quickly became a permanent fixture in Hearts' first-team plans and was selected for U-23 honours. On 3 March 1958, Hammy starred in a World Cup trial match against a Scotland XI in arguably his finest game for Hearts. He displayed amazing pace and dribbling skills and, to top it all, scored an incredible goal. Picking up the ball in front of the players' tunnel on the stand side, he advanced a few yards before unleashing a terrific 35-yard blockbuster which screamed into the net at the School End. Hamilton celebrated many more goals including a crucial equaliser in the 1959 League Cup final but had to wait until March 1965 before recording his first hat-trick.

He moved to Watford where he linked up with a youthful Tony Currie who was later to win full international honours with England. Hammy retired aged 38 in 1973. He assisted Hearts for several years thereafter, combining this with his newsagent's business at the top of Robertson Avenue near Gorgie.

BORN: Glasgow, 7 October 1960

HEIGHT: 5′ 8″ WEIGHT: 10st 11lb (1981)

COMPETITIVE DEBUT: v Ayr United, 3 September 1979 (LC) (H), 2–3 (came on as substitute)

CAREER: Anniesland Waverley; Leicester City; **Hearts, Aug 1979** (free transfer); East Fife, 1981 (free transfer); East Stirling, 1984

Full-back

A small, sturdily-built full-back, Steve's Hearts career got off to a false start due to an ankle fracture in only his third appearance in the first team. He was sidelined for the best part of a year, but made a comeback in November 1980, clocking up a dozen League appearances until he was dropped following three consecutive heavy defeats in March 1981. Hearts were relegated and, in another clear-out, Steve was freed in April 1981.

BORN: Chaplehall, 16 February 1938

DIED: Canada, October 1976

HEIGHT: 5′ 9″ WEIGHT: 10st 10lb (1963)

COMPETITIVE DEBUT: v Dundee, 1 September 1962 (LC) (H), 2–0

CAREER: Drumpellier Amateurs, 1954; Sheffield United, Feb 1956; Middlesbrough, Feb 1961 (£12,000); **Hearts, June 1962** (£5,000); Hibernian, Oct 1963 (£6,000); Aston Villa, Aug 1965 (£25,000); **Hearts, Aug 1967** (free transfer); emigrated to South Africa in 1969; Ross County, 1970; Hamilton Accies, Nov 1971; Ferranti Thistle; emigrated to Canada

HONOURS: 1 full Scotland cap; 2 Scottish League caps; Scottish League Cup winner 1962–63 (Hearts)

Inside-forward

A true footballing genius whose career was hampered due to illness, injury and his liking for Scotland's national drink (not Irn Bru). Willie's marvellous talent as a ball-playing craftsman saw him rise to prominence early in his career as an 18-year-old with Sheffield United. He later moved to Teesside where he failed to settle, and Hearts negotiated his transfer in June 1962.

Willie quickly became a Tynecastle sensation with amazing displays. He was dubbed 'the steal of all time' and 'Hearts' gilt-edged investment in the soccer stock exchange'. After making a major contribution to Hearts' League Cup win in 1962, Willie's career went off the rails during the long winter shutdown of 1962–63. He never really found his way back into manager Walker's favour and, to the disgust of the fans, was transferred to Hibs in October 1963. Hibs later sold him to Aston Villa for a huge fee, but his lifestyle and injuries sustained in a bad car accident hindered his endeavours to re-establish himself in English football. Villa released him and he donned a Hearts jersey again on 16 August 1967 at Annfield Park, Stirling. Goals and appearances were infrequent and, after moving around and emigrating twice, he sadly died in 1976 aged 38. One accolade accorded by Sandy Jardine in later years read: 'I think the sky would've been the limit for Willie Hamilton if his physical preparation had ever matched his skill level. Willie was a character, the type who'd turn up for a match abroad with one shirt in his bag, and maybe they don't make them like that anymore!'

STEVE HANCOCK

Forward

BORN: Sheffield, 10 September 1953

HEIGHT: 5' 8"   WEIGHT: 11st 3lb (1975)

COMPETITIVE DEBUT: v Celtic, 13 August 1975 (LC) (H), 2–0 (scored)

CAREER: St Anthony's Secondary School; Edina Hibs; Newtongrange Star; Celtic S signing; Sheffield Wednesday; **Hearts, 1974**; Meadowbank, 1976; Stenhousemuir, 1979 (£10,000); Forfar Athletic, Aug 1981 (£12,000); retired in 1984

HONOURS: Scotland Schoolboy and Junior international

Not a particular favourite with the Hearts supporters who knew of his liking for a certain football team from Leith! Steve had a reputation for being a real speed merchant and quickly demonstrated his ability to find the net when given his chance at the start of season 1975–76. After scoring three goals in five League Cup appearances, Hancock looked to have a bright future. It was not to be, however. After losing form he completed the season in the reserves and then joined city neighbours Meadowbank. He later commanded nominal transfer fees for Stenhousemuir and Forfar, returning to Tynecastle with the latter in 1982 on Scottish Cup business. Steve scored the only goal that day to knock Hearts out and prompted the late John Fairgrieve to recommend a carpark be built on Tynecastle. Hancock retired in 1984 and later found employment as an insurance agent in Edinburgh.

BORN: Edinburgh, 22 January 1974

HEIGHT: 5' 9"   WEIGHT: 10st 7lb (1991)

COMPETITIVE DEBUT: v Dundee United, 10 February 1991 (PL) (H), 2–1 (came on as substitute)

CAREER: Salvesen Boys Club; **Hearts, April 1990**; freed in Dec 1994; Dunfermline, Jan 1995; freed May 1995; Clyde, Aug 1995

HONOURS: Scotland Schoolboy international

TOMMY HARRISON

Midfield

Hearts beat a host of top Scottish and English clubs to land Tommy's signature. Tipped for the top as a teenager, he had the satisfaction of setting up John Robertson for Hearts' equaliser in his debut match. Having just turned 17, the national press predicted a bright future for Tommy. However, he failed to make an impact the following season and 1992–93 was much the same until Sandy Clark gave him three starts in the remaining League games. He scored his first and only goal in the last game against St Johnstone. The following season he made only one appearance and it looked unlikely that he would ever make a first-team place his own. New team boss Tommy McLean gave Harrison two starts in friendly matches at the beginning of season 1994–95. He then appeared as a substitute in a disastrous League Cup defeat against St Johnstone. His misery was completed when he was himself substituted. Tommy admitted he felt embarrassed about this state of affairs and his free transfer a few months later came as no surprise.

BORN: Edinburgh, 30 July 1950

HEIGHT: 5' 8"   WEIGHT: 10st 7lb (1970)

COMPETITIVE DEBUT: v Celtic, 8 August 1970 (LC) (H), 1–2 (scored)

CAREER: Salvesen Boys Club; Falkirk, 1967; Haddington Athletic; **Hearts, 1969**; Carlisle United, Sept 1971 (swap deal for Tommy Murray); East Fife, 1972; Morton, July 1974; East Fife, Feb 1975; Dunfermline Athletic, 1978; Berwick Rangers, 1983

KEVIN HEGARTY

Forward

After being rejected by Falkirk as a teenager Kevin returned to junior football where he attracted Hearts' interest. After completing his printing apprenticeship he decided to give full-time football his best shot. He left the subs bench to score a memorable debut goal and in a purple patch of good form made a notable contribution throughout season 1970–71 with several well-taken goals. Football reporters forecast a bright future for the young striker but indifferent form in the second part of the season cast doubt on their predictions. After touring America in May 1971, Kevin hoped to start 1971–72 as he had the previous term. However, he couldn't fight his way into contention and manager Seith sprung a surprise when he swapped Hegarty for Carlisle's Tommy Murray. He didn't settle in England and returned to Scotland where he served many senior sides. His brother Paul followed him into senior circles with Hamilton and Dundee United.

JAMES HENDERSON

Defender

HEIGHT: 5' 9" **WEIGHT:** 11st (1949)

COMPETITIVE DEBUT: v Falkirk, 26 February 1949 (Lge) (H), 3–1

CAREER: Linfield; **Hearts, 1947**; Stirling Albion, July 1951 (free transfer); released in 1952

A strapping full-back or centre-half, James enjoyed a profitable debut, completely subduing Falkirk's highly rated outside-left, K. Dawson. Signed from top Irish League side, Linfield, James was strongly fancied to make a challenge for a regular place. However, he didn't quite measure up to the standard Hearts wanted and made only 12 appearances, although he won praise in those matches for his enthusiasm in the tackle. After being confined to the reserves throughout 1950–51, Henderson took the offer of a free transfer to join Stirling Albion.

Forward

BORN: Larkhall, 25 July 1943

HEIGHT: 5′ 3″   WEIGHT: 9st 9lb (1960)

COMPETITIVE DEBUT: v Partick Thistle, 8 October 1960 (Lge) (H), 0–1

CAREER: Leeds United; Celtic; **Hearts, July 1960** (free transfer); St Mirren, Dec 1961 (£2,000); Leeds United, Dec 1962; Bury, June 1965; Swindon Town, Jan 1966; Stockport County, July 1966

HONOURS: Scotland Youth international

A diminutive winger, quick and direct but easily brushed off the ball by big defenders, Tommy had made little impact at his first two senior clubs and it was a similar tale at Tynecastle. In 18 months he managed ten appearances for Hearts. He moved to St Mirren for a nominal fee.

Half-back

BORN: Edinburgh, 15 March 1940

HEIGHT: 6′   WEIGHT: 11st 9lb (1960)

COMPETITIVE DEBUT: v Aberdeen, 19 October 1957 (Lge) (H), 4–0

CAREER: Dalkeith Thistle; (provisional with Rangers); **Hearts, June 1956**; Durban City (South Africa), Apr 1967

HONOURS: 4 Scotland U-23 caps; 1 Scottish League cap; Scottish League winner 1959–60 (Hearts); r-up 1964–65 (Hearts); Scottish League Cup winner 1959–60, 1962–63 (Hearts); r-up 1961–62

Billy was initially a part-timer while training to become a brewers' chemist. He was a left-half with excellent ability who could distribute the ball well and read the game intelligently. His one drawback was a tendency to be one-paced. After winning top honours in the late 1950s and the League Cup again in 1962–63, Billy became a mainstay around which a new team began to form. He was an underrated player in many respects and wasn't noted for power-play despite his physical advantages. Billy preferred to use skill. A serious cartilage injury in August 1965 sidelined him for a lengthy spell. He returned to find George Miller as competition and the new man eventually held down the left-half berth.

Higgins was released in April 1967 to join Durban City in South Africa with the provision that, if he returned to Scotland, he would be deemed a Hearts player. But he never again played at Tynecastle.

GRAEME HOGG

Defender

BORN: Aberdeen, 17 June 1964

HEIGHT: 6′ 1″   **WEIGHT:** 12st 12lb (1991)

COMPETITIVE DEBUT: v St Johnstone, 24 August 1991 (PL) (A), 1–0

CAREER: Aberdeen Boys Club; Manchester United, June 1982; West Brom (on loan) Nov/Dec 1987; Portsmouth, Aug 1988 (£140,000); **Hearts, Aug 1991** (£200,000); Notts County, Jan 1994 (£75,000)

HONOURS: Scotland U-21 international; Premier League r-up 1991–92 (Hearts)

The rugged Aberdonian took time to settle in Scottish football after a lengthy spell in England. Caught out by the quicker pace, Graeme was booked on his debut and sent off the following midweek. He soon adapted, though, and became a fans' favourite. They recognised a real trier. Hoggy tackled with conviction and showed immense strength in the air. He didn't mess around when danger lurked – he cleared his lines in any way he saw fit. Graeme was in and out of the team at first but finally looked to have won a regular place in 1992–93. A suspension then sidelined him and, when he could not get back into the team, he submitted a transfer request. Joe Jordan called his bluff by agreeing and Hogg's relationship with the manager became strained.

After Jordan's dismissal Hogg was restored to the team. His contract was due to expire and Birmingham and Stoke made enquiries. Stoke were later reported to the SFA for trying to 'tap' him. Early in season 1993–94 he put an end to speculation by signing a two-year deal. Misfortune followed when a broken leg in November 1993 put him out of action for three months. An unfortunate punch-up incident with teammate Craig Levein in a pre-season match at Starks Park, Kirkcaldy, in August 1994 had severe repercussions for Graeme. Under club rules, Hearts imposed the maximum fine possible and then the SFA weighed in with a ten-match ban. Hearts were unhappy with the SFA decision and withdrew their own punishment. Hogg made only one more appearance for the club, coming on as a substitute at Ibrox in September 1994. Howard Kendall signed him for English Division I side Notts County a few weeks after he had completed his ten-match ban.

BORN: Glasgow, 3 January 1936

HEIGHT: 5′ 8″   WEIGHT: 12st 2lb (1968)

COMPETITIVE DEBUT: v Airdrie, 24 September 1960 (Lge) (A), 2–2

CAREER: John Street School (Glasgow); Glentyan Thistle; Newhill Amateurs; Lugar Boswell Thistle Juniors; Queens Park, 1954; **Hearts, Sept 1960**; Partick Thistle, 1969 (free transfer); retired *c*.1970

HONOURS: 5 full Scotland caps; Scotland U-23 and Amateur international; 1 Scottish League cap; Scottish League r-up 1964–65 (Hearts); Scottish League Cup winner 1962–63 (Hearts); r-up 1961–62 (Hearts)

DAVID HOLT

Left-back

Small, sturdily-built player who was successfully converted from left-half to left-back, David spent six years as an amateur with Queens Park and represented Great Britain as a member of the 1960 Olympic squad. He joined Hearts in 1960 and quickly filled the void created by George Thomson's departure to Everton. Holt was resolute in the tackle and could time his interceptions to perfection. His consistency and dependability soon brought domestic then long overdue full international honours. A composed individual, Davie put his experience to good use, becoming a mainstay in Hearts' defence. Always a hard yet fair player, he gave excellent service to the club. His appearances decreased in his last few seasons as Arthur Mann emerged then departed. Holt himself moved on in 1969 and served the Firhill Jags for a short spell at the veteran stage.

BORN: Whitburn, 17 August 1940

HEIGHT: 5′ 10″   WEIGHT: 13st (1970)

COMPETITIVE DEBUT: v St Johnstone, 26 August 1967 (LC) (A), 2–3 (came on as substitute)

CAREER: St Mary's School (Bathgate); Edinburgh Athletic; Whitburn Juniors; Dundee United, 1956; Middlesbrough, Apr 1964 (£25,000); **Hearts, July 1967** (£15,000); Barrow, Apr 1970 (free transfer); retired *c*.1972

HONOURS: Scotland Schoolboy international; Division II r-up 1959–60 (Dundee United); Scottish Cup r-up 1967–68 (Hearts)

JIM IRVINE

Forward

Irvine served his apprenticeship as a motor mechanic during his part-time years with Dundee United. He was strongly built and had remarkable speed for such a heavy player. Defenders found him difficult to contain and goalkeepers feared his powerful shooting. Jim always gave 100 per cent. His signing failed to reap expected dividends, however, though Jim was surely one of the unluckiest post-war Hearts players. Many different injuries dogged his Tynecastle career, making him one of the best-known faces in the treatment room. His first season was undoubtedly his best. He led the front line with distinction and appeared in every Scottish Cup tie only to end up with a runners-up medal. Irvine's next two seasons were quite simply a catastrophe of injuries. In his odd appearances he demonstrated his ability to score but, in light of his seemingly never-ending problems, he was released in April 1970. In later years he worked as a spray-painter living in the West Lothian town of Bathgate.

WILLIE JAMIESON
Centre-half

BORN: Barnsley, 27 April 1963

HEIGHT: 5' 11"   **WEIGHT:** 12st (1994)

COMPETITIVE DEBUT: v Falkirk, 3 December 1994 (PL) (H), 1–1

CAREER: Edina Hibs; Tynecastle Boys Club; Hibernian, 1979; Hamilton Accies, 1985; Dundee, Jan 1990 (£120,000); Partick Thistle, Sept 1992; **Hearts, Dec 1994** (swap for Wayne Foster)

HONOURS: Scotland Youth international; Division I winner 1980–81 (Hibs); 1985–86, 1987–88 (Hamilton); 1991–92 (Dundee) B&Q Cup winner 1990–91 (Dundee)

A seasoned campaigner with over 400 League appearances with his senior clubs prior to joining Hearts, Willie started his career as a striker with Hibs before being converted to a central-defender. A gutsy competitor, he attacks the ball powerfully in the air and puts in crunching tackles. Hearts' defensive crisis during November 1994 prompted boss Tommy McLean to move for the experienced cover Jamieson could provide. Many Hearts supporters will view his signing as a stop-gap measure, but Jamieson will be determined to battle for permanent inclusion in the side. He has four Division I winners' medals which he achieved with three different clubs, as well as a B&Q Cup medal. Hearts fans would be delighted to see him add some top domestic honours during the veteran stage of his career.

Midfield

BORN: Irvine, 17 February 1958

HEIGHT: 5′ 10″   WEIGHT: 12st (1988)

COMPETITIVE DEBUT: v Motherwell, 21 September 1985 (PL) (A), 1–2 (scored)

CAREER: Fenwick Amateurs; Irvine Victoria Juniors, July 1975; Kilmarnock, Oct 1976; Partick Thistle, Sept 1979 (swap deal); Anorthosis (Cyprus), 1984; **Hearts, May 1985**; Partick Thistle, Dec 1989 (£25,000); Cumnock Juniors

HONOURS: 1 U-21 cap for Scotland; Premier League r-up 1985–86 (Hearts)

After Premier League experience, Iain sampled Cypriot football before joining Hearts on a free transfer. He scored on his debut at Fir Park after replacing Roddie MacDonald. For the reminder of season 1985–86 Jardine was the engine-room orchestrator in midfield. He had lightning pace, distributed passes accurately, tackled with complete determination and, best of all, could hit the ball with awesome power. He liked to push forward – as is illustrated by his seven well-executed League goals in his first season.

The remainder of his Hearts career was blighted by a series of niggling injuries which included ankle and knee-ligament damage and a fractured ankle. He endured a tough time and was the butt of some jokes – with one fanzine observing in jest that even a pre-match warm-up was not advisable! Iain was restricted predominantly to appearances from the subs bench. When Sandy Clark took over as Partick Thistle manager in 1989, he remembered Iain's early inspired displays for Hearts and a small fee was sufficient to take Jardine back to Firhill for a short spell.

Sweeper

BORN: Edinburgh, 31 December 1948

HEIGHT: 5′ 9″   WEIGHT: 10st 8lb (1985)

COMPETITIVE DEBUT: v Motherwell, 28 August 1982 (LC) (A), 1–2

CAREER: Tynecastle School; United Crossroads; Edinburgh Athletic; Rangers, 1963 (full-time from 1965); **Hearts player/assistant manager, July 1982; Hearts co-manager, 1986–88**

HONOURS: 38 full Scotland caps; 4 Scotland U-23 caps; 2 Scottish League caps; ECWC winner 1971–72 (Rangers); r-up 1966–67 (Rangers); Scottish League winner 1974–75, 1975–76, 1977–78 (Rangers); r-up 1985–86 (Hearts);

Scottish Cup winner 1972–73, 1975–76, 1977–78, 1978–79, 1980–81 (Rangers); r-up 1985–86 (Hearts); Scottish League Cup winner 1970–71, 1975–76, 1977–78, 1978–79, 1981–82 (Rangers); Scottish Football Writers' Association Player of the Year 1974–75 (Rangers); 1985–86 (Hearts)

Sandy occupied several positions in an illustrious career and was a truly world-class player when at his peak with Rangers and Scotland. A stylish, elegant defender with pace and unflappable confidence, his roll of honour speaks volumes for his achievements in football. He supported Hearts as a youngster and hoped to don the maroon jersey one day. He trained with the club as a youth but, while his favourites dallied, Rangers moved in and Sandy took the Ibrox trail where he won countless domestic honours to add to European and international success.

Sandy found his way to Tynecastle eventually in the twilight of his career. He moved to the sweeper role on a permanent basis and simply strolled through games as the mainstay and chief organiser in defence. He recorded his 1,000th first-class appearance as a Hearts player – fittingly in a match against Rangers in 1986. He served Hearts well for six seasons, retiring just short of his 39th birthday. Sandy then concentrated on his co-manager job in conjunction with Alex MacDonald. Poor League form early in 1988–89 saw him dismissed from his position, the reason put down to the dual role being counterproductive. He went on to work as an executive with Scottish & Newcastle Brewers.

JIM JEFFERIES

Defender

BORN: Musselburgh, 22 November 1950

HEIGHT: 6' **WEIGHT:** 12st 2lb (1980)

COMPETITIVE DEBUT: v East Fife, 4 March 1972 (Lge) (A), 2–2

CAREER: Musselburgh Grammar School; Gorgie Hearts; **Hearts, Oct 1967** (amateur form); Haddington Athletic; Gala Fairydean; **Hearts, 1969** (full-time); Berwick Rangers, Nov 1981 (free transfer); Gala Fairydean manager, 1983; Berwick Rangers manager, Dec 1988; Falkirk manager, 1990; **Hearts manager July 1995**

HONOURS: Division I winner 1979–80 (Hearts); r-up 1977–78 (Hearts); Scottish Cup r-up 1975–76; Scottish Cup Second XI winner 1972–73 (Hearts)

Played Schools football before joining the famed Gorgie Hearts who supplied several players to the senior ranks. Jim broke his leg aged 16 and missed out on an SFA U-17 Juvenile cap. He made a quick recovery and signed amateur forms for Hearts in 1967. After being farmed out for two years, Jefferies was called up to Tynecastle at the start of season 1969–70 under the watchful eye of youth coach Jock Wallace. After coming through the ranks Jim broke into the first team in 1972 and demonstrated his potential by holding a place until the end of season 1971–72. Over the next ten years Jim was to be a permanent member of the first-team squad. A rugged, versatile defender, 'Jeff' always looked to inspire those around him, encouraging and shouting instructions at all times. His high points included reaching the 1976 Cup final which saw Hearts gain entry to the European stage and a glory night against Leipzig. The low points would include being a member of three relegated squads in 1977, 1979 and 1981. Jefferies later gained a glowing reputation as a manager with Berwick and Falkirk, both clubs adopting an entertaining, attacking brand of play.

RAOLD JENSEN
Winger

BORN: Eidsvagnesit, Norway, 11 January 1943

DIED: Bergen, 10 October 1987

HEIGHT: 5′ 7″   WEIGHT: 9st 12lb (1969)

COMPETITIVE DEBUT: v Dunfermline, 2 January 1965 (Lge) (A), 2–3

CAREER: SK Brann, April 1953; **Hearts, Dec 1964**; SK Brann, May 1971 (free transfer); retired in May 1973; made a career in banking after his playing days

HONOURS: 31 full Norway caps; Scottish Cup finalist 1967–68 (Hearts); Norwegian Junior Championship 1958–59; Norwegian League Championship 1962–63; Norwegian Cup winner 1972–73 (SK Brann)

Small, dynamic winger who had been a major star in his native Norway as a teenager. Tommy Walker remembered Raold's dazzling displays in friendly matches against Hearts in the early 1960s and moved to secure his services in December 1964 in order to bolster Hearts' Championship challenge. Jensen adjusted quickly to Scottish football and turned in many five-star shows on the right wing as Hearts came so close to the title.

Injury and inconsistency kept Jensen out of the first-team picture in his next two seasons. He returned to form in 1967–68, scoring the goal which took Hearts to the Scottish Cup final. But he failed to produce his best on the Hampden stage, with Dunfermline winning 3–1.

Raold scored seven goals in 22 matches in 1968–69 producing arguably his best performances for Hearts. However, his next two seasons saw a return to indifferent form and ultimately led to a free transfer from new boss Bobby Seith in May 1971. Jensen returned to SK Brann where he ended his playing career in 1973. His sudden death from a heart attack at the young age of 44 was a shock to all fans who marvelled at his touchline trickery. In his will, Raold stated: 'Take care of the youngest, give them the opportunities and teach them to love this sport.' A poignant last testimony to his great love – football.

ALLAN JOHNSTON

Forward

BORN: Glasgow, 14 December 1973

HEIGHT: 5' 9"   WEIGHT: 10st 11lb (1993)

COMPETITIVE DEBUT: v Airdrie, 8 May 1993 (PL) (H), 1–1 (scored)

CAREER: Tynecastle Boys Club; **Hearts, June 1990**

HONOURS: Premier Reserve League winner 1992–93 (Hearts)

Allan was only 19 when he made his League debut and he marked the occasion with a fine goal. He started 1993–94 by appearing mostly as a substitute and came from the bench to sink Hibs in August 1993 with a superb goal. He took a Gary Locke cross, composed himself and sent a raging drive into the roof of the net. Colleagues and fans quickly dubbed him 'Magic' Johnston after the famous American basketball star. The accolade was given in recognition of Allan's 'tanner-ba' skills. His footwork can be dazzling. He is a master of the nutmeg and his body swerves are something else. A joy to watch in full flow, Allan has one or two flaws in his game, as one would expect for a youngster. Given more experience and the chance to further improve his strength and physique, Allan will be one to watch out for in years to come.

DAVID JOHNSTON

Forward

BORN: Nairn, 28 November 1942

HEIGHT: 5' 8"   WEIGHT: 11st (1960)

COMPETITIVE DEBUT: v Kilmarnock, 12 November 1960 (Lge) (A), 1–2

CAREER: Nairn County; **Hearts, Oct 1960**; Nairn County, 1961; Aberdeen, 1966–67

Flying winger from the Highlands who made a quick debut. Despite his inexperience David looked a good prospect and scored a couple of goals in his short stay. After only one season Johnston returned to Nairn due to domestic circumstances. He later played for Aberdeen, having developed into a fine player. He even scored a double for the Dons against Hearts in a League match in 1966–67.

DAVID JOHNSTON
Outside-left

BORN: Edinburgh

HEIGHT: 5′ 8″   WEIGHT: 10st 6lb (1977)

COMPETITIVE DEBUT: v Dundee, 20 August 1977 (Div. I) (H), 2–1

CAREER: George Watson's College; Tartan Boys Club; **Hearts, Aug 1977**; Watsonians Rugby Club

HONOURS: Scotland Schoolboy international; Scottish Rugby Union international during 1980s

A fair-haired flying winger, David made a few brief appearances for Hearts in August 1977 including one single League match. He demonstrated lots of potential but Rab Prentice was the established winger and he kept young Johnston waiting and hoping. Success with Hearts was not to be for David but colleagues and fans who remembered the lad were pleased to see him reach the top with another sport: he became a major national and international rugby union star.

MAURICE JOHNSTON
Forward

BORN: Glasgow, 13 April 1963

HEIGHT: 5′ 10″   WEIGHT: 11st 2lb (1993)

COMPETITIVE DEBUT: v Partick Thistle, 30 October 1993 (PL) (A), 0–0

CAREER: St Roch's School; Milton Battlefield; Partick Thistle, Aug 1980; Watford, Nov 1983 (£200,000); Celtic, Oct 1984 (£380,000); Nantes, July 1987 (£375,000); Rangers, July 1989 (£1,500,000); Everton, Nov 1991 (£1,500,000); **Hearts, Oct 1993** (free transfer); Falkirk, Mar 1995 (free transfer)

HONOURS: 38 full Scotland caps; 3 Scotland U-21 caps; Premier League winner 1985–86 (Celtic), 1989–90, 1990–91 (Rangers); Scottish Cup winner 1984–85 (Celtic); Scottish League Cup r-up 1986–87 (Celtic), 1989–90 (Rangers); English FA Cup r-up 1983–84 (Watford)

A goalscoring penalty-box predator, Mo's pace and finely-tuned reflexes allied to his positional awareness have seen him score goals at all his senior clubs. 'Controversy' could have been his middle name as it has followed him around on and off the field. He crossed the great Glasgow divide by becoming the first known Roman Catholic to sign and play for Rangers. But he continued to score goals and hit the headlines for a variety of reasons in a stormy Ibrox career.

A move to Everton eventually turned sour and amazingly he was granted a free transfer. Hearts moved quickly to obtain his services in the hope he could help end their goalscoring drought of 1993–94. Mo's goal tally for the remainder of the season was moderate, although his general form was good.

His contract expired at the end of season 1993–94 and after considerable speculation that he might move on, Sandy Clark offered him a new two-year deal worth a reported £3,000 per week. The new board and managerial regime who gained control of Hearts in June 1994 quickly identified Johnston as an expensive luxury they could do without. Mo was dropped from the first team in September 1994 and his relationship with Tommy McLean plummeted to rock bottom inside the last five months of his Tynecastle career. After slanging matches which involved Mo, his agent and the Hearts boss, Jim Jefferies negotiated his transfer to Falkirk. Colin Cramb headed in the opposite direction at the same time for a £50,000 fee. Hearts claimed it 'didn't cost them a penny' to dispense with Johnston. However, it was rumoured that the £50,000 paid for Cramb was used to satisfy Johnston's claim for some compensation on the remainder of his Hearts contract.

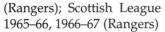

WILLIE JOHNSTON
Winger

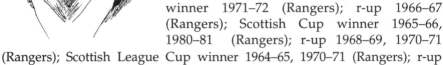

BORN: Glasgow, 19 December 1946

HEIGHT: 5' 7"   **WEIGHT:** 11st 4lb (1984)

COMPETITIVE DEBUT: v St Mirren, 22 September 1982 (LCqf) (H), 2–1

CAREER: Lochore Welfare; Rangers, 1962; West Brom, Dec 1972 (£135,000); Vancouver Whitecaps, Mar 1979 (£100,000); Birmingham City, Oct 1979–Mar 1980 (on loan); Rangers, Aug 1980 (£40,000); **Hearts, Sept 1982** (free transfer); East Fife, Apr 1985; retired in 1985

HONOURS: 22 full Scotland caps; 2 U-23 Scotland caps; 2 Scottish League caps; ECWC winner 1971–72 (Rangers); r-up 1966–67 (Rangers); Scottish Cup winner 1965–66, 1980–81 (Rangers); r-up 1968–69, 1970–71 (Rangers); Scottish League Cup winner 1964–65, 1970–71 (Rangers); r-up 1965–66, 1966–67 (Rangers)

Willie Johnston was a colourful, temperamental character who performed at Tynecastle as his career drew to a close. He had made his name with Rangers as a dashing winger with exceptional pace over 20 to 30 yards and his accuracy with cross balls was legendary. His downfall was a quick temper which landed him in trouble with referees on numerous occasions – he is known to have been sent off at least 19 times. His biggest misfortune was being sent home from the 1978 World Cup in Argentina for testing positive to a banned stimulant drug. It effectively ended his international career in controversial, shameful circumstances. However, despite these altercations, Willie was above all else an entertainer. Allied to his immense skill, he brought some humour to the game with funny antics and histrionics. He was a genuine personality. The fact that he managed to play at the top level well into his late 30s is proof that he was a footballer who ate, slept and generally lived in the correct way. It was for this reason that Alex McDonald brought 'Bud' Johnston to Hearts to impart his experience and good habits to the emerging young talents at the club and to help them avoid some of the traps he fell into.

ROY KAY

Full-back

BORN: Edinburgh, 24 October 1949

HEIGHT: 5' 10"   WEIGHT: 9st 3lb (1972)

COMPETITIVE DEBUT: v Stranraer, 23 January 1971 (SC) (H), 3–0

CAREER: Gracemount School; United Crossroads; **Hearts, 1967**; Celtic, May 1977 (free transfer); York City, July 1978 (free transfer); Northallerton, 1981; retired in 1982

HONOURS: Scotland Juvenile international; Scottish Cup finalist 1975–76 (Hearts)

A slim, skilful full-back who took several years to break into Hearts' first team, Roy received his chance when Peter Oliver sustained a bad injury. The 22-year-old Kay impressed immediately and retained his place for the remainder of the season. He proved to be a versatile defender for the next six seasons, appearing at right-back and in central-defence. Not a noted goal-scorer, Roy always talked of the day his goal won a friendly match against English giants Tottenham. Another strike worth noting was a fine 20-yard shot against Locomotiv Leipzig which gave Hearts a 1–0 lead.

Kay was one of the surprise free transfers in Hearts' 1977 relegation clear-out. Celtic moved quickly to sign the 27-year-old but the situation did not work out and he moved to York City, making 160 League appearances in four seasons before retiring in 1982.

ARCHIE KELLY

Centre-forward

BORN: Glasgow

HEIGHT: 5′ 9″   **WEIGHT:** 11st (1946)

COMPETITIVE DEBUT: v Clyde, 6 March 1943 (S.Lge) (A), 0–1

CAREER: Arthurlie Juniors; **Hearts, Dec 1942**; Aberdeen, Dec 1947 (swapped for George Hamilton, plus £8,000 to Aberdeen); Motherwell, Nov 1949 (£7,000); Stirling Albion, Oct 1953; Ayr United, Jan 1955

HONOURS: Scottish Cup winner 1951–52 (Motherwell); r-up 1950–51 (Motherwell); Scottish League Cup winner 1950–51 (Motherwell)

Fearless leader of the Hearts attack during the immediate post-war period, Archie had a tremendous scoring record using phenomenal pace and physical strength along with his shoot-on-sight policy. Perhaps his most remarkable feat came against Albion Rovers when he scored seven goals in a 10–3 away win in season 1944–45. His courageous enthusiasm had unfortunate repercussions in September 1946 when he dived to meet a cross and smashed into the goalpost. Such was the force of the impact he cracked the post and broke his collarbone. He returned a few months later and was soon scoring again. A lean spell in season 1947–48 which put Hearts in the relegation zone prompted changes. Dave McLean splashed out in the transfer market and Kelly was on his way to Aberdeen in a swap deal. He didn't settle in the Granite City and moved to Motherwell where he scored goals in their successful League Cup and Scottish Cup wins.

BOBBY KEMP

Forward

BORN: Falkirk, 15 August 1941

HEIGHT: 5′ 9″   **WEIGHT:** 11st 6lb (1967)

COMPETITIVE DEBUT: v Dundee United, 10 December 1966 (Lge) (H), 2–1

CAREER: Falkirk; Carlisle United, Nov 1960; Montrose; St Johnstone, Dec 1961; **Hearts, Dec 1966**; emigrated to South Africa in 1968

HONOURS: Division II winner 1962–63 (St Johnstone)

Fast, raiding winger with a range of tricks to upset most full-backs when on form, Bobby could create chances and finish them too. His 36 League goals in 132 games for St Johnstone was enough to convince Hearts he could replace Willie Wallace – no mean feat for anyone to attempt! But Kemp was unable to fill the void left by Wispy's departure. Injuries and inconsistent form didn't help. Bobby still managed a reasonable return of goals before leaving Hearts to sample South African football in 1968. Sadly his new career was cut short with a broken leg. He returned to Scotland where he found himself ordered by his doctor to retire.

DON KERRIGAN

Forward

BORN: Seamill, 7 May 1942

DIED: December 1990

HEIGHT: 5' 7"   WEIGHT: 10st 6lb (1966)

COMPETITIVE DEBUT: v Valerengen, Norway, 18 October 1965 (ICFC) (H), 1–0

CAREER: St Mirren; Aberdeen; **Hearts, June 1965** (swap for Tommy White); Dunfermline, March 1967 (swap for Jim Fleming); Fulham, Dec 1968; Lincoln City, March 1969

HONOURS: Scottish Cup r-up 1961–62 (St Mirren)

A small striker whose Hearts career was blighted by injury, Don was stockily built but quick and linked well with Willie Wallace. He made his club debut against SK Brann on a Norwegian tour friendly match – and was sent off! He scored in his next game against Valerengen but sustained a serious injury late in the game – not the best of starts by any measure! He didn't play again until October and, coincidentally, made his competitive debut against Valerengen in a Fairs Cup tie. He scored his first League goal a week later in a 5–2 win against Motherwell. Don scored one of the goals which prompted the song '1-2-3, Wallace, Kerrigan, McNamee (o.g.)' rendered to the tune of a popular pop song, which referred to a battling 2–3 win at Easter Road on Ne'er Day 1966.

Further injury problems plagued Kerrigan in 1966–67 and in March he found himself involved in another swap deal. Hearts fans were saddened to learn of his tragic death, the result of an accident on a building site, when he was only 48 years old.

WALTER KIDD

Right-back

BORN: Edinburgh, 10 March 1958

HEIGHT: 5' 10"   **WEIGHT:** 12st 3lb (1989)

COMPETITIVE DEBUT: v Montrose, 19 October 1977 (Div. I) (A), 1–3 (came on as substitute)

CAREER: Holyrood School; Links Boys Club; Newtongrange Star; **Hearts, June 1977**; Airdrie, July 1991 (free transfer); **Hearts Reserve XI coach, July 1993**

HONOURS: Premier League r-up 1985–86, 1989–90 (Hearts); Division I winner 1979–80 (Hearts); r-up 1977–78, 1982–83 (Hearts); Scottish Cup r-up 1985–86 (Hearts); Tennents Sixes winner 1984–85 (Hearts); awarded a testimonial match (against Everton) in October 1987

Walter Kidd was a dedicated professional who experienced all the highs and lows under five different managers in his 14 seasons at Tynecastle. Walter received an extended run during his first season after an injury to the established right-back, Jim Brown. Wattie was a determined character, tough in the tackle, a good passer of the ball and probably one of the best man-markers of his time – the late Davie Cooper would have testified to that. The talented Ranger received 'little change' from Wattie in their many encounters. Kidd's hairstyles changed frequently: he was a member of the 'perm crew' until a crop cut brought the brief nickname 'Bald Eagle'. His gutsy midfield displays in the early 1980s saw the fans dub him 'Zico' after the great Brazilian. The latter nickname was partly in jest but it's stuck ever since.

A model of consistency throughout the 1980s, Walter captained Hearts during season 1985–86 as they just missed out on the Premier League and Scottish Cup double. The Cup final was a major disappointment, with Hearts crashing 3–0 and Wattie sent off for a silly incident in which he threw the ball at an opponent. He appeared less often in his last four seasons as the emerging Alan McLaren began to challenge for the right-back slot. He later joined ex-boss Alex MacDonald at Airdrie for two seasons before accepting an offer from Sandy Clark to return to look after Hearts' Reserve XI.

BORN: Bannockburn, 5 December 1931

HEIGHT: 5′ 10″   WEIGHT: 11st 2lb (1952)

COMPETITIVE DEBUT: v Aberdeen, 15 November 1952 (Lge) (A), 0–3

CAREER: Alva Albion; **Hearts, Oct 1952** (£80); Northampton Town, May 1953 (free transfer)

JOHN KILGANNON
Outside-right

John was signed as a part-timer, also working as a commercial traveller with a firm of preserve manufacturers. He made a quick first-team debut, which turned out to be his only appearance. He played regularly in the reserve team and scored several goals, being described as 'a fast and clever ball-player on the right wing' in the Hearts programme. John was on the books only eight months before moving south. English records show he did not play in Northampton's first team and his subsequent moves are not known.

BORN: Kilmarnock, 20 February 1932

HEIGHT: 5′ 8″   WEIGHT: 10st (1953)

COMPETITIVE DEBUT: v Hamilton Accies, 22 August 1953 (LC) (A), 1–1

CAREER: Grange School; Bonnyton Youth Club; Muirkirk Athletic; **Hearts, Oct 1951**; Queen of the South, *c*.1955

WALLACE KING
Half-back

An apprentice bricklayer who worked in the Barony pit in Ayrshire, King was a good all-round player, a neat passer of the ball and a strong tackler. He came in for three League Cup ties at the start of 1953–54, deputising for the injured Davie Laing. He demonstrated good potential but was dropped once Laing was fit again. A painful groin injury interrupted his progress in the reserves and the emergence of another youngster, Dave Mackay, resulted in Wallace moving on in 1955.

HARRY KINNEAR

Forward

BORN: Buckhaven, 5 March 1949

HEIGHT: 6′ 3″   **WEIGHT:** 12st 7lb (1972)

COMPETITIVE DEBUT: v St Johnstone, 5 February 1972 (SC) (H), 2–0

CAREER: Forfar Athletic; **Hearts, Aug 1971** (free transfer); East Fife, Feb 1974 (£5,000); Falkirk (swap deal); Leven Juniors; Wemyss Hearts

A giant, curly-haired striker with an all-action, bustling style, Harry could be cumbersome on the ground but made the most of his height in the air. His chance came in the 1972 Scottish Cup competition when he deputised for Donald Ford, who had been injured in a car crash. The big man did well and kept his place briefly, even partnering Ford on his return. Harry found it difficult to lose his deputy status, though many supporters thought he was worth an extended run to really prove his worth. Others were less than complimentary, however. The arrival of Drew Busby created further competition and Harry was transferred in February 1974. Two months later he returned to Tynecastle with East Fife and hit two goals to earn the Bayview side a draw – and help him prove a point or two!

BOBBY KIRK

Full-back

BORN: Arniston, 12 August 1927

HEIGHT: 5′ 7″   **WEIGHT:** 11st (1959)

COMPETITIVE DEBUT: v Partick Thistle, 13 August 1955 (LC) (A), 2–0

CAREER: Gorebridge School; Newtongrange Hearts Juveniles; Arniston Thistle; Edinburgh Thistle, 1945; Arniston Rangers, 1946; Dunfermline, 1947; Raith Rovers, July 1953 (£750); **Hearts, May 1955** (£2,500); Gala Fairydean player/manager, Apr 1963.

Coaching career: **Hearts Colts, 1967**; Arniston, 1971; Dalkeith, 1973; Penicuik, 1974; Musselburgh, 1975; Linlithgow Rose physio; Craigroyston physio

HONOURS: Scotland Junior international; Scottish League winner 1957–58, 1959–60 (Hearts); Scottish Cup winner 1955–56 (Hearts); Scottish League Cup winner 1958–59, 1959–60 (Hearts); r-up 1949–50 (Dunfermline)

A sturdy, enthusiastic competitor, Bobby excelled in both full-back positions and could provide additional cover as a centre-half. He was a skilled penalty-taker, a job he obtained when regular taker Bobby Parker was out injured. In a match against Hibs in August 1956, Bobby had successfully converted two penalties when Hearts were awarded a third. His effort struck the post to deny him the honour of becoming the first Heart to achieve the feat, but he did manage to score 12 goals in his Hearts career, all from the penalty spot. He was a model of consistency over seven seasons, winning all the domestic honours and enjoying three foreign tours in addition to European games. Bobby read about his free transfer in the paper in April 1963 and was upset at the way he learned of his release. He was a stalwart servant of junior football for many years, and now assists Craigroyston in the east senior leagues.

DAVID KIRKWOOD
Midfield

BORN: St Andrews, 27 August 1967

HEIGHT: 5' 10"   WEIGHT: 11st 7lb (1990)

COMPETITIVE DEBUT: v Celtic, 12 August 1989 (PL) (H), 1–3

CAREER: Leven Royals; East Fife, 1983; Rangers, Mar 1987 (£30,000); **Hearts, July 1989** (£100,000); Airdrie, Dec 1990 (£100,000); Raith Rovers, Aug 1994 (£75,000)

HONOURS: Scotland Schoolboy international; Premier League r-up 1989–90 (Hearts); Division I winner 1994–95 (Raith Rovers)

Dave joined Hearts after failing to establish himself at Ibrox. Following his Tynecastle debut he had an extended run in the team despite some indifferent form. He was eventually dropped but often found a place on the subs bench from where he was tried in several positions. Joe Jordan's arrival presented Kirkwood with a chance to find favour with a new regime. Dave was given his chance and enjoyed a brief spell in the team. He was clearly surplus to requirements, though, given Jordan's decision to sell him to Airdrie.

Kirkwood never really settled at Tynecastle and the fans never took to his style of play. He packed a fair shot which we never saw enough of and could hit precision passes to all areas of the pitch. He made the odd costly mistake which infuriated the fans. He became a regular with Airdrie after his transfer, before quitting Broomfield over a contract dispute in May 1994.

BRIAN LAING

Midfield

HEIGHT: 5′ 9″   **WEIGHT:** 10st 9lb (1971)

COMPETITIVE DEBUT: v Cowdenbeath, 24 April 1971 (Lge) (H), 4–0

CAREER: Liverpool, 1960s; **Hearts, 1970** (free transfer); Queen of the South, Sept 1971 (free transfer)

HONOURS: Scotland Schoolboy international

Brian rubbed shoulders with young players destined to become major stars at Liverpool. But after a double fracture in his arm which needed two operations, Brian quit England feeling homesick. He joined Hearts but his luck didn't change much. He was either out injured or stuck in the reserves throughout 1970–71 until making his League debut in the last fixture of the season. He played in Hearts' next match, the Texaco Cup final second leg at Molineux, and appeared in a friendly against Queen of the South at the start of season 1971–72. A ligament injury in that match sidelined Laing for two months. When he recovered he was offered the chance of a full-time contract with Queen of the South and took a free transfer from Tynecastle.

DAVID LAING

Wing-half

BORN: Strathmiglo, 20 February 1925

COMPETITIVE DEBUT: v Morton, 16 November 1946 (Lge) (A), 1–0

CAREER: Wemyss School; Bayview Youth Club; **Hearts, 1942**; Clyde, Sept 1954 (£5,000); Hibs, 1956; Gillingham, Aug 1957; Canterbury, 1958; **Hearts programme editor, 1969–75**

HONOURS: 2 Scottish League caps; Scottish Cup winner 1954–55 (Clyde)

Davie guested with Bath City while serving as a telegraphist in the navy during the Second World War. He had a tendency to apply the boot in his early days with Hearts, and many supporters felt that wing-half was not his best position. He was a brave player who was able to shake off injuries thanks to his psychological approach. A tough competitor, hard in the tackle and positive in his attitude, Laing was consistent and confident, never hesitating to display his nerve when nominated to take penalty kicks.

Davie was left out when Dave Mackay and John Cumming struck up their half-back partnership. He made one more important contribution before moving on, scoring a goal in the 1954 League Cup sectional match against Celtic which proved crucial. He won a Scottish Cup medal with Clyde in his first season with them. After retiring from football, Davie spent several years as editor of the Hearts programme and then went on to work as a sports editor with a local paper in Dover.

SCOTT LEITCH

Midfield

BORN: Motherwell, 6 October 1969

HEIGHT: 5′ 9″   WEIGHT: 11st 4lb (1993)

COMPETITIVE DEBUT: v Dundee United, 28 August 1993 (PL) (A), 0—0 (came on as substitute)

CAREER: Motherwell, 1986; Shettleston Juniors; Dunfermline, Apr 1990; **Hearts, Aug 1993** (swap for Allan Preston)

Scott was rejected by Motherwell as a teenager and turned junior on his release, but he was spotted by Dunfermline and soon broke into their first team. He stood out in the Pars' matches against Hearts and scored in a 3–1 win in February 1991. Hearts manager Sandy Clark had played with Dunfermline from January to April 1990 and remembered the positive attitude and commitment shown by young Leitch. An approach was made for his signature and an exchange deal was quickly concluded. Scott was thrilled to join Hearts but injuries meant he had to wait for his debut. Before long, he had quietly but effectively played his way into the side. Leitch has good close-control skills and is always looking to make vital linking passes to the forwards. He is strong in the tackle and is willing to shoot when a chance presents itself – in fact, he scored several goals in 1993–94 including the only goal in a win at Pittodrie at a time when Hearts were toiling in the relegation zone. Scott still has youth on his side and here's hoping he can continue to produce the fine form he enjoyed in 1993–94.

CRAIG LEVEIN

Centre-half

BORN: Dunfermline, 22 October 1964

HEIGHT: 6'   **WEIGHT:** 11st 4lb (1990)

COMPETITIVE DEBUT: v Rangers, 3 December 1983 (PL) (A), 0–3

CAREER: Inverkeithing Juveniles; Leven Royals; Lochore Welfare; Cowdenbeath, 1981; **Hearts, Nov 1983** (£30,000)

HONOURS: 16 full Scotland caps; Scotland U-21 international; Premier League r-up 1985–86, 1987–88, 1989–90, 1991–92 (Hearts); Scottish Cup r-up 1985–86 (Hearts); SPFA Young Player of the Year 1984 and 1985

Craig Levein's impressive display in a Cup tie for Cowdenbeath against Hearts in 1983 led to an investment of £30,000 a few months later to take the classy defender to Tynecastle. Craig initially starred in the midfield but was later groomed to replace Sandy Jardine. After winning the SPFA Young Player award twice and coming close to domestic and full international honours, Levein suffered a quite terrible injury – serious ligament damage – which required a pioneering operation before he could return to action one year later. He managed 21 games before the injury recurred and sceptics said he was finished with football. He proved them wrong with a second comeback, in January 1989. He was soon back to his best and played well for Scotland in the 1990 World Cup finals in Italy.

Craig is a star performer with good heading ability and passing skills who can read the game well. His electric pace makes him an ideal sweeper but he can also fill a man-marking role. He has captained Hearts on many occasions, inspiring those around him. Many clubs have made transfer enquiries over the years but Craig has stood by Hearts, remembering how the club did likewise in the dark days of his injury problems. He is also a Hearts shareholder.

An unfortunate punch-up with teammate Graeme Hogg in a pre-season friendly at Kirkcaldy in August 1994 had severe repercussions for Craig. Hearts hit him with the maximum fine possible and stripped him of the club captaincy, only to overturn this punishment when the SFA dished out a huge ten-game ban. Craig is now looking to put this affair behind him, and is looking forward to his testimonial match during season 1995–96.

BORN: Glasgow, 10 June 1925

HEIGHT: 5' 10"   WEIGHT: 11st 8lb (1950)

COMPETITIVE DEBUT: v Stirling Albion, 13 August 1949 (LC) (H), 5–1

CAREER: Albert Secondary School (Glasgow); Queens Park; Morton, 1947; **Hearts, Jun 1949** (£10,000); Rangers, Nov 1951 (swap for Eddie Rutherford); Morton, 1955

HONOURS: Scottish Cup r-up 1947–48 (Morton)

COLIN LIDDELL
Outside-left

A tall, strong-running winger, Colin found difficulty in reproducing the form which had prompted Hearts to pay such a large sum for his services. Dave McLean kept faith with the player initially but eventually had no option but to drop him. Colin had struggled to supply the inside-forwards with the balls they needed. He was given another chance at the start of the season 1950–51 but again failed to impress. Throughout the remainder of that season and up until his transfer, Liddell made only three more League appearances. Hearts decided to cut their losses and arranged a swap deal with Rangers.

BORN: Stirling, 10 July 1953

HEIGHT: 5' 10"   WEIGHT: 12st 7lb (1979)

COMPETITIVE DEBUT: v Aberdeen, 12 August 1978 (PL) (H), 1–4

CAREER: Dunipace Juniors; Alloa Athletic, 1975; **Hearts, May 1978** (£15,000); Australian football, 1982; Dunfermline, 1985; Stenhousemuir, 1985; St Johnstone, Aug 1985; Brisbane Lions, May 1986

HONOURS: Division I winner 1979–80 (Hearts)

FRANK LIDDELL
Centre-half

Tough and uncompromising centre-half, hard in the tackle and dominant in the air, Frank was signed to bolster the defence in preparation for the 1978–79 Premier League campaign. Despite his endeavours, Hearts returned to Division I. He made a major contribution to the 1979–80 Championship success, heading the goal which secured promotion against Berwick and repeating the act with another header against Airdrie to clinch the League title. Frank was mobbed by jubilant supporters who invaded the field at the final whistle.

As before, Hearts struggled in the Premier League and went down again.

Frank appeared briefly at the start of season 1981–82 before falling out of favour. He was granted a free transfer in February 1982 and went down under to try his luck in Australian football. Returning to Scotland in 1985 gave him brief spells at Dunfermline and Stenhousemuir. He signed for St Johnstone in August that year but was never a fans' favourite at Muirton Park, making only 28 competitive appearances before returning to Australia.

GARY LIDDELL

Forward

BORN: Stirling, 27 August 1954

HEIGHT: 5′ 10″   **WEIGHT:** 11st 5lb (1981)

COMPETITIVE DEBUT: v St Mirren, 21 February 1981 (PL) (A), 1–2

CAREER: Leeds United, Sept 1971; Grimsby Town, Mar 1977; **Hearts, Feb 1981** (free transfer); Doncaster Rovers, Apr 1982

Gary trained at Tynecastle as a schoolboy and played several trials for top English sides before signing for Don Revie at Leeds. He later assisted Grimsby Town to win promotion through the English divisions. Hearts negotiated his transfer for a small signing-on fee and the experienced striker provided cover for long-term injury men Chris Robertson and Derek O'Connor. But Gary offered little in the way of goals and was no improvement compared to forwards already on the payroll. He lasted just over a year before returning south.

BILLY LINDORES

Full-back

BORN: Newcastleton, 3 May 1933

HEIGHT: 5′ 8″   **WEIGHT:** 10st 10lb (1956)

COMPETITIVE DEBUT: v Partick Thistle, 3 November 1956 (Lge) (H), 1–0

CAREER: Knox Academy; Edinburgh Thistle; Dunbar United; **Hearts, June 1956**; Barrow, July 1959 (free transfer); Gala Fairydean

HONOURS: Scotland Schoolboy international

A regular at left-back in the reserves, Billy came into the first-team plans in the winter of 1956. He was hard but fair in the tackle and could anticipate the play well. He made 11 appearances in total, finding Kirk, Parker, McKenzie and Thomson all competing for full-back places. He tried his luck in England before returning to Scotland with Gala Fairydean in 1960.

BORN: Edinburgh, 16 June 1975

HEIGHT: 5' 10"   WEIGHT: 10st (1993)

COMPETITIVE DEBUT: v St Johnstone, 15 May 1993 (PL) (A), 1–3 (came on as substitute)

CAREER: Lasswade High School; Hutcheson Vale Boys Club; **Hearts, Sept 1990**

HONOURS: Scotland U-21 international; Premier Reserve League winner 1992–93 (Hearts); BP Youth Cup winner 1992–93 (Hearts)

GARY LOCKE
Midfield

A true Jambo, Locke was only ever going to sign for one club as a schoolboy, and he quickly earned the nickname 'Son of Mackay' due to the fanaticism Gary has for his boyhood favourites. He made rapid progress in Sandy Clark's reserve and youth sides, winning honours in both teams. Clark's promotion to manager resulted in a deserved first-team chance for the Bonnyrigg young- ster who displays soccer maturity beyond his years. A tenacious tackler, excel- lent passer of the ball and accurate crosser, Gary has an incredible ability to strike a dead ball with stunning power and immaculate precision. If this youngster keeps his feet on the ground and works hard and lives right, he will undoubtedly develop into a world-class player.

HEIGHT: 5' 7"   WEIGHT: 10st 6lb (1960)

COMPETITIVE DEBUT: v Raith Rovers, 21 February 1959 (Lge) (H), 2–1

CAREER: Preston Athletic; **Hearts, Apr 1955**; freed *c*.1961

JOHN LOUGH
Full-back

John did well in his early reserve games before heading off for his National Service. Rave reports found their way to Tynecastle from his military base. Following Dave Mackay's trans- fer, George Thomson moved to right-half and Lough was given a run at left-back until the end of season 1958–59. He returned to the reserves the following season but was selected to tour in Canada in 1960. He made a few more appear- ances in 1960–61 but the arrival of David Holt, Willie Polland and the emergence of young Chris Shevlane closed the first- team door to Lough.

ANDY LYNCH

Outside-left

BORN: Glasgow, 24 October 1949

HEIGHT: 5' 10"   **WEIGHT:** 10st 12lb (1970)

COMPETITIVE DEBUT: v Motherwell, 11 November 1969 (Lge) (H), 2–2 (scored)

CAREER: Glasgow Schools; Renfrew Juniors; Queens Park; Kirkintilloch Rob Roy; **Hearts, Aug 1969**; Celtic, Feb 1973 (£30,000); Philadelphia Furies (USA), 1980 (free transfer); Canadian national team assistant manager, 1980s; Albion Rovers assistant manager 1993–94

HONOURS: Scottish League winner 1973–74, 1976–77, 1978–79 (Celtic); Scottish Cup winner 1974–75, 1976–77 (Celtic); Scottish League Cup r-up 1975–76, 1976–77, 1977–78 (Celtic)

Strong-running natural left-winger with a powerful shot, Lynch was quickly elevated to the top team. During his four seasons he scored many important goals in addition to providing his colleagues with many goalscoring opportunities from accurate crosses. Lynch became unsettled during 1972–73 and made his last appearance on a disastrous first day of 1973 as a substitute for Eric Carruthers. Celtic had kept tabs on the talented winger for quite some time and Jock Stein moved to land his man. Andy made little impact as a winger at Parkhead but was successfully converted to a left-back. From this position he collected several honours and his penalty goal decided the 1977 Scottish Cup final. He now runs a guest house in Glasgow.

COLIN McADAM

Forward

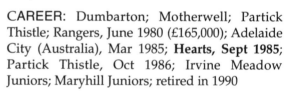

BORN: Glasgow, 28 August 1951

HEIGHT: 6' 1"   **WEIGHT:** 13st (1986)

COMPETITIVE DEBUT: v Motherwell, 4 January 1986 (PL) (A), 3–1 (came on as substitute)

CAREER: Dumbarton; Motherwell; Partick Thistle; Rangers, June 1980 (£165,000); Adelaide City (Australia), Mar 1985; **Hearts, Sept 1985**; Partick Thistle, Oct 1986; Irvine Meadow Juniors; Maryhill Juniors; retired in 1990

HONOURS: Scottish Cup r-up 1980–81 (Rangers); Scottish League Cup winner 1983–84 (Rangers)

A tall, strapping individual, Colin worked aggressively as a capable centre-half or centre-forward. His aerial presence caused panic in many defences. He had served several Scottish clubs, most notably Rangers, and was signed by Hearts to provide cover. Every appearance he made was as a substitute. His single goal was a dramatic equaliser against his old club Rangers in a Scottish Cup third-round tie in January 1986. Colin had come on to replace the injured Sandy Clark and his goal helped Hearts to a 3–2 win. His purpose served, 35-year-old McAdam was released in October 1986. He now teaches PE in a Glasgow list D school.

WILLIE McALPINE
Defender

BORN: Edinburgh, 14 October 1950

HEIGHT: 5′ 8″   WEIGHT: 11st 7lb (1969)

COMPETITIVE DEBUT: v St Johnstone, 23 November 1968 (Lge) (H), 2–2

CAREER: Carrickvale Secondary School; Sighthill Thistle; Gorgie Hearts; **Hearts, 1967**; Arniston Rangers, c.1972

HONOURS: Scotland Youth international

Willie made his debut as a replacement for Arthur Mann after his transfer to Manchester City. Mann was a hard act to follow but Willie initially rose to the challenge, showing authority in the tackle and an assured composure. His inexperience was evident, though, and veteran Davie Holt was soon recalled. The emergence of Peter Oliver in 1969 put Willie further down the selection order. He started off season 1969–70 in the side but a bad injury put him out for 14 months. He only made one more appearance the following season in a Texaco Cup match before going junior after his free transfer.

ATHOLL McARA

Right-back

BORN: Glasgow, 13 July 1921

DIED: Glasgow, January 1981

HEIGHT: 5' 10"   WEIGHT: 11st (1946)

COMPETITIVE DEBUT: v Clyde, 28 April 1942 (S. Lge) (A), 0–2

CAREER: Greenfield School; Glasgow Post Office FC; Benburb Juniors; **Hearts, May 1942**; Celtic, May 1947; Raith Rovers, c.June 1947; Portadown (Northern Ireland)

Atholl's debut match was on a trial basis and he was offered signing terms a few days later. He was a sturdy, reliable defender and appeared in 23 competitive games for Hearts during the war as well as guesting for Crystal Palace. He served in the RAF during the war and did his training in Texas, USA. He made two competitive post-war appearances at the start of season 1946–47, and is known to have played at least once for Celtic, in a testimonial game in May 1947 shortly after his release from Tynecastle.

DUNCAN McCLURE

Full-back

BORN: Troon, 10 June 1913

DIED: Grangemouth, May 1991

HEIGHT: 5' 9"   WEIGHT: 11st (1937)

COMPETITIVE DEBUT: v Celtic, 2 September 1934 (Lge) (A), 0–0

CAREER: Parkhead Juniors; **Hearts, May 1933**; retired, May 1948; **Hearts coach and scout until May 1956**

HONOURS: 1 wartime cap for Scotland

Duncan made his name as a top-class full-back before the Second World War. When hostilities ceased he turned out for Hearts in season 1946–47 at the veteran stage. He was gradually eased out the next season to allow younger men their chance. He continued to assist Hearts by turning out for the reserves when required and even acted as a linesman in one game against Aberdeen in November 1947. He also spent some years as a club scout.

BORN: Glasgow, 24 December 1960

HEIGHT: 5′ 9″   WEIGHT: 10st 3lb (1981)

COMPETITIVE DEBUT: v Aberdeen, 19 August 1981 (LC) (A), 0–3

CAREER: Queens Park, 1978; **Hearts, July 1981**; Falkirk, Mar 1984 (free transfer); Dumbarton, 1985; Partick Thistle, July 1988; Falkirk, Oct 1989 (£30,000); Clyde, Dec 1990; Glenafton Juniors, 1992

HONOURS: Scotland Schoolboy international; Division II winner 1980–81 (Queens Park)

Bustling striker who chased and harried opposition defenders to good effect. Gerry possessed a powerful shot which helped him to a goal tally of 13 in his first season. He performed reasonably well in his first year but encountered disciplinary problems through several bookings and orderings-off. The departure of team boss Tony Ford (who had signed Gerry), signalled a virtual end to his Tynecastle career. He appeared rarely in the next two seasons and eventually moved on in March 1984. He served many senior sides thereafter where he earned a reputation as a consistent goalscorer.

BORN: Stoneyburn, 2 January 1920

HEIGHT: 5′ 10″   WEIGHT: 11st 7lb (1945)

COMPETITIVE DEBUT: v Queens Park, 7 June 1941 (Summer Cup) (H), 8–1

CAREER: Stoneyburn; West Calder Juveniles; Murrayfield Rangers; Haddington Athletic; **Hearts, June 1941**; Charlton Athletic, June 1947 (£9,000); Middlesbrough, Oct 1948 (£10,000); Falkirk, Mar 1953 (£4,500); Stirling Albion manager, Jan 1960; Falkirk manager

An elegant inside-forward who could also mix it with a hard-hitting approach, Alex was endowed with a predatory instinct in the penalty box and was always capable of putting away any chances. The slim striker made his name during the war and continued to score during season 1946–47. Alex then moved to Charlton where he hit eight goals in 43 League games. Another move, this time to Middlesbrough, proved more fruitful, with Alex netting 47 goals in 122 games. He returned to Scotland in 1953, signing for Falkirk. He lost out on a fairytale end to his career in 1957 when injury ruled him out of the 1957 Scottish Cup final. It was cruel luck to miss a possible first domestic honour at the age of 37. He worked in Bathgate with British Leyland until 1985.

DAVID McCREERY
Midfield

BORN: Belfast, 16 September 1957

HEIGHT: 5' 7"   **WEIGHT:** 11st 7lb (1990)

COMPETITIVE DEBUT: v Dundee, 9 September 1989 (PL) (A), 2–2 (came on as substitute)

CAREER: Ashfield Boys Club; Manchester United, Oct 1974; Queens Park Rangers, Aug 1979 (£200,000); Tulsa Roughnecks, March 1981 (£125,000); Newcastle United, Oct 1982 (£75,000); Sundsvall (Sweden), Apr 1989 (free transfer); **Hearts, Sept 1989** (free transfer); Hartlepool, Aug 1991 (free transfer); Carlisle United manager, Sept 1992; Hartlepool United manager until Apr 1995

HONOURS: Northern Ireland full and U-21 international; English FA Cup winner 1976–77 (Manchester United); r-up 1975–76 (Manchester United)

A destructive player in the best sense of the word, Dave could break down opposition moves then initiate attacks for his own team. McCreery starred in the English top flight for 15 years before joining Hearts at the veteran stage. He was instantly recognisable through always wearing cycling shorts under his Hearts kit, a popular fashion at the time. A terrier-like midfielder with a never-say-die attitude, his busy approach was suited to Hearts style of play and he settled quickly. An injury early on in season 1990–91 put him out of action and he did not recover sufficiently to regain his place, managing only a few games before moving to Hartlepool.

BORN: Edinburgh, 2 February 1950

HEIGHT: 5′ 11″   WEIGHT: 12st (1985)

COMPETITIVE DEBUT: v St Patrick's Athletic, 7 September 1988 (UEFA) (A), 2–0 (came on as substitute)

CAREER: Penicuik Athletic; Raith Rovers, 1969; Berwick Rangers, 1981; Arbroath; Morton; **Hearts, Sept 1985**; Berwick Rangers, Oct 1986; Meadowbank, 1987; **Hearts, Aug 1988**; Meadowbank coach

MURRAY McDERMOTT

Goalkeeper

Murray was signed by Hearts twice in the twilight of his career to provide cover for the established goalkeepers on the books. His only major competitive appearance came in Dublin against St Patrick's in the first round of the UEFA Cup. An injury to Henry Smith saw McDermott take the field and he recorded a clean sheet, keeping the Irish side at bay. Remarkably, at the age of 38, Murray had achieved his European debut and a memory to last a lifetime. His other appearances came in East of Scotland Shield matches.

BORN: Glasgow

HEIGHT: 5′ 10″   WEIGHT: 12st 6lb (1969)

COMPETITIVE DEBUT: v Clyde, 29 October 1966 (Lge) (H), 0–1

CAREER: Drumchapel Amateurs; **Hearts, July 1965**; Kilmarnock, Jan 1970 (£8,000); freed in Apr 1972

HONOURS: Scotland U-18 international

ALAN MacDONALD

Half-back

Hard-grafting half-back or inside-forward, Alan was a battler who never gave up and ran his heart out for the Jam Tarts. His downfall at Tynecastle was linked to a poor attitude towards training and his disciplinary record. However, he started as an inside-forward but lacked pace and was moved to the half-back position. He was soon looked on as a hard-man and was often in trouble with referees, collecting too many bookings for the liking of manager John Harvey. MacDonald was dropped as he was considered a liability. The player disagreed with this action and asked for a move. He was transferred to Kilmarnock where he initially encountered the same training and discipline problems. Alan knuckled down in time and later captained the Ayrshire side. He was nicknamed 'Chopper' at Rugby Park.

ALEX MacDONALD

Midfield

BORN: Glasgow, 17 March 1948

HEIGHT: 5′ 6″   **WEIGHT:** 10st 10lb (1982)

COMPETITIVE DEBUT: v Partick Thistle, 9 August 1980 (PL) (A), 2–3

CAREER: Luncarty Juniors; Glasgow United; St Johnstone, Jan 1966; Rangers, Nov 1968 (£50,000); **Hearts, Aug 1980** (£30,000); **Hearts player/manager, Jan 1981**; retired from first team at the end of 1985 but retained his registration; dismissed as manager in Sept 1990; Airdrie manager, July 1991

HONOURS: 1 full Scotland cap; 1 Scottish League cap; ECWC winner 1971–72 (Rangers); Scottish League winner 1974–75, 1975–76, 1977–78 (Rangers); Scottish Cup winner 1972–73, 1975–76, 1977–78, 1978–79 (Rangers); Scottish League Cup winner 1970–71, 1975–76, 1977–78, 1978–79 (Rangers)

Once described as a terrier-like midfielder, 'Doddie' was small but his abilities and determination shone through. He made his mark with St Johnstone as a teenager before a big-money transfer to Ibrox. Alex won full international, European and domestic honours in a 12-year association with the Light Blues. As the midfield powerhouse he sprayed passes all over the field, tackled like a tiger and inspired all those around him. His lack of height meant nothing as Alex was capable of out-jumping much taller players, and his cannonball shot brought countless memorable goals.

He joined newly promoted Hearts in 1980, later taking over as the first player/manager at Tynecastle and the first in the Premier League. He ended the 'yo-yo syndrome' and was awarded a testimonial in 1984 against his old team, Rangers, for his efforts. Doddie almost led Hearts to a League and Cup double in 1986 and instilled tremendous team spirit at the club. He knew the type of player who could serve Hearts well and made many astute signings.

A poor start to season 1990–91 and sacking chants from disgruntled fans led to Alex's dismissal in September 1990. After one year out of football he accepted a post as Airdrie manager, and proceeded to build an Airdrie side with a strong ex-Hearts contingent.

Centre-half

BORN: Dingwall, 30 August 1954

HEIGHT: 6' 1"   WEIGHT: 12st 9lb (1982)

COMPETITIVE DEBUT: v Airdrie, 8 August 1981 (LC) (A), 1–0

CAREER: Brora Rangers; Celtic, 1972; **Hearts, July 1981** (£55,000); Morton, Sept 1987 (£25,000); Partick Thistle, 1989 (free transfer); Irvine Meadow, 1991; Vale of Leven Juniors, 1993

HONOURS: Premier League r-up 1985–86 (Hearts); Scottish Cup winner 1976–77 (Celtic); Scottish League Cup r-up 1975–76, 1976–77, 1977–78 (Celtic)

A solid and reliable centre-half, Roddy cost a record fee from Celtic in 1981 after a bid for Aberdeen's Willie Garner was unsuccessful. The strongly-built pivot was a vital defensive link as Hearts fought out of Division I and consolidated Premier League status. Not noted for his footwork or ball control, Roddy cleared his lines effectively and used his dominance in the air to head cross balls away to safety. He could score goals, too. Opposition defenders panicked when Big Roddy entered their penalty area at set-pieces and corners. This time his heading ability was vital in an attacking sense. Always a popular player with the fans, Roddy provided the necessary cover when Craig Levein suffered his initial knee injury. The signing of Dave McPherson in 1987 created a surplus of central-defenders and MacDonald was sold to Morton. He carried out a grand job for Hearts, and later became a policeman in Strathclyde.

Forward

BORN: Kilmarnock, 20 August 1938

HEIGHT: 6' 1"   WEIGHT: 12st 6lb (1959)

COMPETITIVE DEBUT: v Raith Rovers, 10 November 1956 (Lge) (A), 3–2

CAREER: Kilmarnock YMCA; Troon Juniors; **Hearts, Aug 1956**; St Mirren, Feb 1961 (£3,000); Raith Rovers, Feb 1962; Kilmarnock, May 1963; Ayr United, 1969; Ayr United Reserve XI coach, 1973; Motherwell coach, 1979; Motherwell assistant manager, 1981

HONOURS: Scottish League winner 1964–65 (Kilmarnock)

A giant inside-forward who was an able deputy on many occasions, Jim's appearances were few and far between but he managed to contribute some goals. Successive cartilage operations to first his right then his left knee over a two-year spell interrupted his progress. His best run of games came in 1960–61. He joined St Mirren and in February 1961 was one of several players fined £50 by the SFA for taking part in an illegal game in Spain. He was transferred to Raith a few days later. He joined Kilmarnock in 1963 and was converted to a full-back, ending his career in that position with Ayr United. After taking on several coaching jobs, Jim taught PE in a school in Ayrshire.

WILLIE McFARLANE
Outside-right

BORN: Fallin, 1 October 1923

HEIGHT: 5' 6"   WEIGHT: 9st 12lb (1946)

COMPETITIVE DEBUT: v Albion Rovers, 18 April 1942 (S. Lge) (H), 2–2 (scored)

CAREER: Bathgate Thistle; **Hearts, Mar 1942;** Stirling Albion, Aug 1951 (free transfer); Kilmarnock, Oct 1953; Inverness Caley, Feb 1954

HONOURS: 1 full Scotland cap; 1 Scottish League cap

An electrical engineer with the NCB, Willie was speedy and deceptive with pinpoint crosses a speciality. He hit a rich vein of form in 1947 and was rewarded with a full cap against Luxembourg and a League cap against the Irish League. 'Packie' lost his place to goalscoring outside-right Tommy Sloan early in season 1948–49, effectively ending his Hearts career. He spent the next year in the reserves and received a further setback in April 1950 when an injury necessitated a cartilage operation. Despite recovering to start the 1950–51 season, Willie was unable to recapture sufficient form to challenge the consistency of Tommy Sloan. After enduring another full term of reserve football, he was released in August 1951.

BORN: Glenrothes, 27 October 1960

HEIGHT: 5' 6"   WEIGHT: 10st 6lb (1987)

COMPETITIVE DEBUT: v Celtic, 22 February 1986 (PL) (A), 1–1 (came on as substitute)

CAREER: Glenrothes Schools; Rangers, June 1977; retired due to injury in 1984; **Hearts, Feb 1986**; retired due to injury in Oct 1987

HONOURS: Scotland Schoolboy international

BILLY MACKAY

Winger

A teenage starlet at Ibrox who made his Rangers debut aged 16 in season 1977–78, Billy found his later appearances limited due to stiff competition for places. A terrible knee injury early in 1984 forced him to quit playing after specialist advice, but he kept an interest in football by scouting for his old mate Alex MacDonald at Hearts. Billy joined in several training sessions and, to his surprise and great delight, discovered his damaged left knee had healed. A check from a specialist confirmed his recovery and, to complete his joy, Billy found a contract offer from Hearts on the table. During his two comeback seasons, Mackay's competitive matches were restricted to sub appearances in his basic role as a squad player. Sadly, a recurrence of his injury forced him back into retirement.

BORN: Edinburgh, 14 November 1934

HEIGHT: 5' 9"   WEIGHT: 10st 12lb (1954)

COMPETITIVE DEBUT: v Clyde, 7 November 1953 (Lge) (H), 1–2

CAREER: Slateford Athletic; Newtongrange Star; **Hearts, Apr 1952**; Tottenham Hotspur, March 1959 (£30,000); Derby County, July 1968 (£5,000); Swindon Town player/manager, May 1971; Notts Forest manager, Nov 1972; Derby County manager, Oct 1973; Walsall manager, Nov 1976; Arabic Sporting Club (Kuwait) manager, Aug 1978; Doncaster Rovers manager, Dec 1987; Birmingham City manager, 1989; Zamalec Sporting Club (Egypt), 1991

DAVE MACKAY

Right-half

HONOURS: 22 full Scotland caps; 4 Scotland U-23 caps; Scotland Schoolboy and Junior international; 3 Scottish League caps; 2 English League caps; ECWC winner 1962–63 (Spurs); Scottish League winner 1957–58 (Hearts); Scottish Cup winner 1955–56 (Hearts); Scottish League Cup winner 1954–55,

1958–59 (Hearts); English League winner 1960–61 (Spurs); English Division II winner 1968–69 (Derby); English FA Cup winner 1960–61, 1961–62, 1966–67 (Spurs); Rex Kingsley's Scottish Footballer of the Year 1958; Football Writers' Association Player of the Year 1969; managed Derby County to English Championship in 1974–75

A barrel-chested half-back with the will to win, Dave was an excellent distributor of the ball and was always keen to attack where he could get among the goals. His inspiration and forceful play were features of Hearts' all-conquering 1950s side, Mackay's presence swelling the Tynecastle crowd by thousands. The Old Firm fans hated the sight of him, jeering loudly as he crunched their players in the tackle, while secretly wishing he played for their side. Mackay's powerplay and robust style helped Hearts to League Cup and Scottish Cup success in consecutive seasons. He then skippered the record-breaking 1957–58 League side which won the Championship at a canter. After receiving the 1958 Footballer of the Year award at the Usher Hall in February 1959, Mackay was sensationally transferred one month later. His £30,000 move in the prime of his career totally shattered the fans. Hearts won more honours in the following seasons, but Mackay's departure was the beginning of a general decline at Tynecastle.

As his roll of honour shows, Dave was equally successful away from Hearts as a player and manager. His name was always quoted as a potential Hearts boss whenever the job became vacant but this appointment never materialised.

GARY MACKAY

Midfield

BORN: Edinburgh, 23 January 1964

HEIGHT: 5' 9"   WEIGHT: 10st 5lb (1988)

COMPETITIVE DEBUT: v Ayr United, 24 September 1980 (LC) (A), 0–4 (came on as substitute)

CAREER: Balgreen School; Tynecastle School; Salvesen Boys Club; **Hearts, July 1980**

HONOURS: 4 full Scotland caps; Scotland Schoolboy, Youth and U-21 international; European Youth Championship winner 1982–83; Premier League r-up 1985–86, 1987–88, 1989–90, 1991–92 (Hearts); Scottish Cup r-up 1985–86 (Hearts); Tennents Sixes winner 1984–85, 1990–91 (Hearts)

A lifelong Hearts supporter who signed Schoolboy forms in 1979, Gary made his debut aged 16 and quickly demonstrated his potential. He was soon the main playmaker in midfield and, when on form, brought the best out in his colleagues. His passing, dribbling and penetrating runs are a feature of his play, and he possesses a fierce shot which has yielded many goals. Gary has won honours at every international level, stepping up to gain his first full cap in November 1987. That match saw him come on as a substitute against Bulgaria and he covered himself in glory with a late winning goal, the first Hearts player to score for Scotland since 1960.

Being a true Heart, Mackay reserves his best displays for Edinburgh derby matches with Hibs. He has scored several goals in this fixture and has rarely tasted defeat. Gary has endured periods of poor form at other times, however, but his commitment is never in doubt. His loyalty to the club was rewarded in May 1991 with a testimonial against Everton.

Gary is one of the most likeable and approachable personalities in football. Always willing to give time to a good cause or worthy event, he is a fine ambassador for Hearts. Although he is now entering the veteran stage, Gary still has many good seasons left and, barring any serious injuries, will be hoping to set appearance records.

TAM McKENZIE

Full-back

BORN: Edinburgh

DIED: Peterborough, Nov 1967

HEIGHT: 6'   WEIGHT: 12st 7lb (1953)

COMPETITIVE DEBUT: v Clyde, 28 April 1942 (S. Lge) (A), 0–2

CAREER: Morningside School; Darroch School; Pentland Rovers; Haddington Athletic; **Hearts, 1942**; Wisbech Town, May 1959 (free transfer); March Town player/manager, 1960

HONOURS: Scottish League winner 1957–58 (Hearts); Scottish Cup winner 1955–56 (Hearts); Scottish League Cup winner 1954–55 (Hearts)

The ever-dependable Tam McKenzie was a stalwart member of Hearts' team throughout the 1940s and '50s. A resolute tackler and a good distributor of the ball, he displayed immense strength. The top outside-right of the same era loathed facing McKenzie; Hibernian's Gordon Smith was a highly-rated international, yet Big Tam always had him in his pocket at every Edinburgh derby.

McKenzie skippered the side in 1949–50 and proved an inspirational leader. He was easily recognisable: always smartly dressed on and off the field, with his short hair neatly combed and brylcreemed. He provided top-class service to the club and was justly rewarded with domestic honours. He later played and managed in English non-league football until his tragic, untimely death in 1967 following a road accident.

TOSH McKINLAY

Left-back

BORN: Glasgow, 3 December 1964

HEIGHT: 5' 7"   **WEIGHT:** 10st 3lb (1990)

COMPETITIVE DEBUT: v Rangers, 10 December 1988 (PL) (H), 2–0

CAREER: Celtic Boys Club; Dundee, 1981; **Hearts, Dec 1988** (£300,000); Celtic, Nov 1994 (£350,000)

HONOURS: 1 full Scotland cap; 15 Scotland U-21 caps; Premier League r-up 1989–90, 1991–92 (Hearts); Scottish Cup winner 1994–95 (Celtic); Tennents Sixes winner 1990–91 (Hearts)

A pacy, attacking full-back who overlapped on the left-wing to supply dangerous cross balls. Tosh had such a good left foot that many fans believed he didn't need his right. He was equally at home as a deputy sweeper or driving forward from midfield. An emotional individual, Tosh's temperament often saw him pick up yellow or red cards for rash tackles in the heat of the moment. As such a committed player, this wasn't surprising, and his elation after a goal or the final whistle signalling a Hearts win told its own story.

Tosh broke into Dundee's first team as a highly-rated young teenager but it was always rumoured he might join Celtic. A move to his boyhood favourites didn't materialise with Hearts instead paying a large fee for his transfer in 1988. He was a class act for Hearts during his six years at Gorgie. He was dropped a couple of times under Joe Jordan's managerial reign but came back refreshed and quickly re-established himself. He managed to score a goal or two in almost every season. His best remembered was a 25-yard volley at Pittodrie in 1989.

McKinlay's contract expired in the summer of 1994 and he was unable to agree new terms. He then suffered a personal tragedy with the death of his infant son. He signed monthly deals for Hearts throughout season 1994–95 and eventually got his dream move and a fresh start with Celtic.

BORN: Uddingston, 17 July 1935

HEIGHT: 5′ 9″   **WEIGHT:** 10st 10lb (1953)

COMPETITIVE DEBUT: v Celtic, 18 April 1959 (Lge) (A), 1–2

CAREER: Uddingston Grammar School; Larkhall Thistle; **Hearts, Dec 1951**; freed in May 1959

JOHN MacKINTOSH
Full-back

A plasterer to trade, 'Tosh' was a keen athlete who specialised in sprinting – which accounted for his rapid acceleration to clear up dangerous situations in defence. His first game was a friendly in 1953–54 and he then waited five years before making his only League appearance. It came on the day Hearts lost the race for the 1958–59 League title in a 2–1 defeat at Parkhead. John was released the following month.

BORN: Edinburgh, 4 January 1971

HEIGHT: 5′ 11″   **WEIGHT:** 11st 6lb (1991)

COMPETITIVE DEBUT: v Dundee United, 7 May 1988 (PL) (A), 0–0

CAREER: Calvary Park Boys Club; **Hearts, July 1987**; Rangers, Oct 1994 (£1,250,000, plus David McPherson to Hearts)

HONOURS: 20 full caps for Scotland; Scotland Schoolboy and U-21 international; Premier League winner 1994–95 (Rangers)

ALAN McLAREN
Defender

A powerful, dominant and influential defender, Alan excelled in a man-marker role and was versatile enough to cover every position in defence and midfield. A Hearts supporter as a boy, Alan joined his favourites in 1987 and made rapid progress in the youth and reserve teams. He completed his first season by making a first-team debut. Club manager Alex MacDonald forecast Alan would be a future Scotland captain – and nobody argued.

McLaren starred against Bayern Munich in the 1989 UEFA Cup quarter-finals and continued to develop into a top-class player once he rid himself of early temperamental problems. He was outstanding in season 1991–92 and deservedly won U-21 and full international honours. After a remarkable performance in subduing top Italian star Roberto Baggio in a World Cup qualifier, Alan was widely believed to be worth £2,000,000.

Injury occasionally troubled McLaren and a cartilage operation put him out at the start of season 1993–94. He returned to demonstrate his class once more and played every match in season 1994–95 as if it were his last. Continually the subject of transfer talk, particularly from the Old Firm, most Hearts fans were resigned to the fact that Alan would eventually leave for big money. The most valuable asset on the playing staff joined one of our major competitors, Rangers, in October 1994 after protracted negotiations.

STEWART MacLAREN

Defender

BORN: Larkhall, 6 April 1953

HEIGHT: 5' 10"   **WEIGHT:** 11st 2lb (1982)

COMPETITIVE DEBUT: v Airdrie, 8 August 1981 (LC) (A), 1–0

CAREER: West Brom, 1969; Motherwell, 1974; Dundee, Oct 1978; **Hearts, July 1981** (£25,000); retired in May 1985

HONOURS: Scotland Schoolboy and Professional Youth international

An experienced, no-nonsense defender, MacLaren was a tough tackler, good in the air and a sound pro. His hardened style earned the veteran a chilling nickname: 'Chopper'. Stewart formed a central-defensive partnership with Roddy MacDonald and between them they tightened a defence which had previously lost too many easy goals. Stewart's second season brought a succession of injury problems as Hearts returned to the top flight, but he was able to make a telling contribution in 1983–84 as a European place was achieved and Premier stability secured. He starred in midfield as a hard-grafting ball-winner.

MacLaren's final appearance was the opening League match at Tannadice in 1984–85. Thereafter, a crippling pelvic injury put him out of action. His recovery was slow and medical advisers told Stewart to quit or risk more complications in later life. The popular defender heeded the advice and announced his retirement in May 1985.

BORN: Haddington, 25 September 1960

HEIGHT: 5' 11"   **WEIGHT:** 10st 12lb (1978)

COMPETITIVE DEBUT: v Partick Thistle, 5 May 1979 (PL) (A), 0–2 (came on as substitute)

CAREER: Tranent Juniors, 1977; **Hearts, 1978**; freed in May 1980; Tranent Juniors, 1981

KENNY McLEOD
Forward

Kenny was brought into Hearts' first team at the end of season 1978–79. The club was already relegated and youthful players were given a chance with nothing at stake. Kenny made little impression in his two starts and one substitute appearance. He did not manage any first-team games in 1979–80 and was included in Bobby Moncur's free transfer list in April 1980. He later returned to the ranks of junior football.

BORN: Edinburgh, 22 January 1963

HEIGHT: 5' 10"   **WEIGHT:** 10st 12lb (1986)

COMPETITIVE DEBUT: v Dundee, 3 February 1985 (PL) (H), 3–3 (came on as substitute and scored)

CAREER: Winchburgh Albion; Broxburn Juniors; **Hearts, June 1984**; East Fife, June 1986; Forfar Athletic, 1989; Meadowbank Thistle, Oct 1989; Arbroath, 1992; Broxburn Juniors, Apr 1993; Whitburn Juniors, Aug 1993; Whitburn manager, June 1994

BRIAN McNAUGHTON
Forward

Quick and committed striker who combined his football career with a Post Office job, Brian got off to a grand start with a goal on his debut. He followed this up with the only goal of a Cup replay against Brechin to win Hearts a quarter-final place. McNaughton worked hard to win first-team recognition, completing his first season with two more goals against Eintracht in a friendly and the consolation goal in a 3–1 League defeat at Ibrox. He started 1985–86 with two goals in pre-season matches and then opened the scoring in a League Cup tie against Stirling. He was clearly in Alex MacDonald's plans, making four League appearances early that season. Then came disaster as Brian fractured his collarbone in a reserve match against Dundee in October 1985. He was sidelined for a lengthy spell and, on regaining full fitness, found the first-team door firmly closed with the club in the middle of a record-breaking run. He moved on to

East Fife where he scored regularly, and has continued to be a noted marksman in senior and junior circles.

BRIAN McNEILL
Full-back

BORN: Newcastle-upon-Tyne, 1 April 1956

HEIGHT: 5′ 8″   **WEIGHT:** 10st (1981)

COMPETITIVE DEBUT: v Airdrie, 22 August 1981 (LC) (H), 2–3

CAREER: Newcastle Schools; Bristol City, Apr 1974; Portland Timbers, Feb 1978; Bristol City, Aug 1978; Plymouth Argyle, Nov 1978; **Hearts, Aug 1981** (free transfer)

Stocky full-back who could play on the left, right or centre of defence, Brian's build and short legs made him look a very unlikely footballer. He was one of Tony Ford's so-called 'quality' players – but Ford did not know the meaning of the word! Brian was a trier but he was no improvement on past players already discarded. Halfway through Brian's one and only season, Alex MacDonald took over the manager's job and the player was released early in 1982, MacDonald clearly having no use for him.

DAVE McNICOLL
Centre-half

BORN: Dundee, 23 September 1951

HEIGHT: 5′ 11″   **WEIGHT:** 12st 7lb (1977)

COMPETITIVE DEBUT: v Dumbarton, 22 October 1977 (Div. I) (H), 2–1

CAREER: Butterburn Youth Club; Dunfermline Athletic, 1969; Montrose, 1975 (free transfer); **Hearts, Oct 1977** (£10,000); St Johnstone, Apr 1979 (free transfer); East Fife, 1980; Whitburn, 1983; Dunfermline, 1985

HONOURS: Scotland Youth international; Division I r-up 1977–78 (Hearts)

Dave was a promising youngster at East End Park and a first-team player in his early 20s when injury struck him down. Knee trouble and three operations later, the Pars released him in 1975. His career looked to be over, but McNicoll fought back to full fitness. He was in the Montrose team which gave Hearts a fright in the 1976 Scottish Cup quarter-final, for example. Willie Ormond signed Dave as a part-timer to boost Hearts' promotion push in 1977–78 and the player combined football with a study course in journalism. The hard-tackling McNicoll brought stability to the central-defensive area. He mopped up danger with a minimum of fuss, clearing with his head or feet. Hearts found themselves at the wrong end of the League in 1978–79, however, and their plight worsened when Dave picked up a hip injury in February 1979. He never played another game for the club, and was freed in April 1979.

DAVE McPHERSON
Defender

BORN: Paisley, 28 January 1964

HEIGHT: 6' 3"   WEIGHT: 11st 11lb (1991)

COMPETITIVE DEBUT: v Falkirk, 8 August 1987 (PL) (H), 4–2

CAREER: Gartcosh Juveniles; Rangers, 1980; **Hearts, Jul 1987** (£325,000); Rangers, May 1992 (£1,300,000); **Hearts, Oct 1994** (part-exchange deal involving Alan McLaren)

HONOURS: 27 full Scotland caps; Scotland Youth and U-21 international; Premier League winner 1986–87, 1992–93, 1993–94 (Rangers); r-up 1989–90, 1991–92 (Hearts); Scottish Cup winner 1992–93 (Rangers); r-up 1982–83, 1993–94 (Rangers); Scottish League Cup winner 1983–84, 1984–85, 1992–93, 1993–94 (Rangers)

A teenage star with Rangers, Dave lost his way under the Souness regime at Ibrox. Hearts paid a club record fee for him in 1987 and it was money well spent. Nicknamed 'Hen Broon' by some Hearts fans, Dave matured into a full international and was appointed club skipper. He was always in attack at every opportunity and his dominating height brought Big Mac many goals with his head. Famed for his lengthy runs up the field, he was also an assured defender, using his long legs and natural speed to mop up any danger. His consistency was an asset to Hearts and he won many supporters' club Player of the Year awards. Dave's contract expired in May 1992 and just prior to joining Scotland for the European Championship finals, he signed for his old club Rangers in a shock club record transfer out. Hearts fans were stunned to see the club captain join one of our main competitors but a well-publicised debt problem had necessitated his sale. Dave helped Rangers win the treble in 1992–93 and he almost repeated this in 1993–94.

His return to Tynecastle just over two years later was again linked to Hearts' debt problems and the need to sell Alan McLaren. Dave was a makeweight in a £2,000,000 deal. Hearts required an experienced player to cover not only for Alan McLaren but for the loss of Craig Levein and Graeme Hogg due to long suspensions. All fans hope to see the McPherson of old during his two-and-a-half-year contract.

DENIS McQUADE

Winger

BORN: Glasgow, 6 January 1951

HEIGHT: 6' **WEIGHT:** 10st 10lb (1978)

COMPETITIVE DEBUT: v Partick Thistle, 9 September 1978 (PL) (A), 2–3

CAREER: St Roch's; Partick Thistle, 1970; **Hearts, Sept 1978** (swap deal); Hamilton Accies, Apr 1979 (free transfer); emigrated to Bermuda, Mar 1980

HONOURS: Scotland U-23 international; Scottish League Cup winner 1971–72 (Partick Thistle)

McQuade was a flamboyant left-winger who tormented the opposition using a directness which turned full-backs inside out, though his best years were over when he joined Hearts. His single season at Tynecastle is remembered for two breathtaking goals. The first was a raging 30-yard drive from out on the left-wing into the Beach End goal at Pittodrie. The second was scored against Hibs at the lower altitude Easter Road goal, when he spun on a sixpence and curled the ball into the keeper's top right-hand corner. As the club slid towards Division I Denis was named as a sub most weeks, and was eventually freed in May 1979.

PAT McSHANE

Forward

BORN: Glasgow, 21 October 1960

HEIGHT: 6' 2" **WEIGHT:** 12st 5lb (1979)

COMPETITIVE DEBUT: v Berwick Rangers, 25 August 1979 (Div. I) (A), 3–1 (came on as substitute)

CAREER: Anniesland Waverley; Leicester City; **Hearts, July 1979** (free transfer); East Stirling, 1982; Irish football, 1983

Tall, lean, red-haired striker who had the misfortune to tear his ankle ligaments on his debut, meaning that Pat was sidelined for a considerable period. During the second part of season 1980–81 he was given another opportunity. Alfie Conn had departed and, with Derek O'Connor injured, the young understudy returned. McShane failed to impress, though, scoring only once, in a Premier League fixture against St Mirren at Love Street. He was released in 1982.

BORN: Cleland, 21 January 1920

HEIGHT: 5' 8"   WEIGHT: 11st 7lb (1949)

COMPETITIVE DEBUT: v Rangers, 16 October 1943 (SLC) (A), 3–1

CAREER: Wishaw High School; Newarthill Hearts; Rutherglen Glencairn; **Hearts, July 1942**; freed in April 1952

TOMMY McSPADYEN

Full-back

A draughtsman to trade, Tommy was a hard-tackling full-back who took several years to win a regular place. His progress was halted in March 1948 when continuous back problems necessitated an operation at Law Hospital. He was out of action until January 1949 and found it difficult to regain a place. He played a few more games in 1950–51 and 1951–52 as a deputy for Parker or McKenzie. He played in one of the 1952 Scottish Cup semi-final matches, but within a month was given a free transfer.

BORN: Glasgow, 7 August 1948

HEIGHT: 6' 1"   WEIGHT: 12st 11lb (1980)

COMPETITIVE DEBUT: v Airdrie, 30 July 1980 (ASC) (A), 0–3

CAREER: Lesmahagow; Clyde, 1967; Motherwell, 1975; Toronto Blizzard, 1979; **Hearts, July 1980** (free transfer); Blantyre Victoria, 1981; Stonehouse Violet manager, 1984–85

WILLIE McVIE

Centre-half

Tough central-defender referred to as the 'Honey Monster' by a section of the Hearts support. The nickname was descriptive of his game – Willie took no prisoners, a reputation earned with Clyde and Motherwell. He was signed as a defensive anchorman to improve Hearts' chances of consolidating a Premier League place. He put in plenty of effort but it was clear his best days were long gone. As Hearts toiled they decided to release Willie, who had managed only a dozen games.

ARTHUR MANN

Left-back

BORN: Burntisland, 23 January 1948

HEIGHT: 5′ 10″   **WEIGHT:** 11st (1967)

COMPETITIVE DEBUT: v Kilmarnock, 2 December 1967 (Lge) (A), 2–3

CAREER: Lochore Welfare; **Hearts, July 1967**; Manchester City, Nov 1968 (£65,000); Blackpool, Nov 1971 (on loan); Notts County, July 1972 (£15,000); Shrewsbury Town, Jun 1979; Mansfield, 1981 (£36,000); Boston United player/manager, 1984; Telford United, 1986; Kettering Town; Grimsby Town coach

HONOURS: Scottish Cup r-up 1967–68 (Hearts); English League Cup winner 1969–70 (Man City)

Immensely talented full-back, Mann was good at holding possession and able to link effectively with the forward line. He displayed amazing confidence in his overlapping wing role and his rapid emergence ousted the experienced Davie Holt from the side.

Following his debut Arthur quickly became a permanent fixture in the side and assisted Hearts to the 1968 Cup final. Less than a year after his debut Hearts succumbed to English gold and a large fee took him south – money in the bank perhaps, but a blatant betrayal of the youth policy set in place to re-establish Hearts' position in Scottish football. Disenchanted fans showed their displeasure by voting with their feet. Mann went on to enjoy success with City but fell from favour after it was discovered he had a fear of flying. He did the rounds in English football thereafter and was still playing non-league football in his 40s.

PETER MARINELLO

Winger

BORN: Edinburgh, 20 February 1950

HEIGHT: 5′ 9″   **WEIGHT:** 11st (1982)

COMPETITIVE DEBUT: v East Stirling, 31 October 1981 (Div. I) (H), 0–1 (came on as substitute)

CAREER: St Anthony's School (Edinburgh); Salvesen Boys Club; Hibernian, 1966; Arsenal, Jan 1970 (£90,000); Portsmouth, July 1973 (£100,000); Motherwell, 1975; Fulham, Dec 1978; Phoenix Inferno, 1980; **Hearts, Oct 1981** (free transfer); Partick Thistle, Mar 1983; Whitburn Juniors, 1984

HONOURS: Scotland Youth and U-23 international; Scottish League Cup r-up 1968–69 (Hibs)

Marinello found fame as a youngster with Hibs and earned a big-money transfer to Arsenal. He never realised his potential at Highbury though, and after plying his trade at a number of clubs, Peter found his way back to Edinburgh and Hearts in October 1981. His best years were long gone, but Peter performed competently in his 18 months at Gorgie. His old trademarks were still evident: a jinking, tiptoeing running style, relying more on cunning craft and skill to beat defenders than on pace. The arrival of another veteran, Willie Johnston, in September 1982 saw Marinello lose his place and hastened his departure to Partick. He later became a licensee in Edinburgh.

GORDON MARSHALL
Goalkeeper

BORN: Farnham, Surrey, 2 July 1939

HEIGHT: 6' 1"   WEIGHT: 12st 7lb (1958)

COMPETITIVE DEBUT: v Kilmarnock, 17 November 1956 (Lge) (H), 3–2

CAREER: Balgreen Rovers; Dalkeith Thistle; **Hearts, Aug 1956**; Newcastle United, June 1963 (£18,000); Notts Forest, Oct 1968 (£17,500); Hibernian, 1969; Celtic, Aug 1971; Aberdeen, 1972; Arbroath, July 1972; retired in 1978

HONOURS: 1 England U-23 cap; Scottish League winner 1957–58, 1959–60 (Hearts); Scottish League Cup winner 1958–59, 1959–60, 1962–63 (Hearts); r-up 1961–62 (Hearts); English Division II winner 1964–65 (Newcastle United)

Gordon made his debut aged 17 and was established as Hearts' regular number 1 within a year. He demonstrated brave goalkeeping qualities, often charging from the goal-line to dive on the ball as strikers were about to shoot. He possessed remarkable confidence for one so young and was rated among the best shot-stoppers in Scotland. He used his height to great advantage in cross-ball situations.

After winning a clutch of medals with Hearts, he tried his luck down south with Newcastle. After five seasons at St James's Park he moved around in the late '60s and early '70s before turning part-time with Arbroath in 1972. At the same time he invested in a newsagent/hairdressing business venture at West Maitland Street in Edinburgh. He retired from football in 1978 to concentrate fully on his business, where he can be found serving his customers on a daily basis.

TOMMY MARTIN
Inside-right

BORN: Glasgow, 21 December 1924

HEIGHT: 5' 11"   **WEIGHT:** 11st 10lb (1947)

COMPETITIVE DEBUT: v Queens Park, 3 April 1943 (SLC) (H), 4–1 (scored)

CAREER: Shettleston Juniors; **Hearts, 1942;** Stirling, Mar 1949 (on loan, becoming permanent in Oct 1949 – £3,000); Doncaster Rovers, Jul 1950 (£5,000); Notts Forest, Oct 1952 (£15,000); Hull City, June 1955; retired c.1956–57

A joiner to trade, Tommy trained at various Glasgow club grounds when he lived in the west of Scotland. He can't remember signing for Hearts as on the night in question he'd received a nasty head knock playing for Shettleston. He was propped up receiving treatment when a pen was thrust into his hand and a form was signed in a barely legible scribble – real cunning on the part of Dave McLean.

The tall, fair-haired striker was a scheming inside-forward with superb ball skills. He could pass accurately and had intelligent positional awareness. He played regularly during the war but when hostilities ceased managed very few games thereafter. His failure to win a place alerted many clubs, who all bid unsuccessfully – Hearts wished to retain Tommy and he was committed to the club. The emergence of the Terrible Trio meant a move was inevitable, however, and after a loan spell, Stirling secured his permanent transfer.

BOBBY MASTERTON
Midfield

BORN: Broxburn, 3 August 1956

HEIGHT: 5' 9"   **WEIGHT:** 10st 13lb (1979)

COMPETITIVE DEBUT: v Ayr United, 1 September 1979 (LC) (A), 2–2 (came on as substitute)

CAREER: Bo'ness United; **Hearts, Jun 1979;** Falkirk, 1982; East Fife, 1984; Bo'ness United, 1984; Linlithgow Rose, 1985

HONOURS: Division I winner 1979–80 (Hearts); Junior Cup r-up 1978–79 (Bo'ness)

Fair-haired midfielder already earmarked for Tynecastle before starring in the 1979 Junior Cup final. A hard-working player, Bobby's limitations were exposed in a team struggling for Premier League survival. He had helped Hearts win promotion in 1979–80 but was found out in the cut-throat competitive top flight. His commitment and endeavour were never in doubt and in a better side Bobby's strengths might have been used more. He had earned a reputation as a tremendous finisher with Bo'ness but was unable to demonstrate these talents with Hearts. Bobby is currently Linlithgow's assistant manager.

DOUGAL MATHESON
Full-back

BORN: Glasgow, 22 June 1924

HEIGHT: 5' 10"   WEIGHT: 11st 12lb (1947)

COMPETITIVE DEBUT: v Dundee, 6 October 1947 (Lge) (A), 1–2

CAREER: Yoker Fernlea; Cunard Thistle; Yoker Athletic; Fauldhouse United; **Hearts, June 1947**; Inverness Thistle, Sept, 1951 (free transfer)

HONOURS: 2 Scotland Junior caps

Consistent full-back who partnered Tommy McKenzie in the late 1940s. He was equally capable at right or left-back and played regularly in 1947–48 and 1948–49. Dougal was stocky in build and used his physical strength to win tackles. Bobby Parker's move from central-defence to full-back signalled the beginning of the end for him, though. After failing to make a single appearance in 1950–51, Hearts agreed to release him in September 1951.

ALLY MAUCHLEN
Midfield

BORN: West Kilbride, 29 June 1960

HEIGHT: 5' 7"   WEIGHT: 10st 2lb (1992)

COMPETITIVE DEBUT: v Celtic, 1 August 1992 (PL) (H), 0–1

CAREER: Irvine Meadow; Kilmarnock, 1978; Motherwell, 1982 (£40,000); Leicester City, Aug 1985 (£350,000 including G. McAllister); **Hearts, July 1992** (free transfer); Glenavon, Dec 1993

HONOURS: Division I winner 1984–85 (Motherwell); r-up 1981–82 (Kilmarnock)

A product of Ayrshire Junior football, Ally came to prominence as a teenager with Kilmarnock. He gained a reputation as a tough midfielder with Motherwell and attracted the interest of Leicester in 1985. After seven seasons at Filbert Street, including a period as team captain, Hearts offered the fiery red-head signing-on terms following his free transfer. There was an element of doubt among sections of the Hearts support about his signing, his previous disciplinary record in Scotland and his style of play being the cause of their anxiety. Mauchlen took some time readjusting to the quicker pace of the Premier League and then injury trouble took over. His first season was anything but memorable and the majority of supporters didn't take to him. An unsavoury stamping incident in an Edinburgh derby match didn't help and brought widespread bad publicity. Ally made one competitive appearance in 1993–94 and, to be kind, had an absolute nightmare. He joined Irish club Glenavon on loan before making the move permanent.

SCOTT MAXWELL
Midfield

BORN: Edinburgh, 26 August 1963

HEIGHT: 5′ 10″   WEIGHT: 10st 5lb (1981)

COMPETITIVE DEBUT: v St Mirren, 18 April 1981 (PL) (H), 1–2 (scored)

CAREER: Craigmount High School; Tynecastle Boys Club; **Hearts, July 1980**; Stirling Albion, June 1982 (free transfer)

A thinly built midfielder, Scott was tipped to make the grade with Hearts, finally achieving a first-team debut at the end of season 1980–81. Hearts were doomed to relegation by this point and Maxwell was able to stake his claim in a very relaxed Tynecastle atmosphere, the ground being near empty. Scott had a gangly, awkward style and hit some nice passes, while appearing relatively composed. He failed to make a breakthrough the following season though, and was granted a free transfer. He joined Stirling Albion and served them well for many years.

BILLY MENMUIR

Forward

BORN: Glasgow, 3 February 1952

HEIGHT: 5′ 8″   WEIGHT: 10st (1972)

COMPETITIVE DEBUT: v Celtic, 18 November 1972 (Lge) (A), 2–4

CAREER: Eastbank School; Sandyhills YMCA; Bristol City, June 1969; **Hearts, Sept 1971** (free transfer); released in Apr 1974

A hard-tackling inside-forward and a good passer of the ball, Billy waited over a year for his debut – and what a difficult fixture it arrived on: a trip to Parkhead. He was given a chance to settle in and made a reasonable contribution during a difficult spell when the team's form and confidence were at a low ebb. Billy's only goal was scored against Dumbarton at Boghead in January 1973 in a 0–2 win. He failed to force his way into first-team contention for the duration of season 1973–74 and was consequently granted a free transfer.

JOHN MILLAR

Midfield

BORN: Bellshill, 8 December 1966

HEIGHT: 5′ 8″   WEIGHT: 12st 3lb (1991)

COMPETITIVE DEBUT: v Dunfermline, 10 August 1991 (PL) (A), 2–1

CAREER: Dundee Boys Club; Chelsea, Aug 1984; Hamilton, 1986 (on loan); Northampton, Jan 1987 (on loan); Blackburn Rovers, Jul 1987; **Hearts, Jul 1991** (free transfer)

HONOURS: Scotland U-18 international; Premier League r-up 1991–92 (Hearts)

John was surprisingly freed by Blackburn and Joe Jordan moved quickly to sign him. The quicker pace of Scottish football caught him out in his first few games, and he found it difficult to get involved. However, he soon began to display ball-winning qualities and a willingness to attack. He packed a fair shot and, by the end of 1991–92, had seven League goals to his credit. These goals were all important strikes, with the most memorable coming at Parkhead – the decisive goal in a 1–2 win over Celtic. Season 1992–93 was a washout due to injuries and poor form for Millar but in 1993–94 he managed to perform better and was soon back scoring goals again.

ARCHIE MILLER

Half-back

BORN: Larkhall, 5 September 1913

HEIGHT: 5′ 11″   **WEIGHT:** 11st 4lb (1946)

COMPETITIVE DEBUT: v Airdrie, 31 December 1932 (Lge) (A), 7–2 (scored)

CAREER: Royal Albert; **Hearts, 1932**; Falkirk (guest during the war); Blackburn Rovers, Nov 1947; Kilmarnock, Jun 1948; Carlisle United, Sept 1950; **Hearts, 1951**; Workington player/manager, Feb 1952

HONOURS: 1 full Scotland cap; 1 wartime cap; 1 Scottish League cap

A lithe half-back, Archie was a confident and determined character whose consistency was rewarded with a long overdue cap in 1939. The war interrupted his career as he was reaching his prime, and when hostilities ceased he was well into his 30s. He was still a capable player though, and his experience was put to good use as Hearts attempted to build a new side by blooding young players. He moved south in 1947 and switched clubs every other year, playing on until just short of his 40th birthday. He also returned to Hearts for a short spell, assisting in the reserves.

COLIN MILLER

Full-back

BORN: Lanark, 4 October 1964

HEIGHT: 5′ 7″   **WEIGHT:** 12st (1994)

COMPETITIVE DEBUT: v Dundee United, 19 November 1994 (PL) (A), 2–5

CAREER: Rangers, 1984; Hamilton Steelers (Canada); Hamilton Accies, Sept 1988; St Johnstone, Mar 1994 (£35,000); **Hearts, Nov 1994** (swap deal for Jim Weir and £80,000 to Hearts)

HONOURS: Full Canadian international; B&Q Cup winner 1992–93 (Hamilton)

Solid and reliable full-back who was signed to replace Tosh McKinlay, Colin was born in Scotland but spent his childhood in Canada. He joined Rangers as a youngster but was unable to make the breakthrough at Ibrox and returned to Canada where he starred with the Hamilton Steelers for a short period. He crossed the Atlantic once more to join Hamilton Accies and became a mainstay in their defence alongside Jim Weir. He moved to Perth in 1994 and boss Paul Sturrock appointed him skipper. Colin turned in a very impressive display against Hearts in the

Skol Cup in August 1994 in which Saints won 4–2 and Colin hit a fine goal from 20 yards out. Tommy McLean had been a long-time admirer of Miller and finally got his man after three previous failed attempts to sign him when he was Motherwell boss.

GEORGE MILLER

Half-back

BORN: Larkhall, 20 May 1939

HEIGHT: 6'   WEIGHT: 11st 7lb (1967)

COMPETITIVE DEBUT: v Morton, 20 November 1965 (Lge) (H), 2–1

CAREER: Larkhall Academy; Royal Albert; Dunfermline Athletic, 1959; Wolverhampton Wanderers, Oct 1964 (£28,500); **Hearts, Nov 1965** (£20,000); Falkirk, Nov 1968 (£5,000); Dunfermline Athletic manager, Feb 1972; Falkirk manager, Dec 1976 to 1978; Hamilton commercial manager, 1984

HONOURS: 1 Scottish League cap; Scottish Cup winner 1960–61 (Dunfermline); r-up 1967–68 (Hearts)

Hearts splashed out a record fee for George Miller and he was soon appointed club captain. He excelled in the sweeper role, had a quick turn of pace and was able to fire in powerful long-range shots. He was a spirited performer but many supporters expressed the opinion that he never really justified his large fee. His best season was 1967–68 when he skippered the club to a Scottish Cup final clash with Dunfermline. He scored seven competitive goals that season, three of them from the penalty spot. He moved to Falkirk in 1968 for a modest fee and captained the Bairns for four seasons before becoming the manager of his first senior side.

ANDY MILNE

Forward

BORN: Renfrew, 17 July 1948

HEIGHT: 5′ 11″   **WEIGHT:** 11st 2lb (1967)

COMPETITIVE DEBUT: v Aberdeen, 4 March 1967 (Lge) (A), 0–3

CAREER: Arsenal, 1964; **Hearts, Feb 1967** (free transfer); emigrated to South Africa in 1968; East Fife, 1976–78

Andy joined Arsenal as a young teenager but failed to make the grade. Hearts gave him a chance in Scotland and he knocked in several goals after being introduced at the end of season 1966–67. He scored a hat-trick against relegation-bound Stirling and it looked like Hearts had a bargain striker on a free transfer. Unfortunately, indifferent form the following season saw Milne return to reserve football until his release.

JIMMY MILNE

Centre-half

BORN: Arbroath

HEIGHT: 5′ 11″   **WEIGHT:** 12st 2lb (1956)

COMPETITIVE DEBUT: v Celtic, 29 September 1951 (Lge) (A), 3–1

CAREER: Arbroath Juveniles; Brechin Vics; Arbroath; **Hearts, Aug 1950** (free transfer); Forfar Athletic, Apr 1961 (free transfer); Arbroath director

HONOURS: Scottish League winner 1957–58, 1959–60 (Hearts)

Many eyebrows were raised when Hearts signed Jimmy Milne from Arbroath on a free transfer, but in eleven seasons he proved the doubters wrong with steady, assured defensive play at the centre-half berth. He provided valuable cover after Bobby Dougan's injury in September 1951, and for five seasons thereafter when Fred Glidden took over as centre-half from Dougan. Jimmy won a permanent place when Glidden was eased out in 1958–59 and he assisted Hearts in their two League title wins in the late '50s. He played his part in a changing team during 1960–61 and then returned to his Angus roots. He later lined up for Forfar against Hearts in a Scottish Cup third round tie in January 1963. Hearts won 3–1, with Milne scoring Forfar's consolation goal from the penalty spot. After retiring from football, Jimmy worked for the Post Office in Arbroath.

BORN: Randers, Denmark

HEIGHT: 5' 10"   WEIGHT: 12st 2lb (1969)

COMPETITIVE DEBUT: v Aberdeen, 10 February 1968 (Lge) (A), 0–2

CAREER: Randers Freja; **Hearts, Jan 1968**; Randers Freja, Apr 1970

HONOURS: 4 full and 5 U-23 caps for Denmark; Scottish Cup r-up 1967–68 (Hearts)

Forward

Rene Moller joined his local club Randers Freja, which catered for all age groups, when he was eight. He eventually made it to their first team and spent four years on the payroll of a Randers firm as a freelance photographer. His ambition was to achieve professional status as a footballer, however, and, after a trial for Hearts, he realised his dream and became the club's first and only Danish international.

Moller's second game for Hearts is still talked of to this day – he hit two goals in a famous 6–5 victory against Dundee United in the Scottish Cup. Rene had health problems and missed many games due to heavy winter colds. He was an unorthodox striker who sometimes didn't know what he would do next – and if Rene didn't know, how did his opponents cope? He occasionally fell victim to the boo-boys on his bad days but, in contrast, was a hero when on song. A love-hate relationship developed between him and the Tynecastle punters.

He returned to Denmark feeling unhappy in 1970 but Hearts retained his registration and hoped he would return. He was never heard of again until an official programme from an away match with Falkirk in the early 1980s listed him in Hearts' pool of signed players!

BORN: Glasgow, 25 December 1964

HEIGHT: 5' 6"   WEIGHT: 9st 5lb (1987)

COMPETITIVE DEBUT: v Hamilton Accies, 13 December 1986 (PL) (H), 7–0

CAREER: Possil YM; Dumbarton, 1983; **Hearts, Nov 1986** (£80,000); St Johnstone, June 1989 (£85,000); Dunfermline, Mar 1994 (swap deal)

HONOURS: Div. I winner 1989–90 (St Johnstone)

Winger

A tiny winger with lightning speed, Allan used his pace and deceptive running style to outstrip opposing full-backs and whip in telling crosses, but he found his Tynecastle first-team opportunities limited due to the consistently good form of John Colquhoun. Moore appeared mostly as a substitute, only starting games in the event of injuries or suspension to others. It is fair to say Allan didn't receive an extended run to show his abilities, but equally fair that his form was erratic when he was selected. Frustrated by his lack of progress, Allan jumped at the chance to join rejuvenated St Johnstone in 1989, where he enjoyed popularity with the Saints' fans.

COLIN MORE
Defender

BORN: Edinburgh, 13 November 1960

HEIGHT: 6′ 1″   WEIGHT: 11st 9lb (1979)

COMPETITIVE DEBUT: v Aberdeen, 2 May 1979 (PL) (A), 0–5

CAREER: St Bernard's; **Hearts, July 1978**; Raith Rovers, May 1982 (free transfer)

Colin quit the security of a banking job to sample full-time football with Hearts and, despite being a centre-half, played many of his games at full-back. His debut match was a disaster, a 5–0 drubbing at Pittodrie. Colin was thrown in along with several youngsters when relegation became reality in 1978–79. He made the odd appearance in 1979–80 but went on to enjoy a lengthy run in 1980–81. The arrival of Roddy MacDonald and Stewart MacLaren in July 1981 signalled an end to Colin's genuine chances of first-team action. He was freed early in May 1982, only to answer an SOS to play in a vital promotion match against Kilmarnock.

JOE MORGAN
Winger

BORN: Edinburgh, 22 March 1953

HEIGHT: 5′ 7″   WEIGHT: 9st 12lb (1970)

COMPETITIVE DEBUT: v Cowdenbeath, 24 April 1971 (Lge) (H), 4–0 (came on as substitute)

CAREER: Ainslie Park School; Salvesen Boys Club; **Hearts, 1968**; freed c.1972

A known Hibernian supporter who had played for the Edinburgh Secondary Schools XI on many occasions, Joe was named as a substitute several times without taking the field. In his solitary substitute appearance he made little impact in a match already won.

BORN: Glasgow, 29 November 1942

HEIGHT: 5' 11"   WEIGHT: 11st (1963)

JIM MURPHY
Forward

COMPETITIVE DEBUT: v Aberdeen, 2 November 1963 (Lge) (H), 0–0

CAREER: Larkhall Academy; Larkhall Victoria; Lesmahagow Burnbank; Stonehouse; Larkhall Thistle; Alloa Athletic; **Hearts, Oct 1963** (£2,750); Raith Rovers, Aug 1967 (£5,000); Notts County, Feb 1968; Motherwell

Murphy travelled the junior scene as a teenager before making his mark as a goalscorer with Alloa. Hearts used part of Willie Hamilton's transfer fee to buy Murphy from Alloa as a supposed replacement. He didn't impress on his debut but his next match against East Stirling two months later was explosive – Jim scored all four goals in an easy victory, and his form won him a short run in the team. The remainder of his Hearts career was spent as a deputy. He scored goals when he did appear but he was unable to put together a run of games until season 1966—67. He eventually signed for Tommy Walker again when the famous ex-Hearts manager took over at Raith.

BORN: Elgin, 18 January 1946

HEIGHT: 6'   WEIGHT: 12st (1975)

DON MURRAY
Sweeper

COMPETITIVE DEBUT: v Motherwell, 14 December 1974 (Lge) (A), 3–1

CAREER: Hopeman Junior School; Burghead Thistle Juniors; Cardiff City, Jan 1963; Swansea City, Oct 1974 (on loan); **Hearts, Dec 1974** (£15,000); Newport County, Oct 1976 (free transfer); retired in 1978

HONOURS: 1 Scotland U-23 cap; Captain of the Great Britain Youth side

Murray joined Cardiff City as a 17-year-old and made 406 League appearances in 13 seasons with them. A tough, rugged defender with the will to win, Don often played on after sustaining knocks which would have put other players out of action. He was considered something of a lucky mascot in the first couple of months after signing for Hearts: the team went 13 games without defeat. Don was a natural leader and had a short spell as club captain when he inspired others around him to give their best. The 30-year-old anchorman was released in October 1976.

Inside-right

BORN: Edinburgh, 4 February 1933

HEIGHT: 5' 9"   **WEIGHT:** 11st 6lb (1956)

COMPETITIVE DEBUT: v Stirling Albion, 15 April 1952 (Lge) (H), 5–2 (scored)

CAREER: Edinburgh Schools; Merchiston Thistle; **Hearts, Sept 1950**; Reading (on loan), Feb 1954; Falkirk, May 1961 (free transfer); Clyde, Dec 1962–64; Falkirk assistant manager, 1967–May 1968; Raith Rovers staff, 1968; **Hearts third XI coach 1972**

HONOURS: 5 full Scotland caps; Scotland Schoolboy international; Scottish League winner 1957–58, 1959–60 (Hearts); Scottish League Cup winner 1958–59 (Hearts)

Jimmy Murray scored on his League debut as a 19-year-old and then failed to make a single appearance in the next two seasons. He could be considered a reserve player for seven years, unable to win a place from the established Terrible Trio. He eventually emerged from the reserve-team shadows in season 1956–57: as Alfie Conn's first-team career drew to an end, Jimmy won favour in manager Walker's plans and excelled beyond all expectation in Hearts' record-breaking 1957–58 season. His haul of goals and terrific form was rewarded with a place in Scotland's 1958 World Cup squad for Sweden, where he scored the Scots' first goal in the finals stage. Murray's rich seam of form continued in 1958–59 and he turned in a superlative performance in the 1958 League Cup final with two well-taken goals, helping Hearts to a 5–1 win. He was omitted from the 1959 League Cup final team in favour of the free-scoring Ian Crawford, but Jimmy was soon back in the side and netted 11 goals to assist Hearts to another League Championship. Sadly, his form and goals deserted him during the transitional season 1960–61 and this resulted in a free transfer.

He made attempts to re-establish himself firstly at Falkirk and then Clyde, but struggled without the type of service he had thrived on at Tynecastle. Jimmy moved into management during the 1960s and found his way back to Hearts in the early 1970s, helping out with the third team for a short while. In later years he was employed as a sales manager with an electrical company.

Defender

BORN: Buckie, 26 July 1964

HEIGHT: 5' 11"   WEIGHT: 11st 2lb (1988)

COMPETITIVE DEBUT: v Motherwell, 12 May 1984 (PL) (A), 1–0

CAREER: Leicester City, 1979; Buckie Thistle; **Hearts, March 1983**; Hull City, Apr 1989 (£40,000); Mansfield Town, Dec 1989; Partick Thistle, 1990; Clydebank, Aug 1992; Meadowbank, 1993; Arbroath, July 1994

Malcolm joined Hearts aged 19 and looked to have a bright future in football. He suffered the misfortune of a recurring back injury, however, and this curtailed his progress. He managed several short runs in the side, mostly at right back. The biggest match he played in was the 1987 Scottish Cup semi-final against St Mirren.

Winger

BORN: Fraserburgh, 24 October 1950

HEIGHT: 6' 2"   WEIGHT: 12st 7lb (1970)

COMPETITIVE DEBUT: v Dundee United, 9 August 1969 (LC) (A), 3–2

CAREER: Lossiemouth; Ross County; **Hearts, Mar 1969** (£10,000); Morton, Feb 1973

Neil graduated from Aberdeen University with an MA degree prior to joining Hearts. Initially a part-timer, he quickly went full-time when he gained first-team football. An ungainly winger who was fast and direct, he could be awkward and troublesome to opposing defenders. Neil could operate on either wing and was able to drop deeper into midfield when required. His form could be erratic – brilliant one week then hopeless the next. When Bobby Seith was appointed boss he began to introduce his own players and Murray faded from favour to the point where he moved on in 1973.

TOMMY MURRAY

Midfield

BORN: Caldercruix, 1 June 1943

HEIGHT: 5′ 7″   **WEIGHT:** 9st 6lb (1972)

COMPETITIVE DEBUT: v Dunfermline, 11 September 1971 (Lge) (A), 1–4 (scored)

CAREER: Edinburgh Athletic; Airdrie, 1961; Carlisle United, Mar 1967 (£12,000); **Hearts, Sept 1971** (exchange deal for Kevin Hegarty); Easter FC (Hong Kong), Aug 1975 (free transfer); Arbroath, 1977; Raith Rovers, 1978

Tommy made an immediate impact on his East End Park debut, scoring a fine double in a 1–4 demolition of Dunfermline. A real trier, Tommy packed a fair amount of skill and could create and take goalscoring chances. The best remembered incident involving Tommy came at Ibrox in December 1972 when he cheekily sat on the ball and beckoned the Rangers players to him. They charged towards him, infuriated, but just before they reached him, Tommy jumped to his feet, passed to Jim Brown and, with the Rangers defence posted missing, Brown crossed to Donald Ford who bulleted home a header. That solitary incident demonstrated Murray's contempt for the big guns and is still fondly remembered to this day.

Tommy provided good service to Hearts at the veteran stage of his career. He made a small contribution in assisting the club to win a place in the new Premier League before leaving for Hong Kong.

HUSREF MUSEMIC

Forward

BORN: Janja, Yugoslavia, 4 July 1961

HEIGHT: 6′ 2″   **WEIGHT:** 12st 4lb (1989)

COMPETITIVE DEBUT: v Celtic, 12 August 1989 (PL) (H), 1–3

CAREER: Red Star Belgrade; **Hearts, Jun 1989** (£200,000); Sarajevo, Jan 1990 (free transfer)

HONOURS: 1 full Yugoslavia cap; Yugoslav U-21 international

A prolific goalscorer for Red Star with 122 strikes, Hearts were alerted that he'd lost his first-team place and, after a few scouting missions, Husref became Hearts' first Yugoslavian player. It all started well for the big man dubbed 'Moose' by the Tynecastle fans. He scored on his debut and repeated the act with another goal on his home debut against

Sunderland. His first competitive goal came in a League Cup tie with Montrose but his best effort was the winner against Hibs in his one and only derby, with a well-placed header. Husref was more of a 'touch' player and never really settled into Hearts' pattern of play, which was built around hard work. The biggest problem appeared to be communication – he spoke very little English – and, after losing his first-team place, it came as no surprise when he was released at a considerable loss in January 1990.

TOMMY NEILSON
Half-back

BORN: Armadale, 28 July 1922

HEIGHT: 5' 8"   WEIGHT: 10st 2lb (1946)

COMPETITIVE DEBUT: v Clyde, 6 March 1943 (SLC) (A), 0–1

CAREER: Armadale Thistle; **Hearts, c.1942**; Ipswich Town, May 1948 (free transfer)

Tommy made six competitive appearances in 1946–47 but could not command a place the following season and was freed in 1948. He joined Ipswich but made even less of an impact there, managing only one League match at Portman Road. He appears to have vanished from the football scene after leaving Ipswich.

CRAIG NELSON
Goalkeeper

BORN: Coatbridge. 28 May 1971

HEIGHT: 6' 1"   WEIGHT: 12st 3lb (1994)

COMPETITIVE DEBUT: v Falkirk, 3 December 1994 (PL) (H), 1–1

CAREER: Airdrie, 1988; Ashfield Juniors, 1989; Partick Thistle, Aug 1990; Cork City (on loan); **Hearts, Dec 1994** (£160,000 plus Nicky Walker to Partick)

HONOURS: Scotland B international

A highly-rated young goalkeeper who has been tipped for full international honours, Craig joined Partick from junior football but almost immediately crossed the water for a short period with Cork. He returned to Firhill in April 1991 and quickly set about ousting the established number 1, Andy Murdoch. Once he got his chance, Craig's consistency kept Murdoch out. He is a proven shot-stopper with good reflexes and can command the penalty area with authority. Nelson is a signing for the future and can only get better. The expert guidance and tips available from Henry Smith will ensure Craig's progress – but rest assured that Henry will battle for that number 1 jersey.

PAUL O'BRIEN
Forward

BORN: Edinburgh, 27 July 1962

HEIGHT: 5' 8"   **WEIGHT:** 9st 12lb (1981)

COMPETITIVE DEBUT: v Kilmarnock, 6 December 1980 (PL) (H), 2–0 (scored)

CAREER: North Merchiston BC; Dundee United; **Hearts, Feb 1980** (free transfer); St Johnstone, Nov 1981; Liberton Cropley, 1983; East Stirling, July 1987

Signed by caretaker manager Alex Rennie, who remembered Paul as a nippy winger from his spell alongside him at Tannadice, O'Brien made his debut aged 18 and scored in a 2–0 win. His only other competitive goal was a sliding stab shot against Airdrie on Ne'er Day 1981. Thereafter, Paul managed a short run in the side but failed to maintain his early promise. After a mere handful of appearances in 1981–82 he joined St Johnstone where he made five starts and 13 substitute appearances in two seasons. He returned to the amateur ranks for four years before returning with East Stirling in 1987.

DEREK O'CONNOR
Forward

BORN: Edinburgh, 8 January 1955

HEIGHT: 5' 11"   **WEIGHT:** 11st 7lb (1978)

COMPETITIVE DEBUT: v Aberdeen, 21 October 1978 (PL) (A), 2–1 (scored)

CAREER: Edinburgh Albion; East Fife, 1973; St Johnstone, Oct 1976; **Hearts, Oct 1978** (£25,000); Dunfermline, Jan 1985 (free transfer); Brechin City, Mar 1985; Berwick Rangers, 1986; Broxburn Athletic, 1988; Penicuik Athletic, 1989; retired c.1990

HONOURS: Division I winner 1979–80 (Hearts); r-up 1982–83 (Hearts)

Hearts were attracted by Derek's fine goalscoring rate with St Johnstone, where he managed 24 strikes in 60 appearances. He was a brave, unselfish worker who could head the ball and shoot with considerable power. Derek scored on his Hearts debut at Pittodrie with his first touch of the ball, the first of many fine goals for the club. One of his favourite games was against Rangers in February 1979 when he scored two cracking goals in a 3–2 win at a time when attendance figures were low as a result of a boycott. O'Connor's commitment was never in doubt and he felt genuine sorrow at relegation. He decided to turn part-time in 1981 because of persistent knee trouble, and loan spells later took him to Berwick and Meadowbank. He returned to Tynecastle and later hit a memorable winning goal at Easter Road in August 1984 which prompted the T-shirt heading 'Frankie says Hibs 1 Hearts 2!' Derek celebrated that goal in sheer ecstasy. He took further pleasure from squad involvement as Hearts faced Paris St Germain in the UEFA Cup. A wholehearted Hearts fan, Derek was a player who gave the club his very best during a trying period in its history.

EDDIE O'DONNELL

Outside-right

BORN: Falkirk, 4 March 1947

HEIGHT: 5′ 5″   WEIGHT: 10st 1lb (1965)

COMPETITIVE DEBUT: v Dundee United, 6 November 1965 (Lge) (A), 2–2

CAREER: Falkirk; **Hearts, 1965**; St Johnstone, Aug 1966 (free transfer); Brechin City, Aug 1967 (free transfer)

Eddie O'Donnell was a small but sturdily built winger who joined Hearts after being rejected by Falkirk. His first appearance came in the summer of 1965 in the high-scoring offside trial match against Kilmarnock. Eddie scored in the 8–2 win. He played a mere handful of games the following season, never quite reaching a high enough standard to compete with Hamilton, Jensen or Traynor.

DES O'SULLIVAN

Forward

BORN: Haddington, 12 February 1961

HEIGHT: 5′ 11″   WEIGHT: 10st 12lb (1979)

COMPETITIVE DEBUT: v Morton, 7 May 1979 (PL) (H), 0–1

CAREER: Celtic, 1975; Tranent Juniors, 1977; **Hearts, Jul 1978**; Stirling Albion, Aug 1980 (free transfer); Ormiston Primrose, 1982; Newtongrange, 1984

Des made most of his appearances as a substitute – in fact he scored his only goal in a match which he had begun on the substitutes bench. His magic moment came against Dumbarton on

8 December 1979. He replaced Derek O'Connor with 15 minutes to go and hit a terrific winner with only seconds remaining. His raging half-volley from 20 yards fairly whizzed into the net. He started several games thereafter but a managerial change in January 1980 was bad news for Des. Bobby Moncur clearly didn't look on Des as part of his plans and he was freed in May 1980.

PETER OLIVER
Full-back

BORN: Cowdenbeath, 18 August 1948

HEIGHT: 5' 10"   WEIGHT: 11st 7lb (1969)

COMPETITIVE DEBUT: v Airdrie, 3 September 1969 (Lge) (A), 2–1

CAREER: Beath High School; Lochore Welfare; **Hearts, Sept 1965**; York City, May 1974 (free transfer); Huddersfield Town, May 1976

HONOURS: 1 Scotland U-23 cap

Peter starred as a centre-forward with Hill o' Beath High School and represented the Dunfermline District Schools XI. A studious academic, he had the honour of being school dux. He joined Hearts from prolific Fife nursery side Lochore and progressed through the ranks to establish himself in 1969–70. Peter combined football with work in an Edinburgh insurance office and was known to like playing the stockmarket. The Hearts fans warmed to his enterprising style of play until a horrendous knee ligament injury at Airdrie in January 1971 seriously threatened his career. He made several comeback attempts in following seasons, but failed to maintain form or display his old flair. Increased competition for full-back positions didn't help and it was a sad day when Bobby Seith handed Peter a free transfer.

DONALD PARK
Midfield

BORN: Inverness, 19 July 1953

HEIGHT: 5' 6"   WEIGHT: 10st 1lb (1977)

COMPETITIVE DEBUT: v Arbroath, 28 October 1972 (Lge) (H), 3–0 (scored)

CAREER: Caol School; Lochaber High School; Inverness Caley; **Hearts, July 1972**; Partick Thistle, Sept 1978 (swap deal); **Hearts, May 1983**; Brechin City, July 1985 (free transfer); Meadowbank Thistle, Feb 1986; Meadowbank manager, 1992–Dec 1993; Arbroath manager, Apr 1994; Hibernian coach, July 1994

HONOURS: Scottish Cup r-up 1975–76 (Hearts)

The wee Highlander made a goalscoring debut and quickly found a niche at outside-right in 1972–73. Kenny Aird's arrival brought stiff competition for Parkie and he had to demonstrate his versatility to remain in contention for a first-team place. He settled into the midfield where his busy, all-action style seemed best suited. Donald accumulated a fair number of substitute appearances and even played at left-back in one game against Celtic. He scored many valuable goals and was always guaranteed to give 100 per cent effort. He was never an automatic choice during the roller-coaster years of the late 1970s, but it was one of the club's most shameful decisions that took him to Partick. He was a thorn in Hearts' flesh any time we faced Thistle thereafter, and it was a popular decision by Alex MacDonald to bring Park back to Hearts in 1983. He was a different player five years on. He was more laid-back in his approach and gone were his boyish looks, but he helped Hearts achieve Premier League consolidation.

He later managed Meadowbank Thistle but quit in December 1993 to devote more time to his hotel business interests in Edinburgh.

BOBBY PARKER
Full-back

BORN: Riccarton

HEIGHT: 5' 11"   WEIGHT: 11st 8lb (1952)

COMPETITIVE DEBUT: v Airdrie, 16 August 1947 (LC) (A), 2–3

CAREER: Broxburn High School; Edinburgh Waverley; Bathgate Thistle; Partick Thistle, Aug 1942; **Hearts, April 1947**; retired in 1958; **Hearts Reserve XI coach for short spell in early '60s; Hearts director, 1970; Hearts chairman, 1974–80; director, 1980–93**

HONOURS: 1 Scotland B cap; Scottish League Cup winner 1954–55 (Hearts); Scottish Summer Cup winner 1944–45 (Partick)

Bobby worked as a railwayman and served his time as an electrician. He signed for Hearts in an exchange deal which took Jimmy Walker to Partick. Originally a centre-half or wing-half he later made the right-back position his own. Parker was famed for his crunching tackles and powerful penalty-kick routine – it was jokingly remarked that keepers deliberately dived the wrong way to avoid his G-force kicks. He was an accomplished defensive organiser and gave orders in such a way that his colleagues knew in no uncertain terms what was expected. Such was his ability to motivate, he captained the side for many seasons. He rarely missed games and it was a blow when injury ruled him out of the 1956 Cup final. He made a comeback in 1956–57 but a recurrence restricted him to only four games in the triumphant 1957–58 season. Bobby decided to retire but has since helped Hearts for many years as a coach, scout, club chairman and director, in addition to his business interests.

IAN PATERSON

Forward

BORN: Cardenden, 22 August 1956

HEIGHT: 5′ 11″ **WEIGHT:** 11st 1lb (1977)

COMPETITIVE DEBUT: v Arbroath, 8 April 1978 (Div. I) (H), 3–2 (came on as substitute)

CAREER: Kirkcaldy YM; **Hearts, 1976**; Brechin City, May 1979 (free transfer); Cowdenbeath, 1983; Falkirk, 1985; Montrose, 1986; Brechin City, 1987

Tall, long-striding forward who was given little chance to stake his claim for first-team football at Hearts, playing almost every game as a substitute and making no impact in his brief appearances. Following his free transfer, Ian carved out a career in the lower leagues of Scottish senior football.

DANNY PATON

Forward

BORN: West Calder, 27 January 1936

HEIGHT: 5′ 9″ **WEIGHT:** 11st 2lb (1963)

COMPETITIVE DEBUT: v Partick Thistle, 11 November 1957 (Lge) (A), 3–1

CAREER: Woodmuir Colliery FC; Newtongrange Star, 1956; **Hearts, May 1957**; Yeovil Town, 1959–61 (on loan); Oxford United, Apr 1964 (free transfer); Bedford Town; Cambridge City; Washington Diplomats (USA), *c*.1970; retired in 1972

HONOURS: Scottish League Cup winner 1962–63 (Hearts)

Danny's greatest thrill in football was signing for Hearts in 1957. He made a modest contribution as a first-team fringe player in 1957–58 and 1958–59. His next two years were spent as a guest player with Yeovil as he underwent his compulsory National Service. He returned to Tynecastle in August 1961 and set about winning a first-team place.

Danny's biggest individual success in the eyes of the Hearts supporters was a match at Easter Road. On 8 September 1962 the Hibees were taken apart 4–0 with chief executioner Danny smashing home a glorious hat-trick, his only treble for Hearts. Not surprisingly, he later recalled this game as his fondest memory with the Jam Tarts.

Cartilage trouble spelt the end of his Tynecastle career. He was freed at his own request in April 1964 but managed to recover sufficiently to play on with other teams until the age of 36.

Goalkeeper

BORN: Glasgow, 1928

HEIGHT: 5′ 11″   WEIGHT: 11st 2lb (1947)

COMPETITIVE DEBUT: v Clyde, 13 September 1947 (LC) (A), 2–5

CAREER: Yoker Athletic Juniors; **Hearts, June 1947**; Dumbarton, May 1948 (free transfer)

George came into the first team to cover for the injured Jimmy Brown, and his seven games were something of a nightmare. He played in a winning team just once (thankfully against Hibs) and lost 20 goals in those seven games. The Hearts programme described him as 'A quiet, modest chap with a fine reach'. A free transfer in May 1948 took him to Boghead Park and in his first season there he faced his former colleagues in a Scottish Cup third-round tie. Hearts easily won 3–0, but press reports talked about George's many heroic stops which saved the Sons from a complete thrashing.

Full-back

BORN: Rosewell, 12 April 1943

HEIGHT: 5′ 10″   WEIGHT: 11st 5lb (1966)

COMPETITIVE DEBUT: v Stirling Albion, 23 April 1966 (Lge) (H), 1–1

CAREER: Arniston Rangers; **Hearts, May 1964**; Lincoln City, April 1967 (free transfer)

George was employed as a guillotine operator before joining Hearts aged 21. It was felt that he could add some weight and strength to the defence and he was introduced at the end of season 1965–66. He followed his debut with a run of ten games from September to November 1966 and it looked like he might become a permanent fixture. With additional quality full-backs Shevlane, Holt, Mann and Polland still on the books, however, George was soon left out. He played two further games in March 1967, but at a time of rapid turnover in personnel George was one of many given a free transfer. He joined Lincoln and made 223 League appearances, scoring 15 goals. He left Lincoln in 1973.

STEVE PENNEY

Forward

BORN: Ballymena, 16 January 1964

HEIGHT: 5′ 6″   **WEIGHT:** 10st 6lb (1991)

COMPETITIVE DEBUT: v St Johnstone, 24 August 1991 (PL) (A), 1–0 (came on as substitute)

CAREER: Ballymena United, 1981; Brighton, Nov 1983; **Hearts, July 1991** (free transfer); freed in May 1992; retired through injury in Feb 1994

HONOURS: 17 full Northern Ireland caps

Steve's career looked to be finished after a serious knee injury. Brighton freed him and Hearts hoped to revive his fortunes. Sadly for Penney it was not to be. He made only three full appearances in his single season but performed well in a wide right-wing role. He was quick and supplied good cross balls for the strikers to feed on. Fierce competition for front-line positions forced him to play in reserve football and he was released at the end of season 1991–92.

WILLIE PETTIGREW

Forward

BORN: Motherwell, 2 October 1953

HEIGHT: 5′ 11″   **WEIGHT:** 11st 1lb (1983)

COMPETITIVE DEBUT: v Clydebank, 19 September 1981 (Div. I) (H), 1–0

CAREER: Motherwell Schools; Bonkle Amateurs; Hibernian, 1970; East Kilbride Thistle, 1971; Motherwell, Feb 1972; Dundee United, Aug 1979 (£100,000); **Hearts, Sept 1981** (£120,000); Morton, Jan 1984 (£10,000); Hamilton Accies, 1985 (free transfer); released in May 1986

HONOURS: 5 full Scotland caps; 7 Scotland U-23 caps; Scotland Schoolboy and Junior international; 2 Scottish League caps; Scottish Division I winner 1983–84 (Morton); r-up 1982–83 (Hearts); Scottish Cup r-up 1980–81 (Dundee United); Scottish League Cup winner 1979–80, 1980–81 (Dundee United)

Willie joined Hibs as a teenager but turned junior after failing to make the grade at Easter Road. Motherwell 'rescued' him from East Kilbride and he formed a deadly partnership with Bobby Graham, the slim striker hitting the goal trail with devastating consistency. He displayed remarkable speed and sharpness in and around opposition penalty-boxes. Willie won international honours at all levels although he had to wait for domestic success. A move to Dundee United brought two consecutive League Cup medals.

Hearts paid a record fee to bring Willie to Tynecastle to improve their promotion push. Despite his sixteen League goals, including a hat-trick against Queen of the South and four against Clydebank, Hearts failed to win promotion. Pettigrew continued to score throughout 1982–83 but John Robertson emerged as a hot prospect and Willie began to fall from favour. Jimmy Bone's arrival all but ended his Hearts career. After one appearance in 1983–84, Hearts cut their losses and sold him to Morton.

JAMES PITHIE
Centre-half

BORN: Edinburgh, 1928

HEIGHT: 6'   WEIGHT: 12st 7lb (1946)

COMPETITIVE DEBUT: v Kilmarnock, 19 October 1946 (LC) (A), 0–2

CAREER: Chesser United; Hutcheson Vale; Newtongrange Star; **Hearts, July 1946**; freed in 1948

A strapping centre-half who made five competitive apearances in 1946–47 as a deputy for Bobby Baxter, Jimmy's most notable performances came on the winning side at Ibrox and against Aberdeen at home towards the end of the season. He was hospitalised in Bangour in December 1947 and was later released in 1948. His brother David had a short spell with Hibs at the same time Jimmy was with Hearts. He was a genial personality who apparently liked to sing!

WILLIE POLLAND
Defender

BORN: Armadale, 28 July 1934

HEIGHT: 5' 10"   WEIGHT: 12st 10lb (1964)

COMPETITIVE DEBUT: v Dundee, 29 April 1961 (Lge) (H), 2–1

CAREER: Wallhouse Rose; Raith Rovers, 1955; **Hearts, Apr 1961** (£7,500); Raith Rovers, March 1967 (free transfer); released in Apr 1970

HONOURS: Scottish League r-up 1964–65 (Hearts); Scottish League Cup winner 1962–63 (Hearts); r-up 1961–62 (Hearts)

A steadfast, reliable defender who could play at full-back or in central-defence, Willie served

Hearts well over his six years and starred in many European matches. Despite a willingness to join the attack he managed only one competitive goal, against Dunfermline in 1965. As he approached veteran status Hearts granted him a free transfer. He returned to former club, Raith, where he ended his senior career, working in later years as a publican in Armadale.

BOBBY PRENTICE

Outside-left

BORN: Douglaswater, 27 September 1953

HEIGHT: 5' 9"   WEIGHT: 11st 7lb (1976)

COMPETITIVE DEBUT: v Dundee, 18 August 1973 (LC) (A), 1–2

CAREER: Douglaswater Schools; Thornton BC U-16; Edina Hibs; Dundee, 1971; Newtongrange Star; Celtic, 1972; **Hearts, July 1973** (free transfer); Toronto Blizzard, Apr 1979 (£8,000)

HONOURS: 4 Scotland U-23 caps; Scotland Junior international; 1 Scottish League cap; Division I r-up 1977–78 (Hearts); Scottish Cup r-up 1975–76 (Hearts)

Bobby Prentice was a dazzling, flamboyant, individualist winger. A master of the tease, he could turn defenders inside out with just a slight sway of his hips. He supplied crosses of the highest order which the strikers thrived on. Prentice rated his first goal for Hearts as his most memorable. It came in a 3–0 win at Ibrox in September 1973. His form soon won him U-23 international honours.

Bobby was prone to inconsistent form and his confidence suffered when he was out of the first team. The arrival of Willie Ormond as boss was bad news for Prentice. He never saw eye to eye with the man who had earlier selected him for four U-23 caps and, as the situation steadily deteriorated, Bobby was offloaded to Toronto in 1979.

Prentice left with many happy memories. He was proud to play for Hearts and the often unpredictable, unorthodox style he had endeared him to the fans, who were sad to see a great favourite move on.

BORN: Shotts

HEIGHT: 5′ 9″   WEIGHT: 11st 10lb (1949)

Half-back

COMPETITIVE DEBUT: v Motherwell, 4 March 1950 (Lge) (A), 3–2

CAREER: Carluke Rovers; **Hearts, May 1944;** Rangers, March 1951 (£7,000); Falkirk, Sept 1956 (£2,500); Dumbarton, Jul 1959 (free transfer); Arbroath manager; Clyde manager; Scotland interim manager, 1966; Falkirk manager, Dec 1966; Dundee manager, 1967; Falkirk manager Aug 1973–Aug 1975

HONOURS: 1 Scottish League cap; Scottish League winner 1952–53 (Rangers); Scottish Cup winner 1956–57 (Falkirk)

John experienced weight problems when demobbed from National Service and had to train hard before being considered for a first-team debut. He turned out to be a dominant left-half who displayed fine defensive qualities. He was constructive going forward using a fine turn of pace to good effect. He was reckoned to carry one of the hardest shots in Scottish football in either foot!

Prentice tabled a transfer request in February 1951 because he was unable to maintain a permanent first-team place. An offer from Stirling was rejected before Rangers secured his services. He came back to haunt Hearts two years later when he scored the winning goal in the 1953 Scottish Cup semi-final. He later captained Falkirk to a Scottish Cup win before moving into management later in life.

BORN: Edinburgh, 16 August 1969

HEIGHT: 5′ 10″   WEIGHT: 10st 1lb (1992)

Winger

COMPETITIVE DEBUT: v St Johnstone, 3 October 1992 (PL) (H), 1–1

CAREER: Hutcheson Vale BC; Dundee United, Aug 1985; **Hearts, Oct 1992** (Hearts received £215,000 and Preston for Scott Crabbe); Dunfermline, Aug 1993 (swap for Scott Leitch); St Johnstone, Mar 1994 (swap deal)

HONOURS: Scotland U-18 international

Allan arrived at Tynecastle after failing to establish himself with Dundee United, and the cynics were critical before he even made his debut.

Preston had a difficult task as comparisons would be made with Scott Crabbe, who had moved to Tannadice. To be fair, they were totally different players, but it was evident early on that Allan lacked the essential strength and hardness required for the Premier League.

He scored four goals in his 24 appearances. Two were blistering 25-yard shots in League matches against Celtic and Partick. The others were in Scottish Cup ties against Falkirk and Rangers. The last was a superb flying header which gave Hearts a semi-final lead only for the Gers to overturn the score.

Allan had an unusually deceptive running style and was capable of providing accurate cross balls. A downside to his game was a tendency to become noticeably absent from the play. His departure was hastened after the sacking of Joe Jordan. The new manager, Sandy Clark, soon made it clear that Allan would not be part of his plans. Omitted from Clark's teams as 1992–93 drew to a close, he was then left behind as Hearts toured Germany in late July 1993. Just before the new season started, Dunfermline negotiated his transfer.

BOBBY RANKIN
Inside-forward

HEIGHT: 6'   **WEIGHT:** 12st 6lb (1959)

COMPETITIVE DEBUT: v St Mirren, 9 March 1959 (Lge) (H), 4–0 (scored 2)

CAREER: Cumnock Juniors; Queen of the South, 1955; **Hearts, Mar 1959** (£4,000); Third Lanark, Nov 1959 (£5,000); Queen of the South, 1960; Stenhousemuir

A tall, strapping inside-forward who made a big impact on his arrival at Tynecastle, Bobby Rankin scored 13 goals in his first eight games at the end of season 1958–59. His appearances on the 1959 Australian tour were restricted due to injury, and he missed the start of the new season with a recurrent stomach ailment. Bobby made a brief comeback in reserve football before his surprise transfer to Third Lanark. It was alleged that he was unable to adhere to Tommy Walker's strict disciplinary code and this hastened his departure. How unfortunate that he was unable to continue in the manner he had first exploded onto the Tynecastle scene.

Centre-half

BORN: Edinburgh, 19 August 1967

HEIGHT: 5' 11"   WEIGHT: 12st (1987)

COMPETITIVE DEBUT: v St Mirren, 9 November 1983 (LC) (H), 3–1 (came on as substitute)

CAREER: Tynecastle Boys Club; **Hearts, Sept 1983**; Cowdenbeath, 1988 (free transfer)

HONOURS: Scotland Youth international

As a promising youngster, Alan made two substitute appearances aged 16 in League Cup sectional ties. He had little time to shine during his short periods on the park and never realised his potential. He made only four more appearances, in East of Scotland Shield ties, which, although classed as first-team games, were actually reserve matches.

Inside-forward

BORN: Duns, 7 January 1952

HEIGHT: 5' 11"   WEIGHT: 12st (1972)

COMPETITIVE DEBUT: v Aberdeen, 27 November 1971 (Lge) (A), 3–2

CAREER: Duns Amateurs; Arniston Rangers; Rangers, 1969; **Hearts, 1971** (free transfer); Berwick Rangers, May 1973 (free transfer); emigrated to South Africa; Queen of the South, c.1976; Stenhousemuir, c.1977

HONOURS: Scotland U-16 rugby international

Derek's early sporting experience was as a rugby stand-off at Berwickshire High School. He progressed through amateur and junior football ranks before obtaining a dream ticket to Ibrox. After two years with the Gers, Derek was surprisingly freed. Hearts quickly offered him terms and, after impressing in the reserves, he appeared as a sub in a first-team friendly. The youngster played well and was given an extended run. Renton scored several important goals and it looked like Hearts had pulled off a masterstroke with his signing. However, matters turned sour for Derek in 1972–73 as the team struggled. The goals and appearances dried up and he was released in May 1973.

CHRIS ROBERTSON
Forward

BORN: Edinburgh, 25 December 1957

HEIGHT: 5' 11" **WEIGHT:** 12st 1lb (1981)

COMPETITIVE DEBUT: v Airdrie, 30 July 1980 (ASC) (A), 0–3

CAREER: Portobello School; Rangers, 1974; **Hearts, July 1980** (free transfer); Meadowbank, Oct 1983; Berwick Rangers, Oct 1986; Bonnyrigg Rose Juniors, 1987; assistant manager Newtongrange Star, Jan 1995

HONOURS: Scottish Cup r-up 1976–77 (Rangers)

The older brother of Hearts star John Robertson, Chris joined Rangers straight from school. He appeared infrequently at Ibrox due to strong competition for places in Rangers' strikeforce and Chris was delighted to join his boyhood favourites, Hearts. He scored several goals in his first season, notably a hat-trick against Montrose in a League Cup tie which he managed in only 15 minutes. Injury forced him out of action midway through 1980–81, but he returned to good form the following season. A strong and direct forward, Chris knew the road to goal. Unfortunately, injury would continue to blight his Hearts career. He appeared only once alongside his younger brother, when John came on to make his debut as a substitute. Hearts defeated Queen of the South 4–1 that February evening in 1982. A combination of reasons meant Chris failing to play in any first-team games in his last 18 months at Tynecastle. He moved to city neighbours Meadowbank before turning junior in his last few seasons. Chris later assisted East of Scotland side Craigroyston in the 1990s.

GEORGE ROBERTSON
Centre-half

HEIGHT: 6' **WEIGHT:** 12st 13lb (1959)

COMPETITIVE DEBUT: v Rangers, 13 December 1958 (Lge) (A), 0–5

CAREER: Tranent Juniors; **Hearts, June 1958**; Morton, Apr 1961 (free transfer)

Hearts would have struggled to pick a more difficult debut for big George. He was thrown into the Ibrox cauldron at a time when Rangers were Hearts' greatest opponents. Some players rise to this sort of challenge but George had a nightmare as Rangers handed out a crushing 5–0 defeat. It proved to be Robertson's only competitive match. He played two more recognised first-team games. One was a Canadian tour match in 1960 and the other was at Chirnside just before his release in April 1961.

BORN: Edinburgh, 2 October 1964

HEIGHT: 5' 7"   WEIGHT: 11st 2lb (1991)

COMPETITIVE DEBUT: v Queen of the South, 17 February 1982 (Div. I) (H), 4–1 (came on as substitute)

CAREER: Salvesen Boys Club; Edina Hibs; **Hearts, Jan 1981**; Newcastle United, Apr 1988 (£625,000); **Hearts, Dec 1988** (£750,000)

HONOURS: 13 full Scotland caps; Scotland Schoolboy, Youth and U-21 international; Premier League r-up 1985–86, 1987–88, 1989–90, 1991–92 (Hearts); Scottish Cup r-up 1985–86 (Hearts); Tennents Sixes winner 1984–85, 1990–91 (Hearts); Premier League top goalscorer 1989–90; SPFA Young Player of the Year 1983–84

JOHN ROBERTSON
Forward

A supreme striker and the leading goalscorer on Hearts' books, John is often described as a penalty-box player. He isn't keen on this opinion as he does contribute a fair amount in open play. He made his debut alongside his brother Chris in 1982 and in the following season quickly came to prominence, hitting 21 goals in 23 games – including three hat-tricks. A star was born and Robbo soon became a household name through his exploits on the Premier League stage. One of his best-remembered goals came at Tannadice in April 1986. A loose ball fell to him 25 yards out. John hit a left-foot shot of stunning power and the ball screamed into the keeper's top right-hand corner. It was a magnificent strike.

His best season was 1987–88 with a total of 27 League goals, including his 100th in the League, against Dunfermline. His form attracted English eyes and a disagreement over a new contract eventually led to Robbo joining Newcastle for a record fee. Injury problems, followed by a management change, meant a quick return to Tynecastle. Robbo has continued to score ever since and finally won full international honours in 1991, scoring in his games against Romania and Switzerland.

John is also Hearts' record scorer in Edinburgh derbies against Hibs. He has broken Hibee hearts in every season since 1983–84 and his tally is 20 goals in this fixture. He now has his sights on the League goalscoring records of some famous past players. Willie Bauld's 183 and Tommy Walker's 184 are certainly attainable. Who knows if he might overtake Jimmy Wardhaugh's 206? That would be some achievement.

Season 1993–94 was a difficult one for Robbo. He was dropped for the first time ever and was on the subs bench too often for his liking. The one point to bear in mind with a player such as Robertson is that in some games he can be conspicuous by his absence from the action for 88 minutes. But in those other two minutes he can win the game!

MALCOLM ROBERTSON
Winger

BORN: Edinburgh, 7 July 1951

HEIGHT: 5' 8"   WEIGHT: 10st 4lb (1977)

COMPETITIVE DEBUT: v Aberdeen, 19 March 1977 (PL) (H), 1–1

CAREER: Penicuik Athletic; Raith Rovers, *c.*1971; Ayr United, 1975 (£12,000); **Hearts, Mar 1977** (£25,000); Toronto Blizzard, Jan 1981 (free transfer); Dundee United (one game), 1981; Hibs, 1982; Maltese football, 1984

HONOURS: Division I winner 1979–80 (Hearts); r-up 1977–78 (Hearts)

A nippy winger equally at home on the left or right, Malky joined Hearts at a troubled time when the spectre of relegation was looming. His fifth appearance for the club was against his former side, Ayr United. In an emotion-charged match, Hearts lost 2–1 and Malky was sent off after losing his cool in an exchange with Jim McSherry. The result all but doomed Hearts to Division I. But Robertson settled with Hearts and his skilful wing play and goals helped the club secure promotion in 1977–78 and 1979–80 as Hearts moved between the divisions.

Early in season 1980–81, Malky had a fall-out with manager Bobby Moncur and was dropped from the side. Hearts were heading for relegation for a third time in five years when Robertson joined Toronto as a free agent.

BOBBY ROBINSON
Midfield

BORN: Edinburgh, 10 November 1950

HEIGHT: 5' 9"   WEIGHT: 10st 10lb (1979)

COMPETITIVE DEBUT: v Arbroath, 11 August 1979 (Div. I) (A), 2–1

CAREER: Newtongrange Star; Falkirk; Dundee, 1971 (free transfer); Dundee United, Aug 1977 (£20,000); **Hearts, July 1979** (£20,000); Raith Rovers, May 1981 (free transfer); retired in Apr 1983

HONOURS: 4 full Scotland caps; 1 Scotland U-23 cap; Division I winner 1979–80 (Hearts); Scottish League Cup winner 1973–74 (Dundee)

Nicknamed 'Trigger' in his Dens Park days, Bobby had bags of speed. He gained domestic and international honours before crossing the road to join United. Hearts had attempted to sign him in March 1977 but the move broke down and he chose to move to Tannadice. Willie Ormond had long admired Bobby's abilities and had chosen him for Scotland during his years as the national manager. When his availability was made known in 1979, Ormond moved to sign the experienced operator. He joined on a part-time basis combining football with teacher-training studies. Bobby performed well in his first season as Hearts won the Division I Championship. However, his form dipped the following term and, after relegation, he joined Raith for two years, retiring at the age of 32.

HEIGHT: 6'   WEIGHT: 12st 7lb (1948)

COMPETITIVE DEBUT: v Hibernian, 9 August 1947 (LC) (A), 2–1

JAMES RODGER
Centre-half

CAREER: Larkhall Thistle; Whitburn Juniors; **Hearts, Jul 1947**; Stirling Albion, Feb 1950 (on loan); Third Lanark, Aug 1950 (free transfer); Airdrie, *c.*1952

James Rodger was a towering centre-half who performed to a high standard. He never let himself or the team down and cleared up danger with headed clearances or the hefty boot. He constantly battled with Bobby Dougan and Bobby Parker for a place and managed a good run of games in 1947–48. His competitors eventually forced him into permanent reserve football and Jimmy became unsettled. Although a loan period to Stirling helped ease his frustration, when it became clear that Bobby Dougan was recognised as the main centre-half, James was happy to move on in August 1950.

JIM RODGER
Outside-right

BORN: Cleland, 15 September 1933

HEIGHT: 5' 10"   WEIGHT: 12st 1lb (1963)

COMPETITIVE DEBUT: v Third Lanark, 7 February 1962 (Lge) (H), 2–1

CAREER: Rangers, 1953; St Mirren, May 1955 (free transfer); Newport, Feb 1957 (on loan); **Hearts, Feb 1962**; Queen of the South, Jan 1964

HONOURS: Scottish Cup winner 1958–59; Scottish League Cup r-up 1955–56 (St Mirren)

After being rejected by Rangers, Jim went on to enjoy success with St Mirren and a nominal fee brought him to Tynecastle in 1962. He was tall for a winger but his ungainly style was effective all the same. Jim lost his place early in season 1962–63 when Willie Wallace moved to outside-right to accommodate Willie Hamilton at inside-forward. When the latter picked up an injury Jim was recalled from the fringes of the first team. He held his place with some enterprising wing play which included a four-goal haul in an 8–2 win over a visiting SK Brann XI. The long winter shut-down of 1962–63 ended his run in the side. Rodger played five more League matches as the season dragged into April and May before a broken ankle intervened. He faded from the first-team scene in 1963–64 and moved to Queen of the South. In later years he became a headmaster in the Western Isles.

PAUL RODGER
Defender

BORN: Edinburgh, 2 September 1958

HEIGHT: 5' 11"   WEIGHT: 12st 8lb (1977)

COMPETITIVE DEBUT: v Dundee United, 20 April 1977 (PL) (A), 2–1

CAREER: Tartan Boys Club; **Hearts, 1976**; Alloa Athletic, Jul 1979 (free transfer); Happy Valley FC; Dunfermline, 1984; Bonnyrigg Rose, 1985; Arbroath, 1986

A young defender who was criticised for his over-physical play, Paul's appearances were littered with field indiscretions. He made his debut at a time when Hearts were doomed to relegation and, though he looked a reasonable prospect, failed to become an automatic first choice. He later toured the senior and junior circuits.

BORN: Edinburgh, 18 May 1942

HEIGHT: 5' 9"   WEIGHT: 9st 10lb (1960)

COMPETITIVE DEBUT: v Raith Rovers, 1 April 1961 (Lge) (A), 1–1

CAREER: Tynecastle Athletic; Musselburgh Athletic; **Hearts, Nov 1960**; Shrewsbury Town, May 1963 (free transfer); Brentford, Mar 1966; Cambridge United, Oct 1972

Forward

Bobby hailed from the Whitson district of Edinburgh. He broke into the first team towards the end of season 1960–61 and the eager young forward impressed with a direct attacking style. The following season he appeared 22 times on either wing or at centre-forward and played in such diverse places as Belgium in a Fairs Cup tie and the backwaters of Innerleithen against the local Vale on Scottish Cup business. He looked to have the makings of a very good player. Season 1962–63 saw him assist Hearts to the League Cup final with a good show against St Johnstone in the semi-final. He unfortunately missed out on a winners' medal when Danny Paton took over for the final. Ross made only a couple of appearances thereafter and was freed in May 1963. He went on to score 84 goals in 454 English League games, certainly proving to be a success in the lower divisions down south.

BORN: Keith, 23 October 1946

HEIGHT: 5' 10"   WEIGHT: 10st 3lb (1964)

COMPETITIVE DEBUT: v Partick Thistle, 29 August 1964 (LC) (H), 4–3

CAREER: Keith; Leicester City, 1961; **Hearts, Dec 1962** (free transfer); released in Apr 1968

Full-back

Rutherford returned to Scotland as a 16-year-old after a short, unhappy spell at Leicester. He played most of his Hearts games in the reserves and made only six first-team appearances. Press reports were critical of Rutherford and it was often said that he looked uneasy at left-back, especially when put under pressure. He was allowed to leave when it became obvious he would not make the grade.

EDDIE RUTHERFORD

Winger

BORN: Glasgow, 8 February 1921

HEIGHT: 5′ 9″ **WEIGHT:** 10st 8lb (1952)

COMPETITIVE DEBUT: v Queen of the South, 10 November 1951 (Lge) (H), 4–3

CAREER: Govan High School; Battlefield Amateurs; Mossvale YMCA; Rangers, Aug 1941; **Hearts, Nov 1951** (swap for Colin Liddell); Raith Rovers, Jan 1955 (£500); Hamilton Accies, June 1955; retired in 1956

HONOURS: 1 full Scotland cap; 1 Scottish League cap; Scottish League winner 1948–49, 1949–50 (Rangers); Scottish Cup winner 1947–48, 1948–49, 1949–50 (Rangers); Scottish League Cup winner 1946–47, 1948–49 (Rangers); r-up 1951–52 (Rangers)

Eddie was employed as a commercial traveller in the Glasgow area for a firm of chemists. He joined Rangers in the early years of the war and won full domestic and international honours. He had reached the veteran stage when Hearts negotiated his transfer and starred in his first two seasons at Tynecastle as a foraging winger who could use either foot to devastating effect. A series of knee injuries and a cartilage operation in 1954 took their toll later on. Eddie struggled to maintain the standard of play Hearts demanded and he was eventually sold in 1955.

FRANK SANDEMAN

Inside-forward

BORN: Dundee, 28 August 1936

HEIGHT: 5′ 9″ **WEIGHT:** 10st 11lb (1964)

COMPETITIVE DEBUT: v Dundee United, 14 March 1964 (Lge) (H), 0–4

CAREER: Montrose; East Stirling, 1962; **Hearts, Mar 1964**; Brechin City, May 1965 (free transfer)

HONOURS: Division II r-up 1962–63 (East Stirling

Frank stood out in the East Stirling side which won promotion in 1962–63. He held them together in many games when a complete thrashing looked odds on. Hearts moved to sign him as they felt his ability to battle could be useful. It didn't take long to detect his shortcomings, though. He was considered too slow and this was painfully exposed in a Hearts team with plenty of thrust. Frank made only eight competitive appearances before being offloaded to Brechin.

BORN: Edinburgh, 22 June 1965

Versatile

HEIGHT: 5' 10"   WEIGHT: 10st 10lb (1990)

COMPETITIVE DEBUT: v Rangers, 27 April 1985 (PL) (A), 1–3 (came on as substitute)

CAREER: St Bernard's; Edinburgh Emmet; **Hearts, Aug 1983**; Airdrie, July 1991 (£100,000)

HONOURS: Premier League r-up 1989–90 (Hearts); Tennents Sixes winner 1990–91 (Hearts); B&Q Cup winner 1994–95 (Airdrie); Scottish Cup r-up 1994–95 (Airdrie)

A product of Hearts' youth policy, Jimmy broke through at the end of season 1984–85. A lifelong Hearts supporter, he was very versatile, performing capably at full-back, sweeper, midfield or in a man-marking role. He was basically a reserve for seven years, though, only managing odd appearances or short runs in the side.

One memorable match was the excellent marking job he carried out against Herbert Prohaska of Austria Vienna in a 1988 UEFA Cup tie, a match which culminated in a marvellous 1–0 victory for Hearts in the famous Prater Stadium. Equally memorable was a scorching 25-yard drive which bulged the Aberdeen net at Pittodrie in February 1990. His celebration with Scott Crabbe was straight out of the American football style of celebrating a touchdown.

Jimmy finally held down a place in the team under Joe Jordan, operating in the sweeper position. He later experienced difficulties in agreeing a new contract. Not long after he signed a suitable deal, Airdrie offered £100,000 for his services and he became a Diamond. He later skippered the club.

BORN: Edinburgh, 30 November 1966

Midfield

HEIGHT: 5' 8"   WEIGHT: 10st 7lb (1983)

COMPETITIVE DEBUT: v Clydebank, 30 November 1983 (LC) (A), 3–0 (came on as substitute)

CAREER: Salvesen Boys Club; **Hearts, Sept 1983**; East Fife, Oct 1987 (free transfer); Cowdenbeath, Mar 1989

A small, fair-haired midfielder whose only brief appearance was as a substitute for Alex MacDonald in an unimportant League Cup tie against Clydebank. Colin was confined to reserve-team football though may have made more of an impact had a very serious back injury not held him back.

DAVID SCOTT

Forward

HEIGHT: 5' 9"   WEIGHT: 11st 4lb (1979)

COMPETITIVE DEBUT: v Dundee United, 25 April 1979 (PL) (A), 1–2

CAREER: Tullibody Hearts; **Hearts, Jul 1978**; Alloa Athletic, May 1980 (free transfer); Meadowbank, 1982; Broxburn Athletic, 1985

The son of former Rangers star Alex Scott, David was drafted into first-team action at the age of only 16 and did well enough to earn a full-time professional contract in the summer of 1979. He was making good progress until breaking a bone in his foot in a reserve match. He never really pushed for a place once he recovered, and was freed in May 1980.

FRANK SHARP

Winger

BORN: Edinburgh, 28 May 1947

HEIGHT: 5' 7"   WEIGHT: 9st 7lb (1964)

COMPETITIVE DEBUT: v Partick Thistle, 31 August 1963 (Lge) (A), 2–2

CAREER: Tynecastle Athletic; **Hearts, 1962**; Carlisle United, Mar 1967; Cardiff City, Feb 1969; Barnsley, Aug 1970; Grimsby Town, Jul 1973; Port Vale, May 1974

Frank won a top-team debut aged 16 but the diminutive winger returned to the second string just as quickly. He played in a few friendlies the following season but had to wait until 1965–66 before making more competitive appearances. The pacy winger scored his only League goal, a 20-yard drive, against Stirling Albion at Annfield. Sharp moved to English football when it became obvious that his chances at Tynecastle were limited. He made 223 appearances with his English clubs, scoring 12 goals.

BORN: Edinburgh, 8 October 1951

HEIGHT: 5' 11"   WEIGHT: 11st 12lb (1979)   *Forward*

COMPETITIVE DEBUT: v Dundee, 10 January 1976 (PL) (A), 1–4 (scored)

CAREER: Parsons Green School; Edina Hibs; Albion Boys Club; Musselburgh Athletic, 1970; Dunfermline, 1971; **Hearts, Jan 1976** (£20,000); Arbroath, May 1980 (free transfer); retired in 1986

HONOURS: Division I winner 1979–80 (Hearts); Scottish Cup r-up 1975–76 (Hearts)

Graham came to prominence in senior circles as a consistent scorer with Dunfermline. He was deployed in a deeper role at Hearts, playing just behind the forwards or in the midfield. He revelled in conditions where the going was heavy and was very skilful for a big man with a large build. He scored Hearts' consolation goal in the 1976 Scottish Cup final, which Rangers won 3–1. He was a member of the relegated squad in 1977 but was unable to provide much assistance in 1977–78 or 1978–79. Niggling injuries – in particular a chipped ankle bone and achilles tendon trouble – hampered Shaw's career. The man dubbed 'Shuggie' by the fans recovered sufficiently to make an important contribution to Hearts' 1979–80 promotion challenge. At this time he also moved into a sports shop business venture along with colleague Jim Brown in the Hearts stronghold of Penicuik. Following the League title decider with Airdrie, Graham was released in May 1980 as manager Moncur made room for new signings.

BORN: Edinburgh, 6 May 1942

HEIGHT: 5' 9"   WEIGHT: 10st 10lb (1963)   *Full-back*

COMPETITIVE DEBUT: v St Mirren, 2 April 1963 (Lge) (A), 3–7

CAREER: St Peter's Primary; St Anthony's High School; Edina Hearts; Loanhead Mayflower; **Hearts, Nov 1960**; retired through injury in April 1967; Celtic, May 1967; Hibernian, May 1968; Morton, 1971 (free transfer); released in Apr 1973

HONOURS: 4 Scotland U-23 caps; Scotland Schoolboy international; 2 Scottish League caps; Scottish League r-up 1964–65 (Hearts); Scottish League Cup r-up 1968–69 (Hibernian)

An apprentice bookbinder, Chris signed for Hearts as an 18-year-old at the time of George Thomson's departure for Everton. He was understudy to Bobby Kirk and Davie Holt for two years before breaking into the League side. Chris quickly matured into a tough-tackling, no-nonsense full-back. He had a quick turn of pace and his assured, confident style led to his appointment as club captain in 1964, our youngest ever captain at that time, and was a driving force in the 1964–65 League campaign.

In 1966 Chris suffered a serious ankle injury which kept recurring. Specialist treatment failed to cure the problem and, on doctor's orders, Chris retired aged 24 rather than risk serious disablement. It came as something of a shock when he signed for Celtic just one month later and played on into his thirties! He later worked in the licensed trade, and now runs Shevlane's Bar in Springburn, Glasgow.

PETER SHIELDS
Full-back

BORN: Baillieston 14 August 1960

HEIGHT: 5′ 8″   **WEIGHT:** 10st 9lb (1981)

COMPETITIVE DEBUT: v Morton, 20 September 1980 (PL) (H), 0–1

CAREER: Celtic BC; Ipswich Town, 1977; **Hearts, Sept 1980** (£12,500); Partick Thistle, May 1984 (free transfer); Cowdenbeath, 1986; Cumnock Juniors, Aug 1986

A skilful, pacy left-back who supported the midfield and front line to good effect in his four-year spell with Hearts, Peter played well in his first two seasons and it was a team failure which brought relegation and missing out on promotion. Shields was at his best in 1982–83, his consistency one of the main reasons for a sound defensive record. Sadly, Peter missed the last few weeks of the successful promotion campaign, a fractured ankle in a Scottish Cup quarter-final against Celtic at Parkhead ending his season in agony. When he regained full fitness, George Cowie had taken over the left-back position. He found his chances of a return greatly restricted and only managed another seven games before his free transfer.

BORN: Barrhead, 13 October 1925

HEIGHT: 5′ 7″   WEIGHT: 10st 10lb (1948)

COMPETITIVE DEBUT: v Third Lanark, 17 August 1946 (Lge) (H), 4–1

CAREER: Arthurlie Juniors; **Hearts, Aug 1945**; Motherwell, Dec 1951 (£6,500 plus Charlie Cox); Gloucester City, 1957; Arthurlie Juniors coach, *c.*1960

HONOURS: Scotland Junior international; Scottish Division II winner 1953–54 (Motherwell); Scottish Cup winner 1951–52 (Motherwell)

TOMMY SLOAN
Outside-right

Small winger who supplied ammo to the Terrible Trio in their formative years. Sloan waited a year before making his debut but his dazzling brand of wing trickery soon made him an automatic choice. He performed to a high standard for the five seasons immediately after the war, scoring a good return of goals for a winger but sometimes suffering at the hands of a highly critical press brigade who seemed to hate wingers!

Tommy fell out of favour in November 1951 when Hearts signed veteran Rangers winger Eddie Rutherford. One month later he joined Motherwell and enjoyed more success in Lanarkshire. In later years he was employed as a maintenance engineer at Shanks Barrhead.

BORN: Edinburgh, 25 May 1924

HEIGHT: 5′ 9″   WEIGHT: 11st 6lb (1959)

COMPETITIVE DEBUT: v Kilmarnock, 22 August 1959 (LC) (H), 2–0

CAREER: Montrose South Esk School; Kirriemuir Juveniles; Roselea; Dundee North End; Hibernian, Apr 1941; **Hearts, Aug 1959** (free transfer); Dundee, Apr 1961 (free transfer); Drumcondra, Feb 1964; retired in 1964

HONOURS: 18 full Scotland caps; Scotland Schoolboy international; 10 Scottish League caps; Scottish League winner, 1947–48, 1950–51, 1951–52 (Hibs), 1959–60 (Hearts), 1961–62 (Dundee); Scottish Cup r-up 1946–47 (Hibs); Scottish League Cup winner 1959–60 (Hearts); Scottish Player of the Year 1951

GORDON SMITH
Right-winger

An elegant outside-right who graced Scottish football for 23 years, Gordon is unique in having obtained League Championship medals with his three senior clubs. His pace, ball control, shooting power and crossing ability were the main attributes his admirers marvelled at. He made his name with Hibs in an 18-year association but was handed a surprise free transfer in 1959 as a result of recurrent ankle injuries. Gordon paid for an operation to cure his problems and signed for Hearts. He was warmly welcomed despite his earlier allegiances.

Smith's first appearance in a reserve match drew an amazing 12,000 people to Tynecastle. He played superbly in his first season, winning his first major Cup medal in Hearts' 2–1 League Cup success against Third Lanark. In the League programme he missed only five games, scored 11 goals and made a telling contribution as Hearts clinched the title. Season 1960–61 soon took on a transitional look. Gordon was left out on several occasions in favour of younger men. A free transfer in April 1961 resulted in a move to Dundee, where he formed a potent striking partnership with young Alan Gilzean and completed a unique treble of Championship medals.

Gordon concluded his career in Ireland at the age of 40. He became a publican at the Right Wing in Edinburgh's Willowbrae Road before retiring to his North Berwick home in the mid-1980s.

GORDON SMITH

Forward

BORN: Haddington, 12 June 1959

HEIGHT: 5' 10"   WEIGHT: 11st 1lb (1976)

COMPETITIVE DEBUT: v Kilmarnock, 16 April 1977 (PL) (A), 2–2 (came on as substitute and scored)

CAREER: Musselburgh Windsor; **Hearts, 1976**; Berwick Rangers, Oct 1978 (free transfer); Falkirk, 1981; Meadowbank, 1982; served many junior clubs during the 1980s and 1990s as a player and manager

Signed initially as a part-timer, Gordon combined football with his painting apprenticeship. He broke into Hearts' first team in April 1977 and hit the headlines with two goals in his four appearances. Hearts were already relegated and youth was given a chance. Seventeen-year-old Smith impressed in a situation where no pressure was involved, and press reporters forecast a bright future for the player with a famous name.

Gordon started 1977–78 in the first-team picture but soon fell from favour. He returned to the action near the end of the season but didn't look the same player who had earlier shown such great promise. He appeared once as a substitute in 1978–79 before joining Berwick, remaining in senior football for several years before turning junior, where he also sampled management. He starred at several junior clubs and carried the unusual nickname of 'Pogo' around with him.

Goalkeeper

BORN: Douglaswater, 10 March 1956

HEIGHT: 6' 2"   WEIGHT: 12st (1990)

COMPETITIVE DEBUT: v Airdrie, 8 August 1981 (LC) (A), 1–0

CAREER: Frickley Athletic, 1976; Winterton Rangers, 1977; Leeds United, 1978 (£10,000); **Hearts, July 1981** (£2,000)

HONOURS: 3 full Scotland caps; Scotland U-21 international; Premier League r-up 1985–86, 1987–88, 1989–90, 1991–92 (Hearts); Scottish Cup r-up 1985–86 (Hearts); Tennents Sixes winner 1984–85, 1990–91 (Hearts)

A loyal and consistent servant to Hearts, Henry is the current holder of the club's League shut-out record, a figure unlikely ever to be beaten. Smith is widely recognised as one of Hearts' best ever goalkeepers. His array of skills is plentiful. A superb handler in cross-ball situations, Henry also displays exceptional agility and reflexes. His positional awareness is of a high standard thanks to his excellent reading of the game.

Henry's memorable saves are well documented and remembered and there are three in particular which stand out: one in 1986 from Maurice Malpas where he was unsighted, yet twisted in mid-air to touch a goalbound rocket shot away; a penalty save from Brian Hamilton of Hibs when he moved the wrong way to his left but instinctively stuck out his right hand to tip the ball over the bar; but perhaps the best of all was against Tommy Coyne of Celtic in 1991. Again, Henry was going the wrong way but he turned his body and palmed a shot bound for the top left-hand corner over the bar to safety.

In his first nine seasons Smith missed only four League matches, but the arrival of Joe Jordan as boss saw Henry dropped for the first time in his Hearts career. It was well known that he felt hard done by and that his confidence suffered at times. It is to his credit that he has always battled his way back into contention despite being dropped on several subsequent occasions in favour of Nicky Walker.

Almost every player's career has its unfortunate moments and Henry has suffered more than most with some bad slip-ups in crucial big matches which resulted in the loss of goals. Opposition fans are never slow in reminding the big keeper. Despite these mishaps, Henry's Hearts career is definitely memorable. He has single-handedly saved Hearts from some hammerings down the years and it is better to remember his many great saves than one or two mistakes. He signed a new one-year deal in the sumer of 1995 and he may yet follow in the footsteps of Shilton and Burridge by playing into his 40s. Whether that will be with Hearts or not – well, we'll just have to wait and see.

IAIN SMITH
Centre-forward

BORN: Edinburgh, 2 April 1952

HEIGHT: 6' 2"   WEIGHT: 12st 2lb (1977)

COMPETITIVE DEBUT: v Dumbarton, 13 August 1977 (Div. I) (A), 2–2 (scored)

CAREER: Queens Park; Birmingham City, Mar 1975; **Hearts, Aug 1977** (on trial)

Iain Smith was a towering, curly-haired striker who hit a couple of goals after arriving for a month's trial in August 1977. He scored in his first two matches and again on his League debut. His trial period was extended but he was unable to maintain his early form and, when the established strikers were all fit, he was left out. When his loan spell ended Hearts decided against a permanent offer.

STIRTON SMITH
Outside-left

BORN: Gorebridge, 28 October 1926

COMPETITIVE DEBUT: v Celtic, 12 August 1944 (S. Lge) (A), 1–4

CAREER: Edinburgh Thistle; **Hearts, Jun 1944**; Third Lanark, 1948; Dunfermline Athletic, 1949; Arniston Rangers, 1950; Newtongrange Star, 1960–61; NCB Amateurs, 1966–67

HONOURS: 1 Scotland Junior cap; Scottish League Cup r-up 1949–50 (Dunfermline)

Stirton played in Hearts' first five games of 1944–45, scoring in the fifth match, a 3–1 defeat at Easter Road. He lost his place until December 1945, when he starred in a rare 5–3 victory against Celtic in Glasgow. He had a tough time trying to win selection ahead of Jimmy Walker, but came in for two League Cup matches in March 1946 and scored the decisive goal in a 1–0 win against Hamilton. After appearing in the 1949 League Cup final, Stirton returned to his roots and became a stalwart servant to Arniston Rangers at left-half or left-back. He played into his 40s with works teams and was employed at Bilston Glen Colliery in Midlothian as an electrician until 1983. He now lives in the Woodburn estate in Dalkeith.

BORN: Duntocher, 30 November 1946

HEIGHT: 5' 10"   WEIGHT: 11st 3lb (1969)

COMPETITIVE DEBUT: v St Johnstone, 26 August 1967 (LC) (A), 2–3

CAREER: Clydebank High School; Drumchapel Amateurs; **Hearts, July 1965**; Morton, May 1975 (free transfer)

HONOURS: 2 Scotland Amateur caps; Scottish Cup r-up 1967–68 (Hearts)

IAN SNEDDON
Full-back

A determined right-back who could adapt to the left side or central defence when called upon, 'Sneddy' defended keenly as a resolute tackler. His pace and vision were equally good, with many attacking moves starting from his long passes out of defence. At a time when strong competition existed for the full-back positions, Ian managed almost 200 competitive games in a ten-year association with Hearts, always playing with commitment and endeavour. His appearances in his last few seasons were restricted by injuries, and personal problems outside football didn't help matters. A cartilage operation in December 1974 was the beginning of the end. When he recovered, Hearts decided to release him so that he could resurrect his career elsewhere.

BORN: Rotherham, 14 February 1960

HEIGHT: 5' 7"   WEIGHT: 10st 2lb (1992)

COMPETITIVE DEBUT: v St Johnstone, 14 March 1992 (PL) (H), 2–0 (came on as substitute)

CAREER: Doncaster Rovers, Oct 1977; Sheffield Wednesday, June 1985 (£500,000); Leeds United, July 1987 (£135,000); **Hearts, Mar 1992** (free transfer); Barnsley, May 1993 (free transfer)

GLYNN SNODIN
Full-back

After a senior career spent in England, Glynn rejected terms from Newcastle's Kevin Keegan to join Hearts. His arrival was designed to create more competition in several first-team areas. He pushed Tosh McKinlay hard and succeeded in taking the number 3 jersey a couple of times. A constructive player, he used the ball well, pushing passes forward and moving into position for a return pass. However, he encountered difficulty in coping with some of the Premier League's trickier forwards.

Snodin scored two goals for Hearts, one of which, on his European debut, was particularly memorable. Glynn hit a 30-yard free-kick into the keeper's top right-hand corner at the School End. It brought the house down, totally stunning Slavia Prague. It proved to be the winning goal and will be fondly remembered in Gorgie folklore.

A clear-out after Joe Jordan's dismissal resulted in a free transfer for the wee man nicknamed 'Lord' by the fans.

JIM SOUNESS

Outside-right

BORN: Edinburgh

DIED: September 1990

HEIGHT: 5' 9"   **WEIGHT:** 11st 4lb (1954)

COMPETITIVE DEBUT: v Partick Thistle, 17 January 1953 (Lge) (A), 2–2

CAREER: Murrayfield Athletic; Edinburgh Thistle; Hibernian, 1947; **Hearts, Jan 1953** (£3,600); released in Jan 1956 to pursue his career as an actuary

HONOURS: 1 cap for Scotland at cricket; Scottish League Cup winner 1954–55 (Hearts)

As a Hibs player Jim Souness had found his chances limited as understudy to Gordon Smith. Souness was a speedy, skilful winger and quickly became a star on Hearts' right-wing after his move across the city. He loved running at defences and scored many spectacular solo goals. He made a notable contribution to Hearts' 1954 League Cup success, playing in the later stages of the competition. He scored 17 goals in 64 competitive appearances before requesting release from his contract to concentrate fully on insurance work as an actuary. Hearts agreed, with the provision that they had first option on his signature should he ever return to senior football. Jim subsequently reached the top in the insurance world.

BORN: Gilmerton, 29 March 1942

HEIGHT: 6' **WEIGHT:** 10st 10lb (1961)

Inside-right

COMPETITIVE DEBUT: v Airdrie, 30 September 1961 (Lge) (H), 4–1 (scored)

CAREER: Edina Hearts; Loanhead Mayflower; **Hearts, c.1960**; freed in Apr 1962; Third Lanark, c.1962; Penicuik Athletic

The tall, dark-haired Stenhouse made a big impression on his introduction to the first team in October 1961, scoring four goals in five games. He was then left out, with Tommy Walker supposedly resting him on account of the strain young Robin had endured in some tough games following his debut. For whatever reason, he never played for the first team again and, after completing the remainder of season 1961–62 in the reserves, was given a surprise free transfer in April 1962.

BORN: Glasgow, 13 January 1955

HEIGHT: 5' 11" **WEIGHT:** 11st 2lb (1984)

Centre-half

COMPETITIVE DEBUT: v Partick Thistle, 6 February 1984 (SC) (H), 2–0

CAREER: Baillieston Juniors; Motherwell, 1974; Leicester City, May 1979 (£165,000); Rangers, Sept 1979 (£150,000); **Hearts, Jan–Feb 1984** (on loan); Partick Thistle, May 1984 (free transfer); Brechin City, 1986; Dumbarton, 1987

HONOURS: 1 Scotland U-21 cap

Gregor was renowned as a tough-tackling, dominant centre-half, a hard player noted for the occasional reckless tackle. He had an unenviable disciplinary record containing many bookings and a few orderings-off. He was a committed player, however, and this won admirers. He joined Hearts on loan to cover the loss of Roddy MacDonald through suspension. Stevens provided adequate cover for five games before returning to Ibrox where he was freed two months later. In later years he was a tool company manager.

JOHN STEVENSON

Midfield

BORN: Uddingston, 17 June 1953

HEIGHT: 5′ 6″   WEIGHT: 10st 10lb (1973)

COMPETITIVE DEBUT: v Partick Thistle, 31 March 1973 (Lge) (A), 0–3

CAREER: Coventry City, 1971; **Hearts, Feb 1973** (free transfer); St Johnstone, Oct 1975 (free transfer)

Stevenson joined Hearts a few months short of his 20th birthday and soon won a place in the side. He was a regular in season 1973–74 and his busy style and a willingness to shoot on sight made him popular with the supporters – he possessed a rocket shot. He held his place into season 1974–75 but, after the sacking of Bobby Seith, found it difficult to remain a fixture in John Hagart's squads. He was released in October 1975 but failed to settle with his new club, St Johnstone. He managed one full and two substitute appearances at Muirton Park before deciding to emigrate to Australia in 1976.

RAB STEWART

Forward

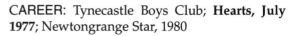

BORN: Edinburgh

HEIGHT: 5′ 10″   WEIGHT: 11st 5lb (1979)

COMPETITIVE DEBUT: v Rangers, 28 April 1979 (PL) (A), 0–4

CAREER: Tynecastle Boys Club; **Hearts, July 1977**; Newtongrange Star, 1980

A hard-working forward or midfielder who broke into a team already doomed to Division I, Rab was one of many young players used at the end of season 1978–79. Early in the new season he was heavily fined after being sent off for retaliation in a reserve game. He managed a few more appearances and scored his only goal with a last-gasp strike against Stirling Albion in January 1980. He was freed in May 1980 to make way for new signings.

BORN: Stoneyburn, 7 November 1959

HEIGHT: 5' 7"   WEIGHT: 10st 7lb (1981)

COMPETITIVE DEBUT: v Dumbarton, 26 September 1981 (Div. I) (H), 2–1 (came on as substitute)

CAREER: Blackburn Academy; Rangers, July 1977; Leicester City, Sept 1979; **Hearts, Jul 1981**; Motherwell, 1982; East Stirling, 1983; Stoneyburn Juniors, 1984; Whitburn manager; Bonnyrigg Rose manager, May 1994

HONOURS: Scotland Schoolboy international

Derek endured a somewhat frustrating senior career by failing to settle or establish himself with five senior clubs. His debut appearance as a substitute was his only game for Hearts.

DEREK STRICKLAND

Forward

BORN: Edinburgh, 25 April 1975

HEIGHT: 5' 11"   WEIGHT: 12st 3lb (1993)

COMPETITIVE DEBUT: v Falkirk, 13 February 1993 (PL) (H), 3–1 (came on as substitute and scored)

CAREER: Royal High School; Salvesen Boys Club; Links United Boys Club; **Hearts, Jun 1990**

HONOURS: Scotland Schoolboy and U-21 international; Reserve League winner 1992–93 (Hearts); BP Youth Cup winner 1992–93 (Hearts)

After a string of impressive displays for Hearts' reserve and youth teams, Kevin made his debut as a substitute and scored with a fine half-volley. He has remarkable confidence for one so young

KEVIN THOMAS

Forward

and reputations don't bother him. He can panic defenders by running straight at them, to create scoring chances for himself or for others. He does show a reluctance to pass the ball, though. Kevin deservedly won U-21 honours with some mature performances in 1993 and he rose to the challenge of the international stage. Hearts supporters hope to see Kevin develop into a top-class player in time. He has the confidence and the ability. His colleagues nick-named him 'The Legend' and he apparently hands out business cards entitled 'Kevin Thomas – professional footballer'! High standards to set and maintain – let's hope he can live up to them.

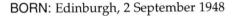

ARTHUR THOMSON

Half-back

BORN: Edinburgh, 2 September 1948

HEIGHT: 6' 1"   **WEIGHT:** 12st 8lb (1968)

COMPETITIVE DEBUT: v Partick Thistle, 3 December 1966 (Lge) (A), 1–1

CAREER: Chelsea, 1963; **Hearts, Apr 1964**; Oldham Athletic, Jan 1970; Raith Rovers, Dec 1970; Dalkeith Thistle, *c*.1972

HONOURS: 3 Scotland U-23 caps; Scotland Schoolboy international; Scottish Cup r-up 1967–68 (Hearts)

Arthur was an intimidating sight for opposing forwards, putting his height to good use and timing his interceptions well in breaking up attacks. He had a short spell in London as a very young teenager and came home to his roots to serve his apprenticeship with Hearts. Following his debut he formed a profitable partnership with Alan Anderson in the centre of the defence.

As more talent came through the ranks, Arthur was left out to accommodate others. He was soon on the move back south. His departure probably pleased a certain *Evening News* journalist who thought Thomson was too rough and rash with his tackling. He didn't like Arthur kicking Hibbies.

EDDIE THOMSON

Half-back

BORN: Edinburgh, 25 February 1947

HEIGHT: 5' 11"   **WEIGHT:** 11st 8lb (1968)

COMPETITIVE DEBUT: v Dunfermline, 22 March 1967 (Lge) (A), 0–1

CAREER: Whitehill Welfare; Penicuik Athletic; **Hearts, Aug 1966**; Aberdeen, Mar 1973 (£60,000); San Antonio coach, 1977; Sydney City manager; Sydney Olympic manager; Australian national 'B' coach, 1984; Australian national coach, 1990

HONOURS: 3 Scotland U-23 caps; 1 Scottish League cap; Scottish Cup r-up 1967–68 (Hearts); Texaco Cup r-up 1970–71 (Hearts)

A fine all-round defender, Eddie combined his early Tynecastle career with his job as an apprentice drawer in the Tweed Mills, Peebles. He starred initially as a full-back but later operated very successfully in either half-back role. He was a more than capable deputy centre-half and even had a spell at centre-forward in 1972–73 – versatile could have been his middle name. Eddie was a spirited performer who launched himself into the fray with great endeavour. His leadership qualities were later rewarded with the club captaincy and he led Hearts to the 1971 Texaco Cup final. His surprise transfer to Aberdeen dismayed the fans – there seemed no need to sell Eddie, despite club statements to the contrary. This was borne out by the excellent service he gave Aberdeen.

GEORGE THOMSON
Left-back

BORN: Edinburgh, 19 October 1936

HEIGHT: 5′ 8″   WEIGHT: 10st 11lb (1956)

COMPETITIVE DEBUT: v Falkirk, 23 February 1957 (Lge) (H), 1–1

CAREER: Craiglockhart School; Tynecastle School; Slateford Athletic; Edinburgh City; **Hearts, Sept 1953**; Everton, Nov 1960 (£18,000); Brentford, Nov 1963; retired c.1967

HONOURS: 2 Scotland U-23 caps; 2 Scottish League caps; Scottish League winner 1957–58, 1959–60 (Hearts); Scottish League Cup winner 1958–59, 1959–60 (Hearts)

George made his debut as a left-half but eventually settled in the side as a left-back. He was an expert penalty-taker and a tireless worker noted for his forceful tackles and surging runs into the opposition half of the field. Thomson was one of the main forces in Hearts' League and Cup triumphs in the late 1950s and was a League ever-present in 1958–59 and 1959–60. He enjoyed a brief period at inside-left in the later part of 1958–59 and scored a tremendous hat-trick against Third Lanark in February 1959. His versatility was a big asset to Hearts, which made the decision to sell him something of a disgraceful mystery. David Holt had just been signed and perhaps the management considered him a better prospect at left-back. George made 73 League appearances for Everton and later moved to Brentford, where he played a further 160 games.

JOHN THOMSON

Full-back

BORN: Glasgow, 22 October 1934

HEIGHT: 5′ 11″   **WEIGHT:** 11st 10lb (1955)

COMPETITIVE DEBUT: v Queen of the South, 11 February 1956 (Lge) (H), 2–2

CAREER: Armadale Thistle; **Hearts, Dec 1954**; Workington, Apr 1958 (free transfer)

John Thomson was a tall, hard-hitting full-back who made his single appearance as a deputy for Bobby Kirk. He was a reliable defender whose hefty clearances could put forwards on the attack immediately. John's move to Workington in 1958 was short-lived and he made only 11 appearances down south.

LAWRIE TIERNEY

Midfield

BORN: Falkirk, 4 April 1959

HEIGHT: 5′ 10″   **WEIGHT:** 11st 7lb (1978)

COMPETITIVE DEBUT: v Dumbarton, 13 August 1977 (Div. I) (A), 2–2 (came on as substitute)

CAREER: Salvesen Boys Club; **Hearts, July 1976**; Hibernian, Feb 1980 (free transfer); Wigan Athletic, July 1980 (free transfer)

HONOURS: Scotland Youth international

Lawrie was an excellent passer of the ball but had a tendency to suffer from inconsistent form. He made his debut at the start of season 1977–78 and his promptings and subtle skills from the midfield assisted Hearts back to the Premier League. Several injuries and a loss of confidence kept Lawrie out of the team during separate periods over the next two seasons. Hearts released him in February 1980 and city neighbours Hibs quickly signed him to help in their fight against relegation.

BORN: Greenock, 2 February 1945

HEIGHT: 5′ 8″   WEIGHT: 11st 8lb (1970)

COMPETITIVE DEBUT: v Motherwell, 29 April 1967 (Lge) (A), 0–1

CAREER: St Columbus School; Woodhall Boys Club Juveniles; Port Glasgow Juniors; St Johnstone, 1961; Middlesbrough, Feb 1964 (£20,000); St Johnstone, 1966 (£7,000); **Hearts, Apr 1967** (£20,000); Morton, Oct 1972 (free transfer)

HONOURS: Scotland Youth and U-23 international; 7 appearances on Scottish XI tour in 1967; Scottish Cup r-up 1967–68 (Hearts); Texaco Cup r-up 1970–71 (Hearts)

JIM TOWNSEND
Half-back

Having quit his joinery apprenticeship at the age of 15, Jim Townsend joined St Johnstone's groundstaff. In a remarkable three-month spell in which he moved from juvenile to junior then senior, the promising teenager won rave notices. English scouts were alerted and Jim made a big-money move to Teesside. He couldn't settle down south, though, and returned to Perth for a knockdown fee. Jim quickly became a fans' favourite during his second stint at Muirton Park, until Hearts identified him as a solution to their lack of midfield thrust. He soon demonstrated why such a big fee was paid with some scintillating displays, but a succession of niggling injuries curtailed his progress during season 1967–68. Jim was playing well in 1968–69 when a sickening injury – a crude challenge from Falkirk's Doug Baillie in a League match at Brockville in October 1968 – saw Townsend suffer a fractured ankle. Sidelined for seven months, he was never quite the same player thereafter.

At his best, 'Townie' could dictate the course of a match with a marvellous display of his all-round talents. Sadly, he produced this kind of form on an infrequent basis. The emergence of Jim Brown and the arrival of Tommy Murray in 1971 increased first-team competition and Jim was dropped. He played on with Morton for several years.

TOMMY TRAYNOR

Winger

BORN: Bonnybridge, 27 September 1943

DIED: Melbourne, Australia, January 1993

HEIGHT: 5′ 6″   WEIGHT: 9st 7lb (1966)

COMPETITIVE DEBUT: v Hibernian, 4 May 1963 (Lge) (H), 3–3

CAREER: St Mungo's School (Falkirk); Denny Boys Club; Dunipace Juniors; **Hearts, 1963**; Dundee United, Apr 1970 (swap for Wilson Wood); Falkirk, 1976 (free transfer); Morton, 1977; retired in 1978; Cowdenbeath coach, *c.*1981

HONOURS: Scottish League r-up 1964–65; Scottish Cup r-up 1967–68 (Hearts), 1973–74 (Dundee United)

A speedy, tricky winger who possessed a deceptive feinting body swerve which often wrong-footed opponents, Tommy knew the way to goal and his sharp footballing brain helped him score many goals. The fans affectionately nicknamed him 'The All-American Boy', probably in reference to his stylish crewcut hairstyle and fine-featured looks. Tommy was a consistent performer in eight years at Tynecastle but despite his skills he won no major honours during his senior career. He was very adaptable, starring on either wing or occasionally at inside-forward. A lively character, Traynor had boundless energy and gave the impression he could run all day. He was more or less an automatic choice when fully fit, until his last season at Gorgie. He suffered a fractured wrist in August 1969, and, although he battled back into contention quickly, his inconsistency saw him in and out of the team. This resulted in Tommy demanding a transfer in December 1969 and in April the following year he got his wish.

Tommy came back to haunt Hearts four years later, hitting a stunning hat-trick as Dundee United hammered Hearts 5–0 in October 1974. His early death in Australia from heart failure aged 49 stunned all who had admired his wing skills.

BORN: Edinburgh, 22 October 1948

HEIGHT: 5' 8"   WEIGHT: 11st (1966)

COMPETITIVE DEBUT: v Partick Thistle, 9 November 1968 (Lge) (H), 2–0 (came on as substitute)

CAREER: Norton Park School; North Merchiston Boys Club; Gorgie Hearts; **Hearts, 1965**; Lincoln City, Sept 1969 (free transfer)

ROY TURNBULL

Forward

Roy had the briefest first-team appearance record possible. His introduction as a late substitute lasted only minutes and, if sports reports on his debut match are to be believed, he took to the field wearing rugby boots. He later moved to Lincoln for a short time.

BORN: Kirkcaldy, 3 February 1925

HEIGHT: 5' 8"   WEIGHT: 11st 8lb (1952)

COMPETITIVE DEBUT: v Dumbarton, 14 October 1944 (S. Lge) (H), 4–0 (scored)

CAREER: Kirkcaldy High School; Kirkcaldy Old Boys; **Hearts, Aug 1944**; Raith Rovers, 1950 (on loan); Raith Rovers, Apr 1956 (£300); Raith Rovers director

HONOURS: 1 Scottish League cap; Scottish League Cup winner 1954–55 (Hearts)

JOHN URQUHART

Forward

A joiner to trade and also a keen Boys Brigade leader in his spare time. John was a penetrative, foraging forward who was forceful and confident in his ability. He had his critics, but could win them over with his determined style. Shortly after signing for Hearts, Urquhart was called into action with the Marines and guested for several sides while in the forces. On his return to Civvy Street John soon won a place in Hearts' first-team. The formation of the Terrible Trio and the signing of new players meant a return to the reserves from 1948 to 1951 interspersed with a loan spell to Raith Rovers in March 1950.

John began to establish himself firmly in the first team in season 1951–52. He performed well in the next four seasons principally as a left-winger although he deputised anywhere in the forward line as required and scored two goals on the path to League Cup glory in 1954. He lost his place to Ian Crawford in 1955 and was later transferred to his home-town team in April

1956. He made his Raith debut against Hearts one week after his move and was on the losing side to the tune of 7–2! He served Raith as a player and director for many years.

PETER VAN DE VEN

Sweeper

BORN: Hunsel, Holland, 8 January 1961

HEIGHT: 6′ 1″   **WEIGHT:** 13st 5lb (1992)

COMPETITIVE DEBUT: v Celtic, 1 August 1992 (PL) (H), 0–1

CAREER: Megaglas Amateurs, 1978; Fortuna Sittard, 1979; Roda JC, 1981 (£150,000); Charleroi SC, 1986; Willem II, Jan 1989; Aberdeen, Aug 1990 (£200,000); **Hearts, July 1992** (£90,000); Racing Genk, Sept 1993 (£90,000)

HONOURS: Holland U-21 international

Following the departure of club skipper Dave McPherson to Rangers, manager Joe Jordan signed Peter as a cut-price replacement. The big Dutchman had occupied a midfield role for Aberdeen but reverted to sweeper at Tynecastle. Peter was familiar with this role from earlier experiences in Holland.

Van de Ven was a cool, confident player with superb footballing skills. He liked to play his way out of sticky situations and the lightning pace of Premier League football saw him caught in possession on odd occasions. For that minor problem alone, Peter could be considered a liability at times. The fans often had their hearts in their mouths watching him. On the plus side, he read the game well and it is an indictment of the Premier League that his skills were inadvisable in defensive situations.

Peter was a regular throughout 1992–93 and started the next season where he left off, despite early speculation that he would follow Joe Jordan out the door. His days were numbered all the same: Hearts quickly agreed to his transfer when Belgian club Racing Genk enquired about him. It was certainly good business to recoup the outlay for 32-year-old Peter.

BORN: Edinburgh, 16 October 1949

DIED: Edinburgh, 16 October 1987

HEIGHT: 5' 10"   WEIGHT: 11st 5lb (1969)

COMPETITIVE DEBUT: v Airdrie, 21 September 1968 (Lge) (A), 1–2

CAREER: Ross High School (Tranent); Elphinstone Primrose; Bonnyrigg Rose 'A'; **Hearts, 1966**; Tranmere Rovers, May 1972; Denver (USA), 1974; Carlisle United, 1974; Halifax Town, Aug 1975; Hartlepool, Aug 1976; Morton, Jan 1977; Airdrie, Feb 1979

HONOURS: Texaco Cup r-up 1970–71 (Hearts)

Tommy was a junior technician at Edinburgh University prior to joining Hearts. He was a product of the club youth policy, coming through the ranks of the Colts and reserve teams to make his debut just before his 20th birthday. A hard-grafting half-back who could double up as a reso-lute defender, Tommy was always on the fringes of the first team, appearing more often as a deputy. He never let anyone down and his attitude and hunger for the game were never in question.

A generally inauspicious club season in 1971–72 saw Bobby Seith attempt to freshen the playing pool and Tommy was one of several departures in May 1972. He moved to Tranmere and captained them in season 1974–75. Tommy later became a man of many clubs before retiring in the early 1980s. Hearts supporters were saddened to hear of his early death from illness on his 38th birthday in 1987.

BORN: Detroit, USA

HEIGHT: 5' 7"   WEIGHT: 10st (1946)

COMPETITIVE DEBUT: v Third Lanark, 30 December 1944 (S. Lge) (A), 2–1 (scored)

CAREER: Moorpark School (Paisley); Renfrew Boys Brigade; Stevens Amateur Works XI; Renfrew Juniors; **Hearts, Oct 1944**; Partick Thistle, Apr 1947 (swap deal for Bobby Parker); Third Lanark, Nov 1956

HONOURS: Scottish League Cup r-up 1953–54 (Partick)

One of the fastest and most profitable wingers in season 1945–46, Jimmy scored 11 League goals. The following season was less rewarding for Jimmy and the club, though. The fans were often verbally critical of Walker during games and this seemed to affect his confidence. After two months out of the team mid-season he was recalled for the second leg of a League Cup quarter-final tie against East Fife – and hit two goals in a 5–2 win which took Hearts to the semi-final. He scored the following week in a 2–1 Scottish Cup third-round tie against Cowdenbeath. All looked rosy for Jimmy until the following Saturday when he failed to report at Gayfield Park for the Scottish Cup quarter-final tie against Arbroath. Hearts crashed out 2–1 to the Division II side and Jimmy was later suspended for what the directors alleged was an 'unsatisfactory explanation'. The suspension was lifted on 2 April 1947 and the next day he was on his way to Partick in exchange for Bobby Parker. He served Thistle well for many years.

NICKY WALKER

Goalkeeper

BORN: Aberdeen, 29 September 1962

HEIGHT: 6' 2"   WEIGHT: 11st 12lb (1990)

COMPETITIVE DEBUT: v Dundee United, 10 February 1991 (PL (H), 2–1

CAREER: Elgin City; Leicester City, Aug 1980; Motherwell, 1981; Rangers, 1983; **Hearts, Aug 1989** (£125,000); Burnley, Feb 1992 (on loan); Partick Thistle, Dec 1994 (swap deal involving Craig Nelson to Hearts and £160,000 plus Walker to Partick)

HONOURS: 1 full Scotland cap; Scottish League Cup winner 1987–88 (Rangers)

Nicky was highly rated by former Hearts coach Jock Wallace, who signed the keeper for Leicester, Motherwell and Rangers. He was relegated to reserve-team football for three years when Rangers signed Chris Woods. Desperate to regain first-team football, he joined Hearts only to become Henry Smith's understudy. After 18 months in the reserves, Joe Jordan gave Nicky his chance in February 1991. He performed well for 13 games until a nasty cheekbone injury put him out of action in the summer of 1991. Henry Smith returned and kept Walker out for the duration of season 1991–92. Nicky returned in December 1992 and his consistency and a good run of shut-outs won him the Tartan Player of the Month in January 1993. Further recognition was just around the corner with his first full cap, against Germany. Nicky lost his first-team place on several occasions as a battle for the number 1 jersey developed with Henry Smith. On his day he produced some fine reflex saves and could command his box with authority. His League shut-out record was reasonable, averaging one in every three games.

Following his move to Partick, Nicky made comments on his last first-team game for Hearts, a 4–2 League Cup disaster against St Johnstone. He acknowledged he didn't perform particularly well but that the manager supposedly treated him like a 'murderer'!

BORN: Livingston, 26 May 1915

DIED: Edinburgh, 11 January 1993

HEIGHT: 5' 8"   WEIGHT: 10st 8lb (1939)

COMPETITIVE DEBUT: v Ayr United, 3 September 1932 (Lge) (H), 4–2 (scored)

CAREER: Berryburn Rangers; Livingston Violet; Broxburn Rangers; Linlithgow Rose; **Hearts, May 1932**; Chelsea, Sept 1946 (£8,000); **Hearts assistant manager, Dec 1948; Hearts manager, Sept 1951**; Dunfermline admin. manager, Nov 1966; Raith Rovers manager, July 1967; Raith Rovers secretary, Jan 1969–1972; **Hearts director, Oct 1974**; retired in 1980

HONOURS: 21 full Scotland caps; 8 wartime caps; Scotland Schoolboy international; Awarded the OBE in 1960

TOMMY WALKER

Inside-forward

Tommy Walker was an all-time great in Hearts history. A dynamic inside-forward with superb all-round ability, his best attribute was his deadly accuracy in front of goal. He won his first cap aged nineteen and quickly became a Scotland regular. His memory is immortalised for twice scoring crucial goals at Wembley. The first, a penalty equaliser, won the Home International Championship in 1936. Two years later, he scored the winner. He was equally revered at Tynecastle. He was Hearts' major asset and fans always threatened boycotts when big English clubs expressed any definite interest in Tommy.

Hearts held on to their star until the war interrupted his career. Seven years later, 31-year-old Walker joined Chelsea after making only a few appearances for Hearts in season 1946–47. Tommy further enhanced his reputation as a footballing gentleman down south while learning managerial skills from Billy Birrell, the Chelsea boss.

He returned to Hearts in 1948 as assistant to Dave McLean and made one more appearance for Hearts against Dundee in January 1949. He then retired from playing and later took the manager's chair in 1951. After guiding Hearts to full domestic success during the '50s and '60s, he left under a cloud in 1966. After a spell away he returned to serve as a club director for six years before retiring in 1980. Tommy passed on in January 1993, aged 77, after a short illness.

WILLIE WALLACE

Centre-forward

BORN: Kirkintilloch, 23 June 1940

HEIGHT: 5' 8"   **WEIGHT:** 12st 1lb (1966)

COMPETITIVE DEBUT: v Dundee, 29 April 1961 (Lge) (H), 2–1

CAREER: Kilsyth Rangers; Stenhousemuir, Aug 1958; Raith Rovers, Oct 1959; **Hearts, Apr 1961** (£15,000); Celtic, Dec 1966 (£29,000); Crystal Palace, Oct 1971 (£30,000 plus J. Hughes to Palace); Dumbarton, Oct 1972 (£10,000); Apia FC (Australia), March 1975; Ross County, 1976; Dundee coach, 1977; Apia FC coach, 1979; Leichhart (Australia) coach; sports shop proprietor in Sydney since 1982

HONOURS: 7 full Scotland caps; 4 Scottish League caps; European Cup winner 1966–67 (Celtic); r-up 1969–70 (Celtic); Scottish League winner 1966–67, 1967–68, 1968–69, 1969–70, 1970–71 (Celtic); r-up 1964–65 (Hearts); Scottish Cup winner 1966–67, 1968–69, 1970–71 (Celtic); Scottish League Cup winner 1962–63 (Hearts), 1967–68, 1968–69 (Celtic); r-up 1961–62 (Hearts); Australian League winner 1974–75, 1975–76 (Apia FC)

A deadly striker of the highest order, 'Wispy' Wallace (as he was known to the fans) was a first-class poacher, capable of scoring goals from anywhere in the penalty box given half a chance. He took time to settle at Hearts but once he gelled with the team style he became the leading scorer from 1962–63 until 1965–66. He won a League Cup medal and came close to a Championship win with Hearts and his consistent form won him three full caps as a Heart. Wallace took over the idol role from Willie Bauld, displaying an incredible appetite for goalscoring.

His popularity crashed with a bang early in season 1966–67. His goals dried up and his commitment level appeared to drop. Rumours abounded that Celtic had 'tapped' Willie and eventually they paid £29,000 for his signature. Wallace won every domestic honour with Celtic, with the 1967 European Cup the icing on the cake. But Hearts fans never forgot or forgave the shameful circumstances which they believed led to his transfer, a feeling which is still evident to this day.

BORN: Marshall Meadows, 21 March 1929

DIED: Edinburgh, 2 January 1978

HEIGHT: 5′ 9″　　WEIGHT: 11st 4lb (1953)

COMPETITIVE DEBUT: v Celtic, 21 August 1946
(Lge) (H), 3–2 (scored)

CAREER: ATC football; Shaftesbury Park; **Hearts, March 1946**; Dunfermline, Nov 1959 (£2,000); retired in 1961

HONOURS: 2 full Scotland caps; 1 Scotland B cap; 8 Scottish League caps; Scottish League winner 1957–58 (Hearts); Scottish Cup winner 1955–56 (Hearts); Scottish League Cup winner 1954–55, 1958–59 (Hearts); post-war League record scorer with 206 goals

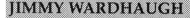

JIMMY WARDHAUGH
Inside-left

A celebrated member of the Terrible Trio, Jimmy made an immediate impact on his debut and appeared 19 times in 1946–47. National Service soon beckoned and he missed most of the following term, but the birth of the Trio in October 1948 established Wardhaugh as a regular for the next 11 seasons. Jimmy set goalscoring records that were second to none and his 206 League goals is a post-war record.

Slimly built and the possessor of a quick football brain, Jimmy outfoxed opponents. Amazing footwork and shooting ability were his best attributes and he used his talents to devastating effect in the penalty box. The fans dubbed him 'Twinkletoes', a glowing tribute to his artistic footwork. But despite his prowess in front of goal he won only two caps – scant reward for such an exceptional player.

Any time Jimmy was out of the Hearts side, for no matter what reason, transfer talk was on the agenda of the sportswriters. This often unsettled Jimmy and on one occasion in 1952 he almost joined Newcastle. Hearts accepted an offer of £26,000 but Newcastle couldn't guarantee him a job and this stumbling block killed the deal. The supporters were relieved and Wardhaugh settled down to help Hearts to glory.

At the age of 30 and entering the veteran stage, Jimmy was transferred to Dunfermline. After two years at East End Park he retired and became a journalist with the *Edinburgh Evening News*. He continued to progress in media circles, enjoying a spell as editor of the official Hearts programme, writing as a sports reporter for the *Daily Express* and later working as a publicity officer with the BBC. Sadly, Jimmy died suddenly in 1978. He collapsed near his Edinburgh home after reporting on a Hearts match at East Fife. He is fondly remembered for the enjoyment he gave to all in his sparkling career.

ANDY WATSON

Midfield

BORN: Aberdeen, 3 September 1959

HEIGHT: 5' 10"   WEIGHT: 10st 10lb (1986)

COMPETITIVE DEBUT: v Morton, 29 December 1984 (PL) (H), 1–0

CAREER: Sunnyside FC; Aberdeen, 1977; Leeds United, June 1983; **Hearts, Dec 1984** (£70,000); Hibernian, Sept 1987 (£30,000); retired due to injury in Aug 1989 and became Hibs coach; Motherwell assistant manager, July 1994

HONOURS: 4 Scotland U-21 caps; Scottish Cup winner 1982–83 (Aberdeen)

Andy was a hard-working midfielder who unfortunately bore the brunt of terracing discontent when the breaks went against him. He was signed to replace Dave Bowman in December 1984 and enjoyed good form in his first season, scoring three League goals, against Rangers, Celtic and Aberdeen respectively. The remainder of his time with Hearts was spent largely as a substitute. When he played, the boo-boys had a field day and this affected Andy's confidence. He never again quite captured the excellent form he once enjoyed at Aberdeen. It was noticeable that his best displays came in away fixtures, particularly tour matches, where he scored regularly.

JIMMY WATTERS

Goalkeeper

BORN: Buckhaven, 12 August 1927

HEIGHT: 5' 10"   WEIGHT: 11st 7lb (1953)

COMPETITIVE DEBUT: v Motherwell, 4 March 1950 (Lge) (A), 3–2

CAREER: Buckhaven High School; **Hearts, 1944**; East Fife, May 1956 (free transfer); released in May 1957; East Fife director in the 1970s; Dunfermline director in the 1980s

Jimmy was a draughtsman/architect by profession who played part-time with Hearts. He waited six years to make his debut such was the form of the man in possession, Jimmy Brown. Watters was initially considered to be a safe, steady, all-round keeper but when he began losing goals the critics were soon on his back. It was said he was unable to hold a hard shot and was forced to palm the ball into the path of incoming forwards, who then scored with ease. His positional awareness was also thought suspect. However, Watters was good enough to keep Jimmy Brown out in 1952–53 and 1953–54 to the point where his competitor moved on. He eventually lost his place to youngster Willie Duff in 1954 but provided cover for two more seasons. A move to East Fife in 1956 suited Watters, who lived in Leven and was employed close to East Fife's Bayview Park. He later moved into a cafeteria business in Kirkcaldy's High Street.

JIM WEIR
Defender

BORN: Motherwell, 15 June 1969

HEIGHT: 6' 1"   WEIGHT: 12st 2lb (1993)

COMPETITIVE DEBUT: v Hibernian, 21 August 1993 (PL) (H), 1–0

CAREER: Orbiston Boys Club; Hamilton Accies, May 1987; **Hearts, Aug 1993** (£300,000); St Johnstone, Nov 1994 (swap deal for Colin Miller and £80,000 to Hearts)

HONOURS: Division I winner 1987–88 (Hamilton); B&Q Cup winner 1992–93 (Hamilton)

After over 300 competitive appearances for Hamilton, constant transfer speculation and trial periods, Jim thought his dream move to a big club would never materialise. August 1993 changed that state of affairs when Hearts beat Dundee United and Blackburn to obtain Jim's signature. He made an impressive debut in the heart of our defence against Hibs and later enjoyed the flavour of a European match against Atletico Madrid. He played most of his games in defence but was also asked to fill a midfield role when required. He played several games on the right side of defence, where he looked very uncomfortable. He was dropped after a run of bad results in December 1993–January 1994 but was recalled for a few more games as the season drew to a close.

Jim had high hopes for a better season in 1994–95 and played in the first two League games. But a poor performance in an embarrassing League Cup defeat against St Johnstone proved to be his last.

IAN WESTWATER

Goalkeeper

BORN: Loughborough, 8 November 1963

HEIGHT: 6'   **WEIGHT:** 13st (1984)

COMPETITIVE DEBUT: v St Mirren, 1 November 1980 (PL) (H), 1–1

CAREER: Currie High School; Balerno Youth Club; Salvesen Boys Club; **Hearts, Jun 1980**; Dunfermline, March 1985 (£4,000); Falkirk, Aug 1991; Dundee, Feb 1994 (swap deal); Dunfermline, Mar 1994

HONOURS: Scotland Youth international; Division I winner 1988–89 (Dunfermline); Division II winner 1985–86 (Dunfermline)

A team lacking quality in general with little strength in depth enabled Ian to make his debut at the tender age of 16. His two League appearances in 1980–81 proved to be his Hearts total. John Brough was the recognised keeper at the time but the arrival of Henry Smith pushed the youngster even further down the pecking order. In his next three and a half seasons Ian made only four appearances in recognised first-team matches. Two were unimportant League Cup ties and the others were in the devalued East of Scotland Shield. A capable enough keeper, Ian has since enjoyed first-team action at Dunfermline and Falkirk.

ARCHIE WHITE

Winger

BORN: Dumbarton, 11 January 1959

HEIGHT: 5' 5"   **WEIGHT:** 9st 10lb (1980)

COMPETITIVE DEBUT: v Raith Rovers, 15 March 1980 (Div. I) (A), 0–0

CAREER: Partick Thistle; Oxford United, Jan 1976; **Hearts, March 1980** (£5,000); freed in May 1981

HONOURS: Division I winner 1979–80 (Hearts)

Archie was Bobby Moncur's first signing as Hearts manager but the tiny winger didn't measure up to the standard of play expected at Hearts at a time when standards were poor. He had a jinking style, but tended to be inconsistent with more off-days than good performances. After playing in the side which won the Division I Championship, he failed to impress in the Premier League and was given a free transfer.

BORN: Musselburgh, 12 August 1939

HEIGHT: 5′ 10″   WEIGHT: 12st (1964)

COMPETITIVE DEBUT: v Dundee United, 16 November 1963 (Lge) (A), 0–0

CAREER: Bonnyrigg Rose; Raith Rovers, 1958; St Mirren, 1962; **Hearts, Nov 1963**; Aberdeen June 1965 (exchange deal for D. Kerrigan); Crystal Palace, June 1966; Blackpool, Mar 1968; Bury, June 1970; Crewe Alexandria, Dec 1971; retired in 1972; Blackpool director

TOMMY WHITE
Centre-forward

Tommy's 20 goals in 35 League appearances for St Mirren was the kind of form which prompted Hearts to secure his transfer. He started his Tynecastle career in similar fashion, with prolific goalscoring. The sportswriters quickly dubbed him 'Goal-a-game Tom White'. Tommy was powerfully built and used his physique and bustling, all-action style to upset even the most assured defenders. He packed a fair shot and was fearsome in the air and this helped him score many goals. However, his progress was brought to a halt when he was injured in a car crash at Wallyford in March 1964. White suffered terrible personal grief at the sudden, tragic death of his brother John, a star with Tottenham and Scotland, but overcame this devastating blow to re-establish his reputation as a top marksman in season 1964–65.

His transfer to Aberdeen was surprising given his scoring record and his relatively young age of 25. He continued to star in top-class football north and south of the border.

BORN: Newtongrange, 1 January 1928

HEIGHT: 5′ 10″   WEIGHT: 10st 7lb (1952)

COMPETITIVE DEBUT: v Partick Thistle, 26 October 1946 (LC) (H), 1–1

CAREER: Inveresk Thistle; **Hearts, 1946**; Stirling Albion, May 1953; Queen of the South, Jan 1955

DICK WHITEHEAD
Half-back

A fringe player throughout his seven years at Tynecastle, Dick deputised in many positions, although most often at wing-half or inside-forward. A workmanlike player, his best seasons were 1946–47 and 1950–51 when he managed brief runs in the first team. He was happy to serve as a covering player but when Stirling enquired about his services, Dick accepted their offer and the chance of a regular first-team game. He later moved to Dumfries and gave good service to the clubs he served throughout his career. Dick emigrated to Canada after his playing days, where he found employment as a real estate agent.

BRIAN WHITTAKER

Defender

BORN: Glasgow, 23 September 1958

HEIGHT: 6'   WEIGHT: 12st 4lb (1988)

COMPETITIVE DEBUT: v Dundee United, 11 August 1984 (PL) (A), 0–2

CAREER: Sighthill Amateurs; Partick Thistle, 1974; Celtic, 1983 (£65,000); **Hearts, May 1984** (£25,000); Falkirk, Aug 1990; **Hearts Reserve XI coach, 1993**

HONOURS: Scottish League international; Premier League r-up 1985–86, 1989–90 (Hearts); Division I r-up 1976–77 (Partick Thistle); Scottish Cup r-up 1985–86 (Hearts); Tennents Sixes winner 1984–85 (Hearts)

A stylish attacking left-back with excellent distribution skills, Brian was a consistent performer in his six seasons at Tynecastle. He proved an able deputy in central-defence during Craig Levein's second knee-ligament injury. 'Roger', as he was known to all, excelled in the European campaigns, most notably in 1988–89. Despite his willingness to assist in attack Brian only scored four goals, three of them in his first season. His last strike was an amazing, looping ball from 30 yards out on the left wing which gave Hearts the lead in the 1988 Scottish Cup semifinal against Celtic. A remarkable goal indeed!

Brian faced stiff competition from Tosh McKinlay for the left-back slot in 1989–90, and, with Craig Levein fit again, he was not an automatic first choice. However, Roger reserved one more exceptional performance, on Ne'er Day 1990, as Hibs were beaten 2–0 at Tynecastle. He moved to Falkirk in August 1990 but retained a Hearts link through his sales executive job in the commercial office. He later returned full-time to assist with Hearts' reserve and youth teams.

BORN: Hamilton, 5 September 1929

HEIGHT: 5′ 10″   WEIGHT: 11st 13lb (1954)

COMPETITIVE DEBUT: v Raith Rovers, 16 December 1950 (Lge) (A), 0–2

CAREER: Hamilton Academy; Cambuslang Rangers; **Hearts, July 1947**; called up 1950; Southampton, Jan 1954 (on loan); Ayr United, 1956

JIMMY WHITTLE
Centre-forward

A qualified chartered accountant, Jimmy Whittle was also a tough inside or centre-forward who was strong in the tackle and useful in the air. He displayed a determined up-and-at-'em style but could not command a regular first-team place due to an abundance of quality forwards on Hearts' books in the early '50s. However, Whittle proved an able deputy on many occasions. He knew the route to goal and came to prominence in 1951–52 and 1952–53. He turned in some fine displays and scored regularly when covering for members of the Terrible Trio. After completing his National Service Jimmy remained a reserve, only being called upon when an injury crisis arose.

Ayr United succeeded in obtaining his signature in 1956 and Jimmy did well at Somerset Park.

BORN: Edinburgh, 13 May 1927

DIED: Edinburgh, 29 September 1985

HEIGHT: 5′ 8″   WEIGHT: 9st 12lb (1947)

COMPETITIVE DEBUT: v Hibernian, 9 August 1947 (LC) (A), 2–1

CAREER: Loanhead Braeside; **Hearts, Jun 1944**; Motherwell, May 1952 (£1,000)

HONOURS: Scottish League Cup r-up 1954–55 (Motherwell)

ARCHIE WILLIAMS
Left-wing

An upholsterer to trade, Archie joined Hearts from Loanhead Braeside, the McTaggart/Scott works team in the Lothian town. But there was no early debut for Archie – he left to serve in the Navy immediately after signing. He returned to Edinburgh in 1947 and played 19 League matches in 1947–48. He was a quick and elusive winger and supplied good crosses to the inside-forwards. However, he often struggled to find consistent form and was not a noted goalscorer. Urquhart, Liddell and Flavell all challenged him for the number 11 jersey during his five seasons. Archie found himself playing mostly reserve-team football although he did manage a brief burst of form in season 1950–51. He was soon out of favour again, though, and became increasingly frustrated at his failure to establish himself. He asked for a transfer in April 1952 and, one month later, a move to Motherwell was negotiated.

BRIAN WILSON
Goalkeeper

HEIGHT: 6'   WEIGHT: 12st (1976)

COMPETITIVE DEBUT: v Dundee, 14 August 1976 (LC) (H), 2–0

CAREER: Arbroath, 1970; **Hearts, July 1976** (free transfer); Nairn County, Apr 1977 (free transfer); Stenhousemuir, 1977

Brian was signed to compensate for the loss of Ken Garland and David Graham who had quit Hearts during the course of season 1975–76. He played in Hearts' sectional League Cup ties before Jim Cruickshank took over. Wilson took part in three major games as a Hearts player. He lost four goals twice to SV Hamburg in the Cup-Winners' Cup, then was in the losing side to Celtic in a League Cup semi-final at Hampden. Brian was dropped in November 1976 after a run of defeats. He returned for one final appearance in Hearts' last Premier League match before relegation in April 1977, and received a free transfer later that week.

TOMMY WILSON
Full-back

BORN: Paisley, 24 August 1961

HEIGHT: 5' 8"   WEIGHT: 9st 7lb (1992)

COMPETITIVE DEBUT: v Slavia Prague, 30 September 1992 (UEFA) (H), 4–2 (came on as substitute)

CAREER: Queens Park, 1978; St Mirren, 1982; Dunfermline, Nov 1989; **Hearts, Aug 1992** (free transfer); Kilmarnock, Nov 1992 (free transfer); Dumbarton, 1993; SFA Community Coach, June 1994

HONOURS: Scotland U-21 international; Scottish Cup winner 1986–87 (St Mirren)

Signed to provide emergency cover and also as a good example to young players, Tommy had a reputation as a clean-living, dedicated professional. It was thought his influence on emerging young reserve players would prove invaluable. His one and only first-team appearance was against Slavia Prague. He replaced hero of the night Glynn Snodin late in the game. His task was to use his experience and close down the midfield, and he certainly buzzed around in those last few minutes. When Kilmarnock offered Tom the chance of first-team action, Hearts did not stand in his way.

ERNIE WINCHESTER
Forward

BORN: Aberdeen, 18 May 1944

HEIGHT: 6'   WEIGHT: 12st 6lb (1970)

COMPETITIVE DEBUT: v St Mirren, 19 April 1969 (Lge) (H), 2–1

CAREER: Torry School (Aberdeen); Aberdeen, 1959; Kansas City (USA), 1969; **Hearts, Apr 1969** (£10,000); Arbroath, May 1972

HONOURS: Scotland Schoolboy international

Ernie spent ten years with Aberdeen before heading for the United States, scoring 13 goals in 17 appearances for Kansas City Spurs. He had made his mark as a rugged, tough leader of the Aberdeen attack. John Harvey remembered his all-action style and hoped he could be an ideal target man to feed Donald Ford at Hearts. The big striker got off to a good start but injuries and illness always interrupted his efforts to settle into the side. He started season 1969–70 with an impressive burst of form and four goals in the League Cup but his goals were thin on the ground thereafter. He moved to midfield in 1971–72 but this didn't work out as had been hoped. Ernie was transferred to Arbroath for a nominal fee at the end of 1971–72.

FRASER WISHART

Full-back

BORN: Johnstone, 1 March 1965

HEIGHT: 5' 8"   **WEIGHT:** 10st 1lb (1995)

COMPETITIVE DEBUT: v Falkirk, 1 April 1995 (PL) (H), 0–1

CAREER: Pollok Juniors; Motherwell, 1984; St Mirren, Aug 1989 (£285,000); Falkirk, Nov 1992 (free transfer); Rangers, July 1993 (free transfer); **Hearts, March 1995** (£50,000)

HONOURS: Scotland U-21 international; Division I winner 1984–85 (Motherwell)

Sturdy defender with short, powerfully-built legs, Fraser has an unusual running style but is deceptively quick over the first 50 yards. He is a constructive player who can create openings with crisp, accurate passes or his dangerous long throw-ins. He is a sound tackler.

Fraser was a highly-rated youngster at Fir Park and was continually linked to the possibility of a transfer to a big club. He moved to a St Mirren side slipping into decline and he was freed when they were relegated in 1992. Frustratingly, Wishart was out of football for six months until Falkirk offered him a short-term contract. He found a new lease of life at Brockville, but the Bairns' relegation meant a new deal was not an option.

A shock move to champions Rangers followed, but Fraser was used principally as a squad player and provided cover when big-money stars were injured or suspended. Sandy Clark tried to sign him for Hearts in February 1994 but a deal was not agreed, and Steve Frail arrived at Tynecastle instead. His former boss at Motherwell, Tommy McLean, took him to Tynecastle in March 1995 to bolster his squad.

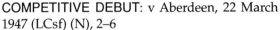

DAVID WOOD

Right-half

BORN: Glasgow

HEIGHT: 6' 1"   **WEIGHT:** 12st (1947)

COMPETITIVE DEBUT: v Aberdeen, 22 March 1947 (LCsf) (N), 2–6

CAREER: Parkhead Juniors; **Hearts, June 1942;** freed, c.1947

David is known to have made at least one guest appearance for Manchester United during the war. A knee injury resulted in a cartilage operation in 1943 for the tall, leggy and rather gangling right-half. His debut and only Hearts game was a nightmare. He headed an own-goal at a time when Hearts were leading 2–1. His game fell apart along with the rest of the defence and Aberdeen won 6–2.

BORN: Whitburn, 25 January 1943

HEIGHT: 5′ 9″   WEIGHT: 11st 7lb (1970)

COMPETITIVE DEBUT: v Celtic, 8 August 1970 (LC) (H), 1–2

CAREER: Whitburn School; Lothian United; Shotts Bon Accord; Newcastle United, 1961; Rangers, 1961 (£2,000); Dundee United, Aug 1967 (exchange deal); **Hearts, Apr 1970** (in exchange for Tommy Traynor); Raith Rovers, May 1973 (free transfer)

HONOURS: Scottish League Cup winner 1964–65 (Rangers); r-up 1965–66 (Rangers); Texaco Cup r-up 1970–71 (Hearts)

WILSON WOOD

Half-back

Having worked as a laboratory assistant with the National Coal Board, Wilson joined Newcastle as a 17-year-old. He became unsettled on Tyneside and soon came home to Rangers. During a six-year association with the Gers, Wood won a League Cup medal as well as many reserve-team medals. He moved to Dundee United in 1967 and joined Hearts three years later after a contract dispute with Jerry Kerr. A Hearts supporter in his youth, Wilson was delighted to end his Tannadice reserve-team nightmare to join his boyhood favourites.

Wilson's debut came in a Shield match against Hibs, and he scored in a 3–2 win. Most of his Hearts career thereafter was plagued by injury problems. The forceful half-back served Hearts well, however, and deputised in several positions when called upon.

A general lack of club achievement in 1972–73 saw Wood granted a free transfer as new players were brought in. A wrangle developed between Raith Rovers and Hamilton Accies when Wilson signed different forms for each club. When the dust settled he was deemed a Raith player. After retiring from football he worked as a physiotherapist in Whitburn.

GEORGE WRIGHT
Versatile

BORN: Johannesburg, 22 December 1969

HEIGHT: 5' 7" **WEIGHT:** 10st 2lb (1991)

COMPETITIVE DEBUT: v Rangers, 5 May 1990 (PL) (H), 1–1 (came on as substitute)

CAREER: Hutcheson Vale Boys Club; **Hearts, July 1986**

HONOURS: Premier League r-up 1991–92 (Hearts); Tennents Sixes winner 1990–91 (Hearts)

George was born in South Africa but brought up in Edinburgh. As a youth he supported Hearts and was delighted to join the club as a 16-year-old. He gradually developed in the reserves as a full-back but made his debut in the midfield as a replacement for Gary Mackay – most of George's appearances have been in midfield but he can cover in defence. In season 1990–91 Wright was performing well in the midfield, showing true effort and getting stuck into the fray. A bad injury in a UEFA Cup tie against Dniepr saw him stretchered off, and, when he regained full fitness, other players had filled the void he left. George had to battle to regain a place and his appearances have been infrequent ever since. Unhappy with his inability to win a regular place in the team, he asked for a transfer midway through season 1993–94.

ALEX YOUNG
Forward

BORN: Loanhead, 3 February 1937

HEIGHT: 5' 8" **WEIGHT:** 10st 10lb (1960)

COMPETITIVE DEBUT: v Partick Thistle, 27 August 1955 (LC) (H), 2–1 (scored)

CAREER: Broughton Star; Musselburgh Union; Newtongrange Star, 1954; **Hearts, Aug 1955**; Everton, Nov 1960 (£42,000); Glentoran player-manager, Aug 1968 (£10,000); Stockport County, Nov 1968 (£14,000); retired through injury in Aug 1969

HONOURS: 8 full Scotland caps; 6 Scotland U-23 caps; Scotland Junior international; 2 Scottish League caps; Scottish League winner 1957–58, 1959–60 (Hearts); Scottish Cup winner 1955–56 (Hearts); Scottish League Cup winner 1959–60 (Hearts); English League winner 1962–63 (Everton); English FA Cup winner 1965–66 (Everton)

Alex was a hero-worshipped blond bombshell. A prolific goalscorer with ability and graceful style, he was effective with both feet and good in the air. Deft touches were his trademark. He exploded on the Tynecastle scene only weeks after his call-up from junior football and made a goalscoring debut. The climax of season 1955–56 saw Alex win a Scottish Cup winners' medal at the age of 19. He was an ever-present in Hearts' record-breaking 1957–58 League campaign, netting 24 of the 132 goals scored that season. He was on target again in the 1959 League Cup final against Third Lanark as Hearts won 2–1. He was idolised by the fans, particularly on Ne'er Day 1960, when a tremendous hat-trick helped Hearts to a crushing 5–1 win over Hibs.

English interest soon arrived in the shape of Mersey giants Everton. A record fee took Young south along with George Thomson, to the dismay of the fans. He was equally revered at Goodison Park, and League and Cup honours soon followed. Alex was even the subject of a television play about his career entitled *The Golden Vision*. He played on for two years after leaving Everton but arthritis in his knee forced his retiral. In later years he was the licensee of the Linton Bar, West Linton, and the owner of a furniture wholesale business.

BORN: Milton of Campsie, 15 March 1950

DREW YOUNG

Forward

HEIGHT: 5' 6"   WEIGHT: 9st 9lb (1970)

COMPETITIVE DEBUT: v Airdrie, 19 October 1970 (Tex. C) (A), 5–0 (scored)

CAREER: Glasgow United; **Hearts, 1967**; Airdrie, Apr 1971 (free transfer); Hamilton Accies, Aug 1972

A small, fair-haired striker, Drew Young was lightweight but determined and full of running. John Harvey likened his style to that of Johnny Hamilton. Drew commented that his debut had come as a complete surprise. Nobody was informed of his inclusion until half an hour before kick-off time and he thought it was a wind-up when his name was read out. His superb volley in scoring that night was no joke, however! Young had a short run in the team thereafter, though the arrival of Bobby Seith as team boss in November 1970 changed things, with George Fleming or Eric Carruthers appearing in the number 7 jersey. The new boss clearly didn't see a future for Drew. He played only a couple more games and was then handed a free transfer. He later played at full-back for Hamilton Accies in the 1970s.

DEREK ADDISON

	LEAGUE CUP		SCOTTISH LEAGUE		SCOTTISH CUP		EUROPE		OTHERS		TOTALS	
SEASON	APPS	GLS	APPS	GLS	APPS	GLS	APPS	GLS	APPS	GLS	APPS	GLS
1981–82	—	—	32	4	2	0	—	—	2	0	36	4

JOHN ADIE

	LEAGUE CUP		SCOTTISH LEAGUE		SCOTTISH CUP		EUROPE		OTHERS		TOTALS	
SEASON	APPS	GLS	APPS	GLS	APPS	GLS	APPS	GLS	APPS	GLS	APPS	GLS
1947–48	—	—	—	—	—	—	—	—	1	0	1	0
1948–49	—	—	4	0	—	—	—	—	4	0	8	0
1949–50	—	—	—	—	—	—	—	—	—	—	—	—
1950–51	—	—	2	0	—	—	—	—	5	0	7	0
1951–52	—	—	10	0	—	—	—	—	2	0	12	0
1952–53	1	0	7	0	1	0	—	—	2+1	0	11+1	0
1953–54	—	—	26	0	3	0	—	—	19	1(1P)	48	1(1P)
1954–55	6	0	7	0	—	—	—	—	4	0	17	0
TOTALS	7	0	56	0	4	0	—	—	37+1	1(1P)	104+1	1(1P)

KENNY AIRD

	LEAGUE CUP		SCOTTISH LEAGUE		SCOTTISH CUP		EUROPE		TEXACO CUP		ANGLO-SCOTTISH CUP		OTHERS		TOTALS	
SEASON	APPS	GLS	APPS	GLS	APPS	GLS	APPS	GLS	APPS	GLS	APPS	GLS	APPS	GLS	APPS	GLS
1972–73	—	—	10	0	—	—	—	—	—	—	—	—	1	0	11	0
1973–74	6	1	17+1	2	6	0	—	—	3	0	—	—	2	0	34+1	3
1974–75	8	3	12+5	0	—	—	—	—	2	0	—	—	6	0	28+5	3
1975–76	—	—	26+2	7	8+1	0	—	—	—	—	1+1	0	6+2	2	41+6	9
1976–77	4	1	13+3	0	1	0	3	0	—	—	—	—	1	0	22+3	1
TOTALS	18	5	78+11	9	15+1	0	3	0	5	0	1+1	0	16+2	2	136+15	16

RAB AITCHISON

	LEAGUE CUP		SCOTTISH LEAGUE		SCOTTISH CUP		EUROPE		OTHERS		TOTALS	
SEASON	APPS	GLS	APPS	GLS	APPS	GLS	APPS	GLS	APPS	GLS	APPS	GLS
1965–66	—	—	2	0	—	—	—	—	1	0	3	0
1966–67	—	—	1	0	—	—	—	—	1	0	2	0
TOTALS	—	—	3	0	—	—	—	—	2	0	5	0

THOMSON ALLAN FIGURES IN BRACKETS REPRESENT SHUT-OUTS

	LEAGUE CUP		SCOTTISH LEAGUE		SCOTTISH CUP		EUROPE		OTHERS		TOTALS	
SEASON	APPS	GLS	APPS	GLS	APPS	GLS	APPS	GLS	APPS	GLS	APPS	GLS
1978–79	—	—	16	(2)	—	—	—	—	—	—	16	(2)
1979–80	2	(0)	8	(0)	—	—	—	—	5	(1)	15	(1)
TOTALS	2	(0)	24	(2)	—	—	—	—	5	(1)	31	(3)

ALAN ANDERSON

SEASON	LEAGUE CUP APPS	GLS	SCOTTISH LEAGUE APPS	GLS	SCOTTISH CUP APPS	GLS	EUROPE APPS	GLS	TEXACO CUP APPS	GLS	ANGLO-SCOTTISH CUP APPS	GLS	OTHERS APPS	GLS	TOTALS APPS	GLS
1963–64	—	—	8	0	—	—	—	—	—	—	—	—	5	0	13	0
1964–65	1	0	33	0	4	0	—	—	—	—	—	—	11	0	49	0
1965–66	5	0	34	1	4	2	5	2	—	—	—	—	5	1	53	6
1966–67	5	0	29	3	1	0	—	—	—	—	—	—	6	1	41	4
1967–68	6	0	22+2	4	4	1	—	—	—	—	—	—	4	0	36+2	5
1968–69	—	—	19+2	3	2	0	—	—	—	—	—	—	7	1	28+2	4
1969–70	6	0	34	2	3	0	—	—	—	—	—	—	8	0	51	2
1970–71	2	0	34	3	2	0	—	—	8	0	—	—	9+2	0	55+2	3
1971–72	6	0	28	2	4	1	—	—	2	1	—	—	4	0	44	4
1972–73	6	1	30	2	2	0	—	—	4	0	—	—	6	3	48	6
1973–74	6	0	27	0	7	2	—	—	4	0	—	—	1	0	45	2
1974–75	—	—	28	0	4	0	—	—	1	0	—	—	2	0	35	0
1975–76	6	0	22	1	2	0	—	—	—	—	3	0	—	—	33	1
TOTALS	49	1	348+4	21	39	6	5	2	19	1	3	0	68+2	6	531+6	37

DAVID ANDERSON   FIGURES IN BRACKETS REPRESENT SHUT-OUTS

SEASON	LEAGUE CUP APPS	GLS	SCOTTISH LEAGUE APPS	GLS	SCOTTISH CUP APPS	GLS	SUMMER CUP APPS	GLS	OTHERS APPS	GLS	TOTALS APPS	GLS
1963–64	—	—	—	—	—	—	1	(0)	—	—	1	(0)
1964–65	—	—	—	—	—	—	2	(0)	—	—	2	(0)
TOTALS	—	—	—	—	—	—	3	(0)	—	—	3	(0)

DOUGLAS ARMSTRONG

SEASON	LEAGUE CUP APPS	GLS	SCOTTISH LEAGUE APPS	GLS	SCOTTISH CUP APPS	GLS	EUROPE APPS	GLS	OTHERS APPS	GLS	TOTALS APPS	GLS
1948–49	—	—	—	—	—	—	—	—	3	0	3	0
1949–50	—	—	—	—	—	—	—	—	—	—	—	—
1950–51	—	—	—	—	—	—	—	—	3	1	3	1
1951–52	—	—	2	0	—	—	—	—	1	0	3	0
1952–53	—	—	19	0	4	0	—	—	7	0	30	0
1953–54	6	0	16	1	—	—	—	—	16	0	38	1
1954–55	—	—	6	0	—	—	—	—	1	0	7	0
TOTALS	6	0	43	1	4	0	—	—	31	1	84	2

IAN BAIRD

SEASON	LEAGUE CUP APPS	GLS	SCOTTISH LEAGUE APPS	GLS	SCOTTISH CUP APPS	GLS	EUROPE APPS	GLS	OTHERS APPS	GLS	TOTALS APPS	GLS
1991–92	3	2	30	6	3	0	—	—	1	1(1P)	37	9(1P)
1992–93	2	0	34	9	4	1	3	1	3	1	46	12
TOTALS	5	2	64	15	7	1	3	1	4	2(1P)	83	21(1P)

EAMONN BANNON

SEASON	LEAGUE CUP		SCOTTISH LEAGUE		SCOTTISH CUP		EUROPE		TEXACO CUP		ANGLO-SCOTTISH CUP		OTHERS		TOTALS	
	APPS	GLS	APPS	GLS	APPS	GLS	APPS	GLS	APPS	GLS	APPS	GLS	APPS	GLS	APPS	GLS
1976–77	—	—	12+1	1	4+1	0	0+1	0	—	—	—	—	—	—	16+3	1
1977–78	7	3	39	13(2P)	3	1(1P)	—	—	—	—	—	—	4	0	53	17(3P)
1978–79	2	1(1P)	19	5(3P)	—	—	—	—	—	—	2	1	3	1	26	8(4P)
1988–89	3+1	0	23+7	2	3	2	7+1	1	—	—	—	—	10+2	0	46+11	5
1989–90	3	1	31+2	2	3	0	—	—	—	—	—	—	6	1(1P)	43+2	4(1P)
1990–91	1+2	1	15+4	2	—	—	3	0	—	—	—	—	1+3	0	20+9	3
1991–92	—	—	10+3	2	4+1	0	—	—	—	—	—	—	1+1	1	15+5	3
1992–93	—	—	8+11	1	0+2	0	2+1	0	—	—	—	—	3+1	0	13+15	1
1994–95	—	—	—	—	—	—	—	—	—	—	—	—	1	0	1	0
TOTALS	16+3	6(1P)	157+28	28(5P)	17+4	3(1P)	12+3	1	—	—	2	1	29+7	3(1P)	233+45	42(8P)

ROY BARRY

SEASON	LEAGUE CUP		SCOTTISH LEAGUE		SCOTTISH CUP		EUROPE		OTHERS		TOTALS	
	APPS	GLS	APPS	GLS	APPS	GLS	APPS	GLS	APPS	GLS	APPS	GLS
1961–62	1	0	3	0	—	—	—	—	5	0	9	0
1962–63	10	0	28	1	2	0	—	—	2	0	42	1
1963–64	4	0	28	0	3	0	3	0	14	1	52	1
1964–65	5	0	16	7	3	0	—	—	12	2	36	9
1965–66	6	1	17	0	2	0	—	—	4	1	29	2
1966–67	6	0	2	0	—	—	—	—	2	0	10	0
TOTALS	32	1	94	8	10	0	3	0	39	4	178	13

WILLIE BAULD

SEASON	LEAGUE CUP		SCOTTISH LEAGUE		SCOTTISH CUP		EUROPE		OTHERS		TOTALS	
	APPS	GLS	APPS	GLS	APPS	GLS	APPS	GLS	APPS	GLS	APPS	GLS
1947–48	—	—	—	—	—	—	—	—	1	1	1	1
1948–49	2	6	24	17	4	1	—	—	7	4	37	28
1949–50	6	8	29	30	3	2	—	—	4	4	42	44
1950–51	6	3	30	15	3	2	—	—	10	6	49	26
1951–52	6	8	29	14	7	5	—	—	5	2	47	29
1952–53	5	5	23	10	4	2	—	—	4	1	36	18
1953–54	6	4	21	10	3	0	—	—	11	8	41	22
1954–55	9	12	25	21	4	6	—	—	4	1	42	40
1955–56	3	0	20	15	5	3	—	—	2	0	30	18
1956–57	6	3	24	12	1	0	—	—	9	3	40	18
1957–58	6	5	9	5	—	—	—	—	10+1	8	25+1	18
1958–59	8	9	20	15	2	0	2	2	17	28	49	54
1959–60	6	3	17	10	—	—	—	—	9	9	32	22
1960–61	4	3	11	3	3	0	1	0	3	3	22	9
1961–62	3	1	10	6	1	1	2	0	—	—	16	8
TOTALS	76	70	292	183	40	22	5	2	96+1	78	509+1	355

BOBBY BAXTER

SEASON	LEAGUE CUP		SCOTTISH LEAGUE		SCOTTISH CUP		EUROPE		OTHERS		TOTALS	
	APPS	GLS	APPS	GLS	APPS	GLS	APPS	GLS	APPS	GLS	APPS	GLS
1946–47	8	1(1P)	25	0	3	1	—	—	—	—	36	2(1P)

BILLY BENNETT

SEASON	LEAGUE CUP		SCOTTISH LEAGUE		SCOTTISH CUP		EUROPE		OTHERS		TOTALS	
	APPS	GLS	APPS	GLS	APPS	GLS	APPS	GLS	APPS	GLS	APPS	GLS
1974–75	—	—	1	0	—	—	—	—	1	1	2	1

NEIL BERRY

SEASON	LEAGUE CUP		SCOTTISH LEAGUE		SCOTTISH CUP		EUROPE		OTHERS		TOTALS	
	APPS	GLS	APPS	GLS	APPS	GLS	APPS	GLS	APPS	GLS	APPS	GLS
1984–85	—	—	2+1	0	3	0	—	—	—	—	5+1	0
1985–86	—	—	32	2	5	0	—	—	7+1	0	44+1	2
1986–87	1	0	30	3	5	0	1	0	7	1	44	4
1987–88	3	1	31+4	0	4	0	—	—	7	2	45+4	3
1988–89	4	0	32	1	3	0	8	0	4	0	51	1
1989–90	2	0	10	1	1+1	0	—	—	4	1	17+1	2
1990–91	2	0	18+1	1	1	0	3	0	3+1	0	27+2	1
1991–92	—	—	—	—	—	—	—	—	0+1	0	0+1	0
1992–93	0+1	0	16+1	1	1	0	1	0	1+1	0	19+3	1
1993–94	1	0	30	0	3	0	—	—	3+3	0	37+3	0
1994–95	1	0	29	0	2	0	—	—	3+1	0	35+1	0
TOTALS	14+1	1	230+7	9	28+1	0	13	0	39+8	4	324+17	14

JIM BETT

SEASON	LEAGUE CUP		SCOTTISH LEAGUE		SCOTTISH CUP		EUROPE		OTHERS		TOTALS	
	APPS	GLS	APPS	GLS	APPS	GLS	APPS	GLS	APPS	GLS	APPS	GLS
1994–95	—	—	26	2(1P)	4	0	—	—	—	—	30	2(1P)

IAN BLACK

SEASON	LEAGUE CUP		SCOTTISH LEAGUE		SCOTTISH CUP		EUROPE		OTHERS		TOTALS	
	APPS	GLS	APPS	GLS	APPS	GLS	APPS	GLS	APPS	GLS	APPS	GLS
1978–79	—	—	10+4	0	2+1	0	—	—	1	0	13+5	0
1979–80	2	0	17+1	0	—	—	—	—	2	0	21+1	0
TOTALS	2	0	27+5	0	2+1	0	—	—	3	0	34+6	0

KENNY BLACK

SEASON	LEAGUE CUP		SCOTTISH LEAGUE		SCOTTISH CUP		EUROPE		OTHERS		TOTALS	
	APPS	GLS	APPS	GLS	APPS	GLS	APPS	GLS	APPS	GLS	APPS	GLS
1984–85	2	0	32	7(5P)	5	0	2	0	6	3(3P)	47	10(8P)
1985–86	2	0	23+6	2(1P)	5	1	—	—	6+3	1	36+9	4(1P)
1986–87	1	0	41+1	1	7	1	2	0	8	1	59+1	3
1987–88	1+1	0	41+1	4	4	0	—	—	10+1	1(1P)	56+3	5(1P)
1988–89	3	1	33	1	0+1	0	8	1	12	2(1P)	56+1	5(1P)
TOTALS	9+1	1	170+8	15(6P)	21+1	2	12	1	42+4	8(5P)	254+14	27(11P)

BOBBY BLACKWOOD

SEASON	LEAGUE CUP		SCOTTISH LEAGUE		SCOTTISH CUP		EUROPE		OTHERS		TOTALS	
	APPS	GLS	APPS	GLS	APPS	GLS	APPS	GLS	APPS	GLS	APPS	GLS
1951–52	—	—	—	—	—	—	—	—	1	0	1	0
1952–53	—	—	14	2	1	2	—	—	5	1	20	5
1953–54	2	0	4	0	—	—	—	—	13	1	19	1
1954–55	7	3	3	0	—	—	—	—	4	0	14	3
1955–56	4	0	5	0	—	—	—	—	1	0	10	0
1956–57	—	—	—	—	—	—	—	—	—	—	—	—
1957–58	—	—	23	4	2	2	—	—	10+2	5	35+2	11
1958–59	5	0	16	4	—	—	2	0	13+1	9	36+1	13
1959–60	9	5	28	12	1	0	—	—	11+1	7	49+1	24
1960–61	7	0	26	11	3	3	2	0	2	0	40	14
1961–62	7	0	17	2	1	1	2	1	5	3	32	7
TOTALS	41	8	136	35	8	8	6	1	65+4	26	256+4	78

JIMMY BONE

SEASON	LEAGUE CUP		SCOTTISH LEAGUE		SCOTTISH CUP		EUROPE		OTHERS		TOTALS	
	APPS	GLS	APPS	GLS	APPS	GLS	APPS	GLS	APPS	GLS	APPS	GLS
1983–84	5	1	34	7	2	1	—	—	6+1	1	47+1	10
1984–85	5	1	16+6	4	—	—	2	0	4	1	27+6	6
TOTALS	10	2	50+6	11	2	1	2	0	10+1	2	74+7	16

ADRIAN BOOTHROYD

SEASON	LEAGUE CUP		SCOTTISH LEAGUE		SCOTTISH CUP		EUROPE		OTHERS		TOTALS	
	APPS	GLS	APPS	GLS	APPS	GLS	APPS	GLS	APPS	GLS	APPS	GLS
1992–93	—	—	0+4	0	0+2	2	—	—	—	—	0+6	2
1993–94	—	—	—	—	—	—	—	—	3+1	1	3+1	1
TOTALS	—	—	0+4	0	0+2	2	—	—	3+1	1	3+7	3

ANDY BOWMAN

SEASON	LEAGUE CUP		SCOTTISH LEAGUE		SCOTTISH CUP		EUROPE		OTHERS		TOTALS	
	APPS	GLS	APPS	GLS	APPS	GLS	APPS	GLS	APPS	GLS	APPS	GLS
1955–56	6	0	2	0	—	—	—	—	0+2	0	8+2	0
1956–57	—	—	3	0	—	—	—	—	6	1	9	1
1957–58	—	—	18	2	3	0	—	—	9	1	30	3
1958–59	5	0	7	0	—	—	1	0	3	0	16	0
1959–60	6	0	24	0	2	0	—	—	12	0	44	0
1960–61	3	1	16	1	3	0	2	0	1	0	25	2
TOTALS	20	1	70	3	8	0	3	0	31+2	2	132+2	6

DAVID BOWMAN

SEASON	LEAGUE CUP		SCOTTISH LEAGUE		SCOTTISH CUP		EUROPE		OTHERS		TOTALS	
	APPS	GLS	APPS	GLS	APPS	GLS	APPS	GLS	APPS	GLS	APPS	GLS
1980–81	4	1	16+2	1	—	—	—	—	3+2	0	23+4	2
1981–82	5	0	16	1	2	0	—	—	4+2	0	27+2	1
1982–83	9	2	39	5	4	0	—	—	6	1	58	8
1983–84	7	0	32+1	0	0+1	0	—	—	8	2	47+2	2
1984–85	4	0	9+2	1	—	—	2	0	3	0	18+2	1
TOTALS	29	3	112+5	8	6+1	0	2	0	24+4	3	173+10	14

CRAWFORD BOYD

SEASON	LEAGUE CUP		SCOTTISH LEAGUE		SCOTTISH CUP		EUROPE		OTHERS		TOTALS	
	APPS	GLS	APPS	GLS	APPS	GLS	APPS	GLS	APPS	GLS	APPS	GLS
1979–80	—	—	28	0	3	0	—	—	2	0	33	0
1980–81	3	0	5	0	—	—	—	—	4+1	0	12+1	0
TOTALS	3	0	33	0	3	0	—	—	6+1	0	45+1	0

JIMMY BRISCOE

SEASON	LEAGUE CUP		SCOTTISH LEAGUE		SCOTTISH CUP		EUROPE		OTHERS		TOTALS	
	APPS	GLS	APPS	GLS	APPS	GLS	APPS	GLS	APPS	GLS	APPS	GLS
1946–47	—	—	2	0	—	—	—	—	—	—	2	0

JOHN BROUGH FIGURES IN BRACKETS REPRESENT SHUT-OUTS

SEASON	LEAGUE CUP APPS	GLS	SCOTTISH LEAGUE APPS	GLS	SCOTTISH CUP APPS	GLS	EUROPE APPS	GLS	TEXACO CUP APPS	GLS	ANGLO-SCOTTISH CUP APPS	GLS	OTHERS APPS	GLS	TOTALS APPS	GLS
1977–78	—	—	5	(2)	—	—	—	—	—	—	—	—	1	(0)	6	(2)
1978–79	2	(0)	2	(0)	2	(1)	—	—	—	—	—	—	—	—	6	(1)
1979–80	—	—	31	(15)	3	(2)	—	—	—	—	—	—	2	(1)	36	(18)
1980–81	4	(0)	34	(5)	2	(1)	—	—	—	—	2	(0)	5	(1)	47	(7)
1981–82	—	—	6	(3)	—	—	—	—	—	—	—	—	1	(0)	7	(3)
1982–83	—	—	—	—	—	—	—	—	—	—	—	—	0+2	(0)	0+2	(0)
1983–84	—	—	—	—	—	—	—	—	—	—	—	—	1+2	(1)	1+2	(1)
TOTALS	6	(0)	78	(25)	7	(4)	—	—	—	—	2	(0)	10+4	(3)	103+4	(32)

GORDON BROWN

SEASON	LEAGUE CUP APPS	GLS	SCOTTISH LEAGUE APPS	GLS	SCOTTISH CUP APPS	GLS	EUROPE APPS	GLS	OTHERS APPS	GLS	TOTALS APPS	GLS
1977–78	0+1	0	0+3	0	—	—	—	—	1	0	1+4	0

JIMMY BROWN FIGURES IN BRACKETS REPRESENT SHUT-OUTS

SEASON	LEAGUE CUP APPS	GLS	SCOTTISH LEAGUE APPS	GLS	SCOTTISH CUP APPS	GLS	EUROPE APPS	GLS	OTHERS APPS	GLS	TOTALS APPS	GLS
1946–47	9	(0)	30	(9)	3	(1)	—	—	3	(0)	45	(10)
1947–48	5	(2)	27	(7)	2	(0)	—	—	4	(1)	38	(10)
1948–49	6	(1)	30	(4)	4	(1)	—	—	5	(2)	45	(8)
1949–50	6	(0)	24	(9)	3	(0)	—	—	1	(0)	34	(9)
1950–51	6	(1)	27	(7)	3	(0)	—	—	10	(3)	46	(11)
1951–52	6	(1)	29	(2)	7	(1)	—	—	2	(0)	44	(4)
TOTALS	38	(5)	167	(38)	22	(3)	—	—	25	(6)	252	(52)

JIMMY BROWN

SEASON	LEAGUE CUP APPS	GLS	SCOTTISH LEAGUE APPS	GLS	SCOTTISH CUP APPS	GLS	EUROPE APPS	GLS	TEXACO CUP APPS	GLS	ANGLO-SCOTTISH CUP APPS	GLS	OTHERS APPS	GLS	TOTALS APPS	GLS
1968–69	—	—	1+1	0	—	—	—	—	—	—	—	—	—	—	1+1	0
1969–70	—	—	20+1	3	2+1	0	—	—	—	—	—	—	3	1	25+2	4
1970–71	3	0	33	4	2	0	—	—	7	1	—	—	6+1	0	51+1	5
1971–72	6	1	34	4	3+1	0	—	—	2	0	—	—	5	2	50+1	7
1972–73	6	0	31+1	2	2	0	—	—	4	0	—	—	4	0	47+1	2
1973–74	1	0	25+3	2	7	0	—	—	2	0	—	—	2	0	37+3	2
1974–75	8	0	18+2	0	2+1	0	—	—	2	0	—	—	5	1	35+3	1
1975–76	5+1	0	33+1	3	9	0	—	—	—	—	3	0	9	1	59+2	4
1976–77	5+2	1	34	3	6	0	4	1	—	—	—	—	—	—	49+2	5
1977–78	4	0	15	0	—	—	—	—	—	—	—	—	3	0	22	0
1978–79	2	0	22+4	0	4	0	—	—	—	—	—	—	1	0	29+4	0
TOTALS	40+3	2	266+13	21	37+3	0	4	1	17	1	3	0	38+1	5	405+20	30

WILSON BROWN

FIGURES IN BRACKETS REPRESENT SHUT-OUTS

SEASON	LEAGUE CUP APPS	GLS	SCOTTISH LEAGUE APPS	GLS	SCOTTISH CUP APPS	GLS	EUROPE APPS	GLS	OTHERS APPS	GLS	TOTALS APPS	GLS
1955–56	4	(2)	1	(1)	—	—	—	—	—	—	5	(3)
1956–57	6	(1)	19	(5)	1	(0)	—	—	4	(2)	30	(8)
1957–58	—	—	3	(1)	—	—	—	—	2	(0)	5	(1)
1958–59	—	—	3	(0)	—	—	—	—	2	(1)	5	(1)
1959–60	—	—	1	(0)	—	—	—	—	—	—	1	(0)
TOTALS	10	(3)	27	(7)	1	(0)	—	—	8	(3)	46	(13)

ANDY BRUCE

FIGURES IN BRACKETS REPRESENT SHUT-OUTS

SEASON	LEAGUE CUP APPS	GLS	SCOTTISH LEAGUE APPS	GLS	SCOTTISH CUP APPS	GLS	EUROPE APPS	GLS	OTHERS APPS	GLS	TOTALS APPS	GLS
1986–87	—	—	1	(1)	—	—	—	—	1+4	(0)	2+4	(1)
1987–88	—	—	—	—	—	—	—	—	1	(0)	1	(0)
TOTALS	—	—	1	(1)	—	—	—	—	2+4	(0)	3+4	(1)

BOBBY BUCHAN

SEASON	LEAGUE CUP APPS	GLS	SCOTTISH LEAGUE APPS	GLS	SCOTTISH CUP APPS	GLS	EUROPE APPS	GLS	OTHERS APPS	GLS	TOTALS APPS	GLS
1948–49	—	—	1	0	—	—	—	—	2	0	3	0
1949–50	—	—	—	—	—	—	—	—	—	—	—	—
1950–51	—	—	—	—	—	—	—	—	—	—	—	—
1951–52	—	—	1	0	—	—	—	—	—	—	1	0
TOTALS	—	—	2	0	—	—	—	—	2	0	4	0

HUGH BURNS

SEASON	LEAGUE CUP APPS	GLS	SCOTTISH LEAGUE APPS	GLS	SCOTTISH CUP APPS	GLS	EUROPE APPS	GLS	OTHERS APPS	GLS	TOTALS APPS	GLS
1987–88	0+1	0	23+1	0	1+1	0	—	—	5+4	1	29+7	1
1988–89	—	—	—	—	—	—	—	—	3+3	0	3+3	0
TOTALS	0+1	0	23+1	0	1+1	0	—	—	8+7	1	32+10	1

SANDY BURRELL

SEASON	LEAGUE CUP APPS	GLS	SCOTTISH LEAGUE APPS	GLS	SCOTTISH CUP APPS	GLS	EUROPE APPS	GLS	TEXACO CUP APPS	GLS	ANGLO-SCOTTISH CUP APPS	GLS	OTHERS APPS	GLS	TOTALS APPS	GLS
1974–75	—	—	2	0	—	—	—	—	1	0	—	—	—	—	3	0
1975–76	—	—	6	0	2+1	0	—	—	—	—	2	0	8+1	0	18+2	0
1976–77	4	0	6+1	0	4	0	—	—	—	—	—	—	3	0	17+1	0
TOTALS	4	0	14+1	0	6+1	0	—	—	1	0	2	0	11+1	0	38+3	0

DREW BUSBY

SEASON	LEAGUE CUP APPS	GLS	SCOTTISH LEAGUE APPS	GLS	SCOTTISH CUP APPS	GLS	EUROPE APPS	GLS	TEXACO CUP APPS	GLS	ANGLO-SCOTTISH CUP APPS	GLS	OTHERS APPS	GLS	TOTALS APPS	GLS
1973–74	6	2	27+1	12	4+1	1	—	—	4	1	—	—	2	0	43+2	16
1974–75	7	1	30	11(1P)	4	3	—	—	2	0	—	—	2	1	45	16(1P)
1975–76	6	3	32	8(4P)	7	3(1P)	—	—	—	—	4	1	9	3(1P)	58	18(6P)
1976–77	9	6(2P)	25+1	3(1P)	6	1	4	2	—	—	—	—	3	1	47+1	13(3P)
1977–78	6	3(1P)	36	15	3	1	—	—	—	—	—	—	4	1(1P)	49	20(2P)
1978–79	1+1	0	25+1	6	3	1	—	—	—	—	—	—	0+1	0	29+3	7
TOTALS	35+1	15(3P)	175+3	55(6P)	27+1	10(1P)	4	2	6	1	4	1	20+1	6(2P)	271+6	90(12P)

PADDY BYRNE

SEASON	LEAGUE CUP APPS	GLS	SCOTTISH LEAGUE APPS	GLS	SCOTTISH CUP APPS	GLS	EUROPE APPS	GLS	OTHERS APPS	GLS	TOTALS APPS	GLS
1981–82	4	0	37	8(3P)	2	1	—	—	6	1(1P)	49	10(4P)
1982–83	10	0	25+3	3	1+2	0	—	—	7+1	4(2P)	43+6	7(2P)
TOTALS	14	0	62+3	11(3P)	3+2	1	—	—	13+1	5(3P)	92+6	17(6P)

RALPH CALLACHAN

SEASON	LEAGUE CUP APPS	GLS	SCOTTISH LEAGUE APPS	GLS	SCOTTISH CUP APPS	GLS	EUROPE APPS	GLS	TEXACO CUP APPS	GLS	ANGLO-SCOTTISH CUP APPS	GLS	OTHERS APPS	GLS	TOTALS APPS	GLS
1973–74	—	—	1	0	—	—	—	—	—	—	—	—	1	2(1P)	2	2(1P)
1974–75	4+1	0	27+1	5(1P)	4	2(1P)	—	—	1	0	—	—	2+1	0	38+3	7(2P)
1975–76	3+1	2	34+1	2	8	2	—	—	—	—	4	1	8+1	2	57+3	9
1976–77	5+2	2	13	2(1P)	2	1	2	0	—	—	—	—	0+1	0	22+3	5(1P)
TOTALS	12+4	4	75+2	9(2P)	14	5(1P)	2	0	1	0	4	1	11+3	4(1P)	119+9	23(4P)

BOBBY CAMPBELL

SEASON	LEAGUE CUP APPS	GLS	SCOTTISH LEAGUE APPS	GLS	SCOTTISH CUP APPS	GLS	EUROPE APPS	GLS	OTHERS APPS	GLS	TOTALS APPS	GLS
1953–54	—	—	2	0	—	—	—	—	—	—	2	0
1954–55	—	—	—	—	—	—	—	—	—	—	—	—
1955–56	—	—	1	0	—	—	—	—	—	—	1	0
TOTALS	—	—	3	0	—	—	—	—	—	—	3	0

GEORGE CAMPBELL

SEASON	LEAGUE CUP APPS	GLS	SCOTTISH LEAGUE APPS	GLS	SCOTTISH CUP APPS	GLS	EUROPE APPS	GLS	OTHERS APPS	GLS	TOTALS APPS	GLS
1955–56	1	0	—	—	—	—	—	—	—	—	1	0
1956–57	—	—	3	2	—	—	—	—	1	2	4	4
TOTALS	1	0	3	2	—	—	—	—	1	2	5	4

JIMMY CANT

SEASON	LEAGUE CUP APPS	GLS	SCOTTISH LEAGUE APPS	GLS	SCOTTISH CUP APPS	GLS	EUROPE APPS	GLS	TEXACO CUP APPS	GLS	ANGLO-SCOTTISH CUP APPS	GLS	OTHERS APPS	GLS	TOTALS APPS	GLS
1972–73	—	—	1	0	—	—	—	—	—	—	—	—	2	0	3	0
1973–74	6	0	26	0	—	—	—	—	4	0	—	—	2	0	38	0
1974–75	8	3	8	0	—	—	—	—	2	0	—	—	4	0	22	3
1975–76	1	0	—	—	—	—	—	—	—	—	1	0	2	0	4	0
1976–77	1	0	1+1	0	—	—	—	—	—	—	—	—	—	—	2+1	0
TOTALS	16	3	36+1	0	—	—	—	—	6	0	1	0	10	0	69+1	3

ERIC CARRUTHERS

SEASON	LEAGUE CUP APPS	GLS	SCOTTISH LEAGUE APPS	GLS	SCOTTISH CUP APPS	GLS	EUROPE APPS	GLS	TEXACO CUP APPS	GLS	ANGLO-SCOTTISH CUP APPS	GLS	OTHERS APPS	GLS	TOTALS APPS	GLS
1969–70	—	—	2	0	—	—	—	—	—	—	—	—	2+1	0	4+1	0
1970–71	1	0	10	2	—	—	—	—	3	0	—	—	7	6	21	8
1971–72	1	1	8+2	2	—	—	—	—	—	—	—	—	0+2	0	9+4	3
1972–73	1	0	24+3	5	0+2	0	—	—	2	0	—	—	5	6	32+5	11
1973–74	—	—	1	0	—	—	—	—	—	—	—	—	—	—	1	0
1974–75	—	—	5+2	1	—	—	—	—	—	—	—	—	—	—	5+2	1
TOTALS	3	1	50+7	10	0+2	0	—	—	5	0	—	—	14+3	12	72+12	23

PAUL CHERRY

SEASON	LEAGUE CUP APPS	GLS	SCOTTISH LEAGUE APPS	GLS	SCOTTISH CUP APPS	GLS	EUROPE APPS	GLS	OTHERS APPS	GLS	TOTALS APPS	GLS
1982–83	—	—	—	—	—	—	—	—	0+1	0	0+1	0
1983–84	—	—	—	—	—	—	—	—	2	0	2	0
1984–85	—	—	0+3	0	—	—	—	—	—	—	0+3	0
1985–86	0+2	1	3+2	0	—	—	—	—	1	0	4+4	1
TOTALS	0+2	1	3+5	0	—	—	—	—	3+1	0	6+8	1

SANDY CLARK

SEASON	LEAGUE CUP		SCOTTISH LEAGUE		SCOTTISH CUP		EUROPE		OTHERS		TOTALS	
	APPS	GLS	APPS	GLS	APPS	GLS	APPS	GLS	APPS	GLS	APPS	GLS
1984–85	—	—	25	8	5	1	—	—	1	1	31	10
1985–86	2	0	33	12	5	0	—	—	8	4	48	16
1986–87	1	0	41	8	7	0	2	1	9	4	60	13
1987–88	3	2	11+24	6	1+1	1	—	—	9+1	2	24+26	11
1988–89	2	0	1+1	1	—	—	—	—	5+4	5	8+5	6
1993–94	—	—	—	—	—	—	—	—	0+3	0	0+3	0
TOTALS	8	2	111+25	35	18+1	2	2	1	32+8	16	171+34	56

DAVID CLUNIE

SEASON	LEAGUE CUP		SCOTTISH LEAGUE		SCOTTISH CUP		EUROPE		TEXACO CUP		ANGLO-SCOTTISH CUP		OTHERS		TOTALS	
	APPS	GLS	APPS	GLS	APPS	GLS	APPS	GLS	APPS	GLS	APPS	GLS	APPS	GLS	APPS	GLS
1965–66	—	—	—	—	—	—	—	—	—	—	—	—	1	0	1	0
1966–67	—	—	0+3	0	—	—	—	—	—	—	—	—	—	—	0+3	0
1967–68	—	—	—	—	—	—	—	—	—	—	—	—	—	—	—	—
1968–69	1	0	15	0	—	—	—	—	—	—	—	—	4	0	20	0
1969–70	6	1	34	3(2P)	3	0	—	—	—	—	—	—	7	0	50	4(2P)
1970–71	6	1	29	1	2	0	—	—	6	0	—	—	12	1	55	3
1971–72	—	—	5	0	—	—	—	—	—	—	—	—	1	0	6	0
1972–73	6	0	25	1	1	0	—	—	4	1(1P)	—	—	7	1	43	3(1P)
1973–74	6	0	31	0	5	0	—	—	4	0	—	—	2	0	48	0
1974–75	1	0	27	0	4	0	—	—	—	—	—	—	5	0	37	0
1975–76	6	0	26	0	6	0	—	—	—	—	4	0	3+1	0	45+1	0
1976–77	7	0	29+1	0	3	0	4	0	—	—	—	—	0+1	0	43+2	0
TOTALS	39	2	221+4	5(2P)	24	0	4	0	14	1(1P)	4	0	42+2	2	348+6	10(3P)

JOHN COCHRANE

SEASON	LEAGUE CUP		SCOTTISH LEAGUE		SCOTTISH CUP		EUROPE		OTHERS		TOTALS	
	APPS	GLS	APPS	GLS	APPS	GLS	APPS	GLS	APPS	GLS	APPS	GLS
1953–54	—	—	2	1	—	—	—	—	2	1	4	2

JOHN COLQUHOUN

SEASON	LEAGUE CUP APPS	GLS	SCOTTISH LEAGUE APPS	GLS	SCOTTISH CUP APPS	GLS	EUROPE APPS	GLS	OTHERS APPS	GLS	TOTALS APPS	GLS
1985–86	2+1	1	36	8	5	2	—	—	8	0	51+1	11
1986–87	1	0	42+1	13	6+1	1	2	0	8+2	5	59+4	19
1987–88	3	0	43+1	15	4	1	—	—	8+2	1	58+3	17
1988–89	4	1	34+2	5	3	2	7+1	1	11+1	3	59+4	12
1989–90	3	0	36	6	3	2	—	—	4	1	46	9
1990–91	2	0	36	7	1	0	4	0	6	2	49	9
1993–94	2	0	38+3	6	3	0	2	1	5	0	50+3	7
1994–95	2	1	23+8	2	2+3	0	—	—	4+2	3	31+13	6
TOTALS	19+1	3	288+15	62	27+4	8	15+1	2	54+7	15	403+28	90

ALFIE CONN (Snr)

SEASON	LEAGUE CUP APPS	GLS	SCOTTISH LEAGUE APPS	GLS	SCOTTISH CUP APPS	GLS	EUROPE APPS	GLS	OTHERS APPS	GLS	TOTALS APPS	GLS
1946–47	6	1	12	3	2	1	—	—	3	3	23	8
1947–48	—	—	—	—	—	—	—	—	—	—	—	—
1948–49	4	3	22	13	2	1	—	—	4	3	32	20
1949–50	5	4	23	13	2	0	—	—	4	3	34	20
1950–51	6	3	28	19	3	2	—	—	8	4	45	28
1951–52	3	3	25	12	7	4	—	—	5	5	40	24
1952–53	3	2	25	11	4	0	—	—	5	2	37	15
1953–54	6	1	26	11	3	1	—	—	20+1	15	55+1	28
1954–55	10	4	22	10	4	1	—	—	4	2	40	17
1955–56	8	5	25	17	5	5	—	—	3	1	41	28
1956–57	6	1	10	2	1	0	—	—	4	5	21	8
1957–58	4	1	5	4	—	—	—	—	5	11	14	16
1960–61	—	—	—	—	—	—	—	—	1	0	1	0
TOTALS	61	28	223	115	33	15	—	—	66+1	54	383+1	212

ALFIE CONN (Jnr)

SEASON	LEAGUE CUP APPS	GLS	SCOTTISH LEAGUE APPS	GLS	SCOTTISH CUP APPS	GLS	EUROPE APPS	GLS	OTHERS APPS	GLS	TOTALS APPS	GLS
1980–81	2	0	13+4	3	—	—	—	—	6	0	21+4	3

IM COWELL

SEASON	LEAGUE CUP APPS	GLS	SCOTTISH LEAGUE APPS	GLS	SCOTTISH CUP APPS	GLS	EUROPE APPS	GLS	OTHERS APPS	GLS	TOTALS APPS	GLS
1984–85	—	—	0+1	0	—	—	—	—	1	0	1+1	0

GEORGE COWIE

SEASON	LEAGUE CUP APPS	GLS	SCOTTISH LEAGUE APPS	GLS	SCOTTISH CUP APPS	GLS	EUROPE APPS	GLS	OTHERS APPS	GLS	TOTALS APPS	GLS
1983–84	7	0	35	1	2	1	—	—	6+2	1	50+2	3
1984–85	5	0	14+1	0	—	—	1	0	2+1	0	22+2	0
1985–86	1	0	8	0	—	—	—	—	2+2	0	11+2	0
1986–87	—	—	9+1	1	4	0	—	—	2	0	15+1	1
TOTALS	13	0	66+2	2	6	1	1	0	12+5	1	98+7	4

CHARLIE COX

SEASON	LEAGUE CUP APPS	GLS	SCOTTISH LEAGUE APPS	GLS	SCOTTISH CUP APPS	GLS	EUROPE APPS	GLS	OTHERS APPS	GLS	TOTALS APPS	GLS
1946–47	7	0	21	1	2	0	—	—	1	0	31	1
1947–48	6	0	10	0	—	—	—	—	2	0	18	0
1948–49	2	0	17	1	4	1	—	—	6	3	29	5
1949–50	6	0	25	0	—	—	—	—	5	0	36	0
1950–51	6	0	22	1	3	0	—	—	4	0	35	1
1951–52	4	0	2	0	—	—	—	—	—	—	6	0
TOTALS	31	0	97	3	9	1	—	—	18	3	155	7

SCOTT CRABBE

SEASON	LEAGUE CUP APPS	GLS	SCOTTISH LEAGUE APPS	GLS	SCOTTISH CUP APPS	GLS	EUROPE APPS	GLS	OTHERS APPS	GLS	TOTALS APPS	GLS
1985–86	—	—	—	—	—	—	—	—	0+1	0	0+1	0
1986–87	—	—	3+2	0	0+1	0	—	—	3+5	0	6+8	0
1987–88	—	—	2+3	0	—	—	—	—	2+6	0	4+9	0
1988–89	—	—	1	0	—	—	—	—	1+3	4(2P)	2+3	4(2P)
1989–90	3	4	27+8	12(2P)	3	1	—	—	3+2	3	36+10	20(2P)
1990–91	1+1	1	13+8	3	1	0	0+1	0	7+2	0	22+12	4
1991–92	3	1	37+4	15(3P)	2+3	1	—	—	4	4	46+7	21(3P)
1992–93	2+1	0	4+4	1	—	—	0+1	0	3+1	1	9+7	2
TOTALS	9+2	6	87+29	31(5P)	6+4	2	0+2	0	23+20	12(2P)	125+57	51(7P)

JOHN CRAIG

SEASON	LEAGUE CUP APPS	GLS	SCOTTISH LEAGUE APPS	GLS	SCOTTISH CUP APPS	GLS	EUROPE APPS	GLS	OTHERS APPS	GLS	TOTALS APPS	GLS
1978–79	—	—	14+5	0	3	0	—	—	1	0	18+5	0

COLIN CRAMB

SEASON	LEAGUE CUP		SCOTTISH LEAGUE		SCOTTISH CUP		EUROPE		OTHERS		TOTALS	
	APPS	GLS	APPS	GLS	APPS	GLS	APPS	GLS	APPS	GLS	APPS	GLS
1994–95	—	—	3+3	1	—	—	—	—	—	—	3+3	1

IAN CRAWFORD

SEASON	LEAGUE CUP		SCOTTISH LEAGUE		SCOTTISH CUP		EUROPE		OTHERS		TOTALS	
	APPS	GLS	APPS	GLS	APPS	GLS	APPS	GLS	APPS	GLS	APPS	GLS
1954–55	—	—	3	1	—	—	—	—	2+1	2	5+1	3
1955–56	—	—	12	5	6	4	—	—	1	0	19	9
1956–57	6	3	30	11	1	0	—	—	5	2	42	16
1957–58	6	2	25	10	1	0	—	—	11	6(2P)	43	18(2P)
1958–59	9	3	19	8	—	—	2	1	13	17	43	29
1959–60	5	8	18	12	2	0	—	—	14	6	39	26
1960–61	5	0	20	11(1P)	3	0	1	0	2	2	31	13(1P)
TOTALS	31	16	127	58(1P)	13	4	3	1	48+1	35(2P)	222+1	114(3P)

JIM CRUICKSHANK   FIGURES IN BRACKETS REPRESENT SHUT-OUTS

SEASON	LEAGUE CUP		SCOTTISH LEAGUE		SCOTTISH CUP		EUROPE		TEXACO CUP		ANGLO-SCOTTISH CUP		OTHERS		TOTALS	
	APPS	GLS	APPS	GLS	APPS	GLS	APPS	GLS	APPS	GLS	APPS	GLS	APPS	GLS	APPS	GLS
1960–61	—	—	4	(0)	1	(1)	—	—	—	—	—	—	1	(1)	6	(2)
1961–62	1	(0)	5	(1)	1	(1)	—	—	—	—	—	—	1	(0)	8	(2)
1962–63	—	—	6	(2)	—	—	—	—	—	—	—	—	—	—	6	(2)
1963–64	6	(2)	34	(9)	3	(1)	3	(0)	—	—	—	—	17	(8)	63	(20)
1964–65	6	(0)	34	(6)	4	(1)	—	—	—	—	—	—	10	(4)	54	(11)
1965–66	6	(1)	34	(10)	4	(0)	5	(1)	—	—	—	—	5	(1)	54	(13)
1966–67	6	(1)	34	(8)	1	(0)	—	—	—	—	—	—	8	(1)	49	(10)
1967–68	3	(0)	20	(2)	5	(1)	—	—	—	—	—	—	5	(2)	33	(5)
1968–69	5	(1)	31	(6)	2	(0)	—	—	—	—	—	—	6	(0)	44	(7)
1969–70	6	(3)	29	(13)	3	(1)	—	—	—	—	—	—	6	(0)	44	(17)
1970–71	6	(1)	32	(11)	2	(1)	—	—	8	(2)	—	—	8	(5)	56	(20)
1971–72	6	(1)	20	(5)	—	—	—	—	2	(1)	—	—	3	(1)	31	(8)
1972–73	—	—	11	(2)	—	—	—	—	—	—	—	—	1	(1)	12	(3)
1973–74	—	—	11	(5)	7	(0)	—	—	—	—	—	—	—	—	18	(5)
1974–75	—	—	27	(7)	4	(2)	—	—	—	—	—	—	6	(2)	37	(11)
1975–76	5	(2)	35	(12)	9	(4)	—	—	—	—	4	(0)	3	(1)	56	(19)
1976–77	3	(0)	27	(3)	6	(3)	2	(0)	—	—	—	—	1	(1)	39	(7)
TOTALS	59	(12)	394	(102)	52	(16)	10	(1)	10	(3)	4	(0)	81	(28)	610	(162)

JOHN CUMMING

SEASON	LEAGUE CUP APPS	GLS	SCOTTISH LEAGUE APPS	GLS	SCOTTISH CUP APPS	GLS	EUROPE APPS	GLS	OTHERS APPS	GLS	TOTALS APPS	GLS
1950–51	—	—	14	4	3	0	—	—	9	2	26	6
1951–52	6	1	12	1	—	—	—	—	6	2	24	4
1952–53	3	0	7	2	1	0	—	—	—	—	11	2
1953–54	4	1	29	0	3	0	—	—	16	3(1P)	52	4(1P)
1954–55	10	1	29	1	4	0	—	—	5	0	48	2
1955–56	8	0	34	1	6	1	—	—	4	1	52	3
1956–57	6	0	25	4	1	0	—	—	8	0	40	4
1957–58	4	0	20	5	—	—	—	—	14	2	38	7
1958–59	8	1	33	2	2	0	2	0	19	3	64	6
1959–60	10	0	32	5	2	0	—	—	3	0	47	5
1960–61	7	2	32	3(2P)	4	0	2	0	3	0	48	5(2P)
1961–62	8	3(3P)	33	3(1P)	2	0	4	0	5	1	52	7(4P)
1962–63	10	0	20	1	2	0	—	—	2	0	34	1
1963–64	5	0	20	0	3	0	3	1	8	0	39	1
1964–65	2	0	—	—	—	—	—	—	4	0	6	0
1965–66	3	0	16	1	2	0	5	0	2	0	28	1
1966–67	—	—	2	0	—	—	—	—	0+1	0	2+1	0
TOTALS	94	9(3P)	358	33(3P)	35	1	16	1	108+1	14(1P)	611+1	58(7P)

KEN CURRIE

SEASON	LEAGUE CUP APPS	GLS	SCOTTISH LEAGUE APPS	GLS	SCOTTISH CUP APPS	GLS	EUROPE APPS	GLS	OTHERS APPS	GLS	TOTALS APPS	GLS
1946–47	7	5	8	0	2	1	—	—	—	—	17	6
1947–48	7	3	16	3	2	2	—	—	2	0	27	8
1948–49	3	0	6	1	—	—	—	—	2	0	11	1
1949–50	—	—	4	0	3	0	—	—	—	—	7	0
TOTALS	17	8	34	4	7	3	—	—	4	0	62	15

TOMMY DARLING

SEASON	LEAGUE CUP APPS	GLS	SCOTTISH LEAGUE APPS	GLS	SCOTTISH CUP APPS	GLS	EUROPE APPS	GLS	OTHERS APPS	GLS	TOTALS APPS	GLS
1948–49	2	0	2	0	—	—	—	—	—	—	4	0

NORMAN DAVIDSON

SEASON	LEAGUE CUP APPS	GLS	SCOTTISH LEAGUE APPS	GLS	SCOTTISH CUP APPS	GLS	EUROPE APPS	GLS	OTHERS APPS	GLS	TOTALS APPS	GLS
1960–61	—	—	6	2	1	0	—	—	—	—	7	2
1961–62	3	1	8	2	—	—	1	2	1	0	13	5
1962–63	9	4	13	10	1	0	—	—	1+1	4	24+1	18
1963–64	5	3	9	4	—	—	2	0	1	2	17	9
TOTALS	17	8	36	18	2	0	3	2	3+1	6	61+1	34

TOMMY DAVIDSON

SEASON	LEAGUE CUP		SCOTTISH LEAGUE		SCOTTISH CUP		EUROPE		OTHERS		TOTALS	
	APPS	GLS	APPS	GLS	APPS	GLS	APPS	GLS	APPS	GLS	APPS	GLS
1966–67	—	—	2+1	0	—	—	—	—	—	—	2+1	0

JIM DENNY

SEASON	LEAGUE CUP		SCOTTISH LEAGUE		SCOTTISH CUP		EUROPE		OTHERS		TOTALS	
	APPS	GLS	APPS	GLS	APPS	GLS	APPS	GLS	APPS	GLS	APPS	GLS
1979–80	—	—	34	0	3	0	—	—	2	0	39	0
1980–81	1	0	19	0	—	—	—	—	3+1	0	23+1	0
TOTALS	1	0	53	0	3	0	—	—	5+1	0	62+1	0

JACKIE DEWAR

SEASON	LEAGUE CUP		SCOTTISH LEAGUE		SCOTTISH CUP		EUROPE		OTHERS		TOTALS	
	APPS	GLS	APPS	GLS	APPS	GLS	APPS	GLS	APPS	GLS	APPS	GLS
1946–47	2	0	3	3	2	0	—	—	2	0	9	3
1947–48	—	—	—	—	—	—	—	—	2	2	2	2
TOTALS	2	0	3	3	2	0	—	—	2	2	11	5

ARTHUR DIXON

SEASON	LEAGUE CUP		SCOTTISH LEAGUE		SCOTTISH CUP		EUROPE		OTHERS		TOTALS	
	APPS	GLS	APPS	GLS	APPS	GLS	APPS	GLS	APPS	GLS	APPS	GLS
1947–48	—	—	24	3(1P)	2	0	—	—	3	2	29	5(1P)
1948–49	4	2	9	1	4	3	—	—	1	0	18	6
1949–50	1	0	—	—	—	—	—	—	1	0	2	0
TOTALS	5	2	33	4(1P)	6	3	—	—	5	2	49	11(1P)

JIM DOCHERTY

SEASON	LEAGUE CUP		SCOTTISH LEAGUE		SCOTTISH CUP		EUROPE		OTHERS		TOTALS	
	APPS	GLS	APPS	GLS	APPS	GLS	APPS	GLS	APPS	GLS	APPS	GLS
1979–80	—	—	1+3	0	0+1	0	—	—	1	0	2+4	0
1980–81	—	—	0+1	0	—	—	—	—	0+1	0	0+2	0
TOTALS	—	—	1+4	0	0+1	0	—	—	1+1	0	2+6	0

JOHN DOCHERTY

SEASON	LEAGUE CUP APPS	GLS	SCOTTISH LEAGUE APPS	GLS	SCOTTISH CUP APPS	GLS	EUROPE APPS	GLS	OTHERS APPS	GLS	TOTALS APPS	GLS
1960–61	—	—	8	1	—	—	—	—	1	0	9	1
1961–62	6	0	1	0	—	—	3	0	2	1	12	1
1962–63	—	—	3	0	—	—	—	—	1	0	4	0
TOTALS	6	0	12	1	—	—	3	0	4	1	25	2

GEORGE DONALDSON

SEASON	LEAGUE CUP APPS	GLS	SCOTTISH LEAGUE APPS	GLS	SCOTTISH CUP APPS	GLS	EUROPE APPS	GLS	OTHERS APPS	GLS	TOTALS APPS	GLS
1974–75	0+1	0	10+4	1	—	—	—	—	5+2	1	15+7	2
1975–76	—	—	2	0	—	—	—	—	2	0	4	0
TOTALS	0+1	0	12+4	1	—	—	—	—	7+2	1	19+7	2

BOBBY DOUGAN

SEASON	LEAGUE CUP APPS	GLS	SCOTTISH LEAGUE APPS	GLS	SCOTTISH CUP APPS	GLS	EUROPE APPS	GLS	OTHERS APPS	GLS	TOTALS APPS	GLS
1947–48	1	0	11	0	—	—	—	—	7	0	19	0
1948–49	6	0	26	0	4	0	—	—	1	0	37	0
1949–50	4	0	28	0	2	0	—	—	6	0	40	0
1950–51	6	0	30	0	3	0	—	—	10	0	49	0
1951–52	6	0	3	0	—	—	—	—	4	0	13	0
1952–53	1	0	18	0	4	0	—	—	5	0	28	0
1953–54	6	0	9	0	—	—	—	—	8	0	23	0
1954–55	—	—	—	—	—	—	—	—	3	0	3	0
TOTALS	30	0	125	0	13	0	—	—	44	0	212	0

WILLIE DUFF   FIGURES IN BRACKETS REPRESENT SHUT-OUTS

SEASON	LEAGUE CUP APPS	GLS	SCOTTISH LEAGUE APPS	GLS	SCOTTISH CUP APPS	GLS	EUROPE APPS	GLS	OTHERS APPS	GLS	TOTALS APPS	GLS
1952–53	—	—	—	—	—	—	—	—	1	(0)	1	(0)
1953–54	—	—	—	—	—	—	—	—	1	(0)	1	(0)
1954–55	9	(2)	26	(8)	4	(2)	—	—	4	(1)	43	(13)
1955–56	4	(2)	32	(6)	6	(5)	—	—	4	(0)	46	(13)
1956–57	—	—	4	(1)	—	—	—	—	1	(0)	5	(1)
TOTALS	13	(4)	62	(15)	10	(7)	—	—	11	(1)	96	(27)

RAY DUNLOP
FIGURES IN BRACKETS REPRESENT SHUT-OUTS

SEASON	LEAGUE CUP		SCOTTISH LEAGUE		SCOTTISH CUP		EUROPE		TEXACO CUP		ANGLO-SCOTTISH CUP		OTHERS		TOTALS	
	APPS	GLS	APPS	GLS	APPS	GLS	APPS	GLS	APPS	GLS	APPS	GLS	APPS	GLS	APPS	GLS
1977–78	7	(3)	34	(14)	3	(0)	—	—	—	—	—	—	4	(2)	48	(19)
1978–79	—	—	18	(4)	2	(1)	—	—	—	—	2	(0)	4	(2)	26	(7)
TOTALS	7	(3)	52	(18)	5	(1)	—	—	—	—	2	(0)	8	(4)	74	(26)

JOHN DURKIN

SEASON	LEAGUE CUP		SCOTTISH LEAGUE		SCOTTISH CUP		EUROPE		OTHERS		TOTALS	
	APPS	GLS	APPS	GLS	APPS	GLS	APPS	GLS	APPS	GLS	APPS	GLS
1950–51	—	—	—	—	—	—	—	—	1	0	1	0
1951–52	—	—	4	0	—	—	—	—	1	0	5	0
1952–53	1	1	5	0	—	—	—	—	—	—	6	1
TOTALS	1	1	9	0	—	—	—	—	2	0	12	1

BOBBY ELGIN

SEASON	LEAGUE CUP		SCOTTISH LEAGUE		SCOTTISH CUP		EUROPE		OTHERS		TOTALS	
	APPS	GLS	APPS	GLS	APPS	GLS	APPS	GLS	APPS	GLS	APPS	GLS
1966–67	—	—	—	—	—	—	—	—	0+1	0	0+1	0
1967–68	—	—	1	0	—	—	—	—	2	0	3	0
1968–69	1	0	—	—	—	—	—	—	—	—	1	0
TOTALS	1	0	1	0	—	—	—	—	2+1	0	4+1	0

MAURICE ELLIOTT

SEASON	LEAGUE CUP		SCOTTISH LEAGUE		SCOTTISH CUP		EUROPE		OTHERS		TOTALS	
	APPS	GLS	APPS	GLS	APPS	GLS	APPS	GLS	APPS	GLS	APPS	GLS
1960–61	—	—	3	0	—	—	—	—	1	0	4	0
1961–62	1	0	7	2	—	—	2	0	3	1	13	3
TOTALS	1	0	10	2	—	—	2	0	4	1	17	3

JUSTIN FASHANU

SEASON	LEAGUE CUP		SCOTTISH LEAGUE		SCOTTISH CUP		EUROPE		OTHERS		TOTALS	
	APPS	GLS	APPS	GLS	APPS	GLS	APPS	GLS	APPS	GLS	APPS	GLS
1993–94	2	0	10+1	1	—	—	2	0	3	0	17+1	1

CHARLIE FERGUSON

SEASON	LEAGUE CUP APPS	GLS	SCOTTISH LEAGUE APPS	GLS	SCOTTISH CUP APPS	GLS	EUROPE APPS	GLS	OTHERS APPS	GLS	TOTALS APPS	GLS
1952–53	—	—	1	0	—	—	—	—	—	—	1	0

DANNY FERGUSON

SEASON	LEAGUE CUP APPS	GLS	SCOTTISH LEAGUE APPS	GLS	SCOTTISH CUP APPS	GLS	EUROPE APPS	GLS	OTHERS APPS	GLS	TOTALS APPS	GLS
1958–59	—	—	—	—	—	—	—	—	1	0	1	0
1959–60	—	—	—	—	—	—	—	—	3	0	3	0
1960–61	—	—	9	0	3	3	—	—	—	—	12	3
1961–62	11	0	26	3	1	0	1	0	—	—	39	3
1962–63	4	0	26	3	2	0	—	—	3	0	35	3
1963–64	6	1	16	2	—	—	3	2	11	0	36	5
1964–65	2	0	18	3	4	0	—	—	10	2	34	5
1965–66	6	0	17	1	—	—	4	0	2	0	29	1
1966–67	—	—	16	1	1	0	—	—	3+1	0	20+1	1
TOTALS	29	1	128	13	11	3	8	2	33+1	2	209+1	21

DEREK FERGUSON

SEASON	LEAGUE CUP APPS	GLS	SCOTTISH LEAGUE APPS	GLS	SCOTTISH CUP APPS	GLS	EUROPE APPS	GLS	OTHERS APPS	GLS	TOTALS APPS	GLS
1990–91	2	0	25+3	2	1	0	0+2	0	7+1	0	35+6	2
1991–92	3	0	37+1	1	6	0	—	—	4	0	50+1	1
1992–93	3	0	37	1	4	1	3	0	2	1	49	3
TOTALS	8	0	99+4	4	11	1	3+2	0	13+1	1	134+7	6

IAIN FERGUSON

SEASON	LEAGUE CUP APPS	GLS	SCOTTISH LEAGUE APPS	GLS	SCOTTISH CUP APPS	GLS	EUROPE APPS	GLS	OTHERS APPS	GLS	TOTALS APPS	GLS
1988–89	3+1	5(1P)	23+6	5	1+1	0	4+2	1	7	6	38+10	17(1P)
1989–90	0+1	0	1+10	1	0+1	0	—	—	5+1	4	6+13	5
1990–91	—	—	7+5	2	—	—	3	1	0+1	0	10+6	3
TOTALS	3+2	5(1P)	31+21	8	1+2	0	7+2	2	12+2	10	54+29	25(1P)

IAN FERGUSON

SEASON	LEAGUE CUP APPS	GLS	SCOTTISH LEAGUE APPS	GLS	SCOTTISH CUP APPS	GLS	EUROPE APPS	GLS	OTHERS APPS	GLS	TOTALS APPS	GLS
1991–92	—	—	12+18	4	4+2	1	—	—	1	0	17+20	5
1992–93	—	—	9+15	4	1+1	1	1+1	0	—	—	11+17	5
1993–94	—	—	3+3	1	—	—	0+1	0	3+3	3	6+7	4
TOTALS	—	—	24+36	9	5+3	2	1+2	0	4+3	3	34+44	14

ALAN FINLAY

SEASON	LEAGUE CUP APPS	GLS	SCOTTISH LEAGUE APPS	GLS	SCOTTISH CUP APPS	GLS	EUROPE APPS	GLS	OTHERS APPS	GLS	TOTALS APPS	GLS
1956–57	—	—	—	—	—	—	—	—	2	1	2	1
1957–58	—	—	—	—	—	—	—	—	—	—	—	—
1958–59	—	—	—	—	—	—	—	—	—	—	—	—
1959–60	—	—	—	—	—	—	—	—	2	0	2	0
1960–61	—	—	9	1	1	1	—	—	1	1	11	3
TOTALS	—	—	9	1	1	1	—	—	5	2	15	4

BOBBY FLAVELL

SEASON	LEAGUE CUP APPS	GLS	SCOTTISH LEAGUE APPS	GLS	SCOTTISH CUP APPS	GLS	EUROPE APPS	GLS	OTHERS APPS	GLS	TOTALS APPS	GLS
1947–48	—	—	17	6	2	1	—	—	3	4	22	11
1948–49	4	2	26	10	4	1	—	—	5	1	39	14
1949–50	1	1	26	11	3	0	—	—	7	4	37	16
TOTALS	5	3	69	27	9	2	—	—	15	9	98	41

GEORGE FLEMING

SEASON	LEAGUE CUP APPS	GLS	SCOTTISH LEAGUE APPS	GLS	SCOTTISH CUP APPS	GLS	EUROPE APPS	GLS	TEXACO CUP APPS	GLS	ANGLO-SCOTTISH CUP APPS	GLS	OTHERS APPS	GLS	TOTALS APPS	GLS
1966–67	—	—	16	1	1	0	—	—	—	—	—	—	8+1	0	25+1	1
1967–68	5	2	19+9	5	1+2	1	—	—	—	—	—	—	3+2	0	28+13	8
1968–69	5	1	30+1	5	2	1	—	—	—	—	—	—	5	0	42+1	7
1969–70	3	0	19+5	3	3	2	—	—	—	—	—	—	6	0	31+5	5
1970–71	3	0	26+4	7	2	0	—	—	5+2	3	—	—	11	1	47+6	11
1971–72	2+1	1	2+1	0	—	—	—	—	—	—	—	—	1	0	5+2	1
TOTALS	18+1	4	112+20	21	9+2	4	—	—	5+2	3	—	—	34+3	1	178+28	33

JIM FLEMING

SEASON	LEAGUE CUP APPS	GLS	SCOTTISH LEAGUE APPS	GLS	SCOTTISH CUP APPS	GLS	EUROPE APPS	GLS	OTHERS APPS	GLS	TOTALS APPS	GLS
1966–67	—	—	9	0	—	—	—	—	5	3	14	3
1967–68	2+1	0	20+3	5	—	—	—	—	5	2	27+4	7
1968–69	0+1	0	13+1	4	1	0	—	—	2	1	16+2	5
TOTALS	2+2	0	43+4	9	1	0	—	—	12	6	57+6	15

DONALD FORD

SEASON	LEAGUE CUP APPS	GLS	SCOTTISH LEAGUE APPS	GLS	SCOTTISH CUP APPS	GLS	EUROPE APPS	GLS	TEXACO CUP APPS	GLS	ANGLO-SCOTTISH CUP APPS	GLS	OTHERS APPS	GLS	TOTALS APPS	GLS
1964–65	—	—	7	2	—	—	—	—	—	—	—	—	7	11	14	13
1965–66	4	2	9	0	2	0	2	0	—	—	—	—	1	0	18	2
1966–67	—	—	5	0	—	—	—	—	—	—	—	—	6	5	11	5
1967–68	6	2	29	11	6	3	—	—	—	—	—	—	5+1	4	46+1	20
1968–69	6	4	23+6	6	2	0	—	—	—	—	—	—	4+2	2(1P)	35+8	12(1P)
1969–70	6	0	24+5	8	3	0	—	—	—	—	—	—	5+1	2	38+6	10
1970–71	6	2	32	11	2	2	—	—	8	8	—	—	12	9	60	32
1971–72	6	3	30	15	3	1	—	—	2	0	—	—	5	0	46	19
1972–73	6	2	32	9	2	1	—	—	4	0	—	—	6	2	50	14
1973–74	6	5(1P)	29+1	18(7P)	7	6	—	—	4	0	—	—	1	1	47+1	30(8P)
1974–75	8	2(2P)	21+1	13(5P)	2	0	—	—	1+1	1(1P)	—	—	9	9(1P)	41+2	28(9P)
1975–76	6	2(1P)	2	0	1	0	—	—	—	—	1	1	2	0	12	3(1P)
TOTALS	60	27(4P)	243+13	93(12P)	30	13	2	0	19+1	9(1P)	1	1	63+4	45(2P)	418+18	188(18P)

WAYNE FOSTER

SEASON	LEAGUE CUP APPS	GLS	SCOTTISH LEAGUE APPS	GLS	SCOTTISH CUP APPS	GLS	EUROPE APPS	GLS	OTHERS APPS	GLS	TOTALS APPS	GLS
1986–87	—	—	23+7	4	4+3	2	2	1	2+4	1	31+14	8
1987–88	0+2	1	33+6	4	3	2	—	—	0+1	0	36+9	7
1988–89	2+1	0	8+1	1(1P)	—	—	3+2	1(1P)	5+2	2	18+6	4(2P)
1989–90	—	—	14+3	1	0+2	0	—	—	0+2	0	14+7	1
1990–91	2	0	21+7	1	0+1	0	2	2	6+1	3	31+9	6
1991–92	0+2	0	1+6	0	0+1	0	—	—	1+2	0	2+11	0
1992–93	2+1	0	7+4	0	0+1	0	1+1	0	1+1	1	11+8	1
1993–94	—	—	8+10	1	1+2	1	—	—	—	—	9+12	2
1994–95	0+1	0	—	—	—	—	—	—	0+2	0	0+3	0
TOTALS	6+7	1	115+44	12(1P)	8+10	5	8+3	4(1P)	15+15	7	152+79	29(2P)

STEPHEN FRAIL

SEASON	LEAGUE CUP APPS	GLS	SCOTTISH LEAGUE APPS	GLS	SCOTTISH CUP APPS	GLS	EUROPE APPS	GLS	OTHERS APPS	GLS	TOTALS APPS	GLS
1993–94	—	—	9	2	—	—	—	—	1+1	0	10+1	2
1994–95	2	0	25	2	4	0	—	—	5	2	36	4
TOTALS	2	0	34	4	4	0	—	—	6+1	2	46+1	6

ANDY FRASER

SEASON	LEAGUE CUP APPS	GLS	SCOTTISH LEAGUE APPS	GLS	SCOTTISH CUP APPS	GLS	EUROPE APPS	GLS	OTHERS APPS	GLS	TOTALS APPS	GLS
1959–60	3	0	—	—	—	—	—	—	—	—	3	0
1960–61	—	—	1	0	—	—	—	—	—	—	1	0
TOTALS	3	0	1	0	—	—	—	—	—	—	4	0

BILLY FRASER

SEASON	LEAGUE CUP APPS	GLS	SCOTTISH LEAGUE APPS	GLS	SCOTTISH CUP APPS	GLS	EUROPE APPS	GLS	OTHERS APPS	GLS	TOTALS APPS	GLS
1965–66	1	0	1	1	—	—	—	—	—	—	2	1

CAMMY FRASER

SEASON	LEAGUE CUP APPS	GLS	SCOTTISH LEAGUE APPS	GLS	SCOTTISH CUP APPS	GLS	EUROPE APPS	GLS	TEXACO CUP APPS	GLS	ANGLO-SCOTTISH CUP APPS	GLS	OTHERS APPS	GLS	TOTALS APPS	GLS
1974–75	—	—	3	0	—	—	—	—	—	—	—	—	1+1	0	4+1	0
1975–76	1	0	5+10	0	1+3	0	—	—	—	—	1	1	7+4	1	15+17	2
1976–77	1+1	0	20+3	0	6	0	0+3	0	—	—	—	—	2+1	2	29+8	2
1977–78	7	0	39	2	3	0	—	—	—	—	—	—	4	0	53	2
1978–79	—	—	36	3(1P)	3	0	—	—	—	—	2	0	3+1	0	44+1	3(1P)
1979–80	2	0	36	12	3	1	—	—	—	—	—	—	7	3	48	16
1980–81	—	—	0+1	1(1P)	—	—	—	—	—	—	—	—	5+1	0	5+2	1(1P)
TOTALS	11+1	0	139+14	18(2P)	16+3	1	0+3	0	—	—	3	1	29+8	6	198+29	26(2P)

JOHN GALLACHER

SEASON	LEAGUE CUP APPS	GLS	SCOTTISH LEAGUE APPS	GLS	SCOTTISH CUP APPS	GLS	EUROPE APPS	GLS	TEXACO CUP APPS	GLS	ANGLO-SCOTTISH CUP APPS	GLS	OTHERS APPS	GLS	TOTALS APPS	GLS
1970–71	—	—	—	—	—	—	—	—	—	—	—	—	1	0	1	0
1971–72	—	—	3	0	—	—	—	—	—	—	—	—	—	—	3	0
1972–73	—	—	5	0	1	0	—	—	—	—	—	—	3	0	9	0
1973–74	—	—	5	0	—	—	—	—	—	—	—	—	1	0	6	0
1974–75	8	0	4	0	—	—	—	—	1	0	—	—	4	0	17	0
1975–76	—	—	14	0	7	0	—	—	—	—	1	0	10	0	32	0
1976–77	9	2	35	4	4	1	4	0	—	—	—	—	3	1	55	8
1977–78	2	0	7	0	—	—	—	—	—	—	—	—	3	1	12	1
TOTALS	19	2	73	4	12	1	4	0	1	0	1	0	25	2	135	9

MIKE GALLOWAY

SEASON	LEAGUE CUP APPS	GLS	SCOTTISH LEAGUE APPS	GLS	SCOTTISH CUP APPS	GLS	EUROPE APPS	GLS	OTHERS APPS	GLS	TOTALS APPS	GLS
1987–88	—	—	22+3	6	3	0	—	—	1	0	26+3	6
1988–89	4	0	30+1	2	3	1	8	5	10+1	8	55+2	16
TOTALS	4	0	52+4	8	6	1	8	5	11+1	8	81+5	22

KENNY GARLAND   FIGURES IN BRACKETS REPRESENT SHUT-OUTS

SEASON	LEAGUE CUP APPS	GLS	SCOTTISH LEAGUE APPS	GLS	SCOTTISH CUP APPS	GLS	EUROPE APPS	GLS	TEXACO CUP APPS	GLS	ANGLO-SCOTTISH CUP APPS	GLS	OTHERS APPS	GLS	TOTALS APPS	GLS
1966–67	—	—	—	—	—	—	—	—	—	—	—	—	3	(2)	3	(2)
1967–68	3	(2)	14	(3)	2	(0)	—	—	—	—			1+1	(2)	20+1	(7)
1968–69	1	(0)	3	(1)	—	—	—	—	—	—	—	—	—	—	4	(1)
1969–70	—	—	5	(1)	—	—	—	—	—	—	—	—	2	(1)	7	(2)
1970–71	—	—	2	(0)	—	—	—	—	—	—	—	—	6+1	(2)	8+1	(2)
1971–72	—	—	14	(4)	4	(2)	—	—	—	—	—	—	2+1	(0)	20+1	(6)
1972–73	6	(2)	23	(10)	2	(1)	—	—	4	(3)	—	—	5	(3)	40	(19)
1973–74	6	(3)	20	(5)	—	—	—	—	4	(2)	—	—	1	(1)	31	(11)
1974–75	8	(4)	7	(0)	—	—	—	—	2	(0)	—	—	2	(1)	19	(5)
1975–76	1	(0)	—	—	—	—	—	—	—	—	—	—	—	—	1	(0)
TOTALS	25	(11)	88	(24)	8	(3)	—	—	10	(5)	—	—	21+3	(12)	153+3	(55)

ARCHIE GARRETT

SEASON	LEAGUE CUP APPS	GLS	SCOTTISH LEAGUE APPS	GLS	SCOTTISH CUP APPS	GLS	EUROPE APPS	GLS	OTHERS APPS	GLS	TOTALS APPS	GLS
1946–47	—	—	4	3	—	—	—	—	—	—	4	3

STUART GAULD

SEASON	LEAGUE CUP APPS	GLS	SCOTTISH LEAGUE APPS	GLS	SCOTTISH CUP APPS	GLS	EUROPE APPS	GLS	OTHERS APPS	GLS	TOTALS APPS	GLS
1980–81	—	—	—	—	—	—	—	—	1	0	1	0
1981–82	—	—	2	0	—	—	—	—	—	—	2	0
1982–83	—	—	14	0	1	0	—	—	1+1	0	16+1	0
1983–84	2	0	2+1	0	—	—	—	—	2+1	0	6+2	0
TOTALS	2	0	18+1	0	1	0	—	—	4+2	0	25+3	0

MARK GAVIN

SEASON	LEAGUE CUP APPS	GLS	SCOTTISH LEAGUE APPS	GLS	SCOTTISH CUP APPS	GLS	EUROPE APPS	GLS	OTHERS APPS	GLS	TOTALS APPS	GLS
1987–88	—	—	5+2	0	—	—	—	—	2	0	7+2	0
1988–89	—	—	0+2	0	—	—	—	—	2+4	1	2+6	1
TOTALS	—	—	5+4	0	—	—	—	—	4+4	1	9+8	1

WILLIE GIBSON

SEASON	LEAGUE CUP APPS	GLS	SCOTTISH LEAGUE APPS	GLS	SCOTTISH CUP APPS	GLS	EUROPE APPS	GLS	TEXACO CUP APPS	GLS	ANGLO-SCOTTISH CUP APPS	GLS	OTHERS APPS	GLS	TOTALS APPS	GLS
1972–73	—	—	—	—	—	—	—	—	—	—	—	—	1+1	2	1+1	2
1973–74	—	—	10+2	6	3+2	4	—	—	—	—	—	—	1	0	14+4	10
1974–75	1	0	27+3	9	4	1	—	—	1	0	—	—	3+1	2	36+4	12
1975–76	0+1	0	24+4	8	7	3	—	—	—	—	3	4	5+2	3	39+7	18
1976–77	7	4	31	15	5	2	2+2	3	—	—	—	—	3	4	48+2	28
1977–78	7	2	36+3	20(1P)	3	1	—	—	—	—	—	—	2+1	0	48+4	23(1P)
1978–79	1	0	33+1	6(3P)	4	1(1P)	—	—	—	—	2	1	4	2	44+1	10(4P)
1979–80	2	1(1P)	39	17(5P)	3	0	—	—	—	—	—	—	7	3(1P)	51	21(7P)
1980–81	2+2	0	30+2	4	2	0	—	—	—	—	—	—	5+1	2(1P)	39+5	6(1P)
TOTALS	20+3	7(1P)	230+15	85(9P)	31+2	12(1P)	2+2	3	1	0	5	5	31+6	18(2P)	320+28	130(12P)

BOSTON GLEGG

SEASON	LEAGUE CUP APPS	GLS	SCOTTISH LEAGUE APPS	GLS	SCOTTISH CUP APPS	GLS	EUROPE APPS	GLS	OTHERS APPS	GLS	TOTALS APPS	GLS
1960–61	2	1	—	—	—	—	—	—	—	—	2	1

FREDDIE GLIDDEN

SEASON	LEAGUE CUP APPS	GLS	SCOTTISH LEAGUE APPS	GLS	SCOTTISH CUP APPS	GLS	EUROPE APPS	GLS	OTHERS APPS	GLS	TOTALS APPS	GLS
1948–49	—	—	—	—	—	—	—	—	1	0	1	0
1949–50	—	—	—	—	—	—	—	—	—	—	—	—
1950–51	—	—	—	—	—	—	—	—	—	—	—	—
1951–52	—	—	21	0	7	1	—	—	4	0	32	1
1952–53	5	0	16	2	—	—	—	—	—	—	21	2
1953–54	—	—	21	0	3	0	—	—	14	0	38	0
1954–55	10	0	30	0	4	0	—	—	2+1	0	46+1	0
1955–56	8	0	32	0	6	0	—	—	4	0	50	0
1956–57	6	0	19	0	1	0	—	—	4	0	30	0
1957–58	6	0	13	0	—	—	—	—	9	0	28	0
1958–59	6	0	13	0	—	—	2	0	2	0	23	0
TOTALS	41	0	165	2	21	1	2	0	40+1	0	269+1	3

ALAN GORDON

SEASON	LEAGUE CUP APPS	GLS	SCOTTISH LEAGUE APPS	GLS	SCOTTISH CUP APPS	GLS	EUROPE APPS	GLS	OTHERS APPS	GLS	TOTALS APPS	GLS
1961–62	1	0	22	5	1	3	—	—	2	1	26	9
1962–63	—	—	16	12	1	0	—	—	3	2	20	14
1963–64	4	2	10	1	—	—	1	0	5	2	20	5
1964–65	3	1	29	19	2	2	—	—	4	1	38	23
1965–66	4	0	15	6	—	—	—	—	4	5	23	11
1966–67	5+1	0	19+1	6	1	0	—	—	9	5	34+2	11
1967–68	—	—	—	—	—	—	—	—	—	—	—	—
1968–69	—	—	15	6	—	—	—	—	0+1	1	15+1	7
TOTALS	17+1	3	126+1	55	5	5	1	0	27+1	17	176+3	80

IAN GORDON

SEASON	LEAGUE CUP APPS	GLS	SCOTTISH LEAGUE APPS	GLS	SCOTTISH CUP APPS	GLS	EUROPE APPS	GLS	OTHERS APPS	GLS	TOTALS APPS	GLS
1951–52	—	—	3	0	—	—	—	—	2	0	5	0
1952–53	—	—	—	—	—	—	—	—	—	—	—	—
1953–54	—	—	—	—	—	—	—	—	1	0	1	0
TOTALS	—	—	3	0	—	—	—	—	3	0	6	0

DAVID GRAHAM   FIGURES IN BRACKETS REPRESENT SHUT-OUTS

SEASON	LEAGUE CUP APPS	GLS	SCOTTISH LEAGUE APPS	GLS	SCOTTISH CUP APPS	GLS	EUROPE APPS	GLS	OTHERS APPS	GLS	TOTALS APPS	GLS
1972–73	—	—	—	—	—	—	—	—	1	(0)	1	(0)
1973–74	—	—	3	(2)	—	—	—	—	1	(0)	4	(2)
1974–75	—	—	—	—	—	—	—	—	1	(1)	1	(1)
1975–76	—	—	1	(0)	—	—	—	—	9	(4)	10	(4)
TOTALS	—	—	4	(2)	—	—	—	—	12	(5)	16	(7)

WILLIAM GRANT

SEASON	LEAGUE CUP APPS	GLS	SCOTTISH LEAGUE APPS	GLS	SCOTTISH CUP APPS	GLS	EUROPE APPS	GLS	OTHERS APPS	GLS	TOTALS APPS	GLS
1954–55	—	—	1	0	—	—	—	—	—	—	1	0

DAVID HAGEN

SEASON	LEAGUE CUP APPS	GLS	SCOTTISH LEAGUE APPS	GLS	SCOTTISH CUP APPS	GLS	EUROPE APPS	GLS	OTHERS APPS	GLS	TOTALS APPS	GLS
1994–95	—	—	16+4	3	5	0	—	—	1	0	22+4	3

ALEX HAMILL

SEASON	LEAGUE CUP APPS	GLS	SCOTTISH LEAGUE APPS	GLS	SCOTTISH CUP APPS	GLS	EUROPE APPS	GLS	OTHERS APPS	GLS	TOTALS APPS	GLS
1980–81	—	—	20+1	1	2	0	—	—	1	0	23+1	1
1981–82	6	0	16+5	2	—	—	—	—	4	0	26+5	2
TOTALS	6	0	36+6	3	2	0	—	—	5	0	49+6	3

BRIAN HAMILTON

SEASON	LEAGUE CUP APPS	GLS	SCOTTISH LEAGUE APPS	GLS	SCOTTISH CUP APPS	GLS	EUROPE APPS	GLS	OTHERS APPS	GLS	TOTALS APPS	GLS
1994–95	—	—	13	2	5	0	—	—	—	—	18	2

GEORGE HAMILTON

SEASON	LEAGUE CUP APPS	GLS	SCOTTISH LEAGUE APPS	GLS	SCOTTISH CUP APPS	GLS	EUROPE APPS	GLS	OTHERS APPS	GLS	TOTALS APPS	GLS
1947–48	—	—	13	6	2	1	—	—	3	2	18	9

JOHNNY HAMILTON

SEASON	LEAGUE CUP APPS	GLS	SCOTTISH LEAGUE APPS	GLS	SCOTTISH CUP APPS	GLS	EUROPE APPS	GLS	OTHERS APPS	GLS	TOTALS APPS	GLS
1955–56	—	—	22	1	2	1	—	—	3	0	27	2
1956–57	—	—	26	4	—	—	—	—	11	6	37	10
1957–58	4	1	4	4	3	1	—	—	11+2	8	22+2	14
1958–59	9	5	27	6	2	0	1	0	19	10	58	21
1959–60	10	4	27	7	2	0	—	—	12	2	51	13
1960–61	1	0	20	4	3	2(1P)	—	—	3	1	27	7(1P)
1961–62	11	3	27	7	1	1	4	0	4	4	47	15
1962–63	10	3	33	10	1	0	—	—	4	1	48	14
1963–64	6	2	34	13(2P)	2	3(3P)	3	1	18	6(1P)	63	25(6P)
1964–65	5	0	32	16(5P)	4	3(1P)	—	—	10	4(2P)	51	23(8P)
1965–66	5	3(2P)	26	4(2P)	3	1	5	0	4	3	43	11(4P)
1966–67	1+1	0	15	0	—	—	—	—	2+1	2(1P)	18+2	2(1P)
TOTALS	62+1	21(2P)	293	76(9P)	23	12(5P)	13	1	101+3	47(4P)	492+4	157(20P)

STEPHEN HAMILTON

SEASON	LEAGUE CUP APPS	GLS	SCOTTISH LEAGUE APPS	GLS	SCOTTISH CUP APPS	GLS	EUROPE APPS	GLS	OTHERS APPS	GLS	TOTALS APPS	GLS
1979–80	0+1	0	5	0	—	—	—	—	—	—	5+1	0
1980–81	—	—	12	0	2	0	—	—	1	0	15	0
TOTALS	0+1	0	17	0	2	0	—	—	1	0	20+1	0

WILLIE HAMILTON

SEASON	LEAGUE CUP		SCOTTISH LEAGUE		SCOTTISH CUP		EUROPE		OTHERS		TOTALS	
	APPS	GLS	APPS	GLS	APPS	GLS	APPS	GLS	APPS	GLS	APPS	GLS
1962–63	5	3	27	10	1	0	—	—	2	2	35	15
1963–64	—	—	3	2	—	—	1	0	—	—	4	2
1967–68	5	0	3+1	0	—	—	—	—	—	—	8+1	0
1968–69	5	0	14+4	7	1	0	—	—	2	0	22+4	7
TOTALS	15	3	47+5	19	2	0	1	0	4	2	69+5	24

STEVE HANCOCK

SEASON	LEAGUE CUP		SCOTTISH LEAGUE		SCOTTISH CUP		EUROPE		TEXACO CUP		ANGLO-SCOTTISH CUP		OTHERS		TOTALS	
	APPS	GLS	APPS	GLS	APPS	GLS	APPS	GLS	APPS	GLS	APPS	GLS	APPS	GLS	APPS	GLS
1974–75	—	—	—	—	—	—	—	—	—	—	—	—	0+2	0	0+2	0
1975–76	5	3	2+2	0	—	—	—	—	—	—	1	0	—	—	8+2	3
TOTALS	5	3	2+2	0	—	—	—	—	—	—	1	0	0+2	0	8+4	3

TOMMY HARRISON

SEASON	LEAGUE CUP		SCOTTISH LEAGUE		SCOTTISH CUP		EUROPE		OTHERS		TOTALS	
	APPS	GLS	APPS	GLS	APPS	GLS	APPS	GLS	APPS	GLS	APPS	GLS
1990–91	—	—	0+3	0	—	—	—	—	0+1	0	0+4	0
1991–92	0+1	0	0+1	0	—	—	—	—	—	—	0+2	0
1992–93	—	—	3+1	1	—	—	—	—	—	—	3+1	1
1993–94	—	—	1	0	—	—	—	—	2	0	3	0
1994–95	0+1	0	—	—	—	—	—	—	2	0	2+1	0
TOTALS	0+2	0	4+5	1	—	—	—	—	4+1	0	8+8	1

KEVIN HEGARTY

SEASON	LEAGUE CUP		SCOTTISH LEAGUE		SCOTTISH CUP		EUROPE		TEXACO CUP		ANGLO-SCOTTISH CUP		OTHERS		TOTALS	
	APPS	GLS	APPS	GLS	APPS	GLS	APPS	GLS	APPS	GLS	APPS	GLS	APPS	GLS	APPS	GLS
1970–71	5+1	3	13+3	4	2	1	—	—	2	1	—	—	2+5	4	24+9	13

JAMES HENDERSON

SEASON	LEAGUE CUP		SCOTTISH LEAGUE		SCOTTISH CUP		EUROPE		OTHERS		TOTALS	
	APPS	GLS	APPS	GLS	APPS	GLS	APPS	GLS	APPS	GLS	APPS	GLS
1947–48	—	—	—	—	—	—	—	—	1	0	1	0
1948–49	—	—	2	0	1	0	—	—	1	0	4	0
1949–50	—	—	4	0	1	0	—	—	2	0	7	0
TOTALS	—	—	6	0	2	0	—	—	4	0	12	0

TOMMY HENDERSON

SEASON	LEAGUE CUP		SCOTTISH LEAGUE		SCOTTISH CUP		EUROPE		OTHERS		TOTALS	
	APPS	GLS	APPS	GLS	APPS	GLS	APPS	GLS	APPS	GLS	APPS	GLS
1960–61	—	—	7	1	—	—	—	—	—	—	7	1
1961–62	2	0	—	—	—	—	—	—	1	0	3	0
TOTALS	2	0	7	1	—	—	—	—	1	0	10	1

BILLY HIGGINS

SEASON	LEAGUE CUP		SCOTTISH LEAGUE		SCOTTISH CUP		EUROPE		OTHERS		TOTALS	
	APPS	GLS	APPS	GLS	APPS	GLS	APPS	GLS	APPS	GLS	APPS	GLS
1957–58	—	—	1	0	—	—	—	—	4+1	1	5+1	1
1958–59	—	—	2	0	—	—	—	—	5+3	0	7+3	0
1959–60	1	0	21	3	1	0	—	—	4	0	27	3
1960–61	4	0	26	0	1	0	—	—	3	0	34	0
1961–62	11	3	28	3	2	0	4	0	3	0	48	6
1962–63	6	0	31	3	2	1	—	—	3	0	42	4
1963–64	4	0	26	0	—	—	2	0	15	0	47	0
1964–65	6	1	32	1	4	0	—	—	6	2	48	4
1965–66	2	0	18	1	3	1	3	0	1	0	27	2
1966–67	3	0	8	0	1	0	—	—	3	0	15	0
TOTALS	37	4	193	11	14	2	9	0	47+4	3	300+4	20

GRAEME HOGG

SEASON	LEAGUE CUP		SCOTTISH LEAGUE		SCOTTISH CUP		EUROPE		OTHERS		TOTALS	
	APPS	GLS	APPS	GLS	APPS	GLS	APPS	GLS	APPS	GLS	APPS	GLS
1991–92	2	0	13+5	1	1	1	—	—	—	—	16+5	2
1992–93	3	0	20+2	2	—	—	3	0	3	0	29+2	2
1993–94	1	0	16+1	0	—	—	1	0	2	1	20+1	1
1994–95	—	—	0+1	0	—	—	—	—	3+1	1	3+2	1
TOTALS	6	0	49+9	3	1	1	4	0	8+1	2	68+10	6

DAVID HOLT

SEASON	LEAGUE CUP		SCOTTISH LEAGUE		SCOTTISH CUP		EUROPE		OTHERS		TOTALS	
	APPS	GLS	APPS	GLS	APPS	GLS	APPS	GLS	APPS	GLS	APPS	GLS
1960–61	—	—	21	0	3	0	—	—	1	0	25	0
1961–62	11	0	34	0	2	0	4	0	5	0	56	0
1962–63	10	0	32	0	2	0	—	—	4	0	48	0
1963–64	1	0	29	0	3	0	1	0	16	0	50	0
1964–65	6	0	32	0	4	0	—	—	7	0	49	0
1965–66	3	0	21	0	1	0	4	0	4	0	33	0
1966–67	6	0	19	0	1	0	—	—	8	0	34	0
1967–68	6	0	18+1	0	—	—	—	—	3	0	27+1	0
1968–69	—	—	24	0	2	0	—	—	1	0	27	0
TOTALS	43	0	230+1	0	18	0	9	0	49	0	349+1	0

JIM IRVINE

SEASON	LEAGUE CUP		SCOTTISH LEAGUE		SCOTTISH CUP		EUROPE		OTHERS		TOTALS	
	APPS	GLS	APPS	GLS	APPS	GLS	APPS	GLS	APPS	GLS	APPS	GLS
1967–68	2+1	1	23	7	7	2	—	—	4	2	36+1	12
1968–69	—	—	5	3	—	—	—	—	2	0	7	3
1969–70	—	—	5+1	1	—	—	—	—	0+1	0	5+2	1
TOTALS	2+1	1	33+1	11	7	2	—	—	6+1	2	48+3	16

WILLIE JAMIESON

SEASON	LEAGUE CUP		SCOTTISH LEAGUE		SCOTTISH CUP		EUROPE		OTHERS		TOTALS	
	APPS	GLS	APPS	GLS	APPS	GLS	APPS	GLS	APPS	GLS	APPS	GLS
1994–95	—	—	13+2	3	2+1	0	—	—	1	0	16+3	3

IAN JARDINE

SEASON	LEAGUE CUP		SCOTTISH LEAGUE		SCOTTISH CUP		EUROPE		OTHERS		TOTALS	
	APPS	GLS	APPS	GLS	APPS	GLS	APPS	GLS	APPS	GLS	APPS	GLS
1985–86	—	—	19+4	7	1+1	0	—	—	2+1	0	22+6	7
1986–87	1	0	12+3	1	—	—	1	0	5	1	19+3	2
1987–88	2+1	0	6+12	2	2+2	0	—	—	3+3	0	13+18	2
1988–89	0+2	1	2+13	1	—	—	1+2	0	3+6	2	6+23	4
TOTALS	3+3	1	39+32	11	3+3	0	2+2	0	13+10	3	60+50	15

SANDY JARDINE

SEASON	LEAGUE CUP		SCOTTISH LEAGUE		SCOTTISH CUP		EUROPE		OTHERS		TOTALS	
	APPS	GLS	APPS	GLS	APPS	GLS	APPS	GLS	APPS	GLS	APPS	GLS
1982–83	10	0	39	2(2P)	4	0	—	—	7+1	0	60+1	2(2P)
1983–84	7	0	33	0	2	0	—	—	8	0	50	0
1984–85	5	0	34	0	5	0	1	0	5+1	0	50+1	0
1985–86	3	0	35	0	5	0	—	—	8	0	51	0
1986–87	1	0	34	1	3	0	2	0	6	0	46	1
1987–88	3	0	9	0	—	—	—	—	6	0	18	0
TOTALS	29	0	184	3(2P)	19	0	3	0	40+2	0	275+2	3(2P)

JIM JEFFERIES

SEASON	LEAGUE CUP APPS	GLS	SCOTTISH LEAGUE APPS	GLS	SCOTTISH CUP APPS	GLS	EUROPE APPS	GLS	TEXACO CUP APPS	GLS	ANGLO-SCOTTISH CUP APPS	GLS	OTHERS APPS	GLS	TOTALS APPS	GLS
1971–72	—	—	7	0	2	0	—	—	—	—	—	—	—	—	9	0
1972–73	—	—	8	0	2	0	—	—	—	—	—	—	2	0	12	0
1973–74	6	0	23+1	0	7	0	—	—	2	0	—	—	2	0	40+1	0
1974–75	6	0	27+1	0	4	0	—	—	1	0	—	—	7	0	45+1	0
1975–76	4	0	26+3	0	8	0	—	—	—	—	3	1	9	0	50+3	1
1976–77	6+1	0	18+2	3	2	0	2+1	0	—	—	—	—	2	0	30+4	3
1977–78	7	0	38	1	2	0	—	—	—	—	—	—	4	0	51	1
1978–79	2	0	26+2	0	4	0	—	—	—	—	2	0	3	0	37+2	0
1979–80	1	0	32	1	3	0	—	—	—	—	—	—	6	0	42	1
1980–81	4	0	12+1	0	—	—	—	—	—	—	—	—	5	0	21+1	0
TOTALS	36+1	0	217+10	5	34	0	2+1	0	3	0	5	1	40	0	337+12	6

RAOLD JENSEN

SEASON	LEAGUE CUP APPS	GLS	SCOTTISH LEAGUE APPS	GLS	SCOTTISH CUP APPS	GLS	EUROPE APPS	GLS	OTHERS APPS	GLS	TOTALS APPS	GLS
1964–65	—	—	15	3	3	0	—	—	4	1	22	4
1965–66	4	0	5	0	—	—	—	—	2	1	11	1
1966–67	5	1	7	0	—	—	—	—	5	0	17	1
1967–68	1	1	15	5	6	3(1P)	—	—	3	0	25	9(1P)
1968–69	2	0	22	7	2	0	—	—	5	0	31	7
1969–70	—	—	5	3	—	—	—	—	5	0	10	3
1970–71	4	1	5	1	0+1	0	—	—	—	—	9+1	2
1975–76	—	—	—	—	—	—	—	—	1	0	1	0
TOTALS	16	3	74	19	11+1	3(1P)	—	—	24	2	126+1	27(1P)

ALLAN JOHNSTON

SEASON	LEAGUE CUP APPS	GLS	SCOTTISH LEAGUE APPS	GLS	SCOTTISH CUP APPS	GLS	EUROPE APPS	GLS	OTHERS APPS	GLS	TOTALS APPS	GLS
1992–93	—	—	2	1	—	—	—	—	0+1	0	2+1	1
1993–94	0+2	0	5+23	1	—	—	—	—	4+3	1	9+28	2
1994–95	2	2	9+12	1	—	—	—	—	4+1	4	15+13	7
TOTALS	2+2	2	16+35	3	—	—	—	—	8+5	5	26+42	10

DAVID JOHNSTON

SEASON	LEAGUE CUP APPS	GLS	SCOTTISH LEAGUE APPS	GLS	SCOTTISH CUP APPS	GLS	EUROPE APPS	GLS	OTHERS APPS	GLS	TOTALS APPS	GLS
1960–61	—	—	5	1	—	—	—	—	2	2	7	3

DAVID JOHNSTON

SEASON	LEAGUE CUP		SCOTTISH LEAGUE		SCOTTISH CUP		EUROPE		OTHERS		TOTALS	
	APPS	GLS	APPS	GLS	APPS	GLS	APPS	GLS	APPS	GLS	APPS	GLS
1977–78	—	—	1	0	—	—	—	—	1+1	0	2+1	0

MAURICE JOHNSTON

SEASON	LEAGUE CUP		SCOTTISH LEAGUE		SCOTTISH CUP		EUROPE		OTHERS		TOTALS	
	APPS	GLS	APPS	GLS	APPS	GLS	APPS	GLS	APPS	GLS	APPS	GLS
1993–94	—	—	31	4(1P)	3	1	—	—	2	0	36	5(1P)
1994–95	1	0	3+1	1	—	—	—	—	2+1	1	6+2	2
TOTALS	1	0	34+1	5(1P)	3	1	—	—	4+1	1	42+2	7(1P)

WILLIE JOHNSTON

SEASON	LEAGUE CUP		SCOTTISH LEAGUE		SCOTTISH CUP		EUROPE		OTHERS		TOTALS	
	APPS	GLS	APPS	GLS	APPS	GLS	APPS	GLS	APPS	GLS	APPS	GLS
1982–83	1+1	0	24+3	6(2P)	3	0	—	—	1+1	0	29+5	6(2P)
1983–84	4+2	1	2+19	2	0+1	0	—	—	8+2	1	14+24	4
1984–85	1+4	1	4+6	1	1+1	0	1+1	0	1+3	0	8+15	2
TOTALS	6+7	2	30+28	9(2P)	4+2	0	1+1	0	10+6	1	51+44	12(2P)

ROY KAY

SEASON	LEAGUE CUP		SCOTTISH LEAGUE		SCOTTISH CUP		EUROPE		TEXACO CUP		ANGLO-SCOTTISH CUP		OTHERS		TOTALS	
	APPS	GLS	APPS	GLS	APPS	GLS	APPS	GLS	APPS	GLS	APPS	GLS	APPS	GLS	APPS	GLS
1968–69	—	—	—	—	—	—	—	—	—	—	—	—	1	0	1	0
1969–70	—	—	—	—	—	—	—	—	—	—	—	—	—	—	—	—
1970–71	—	—	13	0	2	0	—	—	3	0	—	—	8	0	26	0
1971–72	6	0	18	0	—	—	—	—	2	0	—	—	3	1	29	1
1972–73	6	1(1P)	15	0	2	0	—	—	3	0	—	—	3+2	0	29+2	1(1P)
1973–74	—	—	14	1	3	0	—	—	1	0	—	—	—	—	18	1
1974–75	1	0	28	0	3	0	—	—	2	0	—	—	5	0	39	0
1975–76	5	0	23+1	0	4	0	—	—	—	—	1+1	0	7+1	0	40+3	0
1976–77	9	0	29+2	0	5+1	0	4	1	—	—	—	—	3	0	50+3	1
TOTALS	27	1(1P)	140+3	1	19+1	0	4	1	11	0	1+1	0	30+3	1	232+8	4(1P)

ARCHIE KELLY

SEASON	LEAGUE CUP		SCOTTISH LEAGUE		SCOTTISH CUP		EUROPE		OTHERS		TOTALS	
	APPS	GLS	APPS	GLS	APPS	GLS	APPS	GLS	APPS	GLS	APPS	GLS
1946–47	2	1	22	12	1	1	—	—	3	0	28	14
1947–48	6	6	12	5	—	—	—	—	1	0	19	11
TOTALS	8	7	34	17	1	1	—	—	4	0	47	25

BOBBY KEMP

SEASON	LEAGUE CUP APPS	GLS	SCOTTISH LEAGUE APPS	GLS	SCOTTISH CUP APPS	GLS	EUROPE APPS	GLS	OTHERS APPS	GLS	TOTALS APPS	GLS
1966–67	—	—	14	5	1	0	—	—	3	3	18	8
1967–68	2	0	7+1	4	—	—	—	—	0+1	0	9+2	4
TOTALS	2	0	21+1	9	1	0	—	—	3+1	3	27+2	12

DON KERRIGAN

SEASON	LEAGUE CUP APPS	GLS	SCOTTISH LEAGUE APPS	GLS	SCOTTISH CUP APPS	GLS	EUROPE APPS	GLS	OTHERS APPS	GLS	TOTALS APPS	GLS
1964–65	—	—	—	—	—	—	—	—	2	1	2	1
1965–66	—	—	19	5	3	1	5	3	2	1	29	10
1966–67	6	2	17	4	—	—	—	—	3+1	2	26+1	8
TOTALS	6	2	36	9	3	1	5	3	7+1	4	57+1	19

WALTER KIDD

SEASON	LEAGUE CUP APPS	GLS	SCOTTISH LEAGUE APPS	GLS	SCOTTISH CUP APPS	GLS	EUROPE APPS	GLS	TEXACO CUP APPS	GLS	ANGLO-SCOTTISH CUP APPS	GLS	OTHERS APPS	GLS	TOTALS APPS	GLS
1977–78	4	1	21+2	0	3	0	—	—	—	—	—	—	3	0	31+2	1
1978–79	—	—	29+1	0	4	0	—	—	—	—	2	0	4	1	39+1	1
1979–80	2	0	27+7	2	1	0	—	—	—	—	—	—	3+2	0	33+9	2
1980–81	3	0	25	1	2	0	—	—	—	—	2	0	5	0	37	1
1981–82	2+1	0	29+1	0	2	0	—	—	—	—	—	—	5+1	0	38+3	0
1982–83	10	0	37	0	3	0	—	—	—	—	—	—	8	1	58	1
1983–84	7	0	31	1	2	0	—	—	—	—	—	—	8	1	48	2
1984–85	5	0	33	1	4	0	2	0	—	—	—	—	5	0	49	1
1985–86	2	1	28	0	5	0	—	—	—	—	—	—	7	3	42	4
1986–87	1	0	33+2	0	4	0	2	0	—	—	—	—	10+1	0	50+3	0
1987–88	3	0	16+2	0	1	0	—	—	—	—	—	—	8	0	28+2	0
1988–89	1	0	20	0	1+1	0	6	0	—	—	—	—	4	0	32+1	0
1989–90	1+1	1	12+5	1	3	0	—	—	—	—	—	—	1+1	0	17+7	2
1990–91	1+1	0	1+3	0	—	—	0+1	0	—	—	—	—	2+4	0	4+9	0
1994–95	—	—	1	0	—	—	—	—	—	—	—	—	—	—	1	0
TOTALS	42+3	3	342+23	6	35+1	0	10+1	0	—	—	4	0	73+9	6	507+37	15

JOHN KILGANNON

SEASON	LEAGUE CUP APPS	GLS	SCOTTISH LEAGUE APPS	GLS	SCOTTISH CUP APPS	GLS	EUROPE APPS	GLS	OTHERS APPS	GLS	TOTALS APPS	GLS
1952–53	—	—	1	0	—	—	—	—	—	—	1	0

WALLACE KING

SEASON	LEAGUE CUP APPS	GLS	SCOTTISH LEAGUE APPS	GLS	SCOTTISH CUP APPS	GLS	EUROPE APPS	GLS	OTHERS APPS	GLS	TOTALS APPS	GLS
1953–54	3	0	—	—	—	—	—	—	—	—	3	0

HARRY KINNEAR

SEASON	LEAGUE CUP APPS	GLS	SCOTTISH LEAGUE APPS	GLS	SCOTTISH CUP APPS	GLS	EUROPE APPS	GLS	OTHERS APPS	GLS	TOTALS APPS	GLS
1971–72	—	—	4	2	2	2	—	—	1	0	7	4
1972–73	2	0	2	0	—	—	—	—	1	1	5	1
1973–74	—	—	1	0	—	—	—	—	—	—	1	0
TOTALS	2	0	7	2	2	2	—	—	2	1	13	5

BOBBY KIRK

SEASON	LEAGUE CUP APPS	GLS	SCOTTISH LEAGUE APPS	GLS	SCOTTISH CUP APPS	GLS	EUROPE APPS	GLS	OTHERS APPS	GLS	TOTALS APPS	GLS
1955–56	8	0	31	2(2P)	6	0	—	—	4	0	49	2(2P)
1956–57	6	2(2P)	27	2(2P)	1	0	—	—	8	0	42	4(4P)
1957–58	6	1(1P)	30	2(2P)	3	0	—	—	18	0	57	3(3P)
1958–59	10	0	33	0	2	0	2	0	21	0	68	0
1959–60	10	0	34	0	2	0	—	—	12	0	58	0
1960–61	7	0	30	0	2	0	2	0	4	0	45	0
1961–62	6	0	28	2(2P)	2	1(1P)	4	0	6	0	46	3(3P)
TOTALS	53	3(3P)	213	8(8P)	18	1(1P)	8	0	73	0	365	12(12P)

DAVID KIRKWOOD

SEASON	LEAGUE CUP APPS	GLS	SCOTTISH LEAGUE APPS	GLS	SCOTTISH CUP APPS	GLS	EUROPE APPS	GLS	OTHERS APPS	GLS	TOTALS APPS	GLS
1989–90	3	1	10+9	0	1	0	—	—	5	1	19+9	2
1990–91	—	—	8+1	1	—	—	3+1	0	2+4	1	13+6	2
TOTALS	3	1	18+10	1	1	0	3+1	0	7+4	2	32+15	4

BRIAN LAING

SEASON	LEAGUE CUP APPS	GLS	SCOTTISH LEAGUE APPS	GLS	SCOTTISH CUP APPS	GLS	EUROPE APPS	GLS	TEXACO CUP APPS	GLS	ANGLO-SCOTTISH CUP APPS	GLS	OTHERS APPS	GLS	TOTALS APPS	GLS
1970–71	—	—	1	1	—	—	—	—	1	0	—	—	—	—	2	1
1971–72	—	—	—	—	—	—	—	—	—	—	—	—	1	0	1	0
TOTALS	—	—	1	1	—	—	—	—	1	0	—	—	1	0	3	1

DAVID LAING

SEASON	LEAGUE CUP APPS	GLS	SCOTTISH LEAGUE APPS	GLS	SCOTTISH CUP APPS	GLS	EUROPE APPS	GLS	OTHERS APPS	GLS	TOTALS APPS	GLS
1946–47	1	0	9	0	2	0	—	—	3	0	15	0
1947–48	7	1	29	2(1P)	2	0	—	—	3	0	41	3(1P)
1948–49	6	2(2P)	28	3(2P)	4	1	—	—	2	0	40	6(4P)
1949–50	6	0	26	1	3	0	—	—	4	0	39	1
1950–51	5	0	27	3(2P)	3	0	—	—	10	0	45	3(2P)
1951–52	3	0	26	1	7	0	—	—	7	0	43	1
1952–53	6	0	23	1	4	1(1P)	—	—	7	0	40	2(1P)
1953–54	3	0	23	0	3	0	—	—	15+1	1	44+1	1
1954–55	3	1	—	—	—	—	—	—	—	—	3	1
TOTALS	40	4(2P)	191	11(5P)	28	2(1P)	—	—	51+1	1	310+1	18(8P)

SCOTT LEITCH

SEASON	LEAGUE CUP APPS	GLS	SCOTTISH LEAGUE APPS	GLS	SCOTTISH CUP APPS	GLS	EUROPE APPS	GLS	OTHERS APPS	GLS	TOTALS APPS	GLS
1993–94	—	—	24+4	2	3	0	2	0	2	0	31+4	2
1994–95	0+1	0	18+3	0	0+1	0	—	—	3	1	21+5	1
TOTALS	0+1	0	42+7	2	3+1	0	2	0	5	1	52+9	3

CRAIG LEVEIN

SEASON	LEAGUE CUP APPS	GLS	SCOTTISH LEAGUE APPS	GLS	SCOTTISH CUP APPS	GLS	EUROPE APPS	GLS	OTHERS APPS	GLS	TOTALS APPS	GLS
1983–84	—	—	20+2	0	2	0	—	—	3+1	0	25+3	0
1984–85	5	1	35+1	1	4	0	2	0	6	1	52+1	3
1985–86	3	0	33	2	5	0	—	—	8	0	49	2
1986–87	1	0	12	0	—	—	2	0	5	0	20	0
1987–88	—	—	21	0	—	—	—	—	2	0	23	0
1988–89	—	—	8+1	0	2	0	2	0	—	—	12+1	0
1989–90	3	0	35	0	3	0	—	—	6	0	47	0
1990–91	3	0	33	4	—	—	4	0	6	0	46	4
1991–92	3	0	36	2	4	0	—	—	4	1	47	3
1992–93	3	0	37	3	3	0	3	1	3	1	49	5
1993–94	2	0	30	3	3	0	2	0	6	0	43	3
1994–95	2	0	24	0	4	0	—	—	5+1	0	35+1	0
TOTALS	25	1	324+4	15	30	0	15	1	54+2	3	448+6	20

COLIN LIDDELL

SEASON	LEAGUE CUP		SCOTTISH LEAGUE		SCOTTISH CUP		EUROPE		OTHERS		TOTALS	
	APPS	GLS	APPS	GLS	APPS	GLS	APPS	GLS	APPS	GLS	APPS	GLS
1949–50	6	1	11	1	1	0	—	—	6	1	24	3
1950–51	6	0	1	0	—	—	—	—	1	1	8	1
1951–52	—	—	2	0	—	—	—	—	—	—	2	0
TOTALS	12	1	14	1	1	0	—	—	7	2	34	4

FRANK LIDDELL

SEASON	LEAGUE CUP		SCOTTISH LEAGUE		SCOTTISH CUP		EUROPE		TEXACO CUP		ANGLO-SCOTTISH CUP		OTHERS		TOTALS	
	APPS	GLS	APPS	GLS	APPS	GLS	APPS	GLS	APPS	GLS	APPS	GLS	APPS	GLS	APPS	GLS
1977–78	—	—	—	—	—	—	—	—	—	—	—	—	0+1	0	0+1	0
1978–79	2	0	31	0	3	0	—	—	—	—	2	0	4	0	42	0
1979–80	2	0	37	2	3	0	—	—	—	—	—	—	7	0	49	2
1980–81	4	0	24	2	2	0	—	—	—	—	2	0	5+1	0	37+1	2
1981–82	1+1	0	—	—	—	—	—	—	—	—	—	—	—	—	1+1	0
TOTALS	9+1	0	92	4	8	0	—	—	—	—	4	0	16+2	0	129+3	4

GARY LIDDELL

SEASON	LEAGUE CUP		SCOTTISH LEAGUE		SCOTTISH CUP		EUROPE		OTHERS		TOTALS	
	APPS	GLS	APPS	GLS	APPS	GLS	APPS	GLS	APPS	GLS	APPS	GLS
1980–81	—	—	13	2	—	—	—	—	1	0	14	2
1981–82	5	2	9+2	2	—	—	—	—	5+2	2	19+4	6
TOTALS	5	2	22+2	4	—	—	—	—	6+2	2	33+4	8

BILLY LINDORES

SEASON	LEAGUE CUP		SCOTTISH LEAGUE		SCOTTISH CUP		EUROPE		OTHERS		TOTALS	
	APPS	GLS	APPS	GLS	APPS	GLS	APPS	GLS	APPS	GLS	APPS	GLS
1956–57	—	—	2	0	—	—	—	—	3+1	0	5+1	0
1957–58	—	—	1	0	—	—	—	—	4+1	0	5	0
TOTALS	—	—	3	0	—	—	—	—	7+2	0	10+1	0

GARY LOCKE

SEASON	LEAGUE CUP		SCOTTISH LEAGUE		SCOTTISH CUP		EUROPE		OTHERS		TOTALS	
	APPS	GLS	APPS	GLS	APPS	GLS	APPS	GLS	APPS	GLS	APPS	GLS
1992–93	—	—	0+1	0	—	—	—	—	—	—	0+1	0
1993–94	2	0	29+4	0	1+1	0	2	0	4+1	2	38+6	2
1994–95	1	1	3+6	0	—	—	—	—	2+1	0	6+7	1
TOTALS	3	1	32+11	0	1+1	0	2	0	6+2	2	44+14	3

JOHN LOUGH

SEASON	LEAGUE CUP		SCOTTISH LEAGUE		SCOTTISH CUP		EUROPE		OTHERS		TOTALS	
	APPS	GLS	APPS	GLS	APPS	GLS	APPS	GLS	APPS	GLS	APPS	GLS
1958–59	—	—	11	0	—	—	—	—	6	0	17	0
1959–60	—	—	—	—	—	—	—	—	6	0	6	0
1960–61	—	—	3	0	1	0	—	—	1	0	5	0
TOTALS	—	—	14	0	1	0	—	—	13	0	28	0

ANDY LYNCH

SEASON	LEAGUE CUP		SCOTTISH LEAGUE		SCOTTISH CUP		EUROPE		TEXACO CUP		ANGLO-SCOTTISH CUP		OTHERS		TOTALS	
	APPS	GLS	APPS	GLS	APPS	GLS	APPS	GLS	APPS	GLS	APPS	GLS	APPS	GLS	APPS	GLS
1969–70	—	—	13	2	1	0	—	—	—	—	—	—	3+1	0	17+1	2
1970–71	4+1	2	20	4	1	1	—	—	3	1	—	—	12+1	5	40+2	13
1971–72	6	3	16+1	2	4	0	—	—	2	1	—	—	3+1	3	31+2	9
1972–73	5	1	7+3	3	—	—	—	—	2+1	1	—	—	4	1	18+4	6
TOTALS	15+1	6	56+4	11	6	1	—	—	7+1	3	—	—	22+3	9	106+9	30

COLIN McADAM

SEASON	LEAGUE CUP		SCOTTISH LEAGUE		SCOTTISH CUP		EUROPE		OTHERS		TOTALS	
	APPS	GLS	APPS	GLS	APPS	GLS	APPS	GLS	APPS	GLS	APPS	GLS
1985–86	—	—	0+5	0	0+1	1	—	—	0+3	0	0+9	1

WILLIE McALPINE

SEASON	LEAGUE CUP		SCOTTISH LEAGUE		SCOTTISH CUP		EUROPE		TEXACO CUP		ANGLO-SCOTTISH CUP		OTHERS		TOTALS	
	APPS	GLS	APPS	GLS	APPS	GLS	APPS	GLS	APPS	GLS	APPS	GLS	APPS	GLS	APPS	GLS
1968–69	—	—	12	0	2	0	—	—	—	—	—	—	4	0	18	0
1969–70	6	0	1	0	—	—	—	—	—	—	—	—	2	0	9	0
1970–71	—	—	—	—	—	—	—	—	1	0	—	—	—	—	1	0
TOTALS	6	0	13	0	2	0	—	—	1	0	—	—	6	0	28	0

ATHOLL McARA

SEASON	LEAGUE CUP		SCOTTISH LEAGUE		SCOTTISH CUP		EUROPE		OTHERS		TOTALS	
	APPS	GLS	APPS	GLS	APPS	GLS	APPS	GLS	APPS	GLS	APPS	GLS
1946–47	—	—	2	0	—	—	—	—	—	—	2	0

DUNCAN McCLURE

SEASON	LEAGUE CUP		SCOTTISH LEAGUE		SCOTTISH CUP		EUROPE		OTHERS		TOTALS	
	APPS	GLS	APPS	GLS	APPS	GLS	APPS	GLS	APPS	GLS	APPS	GLS
1946–47	1	0	16	0	2	0	—	—	2	0	21	0
1947–48	2	0	1	0	—	—	—	—	2	0	5	0
TOTALS	3	0	17	0	2	0	—	—	4	0	26	0

GERRY McCOY

SEASON	LEAGUE CUP		SCOTTISH LEAGUE		SCOTTISH CUP		EUROPE		OTHERS		TOTALS	
	APPS	GLS	APPS	GLS	APPS	GLS	APPS	GLS	APPS	GLS	APPS	GLS
1981–82	3	1	19+2	9	1	0	—	—	4	3	27+2	13
1982–83	2+1	0	1+5	0	0+2	0	—	—	3+2	1	6+10	1
1983–84	0+1	0	—	—	—	—	—	—	0+1	0	0+2	0
TOTALS	5+2	1	20+7	9	1+2	0	—	—	7+3	4	33+14	14

ALEX McCRAE

SEASON	LEAGUE CUP		SCOTTISH LEAGUE		SCOTTISH CUP		EUROPE		OTHERS		TOTALS	
	APPS	GLS	APPS	GLS	APPS	GLS	APPS	GLS	APPS	GLS	APPS	GLS
1946–47	7	3	24	10	2	0	—	—	—	—	33	13

DAVID McCREERY

SEASON	LEAGUE CUP		SCOTTISH LEAGUE		SCOTTISH CUP		EUROPE		OTHERS		TOTALS	
	APPS	GLS	APPS	GLS	APPS	GLS	APPS	GLS	APPS	GLS	APPS	GLS
1989–90	—	—	20+2	0	3	0	—	—	1	0	24+2	0
1990–91	3	0	4+3	0	—	—	1	0	6+1	0	14+4	0
TOTALS	3	0	24+5	0	3	0	1	0	7+1	0	38+6	0

MURRAY McDERMOTT   FIGURES IN BRACKETS REPRESENT SHUT-OUTS

SEASON	LEAGUE CUP		SCOTTISH LEAGUE		SCOTTISH CUP		EUROPE		OTHERS		TOTALS	
	APPS	GLS	APPS	GLS	APPS	GLS	APPS	GLS	APPS	GLS	APPS	GLS
1985–86	—	—	—	—	—	—	—	—	1+1	(0)	1+1	(0)
1988–89	—	—	—	—	—	—	0+1	(1)	1	(0)	1+1	(1)
TOTALS	—	—	—	—	—	—	0+1	(1)	2+1	(0)	2+2	(1)

ALAN MacDONALD

SEASON	LEAGUE CUP APPS	GLS	SCOTTISH LEAGUE APPS	GLS	SCOTTISH CUP APPS	GLS	EUROPE APPS	GLS	OTHERS APPS	GLS	TOTALS APPS	GLS
1966–67	—	—	15	0	1	0	—	—	3+2	0	19+2	0
1967–68	5	1	7	0	—	—	—	—	1	0	13	1
1968–69	2+2	0	20+1	1	0+1	0	—	—	3	0	25+4	1
1969–70	3	0	16+1	2	—	—	—	—	1+1	0	20+2	2
TOTALS	10+2	1	58+2	3	1+1	0	—	—	8+3	0	77+8	4

ALEX MacDONALD

SEASON	LEAGUE CUP APPS	GLS	SCOTTISH LEAGUE APPS	GLS	SCOTTISH CUP APPS	GLS	EUROPE APPS	GLS	OTHERS APPS	GLS	TOTALS APPS	GLS
1980–81	4	1	28	3	2	1	—	—	1	0	35	5
1981–82	4	0	15+1	1	—	—	—	—	5	0	24+1	1
1982–83	9	3	29+2	5	3	1	—	—	8	0	49+2	9
1983–84	4	0	19+5	1	—	—	—	—	6	1	29+5	2
1984–85	3+1	0	14+8	2	0+1	0	1+1	0	2+1	1	20+12	3
1985–86	—	—	0+1	0	—	—	—	—	1+1	0	1+2	0
1986–87	—	—	—	—	—	—	—	—	—	—		
1987–88	—	—	—	—	—	—	—	—	1	1	1	1
TOTALS	24+1	4	105+17	12	5+1	2	1+1	0	24+2	3	159+22	21

RODDY MacDONALD

SEASON	LEAGUE CUP APPS	GLS	SCOTTISH LEAGUE APPS	GLS	SCOTTISH CUP APPS	GLS	EUROPE APPS	GLS	OTHERS APPS	GLS	TOTALS APPS	GLS
1981–82	4	0	35	6	2	1	—	—	7	1	48	8
1982–83	10	0	39	3	4	1	—	—	8	0	61	4
1983–84	7	0	34	2	—	—	—	—	7	3	48	5
1984–85	5	1	28	1	5	1	—	—	3+2	2	41+2	5
1985–86	3	0	10	2	0+1	0	—	—	3+5	1	16+6	3
1986–87	—	—	27	5	7	0	—	—	4	0	38	5
1987–88	—	—	—	—	—	—	—	—	1	0	1	0
TOTALS	29	1	173	19	18+1	3	—	—	33+7	7	253+8	30

JIM McFADZEAN

SEASON	LEAGUE CUP APPS	GLS	SCOTTISH LEAGUE APPS	GLS	SCOTTISH CUP APPS	GLS	EUROPE APPS	GLS	OTHERS APPS	GLS	TOTALS APPS	GLS
1956–57	—	—	4	1	—	—	—	—	3	1	7	2
1957–58	1	0	—	—	—	—	—	—	—	—	1	0
1958–59	—	—	3	2	—	—	—	—	—	—	3	2
1959–60	1	1	5	1	—	—	—	—	1	0	7	2
1960–61	—	—	13	1	1	2	—	—	—	—	14	3
TOTALS	2	1	25	5	1	2	—	—	4	1	32	9

WILLIE McFARLANE

SEASON	LEAGUE CUP		SCOTTISH LEAGUE		SCOTTISH CUP		EUROPE		OTHERS		TOTALS	
	APPS	GLS	APPS	GLS	APPS	GLS	APPS	GLS	APPS	GLS	APPS	GLS
1946–47	3	1	14	2	2	0	—	—	2	0	21	3
1947–48	7	0	17	2	—	—	—	—	2+1	0	26+1	2
1948–49	—	—	7	0	—	—	—	—	3	1	10	1
1949–50	—	—	—	—	—	—	—	—	—	—	—	—
1950–51	—	—	—	—	—	—	—	—	1	0	1	0
TOTALS	10	1	38	4	2	0	—	—	8+1	1	58+1	6

BILLY MACKAY

SEASON	LEAGUE CUP		SCOTTISH LEAGUE		SCOTTISH CUP		EUROPE		OTHERS		TOTALS	
	APPS	GLS	APPS	GLS	APPS	GLS	APPS	GLS	APPS	GLS	APPS	GLS
1985–86	—	—	0+3	0	0+1	0	—	—	1+3	2(1P)	1+7	2(1P)
1986–87	0+1	0	0+2	0	—	—	—	—	1+2	0	1+5	0
TOTALS	0+1	0	0+5	0	0+1	0	—	—	2+5	2(1P)	2+12	2(1P)

DAVE MACKAY

SEASON	LEAGUE CUP		SCOTTISH LEAGUE		SCOTTISH CUP		EUROPE		OTHERS		TOTALS	
	APPS	GLS	APPS	GLS	APPS	GLS	APPS	GLS	APPS	GLS	APPS	GLS
1953–54	—	—	4	0	—	—	—	—	6	0	10	0
1954–55	7	1	25	2	4	0	—	—	5	0	41	3
1955–56	2	0	28	4	6	0	—	—	3	0	39	4
1956–57	6	0	31	5	1	0	—	—	3	1	41	6
1957–58	6	0	28	12(5P)	3	0	—	—	8	2	45	14(5P)
1958–59	5	1	19	4	2	0	2	0	4	0	32	5
TOTALS	26	2	135	27(5P)	16	0	2	0	29	3	208	32(5P)

GARY MACKAY

SEASON	LEAGUE CUP		SCOTTISH LEAGUE		SCOTTISH CUP		EUROPE		OTHERS		TOTALS	
	APPS	GLS	APPS	GLS	APPS	GLS	APPS	GLS	APPS	GLS	APPS	GLS
1980–81	0+1	0	11+1	0	2	0	—	—	2	0	15+2	0
1981–82	2	0	10+7	2	0+1	0	—	—	1+1	0	13+9	2
1982–83	2+1	0	26+8	6(1P)	4	0	—	—	5+2	4	37+11	10(1P)
1983–84	7+1	2(1P)	29+2	4(2P)	2	0	—	—	7	3	45+3	9(3P)
1984–85	—	—	16+1	2	5	4	1	0	3	3	25+1	9
1985–86	2	0	30+2	4	5	2	—	—	8+1	4	45+3	10
1986–87	1	0	31+5	7(4P)	5+2	2	2	0	4	1	43+7	10(4P)
1987–88	3	1	40+1	5	4	2	—	—	7+1	2	54+2	10
1988–89	4	2	29	2	3	0	6+2	0	11	2(1P)	53+2	6(1P)
1989–90	2	0	31+2	1	1+1	0	—	—	6	1	40+3	2
1990–91	3	0	27+3	3	1	1	1+1	0	8	0	40+4	4
1991–92	3	0	41+2	1	3	1	—	—	4	1	51+2	3
1992–93	3	1	36+1	2	4	0	4	1	4	1	51+1	5
1993–94	2	0	34+2	1	2	0	2	0	7+1	1	47+3	2
1994–95	1	0	21+13	2	4+1	0	—	—	3	0	29+14	2
TOTALS	35+3	6(1P)	412+50	42(7P)	45+5	12	16+3	1	80+6	23(1P)	588+67	84(9P)

TOMMY McKENZIE

SEASON	LEAGUE CUP		SCOTTISH LEAGUE		SCOTTISH CUP		EUROPE		OTHERS		TOTALS	
	APPS	GLS	APPS	GLS	APPS	GLS	APPS	GLS	APPS	GLS	APPS	GLS
1946–47	9	0	21	1	2	0	—	—	2	0	34	1
1947–48	6	0	25	0	1	0	—	—	4	0	36	0
1948–49	6	0	28	0	4	0	—	—	6	0	44	0
1949–50	6	1	27	0	3	0	—	—	5	0	41	1
1950–51	6	0	27	0	3	1	—	—	5	0	41	1
1951–52	3	0	23	0	6	0	—	—	5	1	37	1
1952–53	6	0	24	0	3	0	—	—	5	0	38	0
1953–54	6	0	7	0	—	—	—	—	12	3	25	3
1954–55	4	0	22	1	4	0	—	—	3	0	33	1
1955–56	—	—	22	0	6	0	—	—	3	0	31	0
1956–57	6	0	21	1	—	—	—	—	7+1	1	34+1	2
1957–58	6	0	8	0	—	—	—	—	2	0	16	0
1958–59	—	—	—	—	—	—	—	—	1	0	1	0
TOTALS	64	1	255	3	32	1	—	—	60+1	5	411+1	10

TOSH McKINLAY

SEASON	LEAGUE CUP APPS	GLS	SCOTTISH LEAGUE APPS	GLS	SCOTTISH CUP APPS	GLS	EUROPE APPS	GLS	OTHERS APPS	GLS	TOTALS APPS	GLS
1988–89	—	—	17	1	3	0	2	0	1	0	23	1
1989–90	—	—	29	1	2	0	—	—	1	0	32	1
1990–91	3	0	31+2	2	1	0	4	0	9	0	48+2	2
1991–92	3	0	37+2	2	5	0	—	—	4	1	49+2	3
1992–93	3	1	32+2	1	3	0	4	0	2+1	0	44+3	2
1993–94	2	0	43	0	3	0	2	0	5+1	0	55+1	0
1994–95	1	0	11	0	—	—	—	—	1	0	13	0
TOTALS	12	1	200+6	7	17	0	12	0	23+2	1	264+8	9

JOHN MacKINTOSH

SEASON	LEAGUE CUP APPS	GLS	SCOTTISH LEAGUE APPS	GLS	SCOTTISH CUP APPS	GLS	EUROPE APPS	GLS	OTHERS APPS	GLS	TOTALS APPS	GLS
1953–54	—	—	—	—	—	—	—	—	1	0	1	0
1954–55	—	—	—	—	—	—	—	—	—	—	—	—
1955–56	—	—	—	—	—	—	—	—	—	—	—	—
1956–57	—	—	—	—	—	—	—	—	—	—	—	—
1957–58	—	—	—	—	—	—	—	—	—	—	—	—
1958–59	—	—	1	0	—	—	—	—	1	0	2	0
TOTALS	—	—	1	0	—	—	—	—	2	0	3	0

ALAN McLAREN

SEASON	LEAGUE CUP APPS	GLS	SCOTTISH LEAGUE APPS	GLS	SCOTTISH CUP APPS	GLS	EUROPE APPS	GLS	OTHERS APPS	GLS	TOTALS APPS	GLS
1987–88	—	—	1	0	—	—	—	—	1+1	0	2+1	0
1988–89	—	—	11+1	1	3	0	2	0	3+1	0	19+2	1
1989–90	2+1	0	26+1	1	—	—	—	—	6	0	34+2	1
1990–91	1	0	18+5	1	1	0	3+1	0	8	0	31+6	1
1991–92	1	0	38	1	6	1	—	—	2+1	0	47+1	2
1992–93	2	1	34	1	4	0	2+1	0	2	0	44+1	2
1993–94	—	—	37	1	3	0	2	0	—	—	42	1
1994–95	2	0	10	1	—	—	—	—	5	0	17	1
TOTALS	8+1	1	175+7	7	17	1	9+2	0	27+3	0	236+13	9

STEWART MacLAREN

SEASON	LEAGUE CUP APPS	GLS	SCOTTISH LEAGUE APPS	GLS	SCOTTISH CUP APPS	GLS	EUROPE APPS	GLS	OTHERS APPS	GLS	TOTALS APPS	GLS
1981–82	6	0	34	0	2	0	—	—	6	0	48	0
1982–83	4+2	0	8+6	0	0+1	0	—	—	4	0	16+9	0
1983–84	5	0	18+1	0	2	0	—	—	1+1	0	26+2	0
1984–85	—	—	1	0	—	—	—	—	2+1	0	3+1	0
TOTALS	15+2	0	61+7	0	4+1	0	—	—	13+2	0	93+12	0

KENNY McLEOD

SEASON	LEAGUE CUP		SCOTTISH LEAGUE		SCOTTISH CUP		EUROPE		OTHERS		TOTALS	
	APPS	GLS	APPS	GLS	APPS	GLS	APPS	GLS	APPS	GLS	APPS	GLS
1978–79	—	—	2+1	0	—	—	—	—	1	0	3+1	0

BRIAN McNAUGHTON

SEASON	LEAGUE CUP		SCOTTISH LEAGUE		SCOTTISH CUP		EUROPE		OTHERS		TOTALS	
	APPS	GLS	APPS	GLS	APPS	GLS	APPS	GLS	APPS	GLS	APPS	GLS
1984–85	—	—	3+5	2	0+3	1	—	—	0+1	1	3+9	4
1985–86	1	1	2+2	0	—	—	—	—	2+3	2	5+5	3
TOTALS	1	1	5+7	2	0+3	1	—	—	2+4	3	8+14	7

BRIAN McNEILL

SEASON	LEAGUE CUP		SCOTTISH LEAGUE		SCOTTISH CUP		EUROPE		OTHERS		TOTALS	
	APPS	GLS	APPS	GLS	APPS	GLS	APPS	GLS	APPS	GLS	APPS	GLS
1981–82	2	0	15+2	0	—	—	—	—	1+1	0	18+3	0

DAVE McNICOLL

SEASON	LEAGUE CUP		SCOTTISH LEAGUE		SCOTTISH CUP		EUROPE		TEXACO CUP		ANGLO-SCOTTISH CUP		OTHERS		TOTALS	
	APPS	GLS	APPS	GLS	APPS	GLS	APPS	GLS	APPS	GLS	APPS	GLS	APPS	GLS	APPS	GLS
1977–78	—	—	27	1	3	0	—	—	—	—	—	—	1	0	31	1
1978–79	2	0	16+1	0	1	0	—	—	—	—	2	0	3	0	24+1	0
TOTALS	2	0	43+1	1	4	0	—	—	—	—	2	0	4	0	55+1	1

DAVE McPHERSON

SEASON	LEAGUE CUP		SCOTTISH LEAGUE		SCOTTISH CUP		EUROPE		OTHERS		TOTALS	
	APPS	GLS	APPS	GLS	APPS	GLS	APPS	GLS	APPS	GLS	APPS	GLS
1987–88	3	1	44	4	4	0	—	—	9	1	60	6
1988–89	4	0	32	4	3	1	8	0	10	0	57	5
1989–90	3	0	35	4	3	0	—	—	6	1	47	5
1990–91	3	0	34	2	1	0	3	1	6	1	47	4
1991–92	3	0	44	2	6	0	—	—	3	1	56	3
1994–95	—	—	23	2	5	1	—	—	—	—	28	3
TOTALS	16	1	212	18	22	2	11	1	34	4	295	26

DENIS McQUADE

SEASON	LEAGUE CUP		SCOTTISH LEAGUE		SCOTTISH CUP		EUROPE		OTHERS		TOTALS	
	APPS	GLS	APPS	GLS	APPS	GLS	APPS	GLS	APPS	GLS	APPS	GLS
1978–79	—	—	13+10	4	0+1	0	—	—	—	—	13+11	4

PAT McSHANE

SEASON	LEAGUE CUP APPS	GLS	SCOTTISH LEAGUE APPS	GLS	SCOTTISH CUP APPS	GLS	EUROPE APPS	GLS	OTHERS APPS	GLS	TOTALS APPS	GLS
1979–80	—	—	0+2	0	—	—	—	—	0+1	0	0+3	0
1980–81	—	—	3+2	1	0+1	0	—	—	1	0	4+3	1
TOTALS	—	—	3+4	1	0+1	0	—	—	1+1	0	4+6	1

TOMMY McSPADYEN

SEASON	LEAGUE CUP APPS	GLS	SCOTTISH LEAGUE APPS	GLS	SCOTTISH CUP APPS	GLS	EUROPE APPS	GLS	OTHERS APPS	GLS	TOTALS APPS	GLS
1946–47	9	0	20	0	2	0	—	—	1	0	32	0
1947–48	6	0	10	0	1	0	—	—	1	0	18	0
1948–49	—	—	—	—	—	—	—	—	—	—	—	—
1949–50	—	—	—	—	—	—	—	—	—	—	—	—
1950–51	—	—	3	0	1	0	—	—	4	0	8	0
1951–52	5	0	4	0	1	0	—	—	—	—	10	0
TOTALS	20	0	37	0	5	0	—	—	6	0	68	0

WILLIE McVIE

SEASON	LEAGUE CUP APPS	GLS	SCOTTISH LEAGUE APPS	GLS	SCOTTISH CUP APPS	GLS	EUROPE APPS	GLS	OTHERS APPS	GLS	TOTALS APPS	GLS
1980–81	—	—	12	0	—	—	—	—	3+1	0	15+1	0

ARTHUR MANN

SEASON	LEAGUE CUP APPS	GLS	SCOTTISH LEAGUE APPS	GLS	SCOTTISH CUP APPS	GLS	EUROPE APPS	GLS	OTHERS APPS	GLS	TOTALS APPS	GLS
1967–68	—	—	21	0	7	0	—	—	3	0	31	0
1968–69	6	0	11	0	—	—	—	—	3	0	20	0
TOTALS	6	0	32	0	7	0	—	—	6	0	51	0

PETER MARINELLO

SEASON	LEAGUE CUP APPS	GLS	SCOTTISH LEAGUE APPS	GLS	SCOTTISH CUP APPS	GLS	EUROPE APPS	GLS	OTHERS APPS	GLS	TOTALS APPS	GLS
1981–82	—	—	10+8	2	2	1	—	—	2	0	14+8	3
1982–83	4	1	2+2	1	—	—	—	—	5+1	0	11+3	2
TOTALS	4	1	12+10	3	2	1	—	—	7+1	0	25+11	5

GORDON MARSHALL   FIGURES IN BRACKETS REPRESENT SHUT-OUTS

SEASON	LEAGUE CUP APPS	GLS	SCOTTISH LEAGUE APPS	GLS	SCOTTISH CUP APPS	GLS	EUROPE APPS	GLS	OTHERS APPS	GLS	TOTALS APPS	GLS
1956–57	—	—	11	(3)	—	—	—	—	7	(0)	18	(3)
1957–58	6	(1)	31	(13)	3	(0)	—	—	16	(3)	56	(17)
1958–59	10	(2)	31	(10)	2	(0)	2	(0)	21	(6)	66	(18)
1959–60	10	(2)	33	(5)	2	(0)	—	—	15	(5)	60	(12)
1960–61	7	(0)	30	(5)	3	(0)	2	(0)	3	(0)	45	(5)
1961–62	10	(3)	29	(7)	1	(0)	4	(1)	5	(4)	49	(15)
1962–63	10	(5)	28	(7)	2	(0)	—	—	4	(2)	44	(14)
TOTALS	53	(13)	193	(50)	13	(0)	8	(1)	71	(20)	338	(84)

TOMMY MARTIN

SEASON	LEAGUE CUP APPS	GLS	SCOTTISH LEAGUE APPS	GLS	SCOTTISH CUP APPS	GLS	EUROPE APPS	GLS	OTHERS APPS	GLS	TOTALS APPS	GLS
1946–47	—	—	2	0	—	—	—	—	—	—	2	0
1947–48	—	—	4	2	—	—	—	—	5	2	9	4
1948–49	—	—	1	0	—	—	—	—	1	1	2	1
TOTALS	—	—	7	2	—	—	—	—	6	3	13	5

BOBBY MASTERTON

SEASON	LEAGUE CUP APPS	GLS	SCOTTISH LEAGUE APPS	GLS	SCOTTISH CUP APPS	GLS	EUROPE APPS	GLS	OTHERS APPS	GLS	TOTALS APPS	GLS
1979–80	1+1	0	9+6	0	2	0	—	—	—	—	12+7	0
1980–81	—	—	8+3	0	—	—	—	—	1	0	9+3	0
TOTALS	1+1	0	17+9	0	2	0	—	—	1	0	21+10	0

DOUGAL MATHESON

SEASON	LEAGUE CUP APPS	GLS	SCOTTISH LEAGUE APPS	GLS	SCOTTISH CUP APPS	GLS	EUROPE APPS	GLS	OTHERS APPS	GLS	TOTALS APPS	GLS
1947–48	—	—	24	0	2	0	—	—	6	0	32	0
1948–49	2	0	20	0	3	0	—	—	7	1	32	1
1949–50	6	0	8	0	—	—	—	—	2	0	16	0
1950–51	—	—	—	—	—	—	—	—	1	0	1	0
TOTALS	8	0	52	0	5	0	—	—	16	1	81	1

ALLY MAUCHLEN

SEASON	LEAGUE CUP		SCOTTISH LEAGUE		SCOTTISH CUP		EUROPE		OTHERS		TOTALS	
	APPS	GLS	APPS	GLS	APPS	GLS	APPS	GLS	APPS	GLS	APPS	GLS
1992–93	2	0	16+2	0	3	0	2	0	3	0	26+2	0
1993–94	1	0	—	—	—	—	—	—	3+1	0	4+1	0
TOTALS	3	0	16+2	0	3	0	2	0	6+1	0	30+3	0

SCOTT MAXWELL

SEASON	LEAGUE CUP		SCOTTISH LEAGUE		SCOTTISH CUP		EUROPE		OTHERS		TOTALS	
	APPS	GLS	APPS	GLS	APPS	GLS	APPS	GLS	APPS	GLS	APPS	GLS
1980–81	—	—	1	1	—	—	—	—	0+1	0	1+1	1

BILLY MENMUIR

SEASON	LEAGUE CUP		SCOTTISH LEAGUE		SCOTTISH CUP		EUROPE		OTHERS		TOTALS	
	APPS	GLS	APPS	GLS	APPS	GLS	APPS	GLS	APPS	GLS	APPS	GLS
1972–73	—	—	13+1	1	—	—	—	—	2	0	15+1	1

JOHN MILLAR

SEASON	LEAGUE CUP		SCOTTISH LEAGUE		SCOTTISH CUP		EUROPE		OTHERS		TOTALS	
	APPS	GLS	APPS	GLS	APPS	GLS	APPS	GLS	APPS	GLS	APPS	GLS
1991–92	3	0	40+1	7	5	0	—	—	4	0	52+1	7
1992–93	—	—	23+1	1	1	0	1	0	—	—	25+1	1
1993–94	—	—	16+4	4	2	0	—	—	1	0	19+4	4
1994–95	2	1	25+3	6	3	2	—	—	6	1	36+3	10
TOTALS	5	1	104+9	18	11	2	1	0	11	1	132+9	22

ARCHIE MILLER

SEASON	LEAGUE CUP		SCOTTISH LEAGUE		SCOTTISH CUP		EUROPE		OTHERS		TOTALS	
	APPS	GLS	APPS	GLS	APPS	GLS	APPS	GLS	APPS	GLS	APPS	GLS
1946–47	8	0	20	1	1	1	—	—	2	0	31	2
1947–48	—	—	—	—	—	—	—	—	1	0	1	0
TOTALS	8	0	20	1	1	1	—	—	3	0	32	2

COLIN MILLER

SEASON	LEAGUE CUP		SCOTTISH LEAGUE		SCOTTISH CUP		EUROPE		OTHERS		TOTALS	
	APPS	GLS	APPS	GLS	APPS	GLS	APPS	GLS	APPS	GLS	APPS	GLS
1994–95	—	—	16	1	3+1	1	—	—	1	0	20+1	2

GEORGE MILLER

SEASON	LEAGUE CUP APPS	GLS	SCOTTISH LEAGUE APPS	GLS	SCOTTISH CUP APPS	GLS	EUROPE APPS	GLS	OTHERS APPS	GLS	TOTALS APPS	GLS
1965–66	—	—	17	0	4	0	3	0	—	—	24	0
1966–67	5	0	20	1	—	—	—	—	10	1	35	2
1967–68	6	1(1P)	31	4(2P)	7	2(1P)	—	—	5	1(1P)	49	8(5P)
1968–69	5	0	0+4	0	—	—	—	—	2	0	7+4	0
TOTALS	16	1(1P)	68+4	5(2P)	11	2(1P)	3	0	17	2(1P)	115+4	10(5P)

ANDY MILNE

SEASON	LEAGUE CUP APPS	GLS	SCOTTISH LEAGUE APPS	GLS	SCOTTISH CUP APPS	GLS	EUROPE APPS	GLS	OTHERS APPS	GLS	TOTALS APPS	GLS
1966–67	—	—	5+1	4	—	—	—	—	2+3	2	7+4	6
1967–68	—	—	1	0	—	—	—	—	—	—	1	0
TOTALS	—	—	6+1	4	—	—	—	—	2+3	2	8+4	6

JIMMY MILNE

SEASON	LEAGUE CUP APPS	GLS	SCOTTISH LEAGUE APPS	GLS	SCOTTISH CUP APPS	GLS	EUROPE APPS	GLS	OTHERS APPS	GLS	TOTALS APPS	GLS
1950–51	—	—	—	—	—	—	—	—	1	0	1	0
1951–52	—	—	26	0	7	0	—	—	4	0	37	0
1952–53	6	0	14	0	—	—	—	—	1	0	21	0
1953–54	—	—	—	—	—	—	—	—	6	0	6	0
1954–55	—	—	1	0	—	—	—	—	1	0	2	0
1955–56	—	—	2	0	—	—	—	—	—	—	2	0
1956–57	—	—	15	0	—	—	—	—	7	0	22	0
1957–58	—	—	21	3(3P)	3	0	—	—	9	0	33	3(3P)
1958–59	4	1	20	0	2	0	—	—	16	0	42	1
1959–60	9	0	25	0	2	0	—	—	14	0	50	0
1960–61	7	0	19	0	4	0	2	0	2	0	34	0
TOTALS	26	1	143	3(3P)	18	0	2	0	61	0	250	4(3P)

RENE MOLLER

SEASON	LEAGUE CUP APPS	GLS	SCOTTISH LEAGUE APPS	GLS	SCOTTISH CUP APPS	GLS	EUROPE APPS	GLS	OTHERS APPS	GLS	TOTALS APPS	GLS
1967–68	—	—	8	3	2+2	2	—	—	—	—	10+2	5
1968–69	5	1	13	2	—	—	—	—	5+2	4	22+2	7
1969–70	—	—	32	7	2	0	—	—	3+3	2	37+3	9
TOTALS	5	1	53	12	4+2	2	—	—	8+5	6	70+7	21

ALLAN MOORE

SEASON	LEAGUE CUP APPS	GLS	SCOTTISH LEAGUE APPS	GLS	SCOTTISH CUP APPS	GLS	EUROPE APPS	GLS	OTHERS APPS	GLS	TOTALS APPS	GLS
1986–87	—	—	2+8	0	—	—	—	—	4+2	1	6+10	1
1987–88	—	—	2+5	1	0+1	0	—	—	4+6	4	6+12	5
1988–89	—	—	5+7	2	—	—	1+1	0	3+4	0	9+12	2
TOTALS	—	—	9+20	3	0+1	0	1+1	0	11+12	5	21+34	8

COLIN MORE

SEASON	LEAGUE CUP APPS	GLS	SCOTTISH LEAGUE APPS	GLS	SCOTTISH CUP APPS	GLS	EUROPE APPS	GLS	OTHERS APPS	GLS	TOTALS APPS	GLS
1978–79	—	—	4	0	—	—	—	—	—	—	4	0
1979–80	1	0	6	0	—	—	—	—	5	0	12	0
1980–81	—	—	21+3	0	2	0	—	—	2+1	0	25+4	0
1981–82	6	0	3	0	—	—	—	—	2	0	11	0
TOTALS	7	0	34+3	0	2	0	—	—	9+1	0	52+4	0

JOE MORGAN

SEASON	LEAGUE CUP APPS	GLS	SCOTTISH LEAGUE APPS	GLS	SCOTTISH CUP APPS	GLS	EUROPE APPS	GLS	OTHERS APPS	GLS	TOTALS APPS	GLS
1970–71	—	—	0+1	0	—	—	—	—	—	—	0+1	0

JIM MURPHY

SEASON	LEAGUE CUP APPS	GLS	SCOTTISH LEAGUE APPS	GLS	SCOTTISH CUP APPS	GLS	EUROPE APPS	GLS	OTHERS APPS	GLS	TOTALS APPS	GLS
1963–64	—	—	6	8	3	0	—	—	—	—	9	8
1964–65	2	0	1	0	—	—	—	—	3	2	6	2
1965–66	—	—	7	2	—	—	—	—	1	0	8	2
1966–67	0+2	0	20+2	7	—	—	—	—	6	1	26+4	8
1967–68	—	—	—	—	—	—	—	—	0+1	0	0+1	0
TOTALS	2+2	0	34+2	17	3	0	—	—	10+1	3	49+5	20

DON MURRAY

SEASON	LEAGUE CUP APPS	GLS	SCOTTISH LEAGUE APPS	GLS	SCOTTISH CUP APPS	GLS	EUROPE APPS	GLS	TEXACO CUP APPS	GLS	ANGLO-SCOTTISH CUP APPS	GLS	OTHERS APPS	GLS	TOTALS APPS	GLS
1974–75	—	—	16	0	3	0	—	—	—	—	—	—	6	0	25	0
1975–76	6	0	22	0	5	0	—	—	—	—	3	0	7	0	43	0
1976–77	1	0	—	—	—	—	—	—	—	—	—	—	2	0	3	0
TOTALS	7	0	38	0	8	0	—	—	—	—	3	0	15	0	71	0

JIMMY MURRAY

SEASON	LEAGUE CUP		SCOTTISH LEAGUE		SCOTTISH CUP		EUROPE		OTHERS		TOTALS	
	APPS	GLS	APPS	GLS	APPS	GLS	APPS	GLS	APPS	GLS	APPS	GLS
1950–51	—	—	—	—	—	—	—	—	1	1	1	1
1951–52	—	—	1	1	—	—	—	—	1	0	2	1
1952–53	—	—	—	—	—	—	—	—	—	—	—	—
1953–54	—	—	—	—	—	—	—	—	—	—	—	—
1954–55	—	—	4	0	—	—	—	—	—	—	4	0
1955–56	—	—	4	0	—	—	—	—	0+1	1	4+1	1
1956–57	—	—	12	7	—	—	—	—	4	3	16	10
1957–58	—	—	33	27	3	2	—	—	8	3	44	32
1958–59	8	4	30	12	2	3	1	0	18+1	7	59+1	26
1959–60	5	3	18	11	1	1	—	—	12	6	36	21
1960–61	5	3	13	5	1	2	2	0	2	1	23	11
TOTALS	18	10	115	63	7	8	3	0	46+2	22	189+2	103

MALCOLM MURRAY

SEASON	LEAGUE CUP		SCOTTISH LEAGUE		SCOTTISH CUP		EUROPE		OTHERS		TOTALS	
	APPS	GLS	APPS	GLS	APPS	GLS	APPS	GLS	APPS	GLS	APPS	GLS
1982–83	—	—	—	—	—	—	—	—	0+1	0	0+1	0
1983–84	—	—	1	0	—	—	—	—	4+1	0	5+1	0
1984–85	—	—	4	0	—	—	—	—	1	0	5	0
1985–86	—	—	—	—	—	—	—	—	2+1	0	2+1	0
1986–87	—	—	8	0	1	0	—	—	0+1	0	9+1	0
1987–88	—	—	7	0	1	0	—	—	0+1	0	8+1	0
1988–89	2+1	1	8	0	—	—	—	—	4+3	0	14+4	1
TOTALS	2+1	1	28	0	2	0	—	—	11+8	0	43+9	1

NEIL MURRAY

SEASON	LEAGUE CUP		SCOTTISH LEAGUE		SCOTTISH CUP		EUROPE		TEXACO CUP		ANGLO-SCOTTISH CUP		OTHERS		TOTALS	
	APPS	GLS	APPS	GLS	APPS	GLS	APPS	GLS	APPS	GLS	APPS	GLS	APPS	GLS	APPS	GLS
1968–69	—	—	—	—	—	—	—	—	—	—	—	—	0+1	0	0+1	0
1969–70	6	1	8	1	2	0	—	—	—	—	—	—	1+2	2	17+2	4
1970–71	0+1	0	2	0	—	—	—	—	—	—	—	—	—	—	2+1	0
1971–72	5	2	8+2	1	0+2	0	—	—	2	0	—	—	4	1	19+4	4
1972–73	1+3	0	3	0	—	—	—	—	—	—	—	—	—	—	4+3	0
TOTALS	12+4	3	21+2	2	2+2	0	—	—	2	0	—	—	5+3	3	42+11	8

TOMMY MURRAY

SEASON	LEAGUE CUP APPS	GLS	SCOTTISH LEAGUE APPS	GLS	SCOTTISH CUP APPS	GLS	EUROPE APPS	GLS	TEXACO CUP APPS	GLS	ANGLO-SCOTTISH CUP APPS	GLS	OTHERS APPS	GLS	TOTALS APPS	GLS
1971–72	—	—	29	10(1P)	4	0	—	—	2	0	—	—	2+1	0	37+1	10(1P)
1972–73	6	1	27+1	5	2	0	—	—	4	2	—	—	4	1	43+1	9
1973–74	2+2	0	15+7	0	2+2	0	—	—	1+1	0	—	—	—	—	20+12	0
1974–75	1	0	18+5	2	4	1	—	—	1	0	—	—	3+1	0	27+6	3
TOTALS	9+2	1	89+13	17(1P)	12+2	1	—	—	8+1	2	—	—	9+2	1	127+20	22(1P)

HUSREF MUSEMIC

SEASON	LEAGUE CUP APPS	GLS	SCOTTISH LEAGUE APPS	GLS	SCOTTISH CUP APPS	GLS	EUROPE APPS	GLS	OTHERS APPS	GLS	TOTALS APPS	GLS
1989–90	3	1	4+2	3	—	—	—	—	3+1	2	10+3	6

TOMMY NEILSON

SEASON	LEAGUE CUP APPS	GLS	SCOTTISH LEAGUE APPS	GLS	SCOTTISH CUP APPS	GLS	EUROPE APPS	GLS	OTHERS APPS	GLS	TOTALS APPS	GLS
1946–47	—	—	6	0	—	—	—	—	1	0	7	0
1947–48	—	—	—	—	—	—	—	—	1	0	1	0
TOTALS	—	—	6	0	—	—	—	—	2	0	8	0

CRAIG NELSON   FIGURES IN BRACKETS REPRESENT SHUT-OUTS

SEASON	LEAGUE CUP APPS	GLS	SCOTTISH LEAGUE APPS	GLS	SCOTTISH CUP APPS	GLS	EUROPE APPS	GLS	OTHERS APPS	GLS	TOTALS APPS	GLS
1994–95	—	—	20	(6)	5	(0)	—	—	1	(0)	26	(6)

PAUL O'BRIEN

SEASON	LEAGUE CUP APPS	GLS	SCOTTISH LEAGUE APPS	GLS	SCOTTISH CUP APPS	GLS	EUROPE APPS	GLS	OTHERS APPS	GLS	TOTALS APPS	GLS
1980–81	—	—	13+2	2	2	0	—	—	0+1	1	15+3	3
1981–82	1	0	0+1	0	—	—	—	—	2+1	1	3+2	1
TOTALS	1	0	13+3	2	2	0	—	—	2+2	2	18+5	4

DEREK O'CONNOR

SEASON	LEAGUE CUP APPS	GLS	SCOTTISH LEAGUE APPS	GLS	SCOTTISH CUP APPS	GLS	EUROPE APPS	GLS	OTHERS APPS	GLS	TOTALS APPS	GLS
1978–79	—	—	18	8	4	1	—	—	—	—	22	9
1979–80	1	0	25+2	13	2	0	—	—	6	2	34+2	15
1980–81	4	0	13+3	4	—	—	—	—	5+1	3	22+4	7
1981–82	0+1	0	12+2	4	—	—	—	—	1	0	13+3	4
1982–83	9+1	4	37+2	16	3	2	—	—	1	0	50+3	22
1983–84	4	1	5+6	1	1	0	—	—	2+5	0	12+11	2
1984–85	1+1	1	0+3	1	—	—	0+1	0	1	3	2+5	5
TOTALS	19+3	6	110+18	47	10	3	0+1	0	16+6	8	155+28	64

EDDIE O'DONNELL

SEASON	LEAGUE CUP APPS	GLS	SCOTTISH LEAGUE APPS	GLS	SCOTTISH CUP APPS	GLS	EUROPE APPS	GLS	OTHERS APPS	GLS	TOTALS APPS	GLS
1964–65	—	—	—	—	—	—	—	—	1	1	1	1
1965–66	—	—	3	0	—	—	—	—	1	0	4	0
TOTALS	—	—	3	0	—	—	—	—	2	1	5	1

DES O'SULLIVAN

SEASON	LEAGUE CUP APPS	GLS	SCOTTISH LEAGUE APPS	GLS	SCOTTISH CUP APPS	GLS	EUROPE APPS	GLS	OTHERS APPS	GLS	TOTALS APPS	GLS
1978–79	—	—	2	0	—	—	—	—	—	—	2	0
1979–80	—	—	2+6	1	—	—	—	—	0+1	0	2+7	1
TOTALS	—	—	4+6	1	—	—	—	—	0+1	0	4+7	1

PETER OLIVER

SEASON	LEAGUE CUP APPS	GLS	SCOTTISH LEAGUE APPS	GLS	SCOTTISH CUP APPS	GLS	EUROPE APPS	GLS	TEXACO CUP APPS	GLS	ANGLO-SCOTTISH CUP APPS	GLS	OTHERS APPS	GLS	TOTALS APPS	GLS
1969–70	—	—	33	0	3	0	—	—	—	—	—	—	5	0	41	0
1970–71	6	0	20	0	—	—	—	—	5	0	—	—	4	0	35	0
1971–72	—	—	7+1	0	2	0	—	—	—	—	—	—	1	0	10+1	0
1972–73	—	—	15+2	0	—	—	—	—	3	0	—	—	1	0	19+2	0
1973–74	—	—	1	0	—	—	—	—	—	—	—	—	—	—	1	0
TOTALS	6	0	76+3	0	5	0	—	—	8	0	—	—	11	0	106+3	0

DONALD PARK

SEASON	LEAGUE CUP		SCOTTISH LEAGUE		SCOTTISH CUP		EUROPE		TEXACO CUP		ANGLO-SCOTTISH CUP		OTHERS		TOTALS	
	APPS	GLS	APPS	GLS	APPS	GLS	APPS	GLS	APPS	GLS	APPS	GLS	APPS	GLS	APPS	GLS
1972–73	—	—	16+2	6	2	0	—	—	1	0	—	—	2	0	21+2	6
1973–74	0+1	0	13+5	4	1+1	0	—	—	1	0	—	—	—	—	15+7	4
1974–75	0+2	0	7+4	1	0+1	0	—	—	0+1	0	—	—	7	4	14+8	5
1975–76	0+3	1	18+9	3	3+2	1	—	—	—	—	2	1	6+2	2	29+16	8
1976–77	9	3	26+7	3	6	0	4	1	—	—	—	—	2	0	47+7	7
1977–78	6+1	2	32+1	6	3	1	—	—	—	—	—	—	1+2	0	42+4	9
1978–79	1	0	2+1	1	—	—	—	—	—	—	2	0	3	2	8+1	3
1983–84	7	1	26+4	4	1	0	—	—	—	—	—	—	7+2	3	41+6	8
1984–85	4+1	1	16+6	3	—	—	1	0	—	—	—	—	2+1	1	23+8	5
TOTALS	27+8	8	156+39	31	16+4	2	5	1	2+1	0	4	1	30+7	12	240+59	55

BOBBY PARKER

SEASON	LEAGUE CUP		SCOTTISH LEAGUE		SCOTTISH CUP		EUROPE		OTHERS		TOTALS	
	APPS	GLS	APPS	GLS	APPS	GLS	APPS	GLS	APPS	GLS	APPS	GLS
1947–48	6	0	25	1	2	0	—	—	2	0	35	1
1948–49	6	0	15	0	—	—	—	—	—	—	21	0
1949–50	2	0	28	2(1P)	3	0	—	—	7	1	40	3(1P)
1950–51	6	2(2P)	27	1(1P)	2	1	—	—	9	0	44	4(3P)
1951–52	6	2	29	6(6P)	7	0	—	—	8	0	50	8(6P)
1952–53	6	1(1P)	27	2(1P)	4	0	—	—	6	1	43	4(2P)
1953–54	6	0	26	2(2P)	3	0	—	—	10	1(1P)	45	3(3P)
1954–55	10	1	30	4(3P)	4	0	—	—	5	1	49	6(3P)
1955–56	8	2(2P)	14	0	—	—	—	—	2	1(1P)	24	3(3P)
1956–57	—	—	22	1	1	0	—	—	8	0	31	1
1957–58	—	—	4	0	—	—	—	—	1	0	5	0
TOTALS	56	8(5P)	247	19(14P)	26	1	—	—	58	5(2P)	387	33(21P)

IAN PATERSON

SEASON	LEAGUE CUP		SCOTTISH LEAGUE		SCOTTISH CUP		EUROPE		OTHERS		TOTALS	
	APPS	GLS	APPS	GLS	APPS	GLS	APPS	GLS	APPS	GLS	APPS	GLS
1976–77	—	—	—	—	—	—	—	—	0+1	0	0+1	0
1977–78	—	—	0+2	0	—	—	—	—	1	0	1+2	0
1978–79	—	—	0+2	0	—	—	—	—	0+1	0	0+3	0
TOTALS	—	—	0+4	0	—	—	—	—	1+2	0	1+6	0

DANNY PATON

SEASON	LEAGUE CUP APPS	GLS	SCOTTISH LEAGUE APPS	GLS	SCOTTISH CUP APPS	GLS	EUROPE APPS	GLS	OTHERS APPS	GLS	TOTALS APPS	GLS
1957–58	—	—	3	1	—	—	—	—	3	3	6	4
1958–59	2	1	5	0	—	—	—	—	3	1(1P)	10	2(1P)
1959–60	—	—	—	—	—	—	—	—	—	—	—	—
1960–61	—	—	—	—	—	—	—	—	—	—	—	—
1961–62	3	0	17	4	2	1	—	—	4	5	26	10
1962–63	10	4	19	11	2	1	—	—	1	0	32	16
1963–64	—	—	6	2	1	0	—	—	—	—	7	2
TOTALS	15	5	50	18	5	2	—	—	11	9(1P)	81	34(1P)

GEORGE PATON FIGURES IN BRACKETS REPRESENT SHUT-OUTS

SEASON	LEAGUE CUP APPS	GLS	SCOTTISH LEAGUE APPS	GLS	SCOTTISH CUP APPS	GLS	EUROPE APPS	GLS	OTHERS APPS	GLS	TOTALS APPS	GLS
1947–48	2	(0)	3	(0)	—	—	—	—	3	(0)	8	(0)

GEORGE PEDEN

SEASON	LEAGUE CUP APPS	GLS	SCOTTISH LEAGUE APPS	GLS	SCOTTISH CUP APPS	GLS	EUROPE APPS	GLS	OTHERS APPS	GLS	TOTALS APPS	GLS
1965–66	—	—	1	0	—	—	—	—	—	—	1	0
1966–67	—	—	12	0	—	—	—	—	1	0	13	0
TOTALS	—	—	13	0	—	—	—	—	1	0	14	0

STEVE PENNEY

SEASON	LEAGUE CUP APPS	GLS	SCOTTISH LEAGUE APPS	GLS	SCOTTISH CUP APPS	GLS	EUROPE APPS	GLS	OTHERS APPS	GLS	TOTALS APPS	GLS
1991–92	0+1	0	3+6	0	0+1	0	—	—	1	0	4+8	0

WILLIE PETTIGREW

SEASON	LEAGUE CUP APPS	GLS	SCOTTISH LEAGUE APPS	GLS	SCOTTISH CUP APPS	GLS	EUROPE APPS	GLS	OTHERS APPS	GLS	TOTALS APPS	GLS
1981–82	—	—	35	16	2	0	—	—	3	4	40	20
1982–83	9+1	7	26+7	10	3+1	0	—	—	7+1	3	45+10	20
1983–84	0+1	0	—	—	—	—	—	—	—	—	0+1	0
TOTALS	9+2	7	61+7	26	5+1	0	—	—	10+1	7	85+11	40

JAMES PITHIE

SEASON	LEAGUE CUP		SCOTTISH LEAGUE		SCOTTISH CUP		EUROPE		OTHERS		TOTALS	
	APPS	GLS	APPS	GLS	APPS	GLS	APPS	GLS	APPS	GLS	APPS	GLS
1946–47	1	0	4	0	—	—	—	—	3	0	8	0

WILLIE POLLAND

SEASON	LEAGUE CUP		SCOTTISH LEAGUE		SCOTTISH CUP		EUROPE		OTHERS		TOTALS	
	APPS	GLS	APPS	GLS	APPS	GLS	APPS	GLS	APPS	GLS	APPS	GLS
1960–61	—	—	2	0	—	—	—	—	—	—	2	0
1961–62	10	0	30	0	1	0	4	0	4	0	49	0
1962–63	10	0	26	0	2	0	—	—	4	0	42	0
1963–64	6	0	26	0	3	0	2	0	18	0	55	0
1964–65	6	0	31	0	4	0	—	—	11	1	52	1
1965–66	3	0	20	1	4	0	3	0	4	0	34	1
1966–67	4	0	12	0	—	—	—	—	4	0	20	0
TOTALS	39	0	147	1	14	0	9	0	45	1	254	2

BOBBY PRENTICE

SEASON	LEAGUE CUP		SCOTTISH LEAGUE		SCOTTISH CUP		EUROPE		TEXACO CUP		ANGLO-SCOTTISH CUP		OTHERS		TOTALS	
	APPS	GLS	APPS	GLS	APPS	GLS	APPS	GLS	APPS	GLS	APPS	GLS	APPS	GLS	APPS	GLS
1973–74	3+1	0	26+2	3	5+1	1	—	—	3	0	—	—	0+1	0	37+5	4
1974–75	4	0	5+11	2	1+1	0	—	—	1	0	—	—	8+1	2	19+13	4
1975–76	5+1	2	30+3	4	6	1	—	—	—	—	1	0	9+1	2	51+5	9
1976–77	9	2	25+8	2	3+3	1	4	0	—	—	—	—	3	1	44+11	6
1977–78	4+3	0	17+8	2	0+2	0	—	—	—	—	—	—	4	0	25+13	2
1978–79	1	0	6+6	0	—	—	—	—	—	—	1	0	2+1	1(1P)	10+7	1(1P)
TOTALS	26+5	4	109+38	13	15+7	3	4	0	4	0	2	0	26+4	6(1P)	186+54	26(1P)

JOHN PRENTICE

SEASON	LEAGUE CUP		SCOTTISH LEAGUE		SCOTTISH CUP		EUROPE		OTHERS		TOTALS	
	APPS	GLS	APPS	GLS	APPS	GLS	APPS	GLS	APPS	GLS	APPS	GLS
1947–48	—	—	—	—	—	—	—	—	1	2	1	2
1948–49	—	—	—	—	—	—	—	—	—	—	—	—
1949–50	—	—	2	0	—	—	—	—	3	0	5	0
1950–51	1	0	4	0	—	—	—	—	—	—	5	0
TOTALS	1	0	6	0	—	—	—	—	4	2	11	2

ALLAN PRESTON

SEASON	LEAGUE CUP		SCOTTISH LEAGUE		SCOTTISH CUP		EUROPE		OTHERS		TOTALS	
	APPS	GLS	APPS	GLS	APPS	GLS	APPS	GLS	APPS	GLS	APPS	GLS
1992–93	—	—	19+2	2	3	2	—	—	—	—	22+2	4

BOBBY RANKIN

SEASON	LEAGUE CUP APPS	GLS	SCOTTISH LEAGUE APPS	GLS	SCOTTISH CUP APPS	GLS	EUROPE APPS	GLS	OTHERS APPS	GLS	TOTALS APPS	GLS
1958–59	—	—	5	9	—	—	—	—	3	4	8	13

ALAN REDPATH

SEASON	LEAGUE CUP APPS	GLS	SCOTTISH LEAGUE APPS	GLS	SCOTTISH CUP APPS	GLS	EUROPE APPS	GLS	OTHERS APPS	GLS	TOTALS APPS	GLS
1983–84	0+2	0	—	—	—	—	—	—	1	0	1+2	0
1984–85	—	—	—	—	—	—	—	—	—	—	—	—
1985–86	—	—	—	—	—	—	—	—	1	0	1	0
1986–87	—	—	—	—	—	—	—	—	1	0	1	0
1987–88	—	—	—	—	—	—	—	—	1	0	1	0
TOTALS	0+2	0	—	—	—	—	—	—	4	0	4+2	0

DEREK RENTON

SEASON	LEAGUE CUP APPS	GLS	SCOTTISH LEAGUE APPS	GLS	SCOTTISH CUP APPS	GLS	EUROPE APPS	GLS	TEXACO CUP APPS	GLS	ANGLO-SCOTTISH CUP APPS	GLS	OTHERS APPS	GLS	TOTALS APPS	GLS
1971–72	—	—	17	5	3	1	—	—	—	—	—	—	0+1	1	20+1	7
1972–73	4+1	0	9+1	2	1	0	—	—	0+1	0	—	—	3+1	0	17+4	2
TOTALS	4+1	0	26+1	7	4	1	—	—	0+1	0	—	—	3+2	1	37+5	9

CHRIS ROBERTSON

SEASON	LEAGUE CUP APPS	GLS	SCOTTISH LEAGUE APPS	GLS	SCOTTISH CUP APPS	GLS	EUROPE APPS	GLS	OTHERS APPS	GLS	TOTALS APPS	GLS
1980–81	4	5	12+1	0	—	—	—	—	4+1	4	20+2	9
1981–82	5+1	2	24+5	7	1+1	1	—	—	3+4	2	33+11	12
TOTALS	9+1	7	36+6	7	1+1	1	—	—	7+5	6	53+13	21

GEORGE ROBERTSON

SEASON	LEAGUE CUP APPS	GLS	SCOTTISH LEAGUE APPS	GLS	SCOTTISH CUP APPS	GLS	EUROPE APPS	GLS	OTHERS APPS	GLS	TOTALS APPS	GLS
1958–59	—	—	1	0	—	—	—	—	—	—	1	0
1959–60	—	—	—	—	—	—	—	—	1	0	1	0
1960–61	—	—	—	—	—	—	—	—	1	0	1	0
TOTALS	—	—	1	0	—	—	—	—	2	0	3	0

JOHN ROBERTSON

	LEAGUE CUP		SCOTTISH LEAGUE		SCOTTISH CUP		EUROPE		OTHERS		TOTALS	
SEASON	APPS	GLS	APPS	GLS	APPS	GLS	APPS	GLS	APPS	GLS	APPS	GLS
1981–82	—	—	0+1	0	—	—	—	—	—	—	0+1	0
1982–83	1+1	0	19+4	21	3	0	—	—	2+2	1	25+7	22
1983–84	5+2	4(1P)	34+1	15(2P)	2	1(1P)	—	—	7	3	48+3	23(4P)
1984–85	5	1	33	8(1P)	5	2	2	2	5	3	50	16(1P)
1985–86	3	1	34+1	20(3P)	5	4(1P)	—	—	7+2	6	49+3	31(5P)
1986–87	1	0	31+6	16(4P)	6	2	0+2	1	9+1	2(1P)	47+9	21(5P)
1987–88	3	3(1P)	39	26(10P)	4	2	—	—	9	3(1P)	55	34(12P)
1988–89	—	—	8+7	4(1P)	2+1	0	0+1	0	1	0	11+9	4(1P)
1989–90	0+1	1	25+7	17(4P)	3	4	—	—	1	0	29+8	22(4P)
1990–91	3	1	31	12(2P)	1	0	3	3(1P)	6	5(1P)	44	21(4P)
1991–92	3	2(1P)	42	14(3P)	6	4(1P)	—	—	3+1	3(1P)	54+1	23(6P)
1992–93	3	1	41+1	11(2P)	4	3(1P)	4	0	1+2	0	53+3	15(3P)
1993–94	2	2	32+4	8(2P)	2+1	1	2	1	6+2	2	44+7	14(2P)
1994–95	2	1	27+4	10(2P)	5	3(1P)	—	—	5	4(2P)	39+4	18(5P)
TOTALS	31+4	17(3P)	396+36	182(36P)	48+2	26(5P)	11+3	7(1P)	62+10	32(6P)	548+55	264(51P)

MALCOLM ROBERTSON

	LEAGUE CUP		SCOTTISH LEAGUE		SCOTTISH CUP		EUROPE		TEXACO CUP		ANGLO-SCOTTISH CUP		OTHERS		TOTALS	
SEASON	APPS	GLS	APPS	GLS	APPS	GLS	APPS	GLS	APPS	GLS	APPS	GLS	APPS	GLS	APPS	GLS
1976–77	—	—	7	1	—	—	—	—	—	—	—	—	—	—	7	1
1977–78	4+3	0	26+1	6	3	0	—	—	—	—	—	—	3+1	0	36+5	6
1978–79	2	0	27+2	4	4	2	—	—	—	—	1	0	2+2	0	36+4	6
1979–80	2	1	28+2	3	2	0	—	—	—	—	—	—	6	4	38+2	8
1980–81	0+2	0	6+1	0	—	—	—	—	—	—	—	—	4+1	0	10+4	0
TOTALS	8+5	1	94+6	14	9	2	—	—	—	—	1	0	15+4	4	127+15	21

BOBBY ROBINSON

	LEAGUE CUP		SCOTTISH LEAGUE		SCOTTISH CUP		EUROPE		OTHERS		TOTALS	
SEASON	APPS	GLS	APPS	GLS	APPS	GLS	APPS	GLS	APPS	GLS	APPS	GLS
1979–80	2	0	31+3	1	3	0	—	—	7	0	43+3	1
1980–81	4	0	13+6	0	—	—	—	—	6	0	23+6	0
TOTALS	6	0	44+9	1	3	0	—	—	13	0	66+9	1

JAMES RODGER

	LEAGUE CUP		SCOTTISH LEAGUE		SCOTTISH CUP		EUROPE		OTHERS		TOTALS	
SEASON	APPS	GLS	APPS	GLS	APPS	GLS	APPS	GLS	APPS	GLS	APPS	GLS
1947–48	1	0	15	0	2	0	—	—	5	0	23	0
1948–49	—	—	3	0	—	—	—	—	2	0	5	0
TOTALS	1	0	18	0	2	0	—	—	7	0	28	0

JIM RODGER

SEASON	LEAGUE CUP APPS	GLS	SCOTTISH LEAGUE APPS	GLS	SCOTTISH CUP APPS	GLS	EUROPE APPS	GLS	OTHERS APPS	GLS	TOTALS APPS	GLS
1961–62	—	—	7	2	1	0	—	—	1	0	9	2
1962–63	5	1	13	6	—	—	—	—	3	5	21	12
1963–64	1	0	1	0	—	—	—	—	—	—	2	0
TOTALS	6	1	21	8	1	0	—	—	4	5	32	14

PAUL RODGER

SEASON	LEAGUE CUP APPS	GLS	SCOTTISH LEAGUE APPS	GLS	SCOTTISH CUP APPS	GLS	EUROPE APPS	GLS	OTHERS APPS	GLS	TOTALS APPS	GLS
1976–77	—	—	3	0	—	—	—	—	—	—	3	0
1977–78	3	0	5	0	1	0	—	—	1	0	10	0
1978–79	1	0	2	0	—	—	—	—	—	—	3	0
TOTALS	4	0	10	0	1	0	—	—	1	0	16	0

BOBBY ROSS

SEASON	LEAGUE CUP APPS	GLS	SCOTTISH LEAGUE APPS	GLS	SCOTTISH CUP APPS	GLS	EUROPE APPS	GLS	OTHERS APPS	GLS	TOTALS APPS	GLS
1960–61	—	—	3	0	—	—	—	—	1	0	4	0
1961–62	5	1	13	2	1	0	1	0	2	3	22	6
1962–63	1	0	8	1	—	—	—	—	1	1	10	2
TOTALS	6	1	24	3	1	0	1	0	4	4	36	8

DEREK RUTHERFORD

SEASON	LEAGUE CUP APPS	GLS	SCOTTISH LEAGUE APPS	GLS	SCOTTISH CUP APPS	GLS	EUROPE APPS	GLS	OTHERS APPS	GLS	TOTALS APPS	GLS
1964–65	1	0	—	—	—	—	—	—	—	—	1	0
1965–66	—	—	—	—	—	—	—	—	—	—	—	—
1966–67	—	—	2	0	—	—	—	—	2	0	4	0
1967–68	—	—	—	—	—	—	—	—	1	0	1	0
TOTALS	1	0	2	0	—	—	—	—	3	0	6	0

EDDIE RUTHERFORD

SEASON	LEAGUE CUP APPS	GLS	SCOTTISH LEAGUE APPS	GLS	SCOTTISH CUP APPS	GLS	EUROPE APPS	GLS	OTHERS APPS	GLS	TOTALS APPS	GLS
1951–52	—	—	20	8	7	3	—	—	4	0	31	11
1952–53	3	1	4	1	2	0	—	—	—	—	9	2
1953–54	—	—	14	2	—	—	—	—	4	0	18	2
1954–55	—	—	—	—	—	—	—	—	1	0	1	0
TOTALS	3	1	38	11	9	3	—	—	9	0	59	15

FRANK SANDEMAN

SEASON	LEAGUE CUP APPS	GLS	SCOTTISH LEAGUE APPS	GLS	SCOTTISH CUP APPS	GLS	EUROPE APPS	GLS	OTHERS APPS	GLS	TOTALS APPS	GLS
1963–64	—	—	5	0	—	—	—	—	3	0	8	0
1964–65	3	0	—	—	—	—	—	—	—	—	3	0
TOTALS	3	0	5	0	—	—	—	—	3	0	11	0

JIMMY SANDISON

SEASON	LEAGUE CUP APPS	GLS	SCOTTISH LEAGUE APPS	GLS	SCOTTISH CUP APPS	GLS	EUROPE APPS	GLS	OTHERS APPS	GLS	TOTALS APPS	GLS
1983–84	—	—	—	—	—	—	—	—	1	0	1	0
1984–85	—	—	2+1	0	—	—	—	—	1	0	3+1	0
1985–86	0+2	0	2+1	0	—	—	—	—	2+1	0	4+4	0
1986–87	—	—	12+1	0	4	0	—	—	4+4	0	20+5	0
1987–88	—	—	2	0	0+1	0	—	—	1+2	0	3+3	0
1988–89	—	—	11+3	0	0+1	0	1+1	0	3+5	0	15+10	0
1989–90	—	—	8+4	2	—	—	—	—	1+2	0	9+6	2
1990–91	—	—	24+1	1	1	0	1	0	1+2	0	27+3	1
TOTALS	0+2	0	61+11	3	5+2	0	2+1	0	14+16	0	82+32	3

COLIN SCOTT

SEASON	LEAGUE CUP APPS	GLS	SCOTTISH LEAGUE APPS	GLS	SCOTTISH CUP APPS	GLS	EUROPE APPS	GLS	OTHERS APPS	GLS	TOTALS APPS	GLS
1983–84	0+1	0	—	—	—	—	—	—	—	—	0+1	0
1984–85	—	—	—	—	—	—	—	—	—	—	—	—
1985–86	—	—	—	—	—	—	—	—	1	0	1	0
TOTALS	0+1	0	—	—	—	—	—	—	1	0	1+1	0

DAVID SCOTT

SEASON	LEAGUE CUP APPS	GLS	SCOTTISH LEAGUE APPS	GLS	SCOTTISH CUP APPS	GLS	EUROPE APPS	GLS	OTHERS APPS	GLS	TOTALS APPS	GLS
1978–79	—	—	3+2	0	—	—	—	—	—	—	3+2	0
1979–80	0+2	0	0+2	0	—	—	—	—	—	—	0+4	0
TOTALS	0+2	0	3+4	0	—	—	—	—	—	—	3+6	0

FRANK SHARP

SEASON	LEAGUE CUP APPS	GLS	SCOTTISH LEAGUE APPS	GLS	SCOTTISH CUP APPS	GLS	EUROPE APPS	GLS	OTHERS APPS	GLS	TOTALS APPS	GLS
1963–64	1	0	—	—	—	—	—	—	—	—	1	0
1964–65	—	—	—	—	—	—	—	—	3	1	3	1
1965–66	—	—	6	1	1	0	—	—	1	0	8	1
1966–67	—	—	—	—	—	—	—	—	0+1	0	0+1	0
TOTALS	1	0	6	1	1	0	—	—	4+1	1	12+1	2

GRAHAM SHAW

SEASON	LEAGUE CUP APPS	GLS	SCOTTISH LEAGUE APPS	GLS	SCOTTISH CUP APPS	GLS	EUROPE APPS	GLS	TEXACO CUP APPS	GLS	ANGLO-SCOTTISH CUP APPS	GLS	OTHERS APPS	GLS	TOTALS APPS	GLS
1975–76	—	—	13	2	6+1	4	—	—	—	—	—	—	7+2	0	26+3	6
1976–77	4+2	2	30+5	7	3+2	0	3+1	0	—	—	—	—	2	2	42+10	11
1977–78	4+1	1	23+3	3	0+2	0	—	—	—	—	—	—	4	0	31+6	4
1978–79	1+1	1	8	1	1+1	0	—	—	—	—	2	0	3	0	15+2	2
1979–80	2	0	15+6	2	2	2	—	—	—	—	—	—	5	0	24+6	4
TOTALS	11+4	4	89+14	15	12+6	6	3+1	0	—	—	2	0	21+2	2	138+27	27

CHRIS SHEVLANE

SEASON	LEAGUE CUP APPS	GLS	SCOTTISH LEAGUE APPS	GLS	SCOTTISH CUP APPS	GLS	EUROPE APPS	GLS	OTHERS APPS	GLS	TOTALS APPS	GLS
1961–62	—	—	—	—	—	—	—	—	1	0	1	0
1962–63	—	—	10	0	—	—	—	—	1	0	11	0
1963–64	6	0	31	0	3	0	3	0	17	0	60	0
1964–65	4	0	25	0	1	1	—	—	7	0	37	1
1965–66	3	0	23	0	4	0	1	0	2	0	33	0
1966–67	2	0	15	1	—	—	—	—	3	0	20	1
TOTALS	15	0	104	1	8	1	4	0	31	0	162	2

PETER SHIELDS

SEASON	LEAGUE CUP		SCOTTISH LEAGUE		SCOTTISH CUP		EUROPE		OTHERS		TOTALS	
	APPS	GLS	APPS	GLS	APPS	GLS	APPS	GLS	APPS	GLS	APPS	GLS
1980–81	1	0	30	0	2	0	—	—	—	—	33	0
1981–82	4	0	37	1	2	0	—	—	6	1(1P)	49	2(1P)
1982–83	10	2	25	0	4	1	—	—	7	0	46	3
1983–84	2	0	2+1	0	—	—	—	—	2	0	6+1	0
TOTALS	17	2	94+1	1	8	1	—	—	15	1(1P)	134+1	5(1P)

TOMMY SLOAN

SEASON	LEAGUE CUP		SCOTTISH LEAGUE		SCOTTISH CUP		EUROPE		OTHERS		TOTALS	
	APPS	GLS	APPS	GLS	APPS	GLS	APPS	GLS	APPS	GLS	APPS	GLS
1946–47	6	1	18	5	1	0	—	—	1	1	26	7
1947–48	1	2	10	3	—	—	—	—	4	2	15	7
1948–49	5	1	23	5	4	1	—	—	4+1	0	36+1	7
1949–50	5	2	28	5	3	0	—	—	5	1	41	8
1950–51	6	1	29	7	3	1	—	—	10	3	48	12
1951–52	4	0	2	0	—	—	—	—	1	0	7	0
TOTALS	27	7	110	25	11	2	—	—	25+1	7	173+1	41

GORDON SMITH

SEASON	LEAGUE CUP		SCOTTISH LEAGUE		SCOTTISH CUP		EUROPE		OTHERS		TOTALS	
	APPS	GLS	APPS	GLS	APPS	GLS	APPS	GLS	APPS	GLS	APPS	GLS
1959–60	7	2	29	11	2	0	—	—	15	2	53	15
1960–61	4	0	13	2	3	0	2	0	2	0	24	2
TOTALS	11	2	42	13	5	0	2	0	17	2	77	17

GORDON SMITH

SEASON	LEAGUE CUP		SCOTTISH LEAGUE		SCOTTISH CUP		EUROPE		OTHERS		TOTALS	
	APPS	GLS	APPS	GLS	APPS	GLS	APPS	GLS	APPS	GLS	APPS	GLS
1976–77	—	—	3+1	2	—	—	—	—	1	0	4+1	2
1977–78	—	—	2+3	0	—	—	—	—	0+1	0	2+4	0
1978–79	1+1	0	0+1	0	—	—	—	—	0+1	0	1+3	0
TOTALS	1+1	0	5+5	2	—	—	—	—	1+2	0	7+8	2

HENRY SMITH
FIGURES IN BRACKETS REPRESENT SHUT-OUTS

SEASON	LEAGUE CUP		SCOTTISH LEAGUE		SCOTTISH CUP		EUROPE		OTHERS		TOTALS	
	APPS	GLS	APPS	GLS	APPS	GLS	APPS	GLS	APPS	GLS	APPS	GLS
1981–82	6	(2)	33	(12)	2	(0)	—	—	6+1	(1)	47+1	(15)
1982–83	10	(3)	39	(14)	4	(1)	—	—	8	(2)	61	(20)
1983–84	6	(1)	36	(9)	2	(1)	—	—	8	(4)	52	(15)
1984–85	5	(3)	36	(8)	5	(2)	2	(0)	6	(1)	54	(14)
1985–86	3	(0)	36	(14)	5	(1)	—	—	9	(4)	53	(19)
1986–87	1	(0)	43	(18)	7	(3)	2	(0)	10	(2)	63	(23)
1987–88	3	(1)	44	(21)	4	(2)	—	—	9	(2)	60	(26)
1988–89	4	(2)	36	(12)	3	(1)	8	(6)	11	(3)	62	(24)
1989–90	3	(1)	36	(14)	3	(2)	—	—	6	(2)	48	(19)
1990–91	3	(2)	23	(5)	1	(0)	4	(0)	7+2	(5)	38+2	(12)
1991–92	3	(2)	44	(20)	6	(3)	—	—	3	(1)	56	(26)
1992–93	3	(1)	25	(7)	—	—	4	(0)	4	(2)	36	(10)
1993–94	2	(1)	27	(13)	3	(1)	2	(0)	4	(2)	38	(17)
1994–95	—	—	14+1	(4)	—	—	—	—	3+1	(1)	17+2	(5)
TOTALS	52	(19)	472+1	(171)	45	(17)	22	(6)	94+4	(32)	685+5	(245)

IAIN SMITH

SEASON	LEAGUE CUP		SCOTTISH LEAGUE		SCOTTISH CUP		EUROPE		OTHERS		TOTALS	
	APPS	GLS	APPS	GLS	APPS	GLS	APPS	GLS	APPS	GLS	APPS	GLS
1977–78	—	—	3+5	2	—	—	—	—	4	3	7+5	5

STIRTON SMITH

SEASON	LEAGUE CUP		SCOTTISH LEAGUE		SCOTTISH CUP		EUROPE		OTHERS		TOTALS	
	APPS	GLS	APPS	GLS	APPS	GLS	APPS	GLS	APPS	GLS	APPS	GLS
1946–47	—	—	1	0	—	—	—	—	—	—	1	0
1947–48	—	—	—	—	—	—	—	—	3	0	3	0
TOTALS	—	—	1	0	—	—	—	—	3	0	4	0

IAN SNEDDON

SEASON	LEAGUE CUP		SCOTTISH LEAGUE		SCOTTISH CUP		EUROPE		TEXACO CUP		ANGLO-SCOTTISH CUP		OTHERS		TOTALS	
	APPS	GLS	APPS	GLS	APPS	GLS	APPS	GLS	APPS	GLS	APPS	GLS	APPS	GLS	APPS	GLS
1966–67	—	—	—	—	—	—	—	—	—	—	—	—	0+1	0	0+1	0
1967–68	3	0	31	0	7	0	—	—	—	—	—	—	4	0	45	0
1968–69	2	0	9	0	—	—	—	—	—	—	—	—	2	0	13	0
1969–70	6	0	4+1	0	—	—	—	—	—	—	—	—	5	0	15+1	0
1970–71	5	0	7	0	—	—	—	—	2	0	—	—	7	0	21	0
1971–72	6	0	31	0	4	0	—	—	2	0	—	—	5	0	48	0
1972–73	6	0	22	1	1	0	—	—	1	0	—	—	4	0	34	1
1973–74	6	0	18	0	6	0	—	—	3	0	—	—	1	0	34	0
1974–75	8	0	6	0	—	—	—	—	1	0	—	—	2	0	17	0
TOTALS	42	0	128+1	1	18	0	—	—	9	0	—	—	30+1	0	227+2	1

GLYNN SNODIN

SEASON	LEAGUE CUP APPS	GLS	SCOTTISH LEAGUE APPS	GLS	SCOTTISH CUP APPS	GLS	EUROPE APPS	GLS	OTHERS APPS	GLS	TOTALS APPS	GLS
1991–92	—	—	4+3	0	1	0	—	—	0+1	0	5+4	0
1992–93	0+2	0	16+11	0	1+1	1	2+1	1	2+2	0	21+17	2
TOTALS	0+2	0	20+14	0	2+1	1	2+1	1	2+3	0	26+21	2

JIM SOUNESS

SEASON	LEAGUE CUP APPS	GLS	SCOTTISH LEAGUE APPS	GLS	SCOTTISH CUP APPS	GLS	EUROPE APPS	GLS	OTHERS APPS	GLS	TOTALS APPS	GLS
1952–53	—	—	5	0	1	0	—	—	1	0	7	0
1953–54	—	—	14	6	3	1	—	—	3	3	20	10
1954–55	4	0	28	8	4	1	—	—	2	0	38	9
1955–56	4	1	1	0	—	—	—	—	—	—	5	1
TOTALS	8	1	48	14	8	2	—	—	6	3	70	20

ROBIN STENHOUSE

SEASON	LEAGUE CUP APPS	GLS	SCOTTISH LEAGUE APPS	GLS	SCOTTISH CUP APPS	GLS	EUROPE APPS	GLS	OTHERS APPS	GLS	TOTALS APPS	GLS
1961–62	1	0	3	3	—	—	1	1	—	—	5	4

GREGOR STEVENS

SEASON	LEAGUE CUP APPS	GLS	SCOTTISH LEAGUE APPS	GLS	SCOTTISH CUP APPS	GLS	EUROPE APPS	GLS	OTHERS APPS	GLS	TOTALS APPS	GLS
1983–84	—	—	3	0	2	0	—	—	—	—	5	0

JOHN STEVENSON

SEASON	LEAGUE CUP APPS	GLS	SCOTTISH LEAGUE APPS	GLS	SCOTTISH CUP APPS	GLS	EUROPE APPS	GLS	TEXACO CUP APPS	GLS	ANGLO-SCOTTISH CUP APPS	GLS	OTHERS APPS	GLS	TOTALS APPS	GLS
1972–73	—	—	5	0	—	—	—	—	—	—	—	—	2+1	0	7+1	0
1973–74	6	0	30	4	7	0	—	—	4	0	—	—	2	0	49	4
1974–75	7	1	10+6	1	1+1	0	—	—	—	—	—	—	2	0	20+7	2
1975–76	1	0	—	—	—	—	—	—	—	—	1	0	0+1	0	2+1	0
TOTALS	14	1	45+6	5	8+1	0	—	—	4	0	1	0	6+2	0	78+9	6

RAB STEWART

SEASON	LEAGUE CUP APPS	GLS	SCOTTISH LEAGUE APPS	GLS	SCOTTISH CUP APPS	GLS	EUROPE APPS	GLS	OTHERS APPS	GLS	TOTALS APPS	GLS
1978–79	—	—	4+1	0	—	—	—	—	—	—	4+1	0
1979–80	—	—	3+2	1	—	—	—	—	1+3	0	4+5	1
TOTALS	—	—	7+3	1	—	—	—	—	1+3	0	8+6	1

DEREK STRICKLAND

SEASON	LEAGUE CUP APPS	GLS	SCOTTISH LEAGUE APPS	GLS	SCOTTISH CUP APPS	GLS	EUROPE APPS	GLS	OTHERS APPS	GLS	TOTALS APPS	GLS
1981–82	—	—	0+1	0	—	—	—	—	1+1	0	1+2	0

KEVIN THOMAS

SEASON	LEAGUE CUP APPS	GLS	SCOTTISH LEAGUE APPS	GLS	SCOTTISH CUP APPS	GLS	EUROPE APPS	GLS	OTHERS APPS	GLS	TOTALS APPS	GLS
1992–93	—	—	2+2	2	0+1	0	—	—	—	—	2+3	2
1993–94	0+2	0	7+5	0	—	—	0+2	0	4+3	4	11+12	4
1994–95	—	—	11+7	5	2+3	2	—	—	1+1	0	14+11	7
TOTALS	0+2	0	20+14	7	2+4	2	0+2	0	5+4	4	27+26	13

ARTHUR THOMSON

SEASON	LEAGUE CUP APPS	GLS	SCOTTISH LEAGUE APPS	GLS	SCOTTISH CUP APPS	GLS	EUROPE APPS	GLS	OTHERS APPS	GLS	TOTALS APPS	GLS
1966–67	—	—	14	0	1	0	—	—	5+1	0	20+1	0
1967–68	—	—	30	0	6	0	—	—	2	0	38	0
1968–69	4	0	14	0	2	0	—	—	—	—	20	0
1969–70	3	0	—	—	—	—	—	—	2+1	0	5+1	0
TOTALS	7	0	58	0	9	0	—	—	9+2	0	83+2	0

EDDIE THOMSON

SEASON	LEAGUE CUP APPS	GLS	SCOTTISH LEAGUE APPS	GLS	SCOTTISH CUP APPS	GLS	EUROPE APPS	GLS	TEXACO CUP APPS	GLS	ANGLO-SCOTTISH CUP APPS	GLS	OTHERS APPS	GLS	TOTALS APPS	GLS
1966–67	—	—	9	0	—	—	—	—	—	—	—	—	5	0	14	0
1967–68	3	0	9	1	4+1	1	—	—	—	—	—	—	5	0	21+1	2
1968–69	6	0	34	0	2	0	—	—	—	—	—	—	6	1	48	1
1969–70	—	—	23	0	2	0	—	—	—	—	—	—	4	0	29	0
1970–71	6	0	34	0	1	0	—	—	7	0	—	—	10	1	58	1
1971–72	6	1	29	2	4	0	—	—	2	0	—	—	5	0	46	3
1972–73	—	—	23+1	1	2	0	—	—	3	0	—	—	1+1	0	29+2	1
TOTALS	21	1	161+1	4	15+1	1	—	—	12	0	—	—	36+1	2	245+3	8

GEORGE THOMSON

SEASON	LEAGUE CUP APPS	GLS	SCOTTISH LEAGUE APPS	GLS	SCOTTISH CUP APPS	GLS	EUROPE APPS	GLS	OTHERS APPS	GLS	TOTALS APPS	GLS
1956–57	—	—	7	0	—	—	—	—	4	1	11	1
1957–58	2	0	30	0	3	0	—	—	14	0	49	0
1958–59	10	1	34	10(4P)	2	0	2	0	22	4(2P)	70	15(6P)
1959–60	10	1(1P)	34	4(4P)	2	0	—	—	15	6(6P)	61	11(11P)
1960–61	7	1(1P)	12	0	—	—	2	0	2	0	23	1(1P)
TOTALS	29	3(2P)	117	14(8P)	7	0	4	0	57	11(8P)	214	28(18P)

JOHN THOMSON

SEASON	LEAGUE CUP APPS	GLS	SCOTTISH LEAGUE APPS	GLS	SCOTTISH CUP APPS	GLS	EUROPE APPS	GLS	OTHERS APPS	GLS	TOTALS APPS	GLS
1955–56	—	—	1	0	—	—	—	—	—	—	1	0

LAWRIE TIERNEY

SEASON	LEAGUE CUP APPS	GLS	SCOTTISH LEAGUE APPS	GLS	SCOTTISH CUP APPS	GLS	EUROPE APPS	GLS	TEXACO CUP APPS	GLS	ANGLO-SCOTTISH CUP APPS	GLS	OTHERS APPS	GLS	TOTALS APPS	GLS
1977–78	5+1	0	23+5	2	3	0	—	—	—	—	—	—	1	0	32+6	2
1978–79	1	0	8+6	0	—	—	—	—	—	—	0+1	0	1+1	0	10+8	0
1979–80	—	—	6+1	0	—	—	—	—	—	—	—	—	3	0	9+1	0
TOTALS	6+1	0	37+12	2	3	0	—	—	—	—	0+1	0	5+1	0	51+15	2

JIM TOWNSEND

SEASON	LEAGUE CUP APPS	GLS	SCOTTISH LEAGUE APPS	GLS	SCOTTISH CUP APPS	GLS	EUROPE APPS	GLS	TEXACO CUP APPS	GLS	ANGLO-SCOTTISH CUP APPS	GLS	OTHERS APPS	GLS	TOTALS APPS	GLS
1966–67	—	—	1	0	—	—	—	—	—	—	—	—	2	1	3	1
1967–68	3	0	21	1	6	0	—	—	—	—	—	—	5	0	35	1
1968–69	6	1	11	0	—	—	—	—	—	—	—	—	4	0	21	1
1969–70	4+1	0	20+2	7	3	0	—	—	—	—	—	—	6+1	0	33+4	7
1970–71	—	—	29	1	2	0	—	—	8	0	—	—	11	0	50	1
1971–72	6	0	23	2(1P)	1	0	—	—	2	0	—	—	4	0	36	2(1P)
1972–73	—	—	—	—	—	—	—	—	1	0	—	—	1+1	0	2+1	0
TOTALS	19+1	1	105+2	11(1P)	12	0	—	—	11	0	—	—	33+2	1	180+5	13(1P)

TOMMY TRAYNOR

SEASON	LEAGUE CUP APPS	GLS	SCOTTISH LEAGUE APPS	GLS	SCOTTISH CUP APPS	GLS	EUROPE APPS	GLS	OTHERS APPS	GLS	TOTALS APPS	GLS
1962–63	—	—	1	0	—	—	—	—	—	—	1	0
1963–64	5	2	29	2	3	0	3	1	17	3	57	8
1964–65	6	0	17	3	2	1	—	—	12	2	37	6
1965–66	6	0	30	9	3	1	5	1	4	4	48	15
1966–67	6	2	24+1	1	1	0	—	—	11	4	42+1	7
1967–68	5	3	24+2	6	7	0	—	—	5+1	1	41+3	10
1968–69	4	0	28+1	6	2	1	—	—	5+1	0	39+2	7
1969–70	3+1	0	16	4	1	0	—	—	3	0	23+1	4
TOTALS	35+1	7	169+4	31	19	3	8	2	57+2	14	288+7	57

ROY TURNBULL

SEASON	LEAGUE CUP APPS	GLS	SCOTTISH LEAGUE APPS	GLS	SCOTTISH CUP APPS	GLS	EUROPE APPS	GLS	OTHERS APPS	GLS	TOTALS APPS	GLS
1968–69	—	—	0+1	0	—	—	—	—	—	—	0+1	0

JOHN URQUHART

SEASON	LEAGUE CUP APPS	GLS	SCOTTISH LEAGUE APPS	GLS	SCOTTISH CUP APPS	GLS	EUROPE APPS	GLS	OTHERS APPS	GLS	TOTALS APPS	GLS
1946–47	3	2	11	2	2	0	—	—	3	2	19	6
1947–48	7	1	17	3	2	1	—	—	3	1	29	6
1948–49	2	0	3	0	—	—	—	—	1	0	6	0
1949–50	—	—	1	1	—	—	—	—	—	—	1	1
1950–51	—	—	3	2	—	—	—	—	4	1	7	3
1951–52	5	0	18	2	3	0	—	—	5	0	31	2
1952–53	6	0	28	12	3	1	—	—	6	1	43	14
1953–54	6	1	28	10	3	0	—	—	16	7	53	18
1954–55	10	2	29	10	4	0	—	—	5	4	48	16
1955–56	8	4	19	5	—	—	—	—	3	1	30	10
TOTALS	47	10	157	47	17	2	—	—	46	17	267	76

PETER VAN DE VEN

SEASON	LEAGUE CUP APPS	GLS	SCOTTISH LEAGUE APPS	GLS	SCOTTISH CUP APPS	GLS	EUROPE APPS	GLS	OTHERS APPS	GLS	TOTALS APPS	GLS
1992–93	1	0	37	0	3	0	4	0	4	0	49	0
1993–94	1	0	2	0	—	—	—	—	5	0	8	0
TOTALS	2	0	39	0	3	0	4	0	9	0	57	0

TOMMY VEITCH

SEASON	LEAGUE CUP		SCOTTISH LEAGUE		SCOTTISH CUP		EUROPE		TEXACO CUP		ANGLO-SCOTTISH CUP		OTHERS		TOTALS	
	APPS	GLS	APPS	GLS	APPS	GLS	APPS	GLS	APPS	GLS	APPS	GLS	APPS	GLS	APPS	GLS
1968–69	—	—	6+3	2	0+1	0	—	—	—	—	—	—	0+1	0	6+5	2
1969–70	2	0	18+4	0	2+1	0	—	—	—	—	—	—	2	0	24+5	0
1970–71	5	0	3+1	0	1	0	—	—	1	0	—	—	10+1	0	20+2	0
1971–72	2+1	0	10+2	0	—	—	—	—	—	—	—	—	1	0	13+3	0
TOTALS	9+1	0	37+10	2	3+2	0	—	—	1	0	—	—	13+2	0	63+15	2

JAMES WALKER

SEASON	LEAGUE CUP		SCOTTISH LEAGUE		SCOTTISH CUP		EUROPE		OTHERS		TOTALS	
	APPS	GLS	APPS	GLS	APPS	GLS	APPS	GLS	APPS	GLS	APPS	GLS
1946–47	2	3	8	1	1	1	—	—	—	—	11	5

NICKY WALKER   FIGURES IN BRACKETS REPRESENT SHUT-OUTS

SEASON	LEAGUE CUP		SCOTTISH LEAGUE		SCOTTISH CUP		EUROPE		OTHERS		TOTALS	
	APPS	GLS	APPS	GLS	APPS	GLS	APPS	GLS	APPS	GLS	APPS	GLS
1989–90	—	—	—	—	—	—	—	—	1+1	(1)	1+1	(1)
1990–91	—	—	13	(2)	—	—	—	—	2+4	(2)	15+4	(4)
1991–92	—	—	—	—	—	—	—	—	1	(1)	1	(1)
1992–93	—	—	18	(9)	4	(3)	—	—	—	—	22	(12)
1993–94	—	—	17	(5)	—	—	—	—	3	(1)	20	(6)
1994–95	2	(1)	2	(0)	—	—	—	—	1	(1)	5	(2)
TOTALS	2	(1)	50	(16)	4	(3)	—	—	8+5	(6)	64+5	(26)

TOMMY WALKER

SEASON	LEAGUE CUP		SCOTTISH LEAGUE		SCOTTISH CUP		EUROPE		OTHERS		TOTALS	
	APPS	GLS	APPS	GLS	APPS	GLS	APPS	GLS	APPS	GLS	APPS	GLS
1946–47	—	—	9	3	—	—	—	—	—	—	9	3
1948–49	—	—	1	0	—	—	—	—	1	0	2	0
TOTALS	—	—	10	3	—	—	—	—	1	0	11	3

WILLIE WALLACE

SEASON	LEAGUE CUP		SCOTTISH LEAGUE		SCOTTISH CUP		EUROPE		OTHERS		TOTALS	
	APPS	GLS	APPS	GLS	APPS	GLS	APPS	GLS	APPS	GLS	APPS	GLS
1960–61	—	—	2	1	—	—	—	—	—	—	2	1
1961–62	9	5	26	6	2	0	3	1	6	6	46	18
1962–63	10	6(2P)	34	17(5P)	2	2(1P)	—	—	4	4	50	29(8P)
1963–64	6	3	34	23	3	1	3	1	17	8	63	36
1964–65	4	3	34	21(2P)	4	1	—	—	5	2	47	27(2P)
1965–66	5	4	33	19	4	2	5	3	4	5	51	33
1966–67	6	5	10	4(1P)	—	—	—	—	2	5(1P)	18	14(2P)
TOTALS	40	26(2P)	173	91(8P)	15	6(1P)	11	5	38	30(1P)	277	158(12P)

JIMMY WARDHAUGH

SEASON	LEAGUE CUP		SCOTTISH LEAGUE		SCOTTISH CUP		EUROPE		OTHERS		TOTALS	
	APPS	GLS	APPS	GLS	APPS	GLS	APPS	GLS	APPS	GLS	APPS	GLS
1946–47	6	0	12	2	—	—	—	—	1	0	19	2
1947–48	—	—	1	0	—	—	—	—	—	—	1	0
1948–49	2	0	22	10(1P)	2	3	—	—	4	2	30	15(1P)
1949–50	6	3	30	20	3	1	—	—	4	3	43	27
1950–51	6	6	29	15	3	2	—	—	8	3	46	26
1951–52	6	1	19	14	5	1	—	—	6	15	36	31
1952–53	6	1	26	12	4	1	—	—	7	8	43	22
1953–54	6	4	28	27	3	3	—	—	20	19	57	53
1954–55	10	8	30	15	4	4	—	—	4	5	48	32
1955–56	7	1	32	30	6	3	—	—	3	4	48	38
1956–57	6	7	31	22	1	0	—	—	9+1	9	47+1	38
1957–58	6	7	30	28	3	2	—	—	15+1	22	54+1	59
1958–59	7	2	14	11	2	1	1	0	15	16	39	30
1959–60	4	3	—	—	—	—	—	—	1	0	5	3
1960–61	—	—	—	—	—	—	—	—	1	0	1	0
TOTALS	78	43	304	206(1P)	36	21	1	0	98+2	106	517+2	376(1P)

ANDY WATSON

SEASON	LEAGUE CUP		SCOTTISH LEAGUE		SCOTTISH CUP		EUROPE		OTHERS		TOTALS	
	APPS	GLS	APPS	GLS	APPS	GLS	APPS	GLS	APPS	GLS	APPS	GLS
1984–85	—	—	14+2	3	3+2	0	—	—	1	0	18+4	3
1985–86	3	0	8+4	0	0+1	0	—	—	8+2	4	19+7	4
1986–87	0+1	0	12+17	3	2+4	0	0+2	0	5+5	4	19+29	7
1987–88	—	—	—	—	—	—	—	—	3+3	3	3+3	3
TOTALS	3+1	0	34+23	6	5+7	0	0+2	0	17+10	11	59+43	17

JIMMY WATTERS   FIGURES IN BRACKETS REPRESENT SHUT-OUTS

SEASON	LEAGUE CUP APPS	GLS	SCOTTISH LEAGUE APPS	GLS	SCOTTISH CUP APPS	GLS	EUROPE APPS	GLS	OTHERS APPS	GLS	TOTALS APPS	GLS
1947–48	—	—	—	—	—	—	—	—	1	(0)	1	(0)
1948–49	—	—	—	—	—	—	—	—	1	(0)	1	(0)
1949–50	—	—	6	(1)	—	—	—	—	6	(0)	12	(1)
1950–51	—	—	3	(0)	—	—	—	—	1	(0)	4	(0)
1951–52	—	—	1	(0)	—	—	—	—	6	(1)	7	(1)
1952–53	6	(1)	30	(4)	4	(1)	—	—	6	(1)	46	(7)
1953–54	6	(2)	30	(6)	3	(1)	—	—	21	(7)	60	(16)
1954–55	1	(0)	4	(0)	—	—	—	—	2	(0)	7	(0)
1955–56	—	—	1	(0)	—	—	—	—	—	—	1	(0)
TOTALS	13	(3)	75	(11)	7	(2)	—	—	44	(9)	139	(25)

JIM WEIR

SEASON	LEAGUE CUP APPS	GLS	SCOTTISH LEAGUE APPS	GLS	SCOTTISH CUP APPS	GLS	EUROPE APPS	GLS	OTHERS APPS	GLS	TOTALS APPS	GLS
1993–94	—	—	25+1	0	1+1	0	1	0	—	—	27+2	0
1994–95	1+1	0	2	0	—	—	—	—	0+1	0	3+2	0
TOTALS	1+1	0	27+1	0	1+1	0	1	0	0+1	0	30+4	0

IAN WESTWATER   FIGURES IN BRACKETS REPRESENT SHUT-OUTS

SEASON	LEAGUE CUP APPS	GLS	SCOTTISH LEAGUE APPS	GLS	SCOTTISH CUP APPS	GLS	EUROPE APPS	GLS	OTHERS APPS	GLS	TOTALS APPS	GLS
1980–81	—	—	2	(0)	—	—	—	—	1	(0)	3	(0)
1981–82	—	—	—	—	—	—	—	—	—	—	—	—
1982–83	—	—	—	—	—	—	—	—	0+1	(0)	0+1	(0)
1983–84	2	(1)	—	—	—	—	—	—	1	(0)	3	(1)
TOTALS	2	(1)	2	(0)	—	—	—	—	2+1	(0)	6+1	(1)

ARCHIE WHITE

SEASON	LEAGUE CUP APPS	GLS	SCOTTISH LEAGUE APPS	GLS	SCOTTISH CUP APPS	GLS	EUROPE APPS	GLS	OTHERS APPS	GLS	TOTALS APPS	GLS
1979–80	—	—	9+1	0	—	—	—	—	—	—	9+1	0
1980–81	0+1	0	0+2	0	0+1	0	—	—	1+3	0	1+7	0
TOTALS	0+1	0	9+3	0	0+1	0	—	—	1+3	0	10+8	0

TOMMY WHITE

SEASON	LEAGUE CUP		SCOTTISH LEAGUE		SCOTTISH CUP		EUROPE		OTHERS		TOTALS	
	APPS	GLS	APPS	GLS	APPS	GLS	APPS	GLS	APPS	GLS	APPS	GLS
1963–64	—	—	19	17	3	3	—	—	15	13	37	33
1964–65	4	2	18	13	1	0	—	—	1	0	24	15
TOTALS	4	2	37	30	4	3	—	—	16	13	61	48

DICK WHITEHEAD

SEASON	LEAGUE CUP		SCOTTISH LEAGUE		SCOTTISH CUP		EUROPE		OTHERS		TOTALS	
	APPS	GLS	APPS	GLS	APPS	GLS	APPS	GLS	APPS	GLS	APPS	GLS
1946–47	1	0	7	2	1	0	—	—	—	—	9	2
1947–48	—	—	—	—	—	—	—	—	3	0	3	0
1948–49	—	—	2	0	—	—	—	—	1	0	3	0
1949–50	—	—	1	0	—	—	—	—	—	—	1	0
1950–51	—	—	8	1	—	—	—	—	3	0	11	1
1951–52	3	0	—	—	—	—	—	—	2	2	5	2
1952–53	—	—	1	0	—	—	—	—	1	0	2	0
TOTALS	4	0	19	3	1	0	—	—	10	2	34	5

BRIAN WHITTAKER

SEASON	LEAGUE CUP		SCOTTISH LEAGUE		SCOTTISH CUP		EUROPE		OTHERS		TOTALS	
	APPS	GLS	APPS	GLS	APPS	GLS	APPS	GLS	APPS	GLS	APPS	GLS
1984–85	0+3	1	25+3	1	5	0	2	0	5	1	37+6	3
1985–86	3	0	24+1	0	4	0	—	—	5+3	0	36+4	0
1986–87	—	—	37	0	5	0	2	0	9	0	53	0
1987–88	3	0	42	0	4	1	—	—	8+2	0	57+2	1
1988–89	4	0	24	0	—	—	6	0	13	0	47	0
1989–90	2+1	0	6	0	1	0	—	—	4+2	0	13+3	0
TOTALS	12+4	1	158+4	1	19	1	10	0	44+7	1	243+15	4

JIMMY WHITTLE

SEASON	LEAGUE CUP		SCOTTISH LEAGUE		SCOTTISH CUP		EUROPE		OTHERS		TOTALS	
	APPS	GLS	APPS	GLS	APPS	GLS	APPS	GLS	APPS	GLS	APPS	GLS
1950–51	—	—	1	0	—	—	—	—	—	—	1	0
1951–52	—	—	16	9	5	1	—	—	3	4	24	14
1952–53	2	1	12	4	—	—	—	—	3	0	17	5
1953–54	—	—	—	—	—	—	—	—	2	1	2	1
1954–55	—	—	5	1	—	—	—	—	1	1	6	2
1955–56	—	—	6	2	—	—	—	—	1	0	7	2
1956–57	—	—	1	0	—	—	—	—	—	—	1	0
TOTALS	2	1	41	16	5	1	—	—	10	6	58	24

ARCHIE WILLIAMS

SEASON	LEAGUE CUP APPS	GLS	SCOTTISH LEAGUE APPS	GLS	SCOTTISH CUP APPS	GLS	EUROPE APPS	GLS	OTHERS APPS	GLS	TOTALS APPS	GLS
1947–48	7	0	19	1	—	—	—	—	5	0	31	1
1948–49	4	0	8	0	—	—	—	—	—	—	12	0
1949–50	—	—	1	0	—	—	—	—	3	1	4	1
1950–51	—	—	15	0	—	—	—	—	2	0	17	0
1951–52	—	—	2	0	1	0	—	—	2	1	5	1
TOTALS	11	0	45	1	1	0	—	—	12	2	69	3

BRIAN WILSON   FIGURES IN BRACKETS REPRESENT SHUT-OUTS

SEASON	LEAGUE CUP APPS	GLS	SCOTTISH LEAGUE APPS	GLS	SCOTTISH CUP APPS	GLS	EUROPE APPS	GLS	OTHERS APPS	GLS	TOTALS APPS	GLS
1976–77	6	(2)	9	(1)	—	—	2	(0)	2	(1)	19	(4)

TOMMY WILSON

SEASON	LEAGUE CUP APPS	GLS	SCOTTISH LEAGUE APPS	GLS	SCOTTISH CUP APPS	GLS	EUROPE APPS	GLS	OTHERS APPS	GLS	TOTALS APPS	GLS
1992–93	—	—	—	—	—	—	0+1	0	—	—	0+1	0

ERNIE WINCHESTER

SEASON	LEAGUE CUP APPS	GLS	SCOTTISH LEAGUE APPS	GLS	SCOTTISH CUP APPS	GLS	EUROPE APPS	GLS	TEXACO CUP APPS	GLS	ANGLO-SCOTTISH CUP APPS	GLS	OTHERS APPS	GLS	TOTALS APPS	GLS
1968–69	—	—	1	0	—	—	—	—	—	—	—	—	3	1	4	1
1969–70	6	4	13+3	3	0+1	0	—	—	—	—	—	—	6	1	25+4	8
1970–71	1+2	0	5+4	1	1	0	—	—	1	0	—	—	3	0	11+6	1
1971–72	—	—	21+1	2	1	1	—	—	—	—	—	—	2	1	24+1	4
TOTALS	7+2	4	40+8	6	2+1	1	—	—	1	0	—	—	14	3	64+11	14

FRASER WISHART

SEASON	LEAGUE CUP APPS	GLS	SCOTTISH LEAGUE APPS	GLS	SCOTTISH CUP APPS	GLS	EUROPE APPS	GLS	TEXACO CUP APPS	GLS	ANGLO-SCOTTISH CUP APPS	GLS	OTHERS APPS	GLS	TOTALS APPS	GLS
1994–95	—	—	8	0	—	—	—	—	—	—	—	—	—	—	8	0

DAVID WOOD

SEASON	LEAGUE CUP APPS	GLS	SCOTTISH LEAGUE APPS	GLS	SCOTTISH CUP APPS	GLS	EUROPE APPS	GLS	OTHERS APPS	GLS	TOTALS APPS	GLS
1946–47	1	0	—	—	—	—	—	—	—	—	1	0

WILSON WOOD

SEASON	LEAGUE CUP APPS	GLS	SCOTTISH LEAGUE APPS	GLS	SCOTTISH CUP APPS	GLS	EUROPE APPS	GLS	TEXACO CUP APPS	GLS	ANGLO-SCOTTISH CUP APPS	GLS	OTHERS APPS	GLS	TOTALS APPS	GLS
1969–70	—	—	—	—	—	—	—	—	—	—	—	—	1	1	1	1
1970–71	3	1	15	0	—	—	—	—	6	0	—	—	12	1	36	2
1971–72	2	0	10	0	3	0	—	—	—	—	—	—	2+1	1	17+1	1
1972–73	5	0	17	1	—	—	—	—	4	0	—	—	5	0	31	1
TOTALS	10	1	42	1	3	0	—	—	10	0	—	—	20+1	3	85+1	5

GEORGE WRIGHT

SEASON	LEAGUE CUP APPS	GLS	SCOTTISH LEAGUE APPS	GLS	SCOTTISH CUP APPS	GLS	EUROPE APPS	GLS	OTHERS APPS	GLS	TOTALS APPS	GLS
1986–87	—	—	—	—	—	—	—	—	1	0	1	0
1987–88	—	—	—	—	—	—	—	—	—	—	—	—
1988–89	—	—	—	—	—	—	—	—	1	0	1	0
1989–90	—	—	0+1	0	—	—	—	—	0+1	0	0+2	0
1990–91	—	—	14+3	2	—	—	2	0	5+1	0	21+4	2
1991–92	0+1	0	15+9	1	4+2	0	—	—	0+1	0	19+13	1
1992–93	1	0	8+4	0	1	0	0+1	0	3+1	0	13+6	0
1993–94	2	0	10+2	0	0+1	0	—	—	5+1	1	17+4	1
1994–95	—	—	0+2	0	—	—	—	—	1+1	0	1+3	0
TOTALS	3+1	0	47+21	3	5+3	0	2+1	0	16+6	1	73+32	4

ALEX YOUNG

SEASON	LEAGUE CUP APPS	GLS	SCOTTISH LEAGUE APPS	GLS	SCOTTISH CUP APPS	GLS	EUROPE APPS	GLS	OTHERS APPS	GLS	TOTALS APPS	GLS
1955–56	5	7	27	15	6	1	—	—	2	1	40	23
1956–57	6	1	27	6	1	0	—	—	10	9	44	16
1957–58	3	0	34	24	3	2	—	—	15+1	12	55+1	38
1958–59	4	3	27	7	2	1	—	—	22	25	55	36
1959–60	4	4	28	23	1	1	—	—	2	2	35	30
1960–61	7	3	10	2	—	—	2	1	—	—	19	6
TOTALS	29	18	153	77	13	5	2	1	51+1	49	248+1	150

DREW YOUNG

SEASON	LEAGUE CUP APPS	GLS	SCOTTISH LEAGUE APPS	GLS	SCOTTISH CUP APPS	GLS	EUROPE APPS	GLS	TEXACO CUP APPS	GLS	ANGLO-SCOTTISH CUP APPS	GLS	OTHERS APPS	GLS	TOTALS APPS	GLS
1970–71	—	—	9+5	0	0+1	0	—	—	3+1	2	—	—	1	0	13+7	2